Advance Praise

This book offers a realistic and comprehensive analysis that moves the climate crisis from being merely an environmental issue to the centre of the global economy. With a wide range of sections spanning finance to employment, it stands out by addressing the issue holistically. Its in-depth examination of current market dynamics, such as carbon pricing, green bonds, and climate risk management, makes the work both contemporary and groundbreaking. Its adept blending of critical concepts, such as climate justice and the circular economy, with economic policies enhances the work's academic impact. With these aspects, the book serves as a valuable reference source for researchers and policymakers who wish to understand the economic architecture of a sustainable future. With all these unique contributions, the study will provide significant benefits to the literature on climate economics.

Prof. Dr. Gözde Ersöz Ay
Marmara University, Istanbul, Turkey

This book provides a remarkably comprehensive and incisive analysis of the climate crisis, framing it not merely as an environmental challenge but as a fundamental economic transformation. Its strength lies in its clear and logical progression, moving deftly from identifying macroeconomic risks to detailing the indispensable roles of finance, the private sector, and institutional governance. The argument is particularly compelling in its balanced treatment of both the necessary market mechanisms, such as carbon pricing, and the overarching principle of climate justice, ensuring a holistic perspective. Ultimately, this synthesis offers an invaluable framework for understanding the multifaceted transition to a sustainable and resilient global economy.

Prof. Dr. Burak Darici
Bandirma Onyedi Eylul University, Bandirma, Turkey

The climate crisis is no longer a distant environmental concern but a defining economic challenge shaping global productivity, financial stability, and market dynamics. Escalating environmental disruptions are intensifying systemic risks, deepening inequalities, and threatening the foundations of global trade and development. Bridging the widening gap between ambitious climate targets and actual investment flows requires a transformative mobilisation of finance toward sustainable and low-carbon pathways. Market-based instruments such as green bonds and carbon pricing mechanisms are redefining capital allocation and accelerating structural economic change. At the same time, businesses, financial institutions, and policymakers must embed climate risk, accountability, and justice at the core of governance frameworks. Ultimately, the transition to a resilient, circular, and green economy is not only an environmental necessity but a strategic opportunity for sustainable growth, innovation, and inclusive prosperity. In this regard, this book will contribute to the literature by providing a holistic perspective on the political economy of the climate crisis and addressing the governance aspect of transformation alongside sustainable financing mechanisms.

Prof. Dr. Fatih Mangir
Selcuk University, Selcuklu, Turkey

The climate crisis has moved beyond being just an environmental issue of the future; it now stands as a core economic force reshaping productivity, financial systems, and market behaviour across the globe. Growing ecological disruptions are amplifying systemic vulnerabilities, widening social and economic gaps, and undermining the very pillars of international commerce and progress. To close the growing divide between bold climate pledges and real-world investment, finance must undergo a fundamental shift toward sustainable and low-emission solutions. Tools like carbon pricing and green bonds are transforming how capital is directed, speeding up deep structural changes in the economy. In this regard, this book's multidimensional perspective provides valuable insights for personal and professional development, encouraging readers to think critically about resilience, responsibility, and opportunity in a changing global economy. Carefully and meticulously prepared, the book successfully bridges theory and practice, making it both intellectually enriching and practically relevant.

Assoc. Prof. Dr. Şakir İşleyen
Yuzuncu Yil University, Van, Turkey

Rewriting the Climate Agenda: From Failed Policies to Transformative Action

Rewriting the Climate Agenda: From Failed Policies to Transformative Action

Editor

Meltem Ince-Yenilmez

MDPI

Basel • Beijing • Wuhan • Barcelona • Belgrade • Novi Sad • Cluj • Manchester

Editor
Meltem Ince-Yenilmez
Izmir Democracy University
Izmir, Turkey

Editorial Office
MDPI AG
Grosspeteranlage 5
4052 Basel, Switzerland

For citation purposes, cite each chapter independently as indicated below:

Lastname, A. A., Lastname, B. B., & Lastname, C. C. (2026). Title of Chapter. In M. Ince-Yenilmez (Ed.), *Rewriting the Climate Agenda: From Failed Policies to Transformative Action* (pp. Page range). MDPI.

ISBN 978-3-7258-4402-9 (Hbk)
ISBN 978-3-7258-4401-2 (PDF)
https://doi.org/10.3390/books978-3-7258-4401-2

Dedication

Words cannot express my deepest and heartfelt gratitude to my beloved father, Niyazi Metin, who passed away at the end of November 2025, and to my dear mother, Makbule, for all of the sacrifices that you have made on my behalf. Your love and guidance are with me in whatever I pursue. Furthermore, I am endlessly thankful for my loving and supportive husband, Özgür, and my wonderful, beloved son, Bryan Poyraz, who provides constant inspiration and is a wonderful presence who always lifts my spirits. You are the best thing that has ever come into life. Last but not least, I am so grateful to my dear teacher and colleague, Prof. Dr. M. Hulusi Demir, an honorary family member whose supportive approach and encouragement have guided me throughout this process.

Contents

About the Editor

Meltem Ince-Yenilmez is a Professor at the Department of Economics at Izmir Democracy University who specialises in the economics of gender, labour economics and social work. Prof. Ince-Yenilmez was a Visiting Researcher at the University of California, Berkeley between 2014 and 2015; was at Georg-Universität-Gottingen at summer school in 2015–2016; was a Visiting Researcher at Lund University, was a Research Associate at the University of Massachusetts, Amherst in 2020–2022 and was a Visiting Faculty at IIM Rohtak, India in 2022. Prof. Ince-Yenilmez has been a Visiting Professor at the University of Tohoku, Japan, since 2021. Prof. Ince-Yenilmez is an economist focused on labour economics, discrimination, sustainability, social policy, behavioural economics, and care work. Prof. Ince-Yenilmez has ten books published by Routledge, Palgrave, Rowman, Brill and Peter Lang, while the next book projects are Climate Change, Migration Economy, and Economics of Sports, which will be published by 2026.

Contributors

Saffet Akdağ
Assoc. Prof. Dr., Tarsus University, Mersin, Turkey

Kenan Aydin
Prof. Dr., Istanbul Gelisim University, Avcilar, Turkey

Aykut Balci
Dr., Tekirdag Namık Kemal University, Vocational School of Social Sciences, Tekirdag, Turkey

Isidora Beraha
Dr., Institute of Economic Sciences, Belgrade, Serbia

Aycan Can
Dr., Tekirdag Namik Kemal University, Tekirdag, Turkey

Sonja Đuričin
Dr., Institute of Economic Sciences, Belgrade, Serbia

Nuri Aytuğ Erdemir
Res. Assist., Bakircay University, Seyrek, Izmir, Turkey

Hakan Eygu
Assoc. Prof. Dr., Atatürk University, Erzurum, Yakutiye, Turkey

Melih Kabayel
Dr., Izmir Democracy University, Karabaglar, Turkey

Gökmen Kantar
Assoc. Prof. Dr, Tekirdag Namık Kemal University, Tekirdag, Turkey

Gül Ş. Huyugüzel Kişla
Assoc. Prof. Dr., Ege University, Izmir, Turkey

Isidora Ljumović
Dr., Institute of Economic Sciences, Belgrade, Serbia

Metin Nazlioğlu
Res. Assist., Salihli Faculty of Economics and Administrative Sciences, Department of Public Finance, Salihli/Manisa, Turkey

Kerem Özen
Dr., Independent researcher

Christian Pirker
Dr., Karl-Franzens-University Graz, Graz, Austria

Md. Moshiur Rahman
Dr., Bangladesh Public Administration Training Centre, Savar, Dhaka, Bangladesh

Parimal Kumar Roy
Dr., Bangladesh Public Administration Training Centre, Savar, Dhaka, Bangladesh

Md. Shakhawat Hossain Sojib
Capacity Building Training-Research, Bangladesh, Dhaka, Bangladesh

Zekeriya Şahin
Assist. Prof. Dr., Turkish Military Academy (Kara Harp Okulu), Devlet Mah. Kara Harp Okulu Cd., Ankara, Turkey

Burcu Türkcan
Assoc. Prof. Dr., Ege University, Izmir, Turkey

Serdar Yay
Assoc. Prof. Dr., Izmir Democracy University, Karabaglar, Turkey

Hasan Yazar
Res. Assist., Salihli Faculty of Economics and Administrative Sciences, Department of Public Finance, Salihli/Manisa, Turkey

Durmuş Çağrı Yildirim
Prof. Dr., Tekirdag Namik Kemal University, Tekirdag, Turkey

Hakan Yildirim
Prof. Dr., Istanbul Gelisim University, Avcilar, Turkey

Seda Yildirim
Prof. Dr., Tekirdag Namik Kemal University, Tekirdag, Turkey

Şaban Onur Viga
Assist. Prof. Dr., Istanbul Esenyurt University, Esenyurt, Istanbul, Turkey

Preface

This monograph examines the economic consequences of the climate crisis not merely as a reflection of environmental damage or long-term growth losses, but as a multi-layered and structural transformation process spanning migration dynamics, financial stability, regional inequalities, and global capital flows. Recent studies in the climate economics literature highlight that climate change not only impacts productivity, price stability, and public finances but also reshapes economic structures through population movements and spatial inequalities. In this context, the book conceptualises climate risk not as a temporary shock, but as an element that permanently transforms the functioning of the economic system.

Climate-induced migration holds a central place in the economic analysis of this monograph. Rising temperatures, water scarcity, agricultural yield losses, and extreme weather events are triggering forced migration movements both domestically and internationally. The current literature shows that the effects of these migration waves on labour supply, wages, housing markets, and public spending vary from region to region and have the potential to deepen existing inequalities. This monograph analyses climate migration not only as a humanitarian crisis but also as an economic phenomenon with long-term effects on regional labour markets, production structures, and public finances.

Climate finance is another fundamental axis of the book. As frequently emphasised in the existing literature, there is a significant mismatch between global climate targets and the financial resources needed to achieve them. This collection examines green bonds, sustainable finance instruments, and the role of development banks not only in terms of investment volume but also within the context of the geographical distribution of capital and its impact on regional inequalities. The structural constraints faced by developing countries and regions highly vulnerable to climate change in accessing finance bring up the justice dimension of global climate finance.

In this context, the book argues that climate finance, in its current state, can sometimes reproduce rather than reduce regional and global inequalities. The fact that capital flows are predominantly directed toward countries with low risk and high return potential deprives the regions most affected by the climate crisis of adaptation and mitigation investments. This situation is deepening both economic development disparities and threatening global economic stability by increasing climate-related migration pressures.

At the macroeconomic level, the climate crisis creates new risk channels in terms of inflation dynamics, financial stability, and public debt sustainability. This monograph discusses the current approaches of central banks and regulatory institutions that treat climate risk as an integral part of financial stability within a theoretical and institutional framework. In addition to physical risks, policy uncertainties arising from the transition to a low-carbon economy and sudden corrections in asset valuations are increasing systemic risks in the financial system.

Finally, the relationship between regional inequalities and labour markets is examined from a green transition perspective. While the circular economy and green job opportunities create new growth areas in certain regions, job losses and income declines can occur in regions dependent on fossil fuels. This monograph emphasises the necessity of inclusive policy frameworks that consider the asymmetric regional and sectoral effects of climate policies.

With this holistic approach, the book establishes a strong connection with current academic debates in the climate economics literature, offering an original and in-depth contribution that addresses the climate crisis through the lenses of migration, financing, and regional inequalities and focuses on the structural transformation of the economic system.

Meltem Ince-Yenilmez
Editor

Economic Implications of the Climate Crisis

Saffet Akdağ

Abstract: This study explores how climate risks shape financial market dynamics, focusing on two distinct measures: the Physical Risk Index (PRI) and the Transition Risk Index (TRI). Drawing on daily data spanning from January 2005 to June 2025, this study examines how these risk indicators relate to the VIX (volatility index), gold, and oil prices, applying both the 1969 Granger causality test and Frequency Domain Approaches. The analysis shows that physical risks, as captured by the PRI, have a notable short-term impact on all three market variables, while transition risks influence only gold, and again only in the short run. Gold's sensitivity to both forms of climate risk helps to explain its continuing appeal as a safe-haven asset. In contrast, the VIX and oil prices seem to react mainly to physical risk factors. From an investment standpoint, the findings point to the importance of preparing strategies that can address sudden climate-related shocks over different time horizons. For regulators and policymakers, the results reinforce the case for embedding climate risk into financial stability assessments, stress-testing procedures, and broader supervisory planning. By identifying how the effects of climate risk vary across asset classes, the study adds a fresh perspective to ongoing debates on the intersection between environmental change and financial stability.

1. Introduction

Scholars have long been interested in how climate and geographical conditions shape human behaviour and social organisation. Centuries ago, Montesquieu, in *The Spirit of the Laws* (1750), argued that high temperatures could sap people's energy and morale, making them less industrious—an observation that, in his view, underscored the influence of climate on both human nature and the structure of society (Dell et al., 2012, p. 66). This perspective treats climate not just as an environmental backdrop but as a fundamental force that can guide patterns of economic and social development. In modern economics, researchers often return to related themes. Geography, climate, transport connectivity, and access to natural resources are widely cited as important drivers of growth and development (Sachs & Warner, 1997; Gallup et al., 1999; Nordhaus, 2006). These structural factors shape a country's long-term growth potential while also determining how exposed it may be to global disruptions—including climate change.

The climate crisis today stands out as one of the most complex and far-reaching challenges for mankind, cutting across environmental, social, and economic domains. Rising greenhouse gas concentrations, warmer global averages, increasingly frequent extreme weather events, and the gradual but relentless rise in sea levels threaten not only ecosystems but also the underlying stability of the global economy. Because of this, climate change has shifted from being seen as a narrow environmental matter to becoming central in debates on economic sustainability, policy design, and the protection of social welfare (Katyal, 2009).

Modern global warming—regarded as one of the most pressing environmental and economic issues of this century—has been driven in large part by fossil fuel-dependent industrial activity, which has disrupted the planet's natural equilibrium (Demirbaş & Aydın, 2020). The consequences go beyond environmental decline, creating direct threats to productivity, public health, and overall social well-being. Disasters such as floods, droughts, wildfires, and heatwaves now occur more often and with greater intensity, leaving no economy untouched, regardless of national borders (Gozzini et al., 2022).

For much of the past, climate change was framed mainly in environmental terms, but over the last few decades, its economic dimensions have come sharply into focus. Severe weather events have caused substantial production losses, imbalances between supply and demand, and volatile prices—especially in sectors like agriculture, energy, transport, and tourism, which are closely tied to climate conditions. The harm is not limited to visible, physical damage; it also works indirectly, for example, by breaking supply chains, damaging key infrastructure, and increasing financial uncertainty. Developing countries tend to face the brunt of these effects, as structural vulnerabilities and limited capacity to adapt amplify the shock. According to the European Environment Agency, climate-related events cost Europe EUR 433 billion between 1980 and 2015. Globally, disasters in 2017–2018 alone caused a record USD 515 billion in damages (Gozzini et al., 2022). These numbers make it clear that the climate crisis is a multi-dimensional threat with deep and lasting consequences for growth and social progress.

Empirical research confirms that the economic toll of climate change falls unevenly, often hitting poorer and tropical countries hardest. Dell et al. (2012), studying 125 countries, found that each 1 °C rise in temperature cut growth in low-income countries by an average of 1.3 percentage points, affecting not just agriculture but also industrial activity and even political stability. Carleton and Hsiang (2016) report that higher temperatures have reduced U.S. corn yields by 45% and slowed global growth by about 0.28% per year. Similarly, Pretis et al. (2018) warn that a 2 °C increase could cause larger-than-expected output losses for most nations. Projections by Kalkuhl and Wenz (2020) suggest a 7–14% drop in global output by 2100 if warming reaches 3.5 °C, while Kahn et al. (2021) estimate that continued warming could lower real GDP per capita by more than 7% by the end of the century.

One of the most directly affected sectors is agriculture. Rising temperatures, shifting precipitation patterns, and the spread of pests and diseases significantly impact both the quantity and quality of agricultural output. Water scarcity and increased irrigation costs raise production expenses, leading to higher food prices. According to recent studies, climate change increases food costs by 1.49–1.79% annually and exerts upward pressure on overall inflation by 0.76–0.91 percentage points per year. Projections by the Potsdam Institute for Climate Impact Research and the European Central Bank estimate that by 2035, global warming could raise food inflation by 0.92–3.23% and headline inflation by 0.32–1.18%. Southern regions are expected to face more intense inflationary pressures due to prolonged high temperatures, while northern regions will experience milder seasonal effects. Africa and South America are anticipated to be among the most affected areas (Tanboğa, 2024). Studies focusing on Turkey support these global trends. Akyol

(2022) found that rising temperatures negatively impact Turkey's economic growth, while Memiş and Aydın (2023) identified a positive relationship between carbon emissions and national income, though they questioned the sustainability of this correlation. Hayaloğlu (2018) concluded that CO_2 emissions negatively affect both economic growth and agricultural value added. These effects, particularly in climate-sensitive sectors such as agriculture, threaten both economic development and food security.

The economic consequences of the climate crisis extend far beyond the confines of individual sectors, producing highly asymmetric impacts across countries, regions, and socioeconomic strata. The acceleration of inequality, the disproportionate exposure of vulnerable populations, and the mounting strain on social protection systems all illustrate the deeply rooted socioeconomic dimensions of climate change. This phenomenon has progressed beyond merely acting as a drag on economic performance; it now constitutes a structural transformation challenge that shapes development trajectories, poverty reduction agendas, and broader social justice objectives. Insights from general equilibrium modelling (Roson & Van der Mensbrugghe, 2012; Dellink et al., 2019) indicate considerable variation in the magnitude and distribution of these effects across both sectors and regions. Developing economies—owing to their greater susceptibility to climate-induced shocks—frequently encounter more severe constraints on growth prospects. Ethiopia stands as a notable example, with projections suggesting that climate change could reduce its GDP by as much as 10% while widening income inequality by nearly 20% (Mideksa, 2010). At the global level, direct economic losses attributable to climate-related disasters over the past decade are estimated at approximately USD 1.3 trillion (Suntheim & Vandenbussche, 2020). Even within Europe, the distribution of outcomes is uneven: while southern and western regions are expected to incur welfare losses, certain northern economies may experience modest welfare gains (Ciscar et al., 2011).

These patterns make it evident that the economic repercussions of climate change are shaped not only by rising temperatures but also by pre-existing structural conditions, localised vulnerabilities, and the specific nature of policy responses. Increasingly, such economic impacts are becoming integral to the policy agenda. Mechanisms like carbon pricing, targeted green investment programmes, and the expansion of renewable energy infrastructure aim not only to mitigate environmental threats but also to reconfigure underlying economic systems. Achieving fairness in cost distribution, enhancing public–private cooperation, and strengthening policy coordination at the multilateral level are critical to ensuring that climate policies do not inadvertently deepen inequality or compromise societal resilience. As such, effective strategies require a calibrated blend of global policy harmonisation and region-specific adaptation measures.

Within this analytical setting, the present study examines the causal linkages between climate-related risks and three core financial market indicators: the VIX, representing market volatility; gold, traditionally perceived as a safe-haven asset; and crude oil, a central component of the global energy system. The analysis centres on two high-frequency measures of climate risk—the Physical Risk Index (PRI) and the Transition Risk Index (TRI)—derived through systematic text-mining techniques applied to the Reuters News Archive. Updated daily since January 2005 (Bua et al., 2024), these indices capture two distinct risk dimensions: the PRI reflects unexpected developments associated with physical climate impacts such as extreme weather events, droughts, or sea level rise, while the TRI measures unanticipated developments in the transition toward climate policy targets, including the introduction of carbon taxation, net-zero commitments, and renewable energy policy initiatives.

By investigating the causal interactions between these risk measures and macro-financial variables such as the VIX, gold, and oil prices, this research offers an original contribution to the literature on climate-finance linkages. Beyond exploring statistical relationships, it also addresses the temporal nature of such linkages, distinguishing between short-term market reactions to acute shocks and longer-term adjustments to structural policy shifts. In doing so, the study not only enriches the empirical understanding of how climate risks permeate financial markets but also provides actionable insights for policymakers, investors, and regulatory authorities. The findings may inform risk management strategies, contribute to the refinement of volatility forecasting models, and support the design of adaptive financial instruments capable of mitigating the adverse effects of climate-driven uncertainty. The paper is structured into four sections: the first outlines the theoretical and empirical background; the second presents the data sources and methodological framework; the third discusses the empirical results; and the final section synthesises the conclusions and offers targeted policy recommendations for enhancing financial resilience in the face of climate risks.

2. Research Methodology

In this study, the analysis employs daily observations spanning the period from January 2005 to June 2025 for the Physical Risk Index (PRI), the Transition Risk Index (TRI), and three financial market variables: the VIX, gold prices, and crude oil prices. Gold values are expressed in terms of troy ounces, while crude oil prices are denominated in U.S. dollars based on Brent benchmark quotations, with both series obtained from www.investing.com. The PRI and TRI represent high-frequency measures of climate-related risk, constructed through a systematic text-based methodology applied to the Reuters News Archive. Specifically, the PRI quantifies the intensity of unanticipated news related to physical climate hazards, including sudden-onset natural disasters, extended drought periods, and sea level rise. By contrast, the TRI reflects news-driven shocks associated with the structural transition toward climate policy objectives, such as the implementation of carbon pricing mechanisms, commitments to net-zero emissions, and the expansion of renewable energy capacity. The construction of these indices followed a multi-step process. First, distinct text corpora were compiled to capture the conceptual domains of the Physical Risk Index (PRI) and Transition Risk Index (TRI), drawing from both academic publications and institutional reports. These corpora were transformed into vector representations using the Term Frequency–Inverse Document Frequency (TF-IDF) method. Subsequently, cosine similarity scores were computed between the daily news vectors and the PRD/TRD dictionaries, yielding continuous time series that measure daily news intensity for each category of risk. To isolate the unexpected components of these series, autoregressive (AR(1)) residuals were extracted, forming the PRI and TRI indices as indicators of unanticipated climate risk shocks (Bua et al., 2024). The final versions of the PRI and TRI datasets were sourced from www.policyuncertainty.com (accessed on 14 July 2025).

The Volatility Index (VIX) was introduced in 1993 by the Chicago Board Options Exchange (CBOE) to measure market volatility (Xin, 2011). It is calculated based on the difference between call and put option prices on equity indices (Fountain et al., 2008). As the difference narrows, the VIX decreases. The index reflects investors' expectations of stock market volatility over the next 30 days and is commonly referred to as the "investor fear gauge". A higher VIX indicates greater market fear (Whaley, 2000, p. 12). VIX data were sourced directly from the CBOE website (CBOE, 2025).

One of the earliest studies addressing the stationarity of macroeconomic data was conducted by Yule (1926). Granger and Newbold (1974) demonstrated that employing non-stationary datasets in empirical analyses could give rise to the problem of spurious regression. Similarly, Nelson and Plosser (1982) emphasised that conventional statistical techniques are not applicable when dealing with non-stationary time series. Consequently, ensuring that the data satisfy the stationarity condition is regarded as a fundamental prerequisite for analyses carried out using traditional econometric methods. To test whether the variables used in the study contain unit roots and are therefore stationary, three unit root tests were applied: the Augmented Dickey–Fuller (ADF) test, the Phillips–Perron (PP) test, and the Zivot–Andrews structural break unit root test. The ADF test is an extended version of the classical Dickey–Fuller test developed by Dickey and Fuller (1979), later expanded by Said and Dickey (1984) through the inclusion of multiple lag terms. This test incorporates lagged differences to control for autocorrelation in the error terms and assesses the null hypothesis:

H0: $\gamma = 0 \rightarrow$ *indicating the presence of a unit root.*

The PP test, developed by Phillips and Perron (1988), accounts for potential autocorrelation and heteroskedasticity in the error terms, unlike traditional Dickey–Fuller-type tests. It provides a non-parametric correction using Newey–West standard errors. The base regression model and null hypothesis are identical to the ADF test.

The Zivot and Andrews (1992) test, unlike traditional unit root tests, allows for a single unknown structural break in the time series, determined endogenously from the data. This test is particularly useful for modelling the effects of policy shifts or crises in economic and financial time series.

Causality analyses are used to assess the predictive relationship between variables. The Granger (1969) causality test evaluates the statistical causality between variables and requires the data series to be stationary. The model assumes that the error terms of x and y are uncorrelated (Asteriou & Hall, 2011, pp. 322–323).

$$y_t = a_1 + \sum_{i=1}^{n} \beta_i x_{t-i} + \sum_{j=1}^{m} \gamma_i y_{t-j} + \varepsilon_{1t} \tag{1}$$

$$x_t = a_2 + \sum_{i=1}^{n} \theta_i x_{t-i} + \sum_{j=1}^{m} \delta_i y_{t-j} + \varepsilon_{2t} \tag{2}$$

Another causality test is the Frequency Domain Causality Test, developed in a study by Breitung and Candelon (2006). This test examines whether causality between variables is permanent or temporary. In their work, Breitung and Candelon (2006) propose a single testing procedure based on a bivariate vector autoregressive (VAR) model and a linear hypothesis on autoregressive parameters. As a result of the analysis, the test statistics are used to determine the existence of a causal relationship between the variables. Additionally, the test allows researchers to identify whether this relationship is persistent or transitory (Bozoklu & Yılancı, 2013, p. 877).

$$M_{a\to b}(\omega) = \log\left[\frac{2\pi f_x(\omega)}{\left|\Psi_{11}\left(e^{-i\omega}\right)\right|^2}\right] = \log\left[1+\frac{\left|\Psi_{12}\left(e^{-i\omega}\right)\right|^2}{\left|\Psi_{11}\left(e^{-i\omega}\right)\right|^2}\right] \tag{3}$$

According to the equation, if $\Psi_{12}\left(e^{-i\omega}\right) = 0$, then there will be no causality from variable a to variable b at any frequency ω (Ciner, 2011, p. 500). In their study, Breitung and Candelon (2006) propose a new method to test the null hypothesis of no causality.

$$\text{If } M_{a\to b}(\omega) = 0,\ \Psi_{12}\left(e^{-i\omega}\right) = 0 \tag{4}$$

$$\Psi(L) = \Theta(L)^{-1}G^{-1} \text{ ve } \Psi_{12}(L) = -\frac{g^{22}\Theta_{12}(L)}{\Theta(L)} \tag{5}$$

The expression g^{22} represents the determinant of $\Theta(L)$, where $\Theta(L)$ are the lower diagonal elements of the matrix G^{-1}.

3. Results and Discussion

Descriptive statistics were first calculated for the data used in the study. These are presented in Table 1.

Table 1. Descriptive statistics of the study variables.

Variables	Mean	Minimum	Maximum	Std. Dev.	Skewness	Kurtosis
PRI	−0.00012	−0.0631	0.1225	0.0208	0.7494	4.4632
TRI	0.00008	−0.0782	0.1907	0.0233	0.9994	7.1375
Gold	1386.02	414.30	3452.80	549.49	0.7169	4.2219
Oil	71.7264	11.5700	145.290	20.9670	0.3061	2.7204
VIX	19.1969	9.1400	82.6900	8.7230	2.5089	12.3673

PRI—Physical Risk Index; TRI—Transition Risk Index; VIX—The Volatility Index. Source: Table by author.

When the statistical values for the variables in Table 1 are examined, it can be stated that the variability in these series is significant, as the mean of the PRI and TRI variables is smaller than the relevant standard deviation. The positive skewness and elevated kurtosis observed in the PRI and TRI variables suggest that these indices can, at times, exhibit unexpected upward movements, a feature that warrants attention in risk management considerations. For the VIX, gold, and oil variables, the mean values exceed their respective standard deviations, indicating that the data are more tightly clustered around the average and thus reflect relatively lower volatility. Notably, the pronounced skewness and kurtosis in the VIX and gold series point to their tendency to rise during periods of market turmoil. This pattern reinforces the view that the VIX functions as a barometer of financial stress, while gold retains its role as a safe-haven asset in times of economic uncertainty. In contrast, the relatively low skewness and kurtosis in oil prices suggest a more balanced, near-normal distribution. Table 2 shows the ADF and PP test results used to test whether the variables used in the analysis are stationary.

Table 2. Unit root test results for the study variables.

Variables	ADF		PP	
	Constant	Constant and Trend	Constant	Constant and Trend
PRI	−12.3091 *	−13.1251 *	−102.6757 *	−98.1143 *
TRI	−11.5110 *	−12.3939 *	−105.7189 *	−100.5334 *
Gold	1.3869	0.1428	1.4653	0.1748
ΔGold	−19.8337	−19.8971 *	−73.7394	−73.8248
Oil	−2.7422	−2.8360	−2.8050	−2.9059
ΔOil	−19.3253 *	−19.3292 *	−75.1226	−75.1208
VIX	−5.6885 *	−5.6981 *	−6.6957 *	−6.7038 *

* Significant at 1% significance level. ADF—the Augmented Dickey–Fuller test; PP—the Phillips–Perron test. Source: Table by author.

According to the ADF and PP test results, the PRI, TRI, and VIX variables were found to be stationary at the level. This result indicates that the relevant variables fluctuate around a certain mean over time and do not contain a unit root. Gold and oil prices, on the other hand, were not stationary at the level but were found to be stationary when the different series were taken.

Financial time series often contain structural breaks. Because classical unit root tests (ADF, PP) do not account for such breaks, they can reduce the power of the test and pose a risk of incorrectly assuming non-stationary series to be stationary. Therefore, in this study, the Zivot & Andrews Breakpoint Unit Root (ZA) Test was applied under the assumption that the series may contain a structural break. The ZA test endogenously determines the unknown structural break date in the series and performs the stationarity test by considering this break point. Table 3 presents the results of the Zivot & Andrews Breakpoint Unit Root Test.

Table 3. Zivot & Andrews Breakpoint Unit Root Test for the study variables.

Variables	Zivot & Andrews Test	
	Constant	Constant and Trend
PRI	−14.1221 *	−14.2558 *
TRI	−14.5263 *	−14.6256 *
Gold	−1.9736 *	−2.5424
ΔGold	−20.3301 *	−20.3294 *
Oil	−4.5574 *	−4.4833 *
ΔOil	−19.5128 *	−19.5944 **
VIX	−6.2895 *	−7.0445 *

* Indicates significance at 1% and ** at 5% levels of significance, respectively. Source: Table by author.

An examination of the Zivot & Andrews Breakpoint Unit Root test results revealed that the PRI, TRI, and VIX variables are stationary at the level, while oil prices are stationary in both the level and difference series, taking into account structural breaks. This indicates that sudden regime changes, particularly during crisis periods, do not alter the stationarity of the series. Gold prices, on the other hand, are found to contain a unit root at the level and are stationary in the difference series. Therefore, structural breaks in gold prices do not alter the unit root test results.

Following the unit root tests, causality tests were conducted from the climate risk indices to the VIX, gold, and oil prices. The test results are presented in Table 4.

Table 4. Granger causality test results for the study variables.

Direction of Causality	F-Statistic	Lag	Result
PRI → VIX	2.1547 *	7	Granger causality exists.
TRI → VIX	0.5255	11	Granger causality does not exist.
PRI → Gold	2.7922 *	3	Granger causality exists.
TRI → Gold	2.8011 *	4	Granger causality exists.
PRI → Oil	1.8765 *	8	Granger causality exists.
TRI → Oil	0.4898	7	Granger causality does not exist.

* Significant at 5% significance level. Source: Table by author.

According to the Granger (1969) causality results in Table 4, a direct causal relationship was found from the PRI to the VIX and to gold and oil prices. The causal relationship found from the PRI to the VIX indicates that physical climate risks can affect the volatility index by increasing investor uncertainty and market volatility. This suggests that climate-related disasters such as floods, forest fires, and droughts can quickly trigger risk perception in financial markets. Furthermore, the causal relationship found for gold prices reflects investors' tendency to seek safe-haven assets during periods of increased physical climate-related risks. Similarly, the causal relationship found for oil prices reveals that climate events also affect commodity markets through their effects on the supply–demand balance and energy infrastructure. These findings demonstrate that the PRI plays a significant role in financial market dynamics as a leading indicator reflecting climate-related shocks and demonstrate that it is an important risk factor for investors to consider in short-term pricing behaviour. A causal relationship was found only from the TRI to gold prices. This may suggest that transition risks such as policy changes towards a low-carbon economy, carbon pricing, and technological transformation are not directly reflected in financial markets in the short term. The causal relationship identified in the gold market can be attributed to investors' tendency to seek traditional safe havens in uncertain environments. On the other hand, the ineffectiveness of the TRI in shorter-term and volatility-sensitive markets such as the VIX and oil suggests that transition risks are priced in through longer-term processes. In this context, the impact of the TRI on financial markets may emerge over time and may not be fully captured by short-term analyses such as Granger (1969) causality analysis. Consequently, the impact of transition risks on financial markets should be evaluated primarily in the context of long-term investment decisions and sustainable financial policies.

The results of the Frequency Domain Causality test, conducted to test the periodic extent of the causal relationship between variables, are presented in Table 5.

When the results of the Frequency Domain Causality test in Table 5 are evaluated, a short-term causality relationship from the PRI to the VIX is identified, while no causality from the TRI to the VIX is identified in any period. The situation is different for gold prices. Causality from the PRI to gold prices is found to exist in all periods, but causality from the TRI to changes in gold prices is only effective in the short term. When the causality relationship from the PRI to changes in oil prices is examined, a causality relationship is found only in the short term, and no causality relationship from the TRI to changes in oil prices is found in any period. Graphs of the test results are provided in Appendix A.

Table 5. Frequency Domain Causality test results for the study variables.

Direction of Causality	Long Term		Mid Term		Short Term	
	0.1	0.5	1	1.5	2	2.5
PRI → VIX	1.8441	0.0669	1.2446	4.3562	9.0573 *	0.5854
TRI → VIX	3.0702	1.2865	0.0798	0.1406	2.3210	0.2108
PRI → ΔGold	7.8509 **	7.9479 **	8.2441 **	8.2574 **	7.1462 **	6.5106 **
TRI → ΔGold	0.4700	0.2769	1.6153	5.7276	8.2261 **	10.9856 *
PRI → ΔOil	0.3399	0.2561	0.8867	0.0060	8.9056 *	8.4859 *
TRI → ΔOil	1.9573	2.2044	2.6132	0.1337	0.5904	0.0774

* Indicates significance at 1% and ** at 5% levels of significance, respectively. Source: Table by author.

The present analysis investigates the influence of both physical and transition-related climate risks on key indicators within global financial markets, applying Granger causality techniques (Granger, 1969) alongside Frequency Domain Causality approaches. The empirical findings indicate that physical climate risks (PRI) exert a wider and more substantial influence on market dynamics and investor sentiment compared to transition-related risks (TRI). Results from the Granger causality framework reveal a statistically significant unidirectional causal flow from the PRI toward the VIX, gold prices, and crude oil prices. Among these, the PRI–VIX linkage emerges as particularly robust, underscoring the pronounced sensitivity of market volatility to climate-induced physical disruptions. Severe events—such as large-scale flooding, extensive wildfires, and prolonged drought conditions—can rapidly erode market confidence, prompting abrupt yet transient surges in volatility levels. This tendency suggests that investors perceive such episodes primarily as acute shocks rather than long-term structural shifts. Corroborating this interpretation, the Frequency Domain Causality Test results demonstrate that the causal effect of PRI on the VIX retains statistical significance only over shorter time horizons, implying that financial markets tend to absorb and normalise the impact of these disturbances relatively quickly. Taken together, these findings emphasise the necessity of incorporating climate-related physical risk assessments into volatility forecasting models, particularly for risk-sensitive asset classes, while recognising the temporal nature of such market responses.

For gold prices, the analysis identifies a significant causal link from PRI across all frequency ranges. This pattern indicates that physical climate risks tend to boost demand for safe-haven assets, reinforcing the perception of gold as a financial refuge during periods of crisis. By contrast, the influence of transition risks (TRI) on gold prices emerges as statistically significant only in the short term. This finding suggests that developments tied to climate transitions, such as carbon taxation, environmental regulation, and the expansion of renewable energy policies, have yet to establish lasting effects on investor pricing behaviour. Instead, these factors appear to be viewed primarily as short-lived sources of market uncertainty.

Regarding oil prices, the study finds a short-term causal relationship only from the PRI, indicating that events such as hurricanes, floods, and other physical shocks can temporarily disrupt the supply–demand balance in energy markets. The analysis reveals no evidence of a causal relationship between TRI and oil prices, indicating that transition-related policies have not yet meaningfully shaped the behaviour of oil markets. This outcome suggests that market participants tend to view transition risks as gradual, long-term processes, carrying little immediate influence on short-term pricing dynamics.

Likewise, the results show no statistically significant causal link between TRI and the VIX at any frequency. This supports the view that transition risks influence market volatility only indirectly and are more likely to manifest their effects over extended time horizons. Factors such as carbon pricing, environmental regulations, and technological transformation appear to influence volatility not through immediate shocks but rather through gradually unfolding structural adjustments.

Overall, the evidence suggests that physical climate risks (PRI) exert sharper and more immediate impacts on financial markets, whereas transition risks (TRI) emerge more slowly and are largely long-term in character. As a result, the way market participants perceive and respond to climate risks depends not only on whether the risk is physical or transition-related, but also on its time horizon—whether it is short-, medium-, or long-term. For example, while the gold market shows sensitivity to both the PRI and TRI, the VIX and oil prices are predominantly responsive to physical risks. This divergence highlights the need for differentiated investor responses based on asset type and time horizon.

Consistent with the literature, these results confirm that climate change should no longer be viewed solely as an environmental concern but as a systemic economic and financial risk. From an investor's perspective, physical risks play a decisive role in short-term pricing. The short-term influence of the PRI on the VIX and on gold and oil prices suggests that investors must adopt more cautious positions in anticipation of sudden climate shocks such as floods, wildfires, or storms. Such events can increase volatility and elevate the risk of speculative investment positions. In this context, gold emerges as a prominent safe-haven asset. Given its statistically significant relationship with both the PRI and TRI, gold can serve as an effective hedge during periods of uncertainty, making gold-inclusive portfolios potentially more resilient to climate-related shocks.

Although the TRI currently has a limited observable impact, particularly in the short term and primarily on gold, this does not negate the importance of long-term sustainability strategies. Transition-related developments such as carbon regulation, green finance policies, and technological innovation possess the potential to exert substantial influence on asset prices over time. As the effects of physical risks tend to be more visible in the short term, and transition risks unfold over longer horizons, investors must develop portfolio strategies that are resilient to both immediate shocks and long-term structural changes.

From the perspective of market regulators, the findings underscore the urgent need to systematically analyse the macro-financial effects of climate risks and incorporate them into policy frameworks to ensure financial stability. The observed impact of the PRI on the volatility index highlights the capacity of climate shocks to trigger sudden and unforeseen fluctuations in the financial system. This underlines the importance of treating climate risks not only as environmental threats but also as key factors for financial stability. The PRI and TRI should be integrated into financial stress tests, risk assessment frameworks, and financial stability reports.

Additionally, the limited short-term pricing of the TRI in financial markets suggests that the effects of transition risks are likely to emerge gradually and may be delayed. This, however, does not imply that these risks are insignificant. On the contrary, if policymakers adopt abrupt or poorly communicated regulatory measures, the potential for sudden and severe market corrections increases. Therefore, the regulatory framework must be gradual, consistent, and predictable. To reduce uncertainty surrounding the transition process, central banks and regulatory authorities should provide clear, time-aligned roadmaps toward decarbonisation, enabling market participants to price such risks more accurately and promptly.

Moreover, to facilitate the integration of climate risks into financial markets, the design and promotion of green bonds, carbon-linked securities, and other sustainable investment instruments must be revisited. Developing and supporting such instruments would help investors diversify and hedge climate-related risks, while also enabling regulators to align climate policy more effectively with financial system dynamics.

This study is not without limitations. First, the Granger (1969) causality and Frequency Domain Causality Tests used focus primarily on short- and medium-term relationships and may not fully capture the long-term dynamics associated with transition risks. Additionally, the constructed indices may not encompass all dimensions of physical and transition risks. Factors such as data quality, frequency, and representativeness may also influence the sensitivity of the causality tests. Future research could apply panel data models, structural VAR approaches, or macroeconomic impact simulations to explore more comprehensive and time-extended effects of climate risks. Micro-level analyses focusing on risk contagion, systemic risk formation, and investor sentiment across financial asset classes would also offer valuable contributions.

4. Conclusions

This study evaluates the impact of climate risks on financial markets through the lens of both physical and transition risks by testing the causal relationships of the Physical Risk Index (PRI) and the Transition Risk Index (TRI) with the VIX and with gold and oil prices using Granger (1969) causality and Frequency Domain Causality tests. The study offers significant findings regarding investor behaviour and market responses. It is observed that physical risks play a determining role, particularly in short-term pricing, whereas transition risks have more limited effects. Safe-haven assets such as gold appear to be more sensitive to both types of risks, while indicators like the VIX and oil prices predominantly respond to physical shocks. The results highlight that market participants need to develop distinct strategies depending on the type and temporal characteristics of the risk. From the perspective of policymakers, the findings emphasise the importance of regulatory framework predictability as a critical factor in managing climate risks effectively within the financial system.

Funding: This research received no external funding.

Conflicts of Interest: The author declares no conflicts of interest.

Author Name and Affiliation: Saffet Akdağ, Department of Finance and Banking, Tarsus University, Mersin, Turkey.

Keywords: climate risk; Physical Risk Index; Transition Risk Index; 1969 Granger causality test; Frequency Domain Test; VIX; financial market; gold; oil.

Appendix A

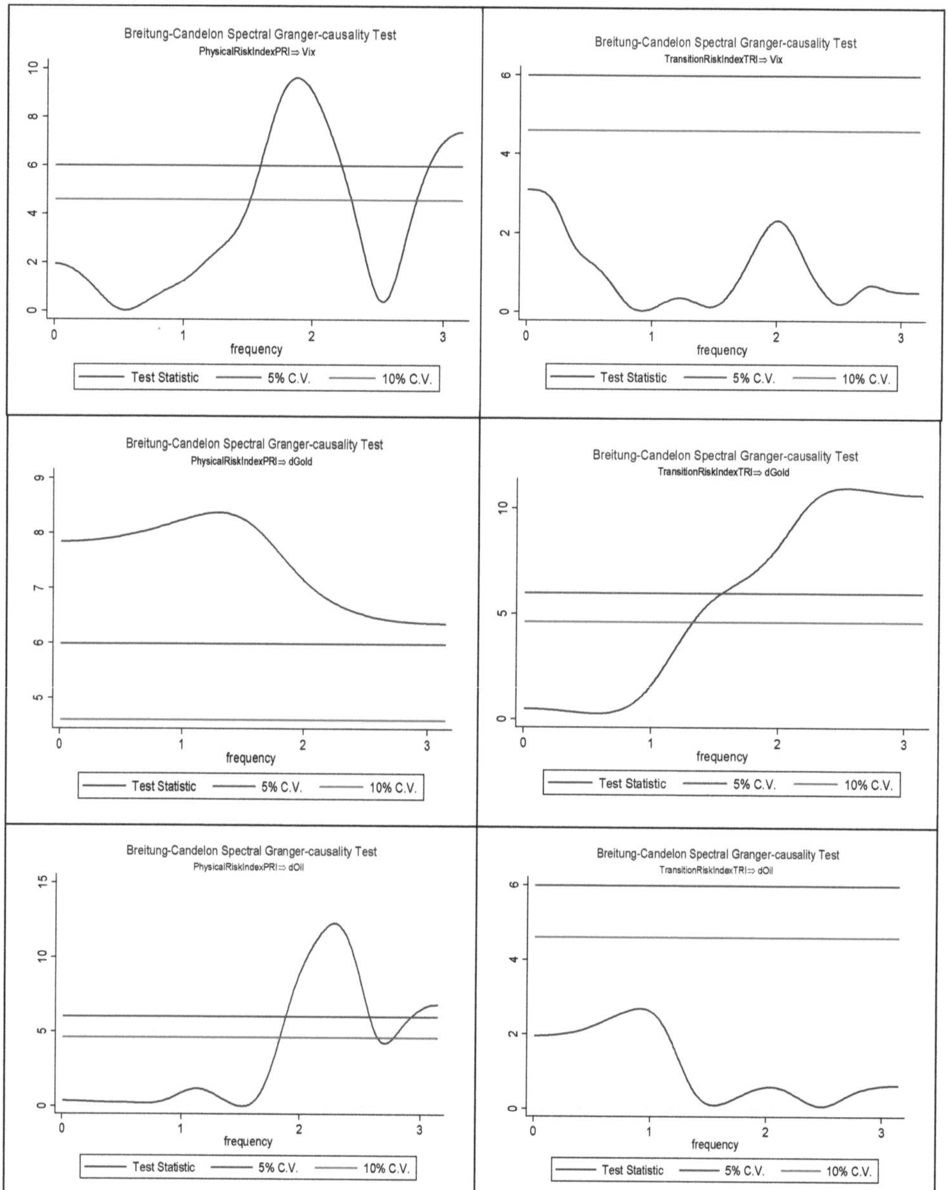

Source: Figure by author.

References

Akyol, H. (2022). İklim değişikliği Türkiye'de ekonomik büyüme için bir risk oluşturur mu? *Afet ve Risk Dergisi*, *5*(1), 179–195. [CrossRef]

Asteriou, D., & Hall, S. G. (2011). *Applied econometrics* (2nd ed.). Macmillan International Higher Education.

Bozoklu, S., & Yılancı, V. (2013). Energy consumption and economic growth for selected OECD countries: Further evidence from the Granger causality test in the frequency domain. *Energy Policy*, *63*, 877–881. [CrossRef]

Breitung, J., & Candelon, B. (2006). Testing for short and long-run causality: A frequency domain approach. *Journal of Econometrics*, *132*(2), 363–378. [CrossRef]

Bua, G., Kapp, D., Ramella, F., & Rognone, L. (2024). Transition versus physical climate risk pricing in European financial markets: A text-based approach. *The European Journal of Finance*, *30*(17), 2076–2110. [CrossRef]

Carleton, T. A., & Hsiang, S. M. (2016). Social and economic impacts of climate. *Science*, *353*(6304). [CrossRef] [PubMed]

CBOE. (2025). *Chicago board options exchange, VIX*. Available online: http://www.cboe.com/vix (accessed on 14 July 2025).

Ciner, Ç. (2011). Eurocurrency interest rate linkages: A frequency domain analysis. *International Review of Economics and Finance*, *20*(4), 498–505. [CrossRef]

Ciscar, J. C., Iglesias, A., Feyen, L., Szabó, L., Van Regemorter, D., Amelung, B., Nicholls, R., Watkiss, P., Christensen, O. B., Dankers, R., Garrote, L., Goodess, C. M., Hunt, A., Moreno, A., Richards, J., & Soria, A. (2011). Physical and economic consequences of climate change in Europe. *Proceedings of the National Academy of Sciences*, *108*(7), 2678–2683. [CrossRef]

Dell, M., Jones, B. F., & Olken, B. A. (2012). Temperature shocks and economic growth: Evidence from the last half century. *American Economic Journal: Macroeconomics*, *4*(3), 66–95. [CrossRef]

Dellink, R., Lanzi, E., & Chateau, J. (2019). The sectoral and regional economic consequences of climate change to 2060. *Environmental and Resource Economics*, *72*(2), 309–363. [CrossRef]

Demirbaş, M., & Aydın, R. (2020). 21. yüzyılın en büyük tehdidi: Küresel iklim değişikliği. *Ecological Life Sciences*, *15*(4), 163–179.

Dickey, D. A., & Fuller, W. A. (1979). Distribution of the estimators for autoregressive time series with a unit root. *Journal of the American Statistical Association*, *74*(366a), 427–431. [PubMed]

Fountain, R. L., Herman, J. R., Jr., & Rustvold, D. L. (2008). An application of Kendall distributions and alternative dependence measures: SPX vs. VIX. *Insurance: Mathematics and Economics*, *42*(2), 469–472. [CrossRef]

Gallup, J. L., Sachs, J. D., & Mellinger, A. D. (1999). Geography and economic development. *International Regional Science Review*, *22*(2), 179–232. [CrossRef]

Gozzini, B., Giorgio, B., & Grifoni, D. (2022). The climate crisis and its impact on the territory, economic and social effects. *Modern Environmental Science and Engineering*, *7*(9), 871–881.

Granger, C. W. J. (1969). Investigating causal relations by econometric models and cross-spectral methods. *Econometrica*, *37*(3), 424–438. [CrossRef]

Granger, C. W. J., & Newbold, P. (1974). Spurious regressions in econometrics. *Journal of Econometrics, 2*(2), 111–120. [CrossRef]

Hayaloğlu, P. (2018). İklim değişikliğinin tarım sektörü ve ekonomik büyüme üzerindeki etkileri. *Gümüşhane Üniversitesi Sosyal Bilimler Dergisi, 9*(25), 51–62.

Kahn, M. E., Mohaddes, K., Ng, R. N., Pesaran, M. H., Raissi, M., & Yang, J. C. (2021). Long-term macroeconomic effects of climate change: A cross-country analysis. *Energy Economics, 104*, 105624. [CrossRef]

Kalkuhl, M., & Wenz, L. (2020). The impact of climate conditions on economic production. *Environmental and Resource Economics, 103*, 102360.

Katyal, A. K. (2009). Climate change: Social, economic, and environmental sustainability. *Environmental Forensics, 10*(3), 177–182. [CrossRef]

Memiş, O. B., & Aydın, R. (2023). İklim değişikliğinin ekonomik büyüme üzerine etkisi: Türkiye örneği. *Üçüncü Sektör Sosyal Ekonomi Dergisi, 58*(2), 1065–1080.

Mideksa, T. K. (2010). Economic and distributional impacts of climate change: The case of Ethiopia. *Global Environmental Change, 20*(2), 278–286. [CrossRef]

Nelson, C. R., & Plosser, C. R. (1982). Trends and random walks in macroeconomic time series: Some evidence and implications. *Journal of Monetary Economics, 10*, 139–162. [CrossRef]

Nordhaus, W. D. (2006). Geography and macroeconomics: New data and new findings. *Proceedings of the National Academy of Sciences, 103*(10), 3510–3517. [CrossRef]

Phillips, P. C. B., & Perron, P. (1988). Testing for a unit root in time series regression. *Biometrika, 75*(2), 335–346. [CrossRef]

Pretis, F., Schwarz, M., Tang, K., Haustein, K., & Allen, M. R. (2018). Uncertain impacts on economic growth when stabilizing global temperatures at 1.5 °C or 2 °C warming. *Philosophical Transactions of the Royal Society A: Mathematical, Physical and Engineering Sciences, 376*(2119), 20160460. [CrossRef]

Roson, R., & Van der Mensbrugghe, D. (2012). Climate change and economic growth: Impacts and interactions. *International Journal of Sustainable Economy, 4*(3), 270–285. [CrossRef]

Sachs, J. D., & Warner, A. M. (1997). Sources of slow growth in African economies. *Journal of African Economies, 6*(3), 335–376. [CrossRef]

Said, S. E., & Dickey, D. A. (1984). Testing for unit roots in autoregressive-moving average models of unknown order. *Biometrika, 71*(3), 599–607. [CrossRef]

Suntheim, F., & Vandenbussche, J. (2020). Equity investors must pay more attention to climate change physical risk. *IMF Blog: Climate and the Economy*. Available online: https://www.imf.org/en/blogs/articles/2020/05/29/blog-gfsr-ch5-equity-investors-must-pay-more-attention-to-climate-change-physical-risk. (accessed on 1 July 2025).

Tanboğa, S. (2024). *İklim değişikliği ve ekonomik etkileri*. Türkiye İhracatçılar Merkezi. Available online: https://tim.org.tr/files/downloads/Mevzuat/Iklim_Degisikligi_ve_Ekonomik_Etkileri.pdf (accessed on 14 July 2025).

Whaley, R. E. (2000). The investor fear gauge. *Journal of Portfolio Management, 26*(3), 12–17. [CrossRef]

Xin, M. (2011). *The VIX volatility index (2011–7)*. Uppsala University.

Yule, G. U. (1926). Why do we sometimes get nonsense-correlations between time-series?—A study in sampling and the nature of time-series. *Journal of the Royal Statistical Society, 89*(1), 1–63. [CrossRef]

Zivot, E., & Andrews, D. W. (1992). Further evidence on the great crash, the oil-price shock, and the unit-root hypothesis. *Journal of Business & Economic Statistics, 10*(3), 251–270.

The Relationship Between Investment, Economic Growth, and Renewable Energy in Japan: The Gap Between Goals and Investment

Aycan Can and Gökmen Kantar

Abstract: The rapid changes taking place around the world also have a strong impact on the financial world. In particular, the climate crisis and environmental degradation are making it necessary to re-evaluate financial investments in terms of sustainability. In this context, green finance is coming to the fore. This approach, which aims to be both environmentally conscious and economically profitable, is gaining traction worldwide. This study empirically tests the relationship between renewable energy consumption, foreign direct investment, and economic growth in Japan between 1990 and 2021. Additionally, despite progress in the field of green finance in Japan, this study addresses the fundamental challenges between targets and investments, offering areas for development and recommendations.

1. Introduction

Green finance is the entirety of the financial processes and tools that support environmental sustainability. This method, which is used to combat climate change, increase energy efficiency, and protect natural resources, represents an environmentally conscious financial approach. Furthermore, unlike traditional financial models, it aims to reduce environmental impacts and provide social benefits (Wang et al., 2025). Methodological foundations of bootstrap ARDL and related empirical applications are further supported by McNown et al. (2018), Saleem et al. (2019), Fatima et al. (2022), Wall et al. (2019), and Cao et al. (2025).

The new financing model not only protects the environment but also puts economic growth on a sustainable footing. For example, funds provided for renewable energy projects reduce carbon emissions while creating new employment opportunities. In addition, companies that adopt environmentally friendly strategies gain a more reputable position in the eyes of consumers. Thus, financial success can be achieved in the long term. Therefore, green financing is a good opportunity for both individual and institutional investors (Tong et al., 2020).

Environmentally focused investments aim to improve today's world while providing a more sustainable life for future generations. However, the goal is not only sustainability or resource conservation. Green investments also provide long-term economic advantages. The main benefits of these investments can be listed as follows (Zheng et al., 2025):

- Green investments contribute to minimising carbon emissions.
- Investments in renewable energy sources reduce energy costs.

- Environmentally friendly projects increase profitability with sustainable business models.
- The growth of the green economy creates employment opportunities in new sectors.
- Projects that minimise environmental impacts contribute to public health by improving air and water quality.
- Companies that adopt environmentally friendly strategies gain a competitive advantage in the market.

Each of the various financial mechanisms that support environmental sustainability is considered a green finance tool. The primary purpose of these tools is to provide funding for environmentally friendly projects and reduce carbon emissions. Although they may appear different from one another, each tool aims to reduce environmental impacts and provide economic benefits. For example, carbon markets, which offer trading systems aimed at reducing carbon emissions, are green finance tools. Through this financing, it is possible to purchase carbon credits to avoid exceeding the specified carbon emission limits (Balli et al., 2023).

Sustainability funds are financing models used to invest in environmentally friendly technologies and innovations. These funds focus on projects with a low carbon footprint. As an investor, environmentally conscious investments can be made through these funds. As can be seen from the examples, green financing instruments play an important role in combating environmental problems (Alzaidy et al., 2017).

On the other hand, although green finance is seen as an important tool in the fight against climate change, there is a serious gap between targets and actual investments. Financial institutions support climate-resilient projects and renewable energy investments to reduce carbon emissions and support sustainable development. However, their participation in this process is shaped by both opportunities and challenges. In this regard, the role of financial institutions is crucial. As financial institutions, banks, investment funds, insurance companies, and development finance institutions play a fundamental role in the green transition in four distinct ways (Zhu et al., 2025).

1. Green Bonds and Sustainability Bonds

Institutions issue green bonds to finance environmentally friendly projects. These bonds are used in solar and wind energy projects, energy efficiency investments, or projects with carbon reduction targets.

2. Credit Policies and ESG Criteria

Banks are developing lending policies based on environmental, social, and governance (ESG) criteria. Loans to carbon-intensive sectors are being restricted, and priority is being given to low-carbon investments.

3. Portfolio Transformation and Risk Management

Institutions are reshaping their investments to reduce climate risks. Investments in fossil fuel companies are being reduced, and renewable energy companies are being supported.

4. Development Banks and Public Finance

Institutions such as the World Bank and the European Investment Bank provide financing for climate-resilient projects in developing countries. These institutions also offer risk-sharing mechanisms to encourage the private sector.

As a result, even though the targets are ambitious, progress in green investments may be insufficient. The main reasons for this are (Jiang & Ma, 2025) as follows:

- Insufficient incentives: Carbon pricing, subsidies, and tax incentives are not sufficiently robust.
- Risk perception: Projects in developing countries are perceived as high-risk by investors.
- Data deficiency: There is a lack of reliable and comparable data to measure ESG performance.
- Short-term profit focus: Since a large part of the financial system focuses on short-term returns, long-term climate investments are being pushed into the background.

This study empirically tests the relationship between renewable energy consumption, foreign direct investment, and economic growth in Japan between 1990 and 2021. In addition, this study addresses the fundamental challenges between targets and investments despite advances in green finance in Japan and offers areas for development and recommendations. The first section of the study covers materials and methods, the second section presents the results obtained from the empirical analysis, the third section includes a discussion, and the final section concludes by addressing the fundamental challenges between targets and implementation in the field of green finance in Japan, despite the progress made, and offers areas for development and recommendations.

2. Materials and Methods

This study analyses the relationship between RENE, GDP, and FDI in Japan. The econometric equation used in the analysis is generally as follows:

$$lnRENE_{2t} = \gamma_0 + \gamma_1 lnGDP_t + \gamma_2 lnFDI_{it} + \varepsilon_{it} \quad (1)$$

R, R-Studio, and Eviews 10 programs were used to perform the analyses in this study. γ_0 represents the constant term, ε_{it} represents the error term, and γ_1 and γ_2 represent the coefficients of each variable. In the equation, GDP_t represents per capita GDP at constant 2015 USD prices, which is a measure of economic growth; FDI_t represents the share of FDI inflows in GDP; and $RENE_t$ represents the share of renewable energy consumption in total final energy consumption, which is a measure of renewable energy consumption. Renewable energy data were obtained from the OECD, while all other data were obtained from the World Bank database. Detailed definitions of the variables are provided in Table 1.

Table 1. Variables and definitions.

Variables	Symbols	Measurement	Source
Renewable Energy Consumption	RENE	Percentage of total final energy consumption	OECD
Economic Growth	GDP	GDP per capita (2015 US dollars)	WB
Foreign Direct Investment	FDI	Net investment inflows (as a percentage of GDP)	WB

Source: Table by authors.

Table 2 provides descriptive statistics for Japan. This table shows the means, medians, and other statistical findings for variables from 1990 to 2021.

Table 2. Descriptive statistics for Japan (1990–2021).

	lnREN	lnGDP	lnFDI
Mean	4.890938	4.12×10^{12}	0.252721
Median	4.385000	4.19×10^{12}	0.141526
Maximum	8.800000	4.58×10^{12}	1.237932
Minimum	3.340000	3.51×10^{12}	−0.052088
Std. Dev.	1.489320	3.06×10^{11}	0.296694
Skewness	1.336360	−0.288961	1.562960
Kurtosis	3.678734	2.009980	5.213504
Jarque–Bera	10.13881	1.752176	19.56130
Probability	0.006286	0.416409	0.000057
Sum	156.5100	1.32×10^{14}	8.087058
Sum Sq. Dev.	68.76027	2.90×10^{24}	2.728850
Observations	32	32	32

Source: Authors' compilation based on data from OECD (2024) and World Bank (2024) data.

Long-term relationships between variables were examined using an ARDL model with RENE as the dependent variable. The model was estimated to use a dataset containing annual data from the World Bank (WB) from 1990 to 2021. The ADF unit root test was performed using data in logarithmic form. Subsequently, the cointegration relationship between the series was tested using the bootstrap ARDL cointegration analysis (Caglar, 2020).

3. Results

In this study, the logarithmic values of the series were taken, and the ADF unit root test was performed. The unit root results of the variables related to the Japanese economy were found to be stationary in the first difference when the level values and first differences of the series were taken. The results are presented in Table 3.

Table 3. ADF unit root results.

Variables	Level Values	*p*-Value	First Difference Values	*p*-Value
	ADF		ADF	
LnRENE	2.692	1.000	−5.003	0.000
lnGDP	−1.706	0.618	−5.793	0.000
lnFDI	−2.364	0.159	−7.884	0.000

ADF—the Augmented Dickey–Fuller test. Source: Authors' compilation based on data from OECD (2024) and World Bank (2024) data.

Table 4 presents the results of the Bootstrap ARDL cointegration test. To investigate whether there is a long-term relationship between RENE and other variables, boundary and bootstrap tests were applied for Cases II and III. The results reveal that there is cointegration between the dependent variable RENE and other variables for Japan (Bertelli et al., 2022).

Table 4. Bootstrap ARDL cointegration test results.

		Fov (C)	Fov (UC)	t (C)	t (UC)	Find (C)	Find (UC)
CASE II	STATISTICS	2.621	6.819	−2.170	−3.264	5.403	10.500
	I (0) 5%	3.272	5.018	-	-	-	-
	I (1) 5%	4.306	6.380	-	-	-	-
	Boot Critical Value (%5)	6.670	5.770	−2.350	-	-	-
CASE III	STATISTICS	4.909	3.262	−2.17	-	-	-
	I (0) 5%	3.71	3.71	−2.86	−2.86	2.96	2.96
	I (1) 5%	5.02	5.02	−3.78	−3.78	5.14	5.14
	Boot Critical Value (%5)	6.80	6.380	−3.510	−1.450	6.260	6.420

ARDL—Autoregressive Distributed Lag. Source: Authors' compilation based on data from OECD (2024) and World Bank (2024).

4. Discussion

Japan aims to be carbon-neutral by 2050. In line with this goal, it has committed to reducing greenhouse gas emissions by 46% by 2030 compared to 2013 levels. According to Japan's Basic Energy Plan, the share of renewable energy in the energy mix is targeted to reach 36–38% by 2030 (IPCC, 2013). Additionally, Japan's Green Growth Strategy was announced at the end of 2020. This strategy includes special incentives for 14 priority sectors (hydrogen, ammonia, offshore wind, mobility, energy efficiency, etc.). In this context, the role and participation of financial institutions is important for the Japanese economy. To this end, the Japanese economy uses certain tools. These are summarised below (Wang et al., 2025).

(a) Green Bonds and the Sustainable Finance Market

Japan is the second-largest exporter of green bonds in Asia after China. As of 2023, the volume of green bonds issued by Japanese companies has exceeded USD 20 billion. The Japanese government issued its first "Climate Transition Bond" in 2024. This bond aims to finance the low-carbon transformation of industry.

(b) Financial Institutions and ESG Policies

Japanese banks (e.g., MUFG, Mizuho, Sumitomo Mitsui) have committed to gradually reducing fossil fuel financing in their energy project lending and aligning their portfolios with net-zero targets. The Bank of Japan (BOJ) has been offering banks low-interest funding mechanisms for green investments and loans since 2021.

(c) Corporate Reporting and TCFD

Japan is one of the global leaders in TCFD (Task Force on Climate-related Financial Disclosures) implementation. The Tokyo Stock Exchange has made climate-related financial disclosures mandatory for large companies since 2022. In addition to all this, despite progress in the field of green finance in Japan, there are still some fundamental challenges between targets and implementation. These are mainly categorised as investment and implementation gaps, dependence on fossil fuels, and quality issues in ESG investments.

- Investment–Implementation Gap: Japan's renewable energy investments are not progressing at the targeted pace. Bureaucracy, land constraints, and grid capacity are creating problems in solar and wind energy.
- Dependence on Fossil Fuels: Japan remains heavily dependent on fossil fuels such as LNG (liquefied natural gas) and coal. This dependence has increased even further since the 2011 Fukushima nuclear disaster. Financial institutions continue to provide financing for fossil fuel projects in some cases. The Japan Exim Bank is an example of this, providing loans for overseas coal projects (Liu, 2022).
- Quality Issues in ESG Investments: Despite the growth of ESG funds, some funds are subject to criticism of "greenwashing". Investments that are not truly environmentally friendly are being marketed with ESG labels (Rafindadi et al., 2018).

5. Conclusions

Japan stands out as one of the leading countries in Asia in terms of green finance. However, it is an undeniable fact that the financial system needs to be restructured in a stronger, more comprehensive, and ambitious manner to achieve net-zero targets. In this regard, coordination between public policies, private sector investments, and sustainable financing instruments in Japan should be increased.

In addition, Japan has a strong framework for effectively using green finance as a public policy tool compared to many developed countries. The state's role is not only regulatory; it also acts as a direct investor, incentive provider, and guiding actor. However, fossil fuel dependency, inadequate carbon pricing, and slow implementation limit the effectiveness of public policies. Therefore, the Japanese government should support the transformation of the financial system, infrastructure investments, and more ambitious climate laws.

In addition, Japan needs a clearer "green investment definition" system, similar to the EU Taxonomy in Europe. ESG data providers should be strengthened, and companies should be encouraged to produce higher-quality climate reporting. In the context of financial innovation, new instruments such as sustainability-linked bonds, carbon markets, and transition finance need to be promoted. Finally, Japan's provision of green finance support to Asian countries would both enhance its regional influence and accelerate green growth.

Author Contributions: Conceptualization, A.C. and G.K.; methodology, A.C.; software, A.C.; validation, A.C. and G.K.; formal analysis, A.C.; investigation, A.C.; resources, G.K.; data curation, A.C.; writing—original draft preparation, A.C.; writing—review and editing, A.C. and G.K.; visualization, A.C.; supervision, G.K.; project administration, G.K. All authors have read and agreed to the published version of the manuscript.

Funding: No funding was used for this study.

Conflicts of Interest: There is no conflict of interest among the authors.

Author Names and Affiliations: Aycan Can, Department of Economics, Tekirdağ Namık Kemal University, Tekirdağ, Turkey; Gökmen Kantar, Political Science and Public Administration, Tekirdağ Namık Kemal University, Tekirdağ, Turkey.

Keywords: green finance; renewable energy consumption; foreign direct investment; economic growth.

References

Alzaidy, G., Ahmad, M. N., & Lacheheb, Z. (2017). The impact of foreign-direct investment on economic growth in Malaysia: The role of financial development. *International Journal of Economics and Financial Issues*, *7*(3), 382–388.

Balli, E., Sigeze, C., Ugur, M. S., & Çatık, A. N. (2023). The relationship between FDI, CO_2 emissions and energy consumption in Asia-Pacifc economic cooperation countries. *Environmental Science and Pollution Research*, *30*, 42845–42862. [CrossRef]

Bertelli, S., Vacca, G., & Zoia, M. (2022). Bootstrap cointegration tests in ARDL models. *Economic Modelling*, *116*, 1–15. [CrossRef]

Caglar, A. E. (2020). The importance of renewable energy consumption and FDI inflows in reducing environmental degradation: Bootstrap ARDL bound test in selected 9 countries. *Journal of Cleaner Production*, *264*, 1–15. [CrossRef]

Cao, W., Zhang, X., & Iqbal, K. (2025). Using green finance to study energy elasticity, coal subsidy, energy transition and energy dependence in E7 economies: An efficiency analysis with data envelopment analysis. *Energy Strategy Reviews*, *60*, 101794. [CrossRef]

Fatima, N., Yanting, Z., & Guohua, N. (2022). Effect of economic growth, FDI inflows, trade openness, environment related technologies and environment related revenues taxes on CO_2 emission with pooled mean group (PMG) panel ARDL. *Research Square*, 1–15. [CrossRef]

IPCC. (2013). *Climate change 2013: The physical science basis. Contribution of working group I to the fifth assessment report of the intergovernmental panel on climate change*. Cambridge University Press.

Jiang, M., & Ma, J. (2025). Policy, investment, and growth: How green finance drives corporate sustainable development? *International Review of Economics & Finance*, *102*, 104326. [CrossRef]

Liu, C. (2022). Empirical analysis of the relationship between renewable energy consumption and economic growth based on the grey markov model. *Hindawi Journal of Mathematics*, *2022*, 5679696. [CrossRef]

McNown, R., Sam, C. Y., & Goh, S. K. (2018). Bootstrapping the autoregressive distributed lag test for cointegration. *Applied Economics*, *50*(13), 1509–1521. [CrossRef]

OECD. (2024). *Renewable energy consumption data*. OECD Statistics Database. Available online: https://stats.oecd.org (accessed on 2 March 2024).

Rafindadi, A. A., Muye, I. M., & Kaita, R. A. (2018). The effects of FDI and energy consumption on environmental pollution in predominantly resource-based economies of the GCC. *Sustainable Energy Technologies and Assessments*, *25*, 126–137. [CrossRef]

Saleem, H., Shabbir, M. S., & Khan, M. B. (2019). The short-run and long-run dynamics among FDI, trade openness and economic growth: Using a bootstrap ARDL test for co-integration in selected south asian countries. *South Asian Journal of Business Studies*, *9*(2), 279–295. [CrossRef]

Tong, T., Ortiz, J., Xu, C., & Li, F. (2020). Economic growth, energy consumption and carbon dioxide emissions in the E7 countries: A bootstrap ARDL bound test. *Energy, Sustainability and Society*, *10*(20), 2–17. [CrossRef]

Wall, R., Grafakos, S., Gianoli, A., & Stavropoulos, S. (2019). Which policy instruments attract foreign direct investments in renewable energy? *Climate Policy*, *19*(1), 59–72. [CrossRef]

Wang, W., Zhang, P., & He, T. (2025). Climate investment and financing, economic growth target constraints and urban green development efficiency. *Journal of Environmental Management*, *382*, 125369. [CrossRef]

World Bank. (2024). *World Development Indicators*. World Bank Open Data. Available online: https://data.worldbank.org (accessed on 2 March 2024).

Zheng, L., Wang, J., & Zhu, X. (2025). The impact of green financing on renewable energy growth in China: Insights from provincial data. *Renewable Energy*, *251*, 123385. [CrossRef]

Zhu, Y., Lin, B., & Zhu, R. (2025). Impact assessment of green finance reforms on renewable energy development. *Environmental Impact Assessment Review*, *114*, 107913. [CrossRef]

Divestment from Fossil Fuels: Redirecting Capital for a Sustainable Future

Durmuş Çağrı Yıldırım and Seda Yıldırım

Abstract: The fight against climate change has made sustainable development necessary. As a result of the sustainable transformation movement initiated by the 2030 SDGs, world leaders have begun to develop sustainable practices and policies in many basic areas, such as health, education, employment, energy, and food. Regarding energy policies, changes have begun to be made in policies based on fossil-based energy sources. Green transformation in energy is important within the scope of the clean energy and accessible energy targets included in the 2030 SDGs. This study aims to determine a framework for investments in renewable and clean energy sources within the scope of green energy transformation. A literature review will be conducted, and international reports and current data will be interpreted. Furthermore, basic indicators for investments in fossil-based energy sources, renewable energy sources, and new energy initiatives will be examined.

1. Introduction

The sustainability problem is a global reality in the 21st century. The Industrial Revolution was an important step in the development of humanity, but it cannot be said that it led to positive developments for the ecosystem. While climate change is a normal weather event, rapid industrialisation, urbanisation, increased production and consumption, etc.—human activities that started during the Industrial Revolution—have brought about climate change and global warming faster and more severely than normal (Yildirim et al., 2023; NASA, n.d.). On the other hand, the limits of natural resources have become more noticeable in today's conditions. *The Limits to Growth* was the first to suggest that the sustainability problem would emerge in the future (Meadows et al., 1972; Yildirim & Yildirim, 2020). After this publication, which clearly stated that economic growth would not be sustainable in the future and that there would be a shortage of resources, global initiatives for sustainability did not progress very quickly. Historical and official progress towards a sustainable future is summarised in Table 1.

The 17 key goals in the 2030 SDGs were the first set of guidelines to show people how to continue growing by considering the balance between economic and social well-being and the environment. As summarised in Table 1, world leaders outlined theoretical approaches to sustainability in the 2000s. In the 2000s, the UN launched the Millennium Development Goals and then the 2030 SDGs to be achieved globally. In 2015, the 2030 Agenda and 2030 SDGs were launched, and 17 key goals were presented officially (UN General Assembly, 2015; Yildirim & Yildirim, 2020; Yildirim, 2022a).

Table 1. Official progress towards a sustainable future.

Year	Issue
1972	*Limits to growth* (Meadows et al., 1972)
1972	United Nations Conference on the Human Environment—Stockholm (UN, 1973)
1987	Brundtland Report—Our Common Future (UN, 1987)
1989	Blueprint for a Green Economy (Pearce et al., 1989)
1992	Rio Conference (UN, 1993)
1997	Rio +5 (UN General Assembly, 1997)
2002	World Summit on Sustainable Development (UN, 2002)
2005	2005 World Summit (UN General Assembly, 2005)
2008	High-level meeting on the Millennium Development Goals (UN, 2008)
2010	Millennium Development Goals Summit (UN General Assembly, 2010)
2012	United Nations Conference on Sustainable Development (UN, 2012)
2015	2030 Agenda, 2030 SDGs (UN General Assembly, 2015)
2022	Stockholm+50 (Stockholm50, 2022)

Source: Authors' compilation based on data from Yildirim and Yildirim (2020).

The energy theme is also an important key goal within the 2030 SDGs. Goal 7, which aims for a green transformation in energy, points to investment in clean and accessible energy sources as a practice and policy. While focusing on access to energy for everyone globally, it advocates that energy sources should be renewable and that clean energy should be prioritised for zero-carbon emissions (Yildirim et al., 2024). The realisation of Goal 7 is considered a basic goal that also supports the other 2030 SDGs. Goal 7 serves the purpose of achieving a balance (Yildirim, 2022b) between the three main areas of sustainable development: economic, social, and environmental continuity (Munasinghe, 2002).

Achieving Goal 7 will also support the other 2030 SDGs in the long term. Energy has an important place in building a sustainable future. The following aspects summarise how energy supports economic, social, and environmental issues in the context of the 2030 SDGs (Yildirim, 2022b; International Atomic Energy Agency—IAEA, 2005):

- Social issues and energy: The themes of "health and equality" are included in the scope of social welfare. Issues such as access to energy, the affordability of energy, and the availability of energy to groups with varying levels of household income indicate the relationship between social welfare and energy. When access to energy and accessibility become balanced, equality is achieved in society. In addition, fatal accidents in fossil-based energy production are also important in terms of how they affect health.
- Economic issues and energy: Energy use, production, and energy security issues are important from an economic perspective. These include energy usage rates, energy production, energy supply and distribution, industrial usage rates, the amount of energy allocated to agriculture, the amount of energy used by households, energy prices, and energy security.

- Environmental issues and energy: When the relationship between energy and the environment is examined, issues such as atmospheric effects, air quality, climate change effects, water quality, forest areas, land pollution, and waste should be considered.

Directing capital towards green and clean energy sources can be considered a policy that started with the 2030 SDGs. The 2030 SDGs can be considered as the official beginning of actual actions aimed at green transformation. Green transformation in energy will be an important action to stop the damage caused by fossil-based energy.

As fossil-based energy sources, "coal, oil and petroleum derivatives" have provided great advantages to many countries and have greatly supported and powered their development. Although the term resource curse (Badeeb et al., 2017; Beck, 2012) and the subject of "curse versus gift" often come to the fore, fossil-based energy has long been a source of resource wealth (Yildirim et al., 2022). On the other hand, there is a limit to using fossil-based energy sources in the long term, and transitioning to clean and renewable energy sources is a key goal for the energy sector in order to prevent climate change and carbon emissions. Various types of environmental damage have occurred in the extraction and production of fossil fuels. Environmental pollution in the form of soil pollution, water pollution, and air pollution has increased globally (ClientEarth Communications, 2025). In this context, a general framework will be drawn in this study, focusing on the importance of investments in clean and renewable energy sources.

2. Aim and Research Design

This study aims to examine the main indicators of the transition from fossil-based energy sources to renewable sources. Within the scope of green transformation in energy, the importance of renewable energy policies within the 2030 SDGs, the importance of investment in renewable energies in terms of energy security, and the importance of green energy policies in terms of energy security in crises will be discussed. Current reports, as well as data and indicators obtained from open and accessible data sources, will be used in this study. The results will be interpreted with a literature review based on secondary sources.

3. Results

This section will examine clean and renewable energy sources and present indicators of clean and renewable energy sources. When reviewing the main indicators of clean and renewable energy sources, the development trend for green transition in the energy sector will be examined clearly.

Investments in Clean and Renewable Energy Sources

Renewable energy can be based on clean energy sources such as "solar, wind, hydro and biomass" sources. Investment in one or more of these is considered an investment in renewable energy sources. It can be said that the main investments are in the solar, wind, hydro, biomass, and ocean energy fields (The Business Research Company, 2025).

According to a report by The Business Research Company (2025), investments in renewable energy sources (as seen in Table 2) have achieved faster growth in recent years. For example, investment in alternative energy sources was 309.77 billion dollars in 2024 and 344.5 billion dollars in 2025. Among clean energy investments, it is seen that the largest amount of resources is directed to solar energy and solar energy-related projects. The increase in investment in and use of solar energy and other renewable energy sources has also led to an increase in infrastructure and investments in the storage and distribution of renewable energy sources. When countries are examined in terms of investment in renewable energy sources, China, America, and the European Union are seen to be in the lead. Developing countries other than China still have low levels of investment in renewable energy sources (Klein, 2024).

Table 2. Investment in renewable energy sources—future trends.

Year	Investment (USD Billion)
2024	309.77
2025	344.5
2029	488.67

Source: Adapted from The Business Research Company (2025).

China invested USD 177 billion in renewable energy in the first half of 2023, making it the largest market. China's renewable energy market investment increased by 16% compared to 2022. Overall, capital investment in renewable energy companies increased in 2023 compared to the previous year. Investments in solar energy came in first place in this period. Solar energy investments grew in 2023 compared to 2022, but investments in wind energy did not grow in the same way. It can also be said that the zero-carbon target will be achieved with further increases in investments in renewable energy (BloombergNEF, 2023).

The Renewable Energy Country Attractiveness Index is a good indicator of countries' investments in renewable energy (Reglobal, 2022). The relationships of different countries with renewable energy for 2022 are shown in Table 3.

Table 3. Renewable Energy Country Attractiveness Index, 2022.

Countries	Decreased	Increased	No Change
Argentina	X		
Australia		X	
Austria		X	
Belgium	X		
Brazil	X		
Canada		X	
Chile	X		
China			X
Denmark		X	
Egypt	X		
Finland		X	
France	X		
Germany		X	
Greece		X	
India	X		

Table 3. *Cont.*

Countries	Decreased	Increased	No Change
Ireland		X	
Israel	X		
Italy	X		
Japan			X
Jordan	X		
Kazakhstan			X
Mexico		X	
Morocco	X		
Netherlands		X	
Norway	X		
Philippines	X		
Poland		X	
Portugal			X
Saudi Arabia		X	
South Africa	X		
South Korea	X		
Spain		x	
Sweden		X	
Switzerland		X	
Taiwan	X		
Thailand		X	
Turkey		X	
UK		X	
US			X
Vietnam	X		

Source: Adapted from Reglobal (2022).

With the COVID-19 pandemic, the energy security issue has become a priority globally. The energy problem has increased following the COVID-19 pandemic and the Russia–Ukraine war. The problem of dependence on fossil-based energy sources has become more stressful. In this context, investment in renewable energy sources has increased and has come to the fore. For example, a greater shift towards renewable energy production has been observed in European Union countries. In Germany, onshore wind energy and solar energy have increased by three times. After the onset of the Russia–Ukraine conflict, it has been seen that the goal of green transformation in energy has been brought forward in Germany. Italy has also made serious plans for renewable energy investments in the coming years. Türkiye has also aimed at increasing its renewable energy capacity in the short term (Reglobal, 2022). SolarPower Europe (2025) reported on Solar Energy 2024 in detail. According to a SolarPower Europe (2025) press release, the top 10 countries for global solar energy in the world in 2024 were as follows: "China (55%); United States (8%); India (5%); Brazil (3%); Germany (3%); Spain (2%); Türkiye (2%); Italy (1%); Japan (1%) and France (1%)".

Wind energy is one of the most widely used energy sources after solar energy, as it is one of the cleanest energy sources. Approximately 6.59% of global electricity production comes from wind energy. In the United States, the share of wind energy-based electricity is 9.2 percent. In essence, the efficiency rate of a wind turbine varies between 20% and 45%. The efficiency rate gives the rate at which the turbine converts wind energy into electricity. China still seems to be the world leader in energy production from renewable energy sources. It has the largest share of wind and solar energy production in the world. The world's largest wind farm is also located in China (Cole, 2024). The US is the second-largest market for wind energy. There was a significant increase in the number of wind turbines in the US from 2004 to 2020. As of the end of 2020, a total of 118 GW of wind energy capacity had been reached. Some states have invested more in wind energy. For example, in 2020, Texas was the state that produced the most electricity from wind. Iowa, Oklahoma and Kansas are the leading states in wind energy production (EIA, 2021). According to European records from 2019, wind energy capacity in European countries reached 15.4 GW. In fact, wind energy capacity increased compared to 2018, but it was evaluated as low compared to 2017. The share of wind energy-based electricity in the EU-28 is 15 percent. Onshore wind installations are seen to be more prominent. For example, Spain was the country with the highest onshore wind installation capacity in 2019, with a capacity of 2.2 GW. Denmark was also the country with the highest wind energy demand in 2019, with 48 percent. Then, Ireland (33 percent) and Portugal (27 percent) had the highest wind energy share in electricity demand in 2019. The UK installed the most wind energy in 2019 (WindEurope, 2020). According to 2023 records, in Europe, a total of 16.2 GW wind energy capacity was installed for the EU-27. However, this is still a small number to meet the 2030 targets. A wind energy capacity of 260 GW is planned in Europe for the period 2024–2030. Investments in onshore wind in Germany are expected to grow. According to 2023 records, Denmark and Ireland are still the European countries with the most wind-based energy in their electricity production (WindEurope, 2024).

Wind turbines are considered a clean and renewable energy source with the least greenhouse gas emissions during energy production. Wind energy installation costs may be high, but it provides clean and affordable energy. When wind turbines are designed for a long life, more economical energy production can be possible. However, wind turbine maintenance, high installation costs, geographical constraints, etc., are hindering investments in wind energy (Spherical Insights, 2023).

In the WWEA's 2023 annual report, countries and regions for wind energy globally are summarised as follows (WWEA, 2024):

- Asia region: China became the leading country in wind energy development in 2023 in terms of renewable energy sources in Asia. Approximately 65 percent of the global wind turbine market is concentrated in China. India (3.1 GW) has also become a good market for wind energy in Asia. Japan (5.2 GW) and Vietnam (4.9 GW) have also become important markets.
- Europe region: Germany (3.2 GW) has taken the lead in wind energy installations in Europe according to 2023 records. For countries in the European region, getting rid of their dependence on fossil energy sources in accordance with the 2030 SDGs has been an important motivation in the transition to renewable energy.
- North America: In the USA, a wind energy capacity of 150 GW was reached in 2023. Canada has installed 1.8 GW of wind energy. Mexico has exceeded 8 GW.
- South America: Brazil has become the third largest country globally. With 28.6 GW of wind energy capacity, Brazil was the leading country in South America in 2023.
- Oceania: A total of 11.5 GW of wind energy has been installed in Australia.

- Africa: Africa experienced very little growth in wind energy in 2023. Morocco and Egypt are the leading countries in terms of wind energy in Africa.

According to IEA (2024a) projections, global renewable energy is projected to exceed 17,000 TWh by 2030. Solar and wind energy are expected to surpass hydroelectricity in 2024. Wind and solar energy are projected to surpass nuclear energy in 2026 (IEA, 2024b).

Bioenergy is considered an energy source produced from plant materials, particularly waste organic matter. The production of waste may have increased the use of this energy source. The global waste-to-energy market is expected to exceed USD 50 billion by 2027 (Statista Research Department, 2024). Bioenergy, as an important renewable energy source, can produce more energy than solar and wind sources. Bioenergy plays a significant role in heating. It is expected to account for 95 percent of the total renewable fuel market by 2030 (IEA, 2024b). In 2018, approximately 5.13 quadrillion British thermal units (GBT) of energy from biomass was consumed in the US, and this share is expected to reach 5.54 quadrillion British thermal units (GBT) by 2050. Biomass energy is an alternative to fossil-based energy sources (Fernández, 2024).

Some indicators were created using data from Our World in Data. Below are some tables showing key data for the renewable energy market. Our World in Data provides open access data for users.

Table 4 shows the remaining reserve years for fossil fuels on Earth. According to 2020 records, there are 139 years left for coal, 56 years for oil, and 49 years for gas. The expiration of fossil fuel limits can be considered an important motivation for countries to switch to renewable and alternative energy sources.

Table 4. Years of fossil fuel reserves left, 2020 year.

Fossil-Based Fuel	Reserve Years (Recorded in 2020)
Coal	139
Oil	56
Gas	49

Source: Adapted from Our World in Data (2025g)—Energy Institute—Statistical Review of World Energy (2025)—with major processing by Our World in Data.

According to Freeing Energy (2021), there are 150 years left for coal, 50 years for oil, 50 years for natural gas, and 90 years for uranium (see Table 5).

Table 5. Reserve years of fossil-based energy sources.

Fossil-Based Energy Sources	Reserve Years
Coal	150
Oil	50
Natural Gas	50
Uranium	90

Source: Adapted from Freeing Energy (2021).

Table 6 shows the annual changes in consumption of energy obtained from renewable sources in TWh for 2000 and 2023. The latest calculation was made regarding the changes based on the previous year. Accordingly, while consumption in the African region was 15.85 TWh in 2000, this number increased to 28.50 TWh in 2023. Compared to 2022, consumption of renewables in the Africa region increased by 12.68 TWh. While consumption in the Asia region was 62.07 TWh in 2000, this number increased to 676.46 TWh in 2023. Compared to 2022, consumption of renewables in the Asia region increased by 614.39 TWh. While consumption in the Europe region was 116.98 TWh in 2000, this number increased to 412.77 TWh in 2023. Compared to 2022, consumption of renewables in Europe increased by 295.80 TWh. While consumption in North America was −85.21 TWh in 2000, this consumption was −38.16 TWh in 2023. Compared to 2022, consumption of renewables in North America increased by +47.05 TWh, and negative consumption decreased slightly. While consumption in Oceania was 5.32 TWh in 2000, this consumption was 20.19 TWh in 2023. Compared to 2022, consumption of renewables in Oceania increased by +14.87 TWh. While consumption in South America was 72.35 TWh in 2000, this consumption was 157.20 TWh in 2023. Compared to 2022, consumption of renewables in South America increased by 84.85 TWh. When examined by region, Asia has the highest renewables consumption in TWh globally. From 2000 to 2023, the largest increase occurred in Asia.

Table 6. Annual change in consumption of renewables (TWh).

Region	2000	2023	Absolute Change
Africa	15.82	28.50	+12.68
Asia	62.07	676.46	+614.39
Europe	116.98	412.77	+295.80
North America	−85.21	−38.16	+47.05
Oceania	5.32	20.19	+14.87
South America	72.35	157.20	+84.85

Source: Adapted from Our World in Data (2025b)—Energy Institute—Statistical Review of World Energy (2025)—with major processing by Our World in Data.

Table 7 shows the annual changes (TWh) in solar power consumption for specific regions in the world.

Table 7. Annual change in solar power consumption (TWh).

Region	2000	2023
Africa	0.04	3.51
Asia	0.40	517.85
Europe	−0.02	106.96
North America	0.01	105.44
Oceania	0.02	19.24
South America	0.01	64.50

Source: Adapted from Our World in Data (2025c)—Energy Institute—Statistical Review of World Energy (2025)—with major processing by Our World in Data.

Table 8 shows the annual changes in wind energy generation (TWh). Accordingly, wind energy generation in Africa increased from 0.5 TWh in 2000 to 8.8 TWh in 2023. In Asia, it increased from 1.0 TWh in 2000 to 361.2 TWh in 2023; in Europe, it increased from 24.2 TWh in 2000 to 152.1 TWh in 2023. In North America, wind energy generation increased from 3.7 TWh in 2000 to −24.4 TWh in 2023. In Oceania, it increased from 0.5 TWh in 2000 to 5.4 TWh in 2023. In South America, wind energy generation increased from 0.0 TWh in 2000 to 39.9 TWh in 2023.

Table 8. Annual change in wind energy generation (TWh).

Region	2000	2023
Africa	0.5	8.8
Asia	1.0	361.2
Europe	24.2	152.1
North America	3.7	−24.4
Oceania	0.5	5.4
South America	0.0	39.9

Source: Adapted from Our World in Data (2025d)—Energy Institute—Statistical Review of World Energy (2025)—with major processing by Our World in Data.

Table 9 shows the annual changes in hydropower consumption (TWh). In the Africa region, hydropower consumption was 13.53 TWh in 2000 and decreased to 12.52 TWh in 2023. In the Asia region, hydropower consumption was 49.13 TWh in 2000 and −303.47 TWh in 2023. In the Europe region, it was 79.37 TWh in 2000 and 202.99 TWh in 2023. In the North America region, it was −96.43 TWh in 2000 and −172.71 TWh in 2023. In the Oceania region, it was 5.03 TWh in 2000 and −3.44 TWh in 2023. In the South America region, it was 84.81 TWh in 2000 and 22.46 TWh in 2023. Hydropower consumption generally declined from the early 2000s to 2023. However, hydropower consumption increased in the Europe region.

Table 9. Annual change in hydropower consumption (TWh).

Region	2000	2023	Absolute Change
Africa	13.53	12.52	−1.02
Asia	49.13	−303.47	−352.60
Europe	79.37	202.99	+123.63
North America	−96.43	−172.71	−76.27
Oceania	5.03	−3.44	−8.47
South America	84.81	22.46	−62.35

Source: Adapted from Our World in Data (2025a)—Energy Institute—Statistical Review of World Energy (2025)—with major processing by Our World in Data.

Table 10 shows the annual percentage changes in hydropower consumption. In Africa, hydropower consumption was 6.48% in 2000 and 3.25% in 2023. In Asia, hydropower consumption was 3.02% in 2000 and −5.48% in 2023. In Europe, hydropower consumption was 3.71% in 2000 and 11.60% in 2023. In North America, hydropower consumption was −4.68% in 2000 and −9.32% in 2023. In Oceania, hydropower consumption was 4.34% in 2000 and −2.72%. In South America, hydropower consumption was 5.68% in 2000 and 1.58% in 2023.

Table 10. Annual percentage change in hydropower consumption (%).

Region	2000	2023
Africa	6.48	3.45
Asia	3.02	−5.48
Europe	3.71	11.60
North America	−4.68	−9.32
Oceania	4.34	−2.72
South America	5.68	1.58

Source: Adapted from Our World in Data (2025e)—Energy Institute—Statistical Review of World Energy (2025)—with major processing by Our World in Data.

Table 11 shows the share of primary energy consumption that comes from renewables (%). In some countries, the share of primary energy consumption is higher. From 2022 to 2023, some countries saw an increase of over 10 percent. The countries that obtained more than 10 percent of their primary renewable energy inputs in 2023 compared to 2022 are as follows: "Australia (+10.99); Belgium (+12.09); Bulgaria (+11.43); Chile (+10.75); China (+10.51); Croatia (+11.80); Denmark (+35.64); Estonia (+15.18); Europe (+10.15); Europe (EI) (+14.63); European Union (27) (+15.15); Finland (+16.12); France (+10.22); Germany (+21.51); Greece (+18.36); Hungary (+10.72); Ireland (+20.27); Italy (+12.12); Lithuania (+16.19); Luxembourg (+10.38); Netherlands (+16.86); Poland (+11.47); Portugal (+23.00); Romania (+11.46); Spain (+17.95); Sweden (+16.02); United Kingdom (+19.39)".

Table 11. Share of primary energy consumption that comes from renewables (%).

Countries	2000	2023	Absolute Change
Africa	7.20%	9.83%	+2.62 pp
Africa (EI)	7.20%	9.83%	+2.62 pp
Algeria	0.05%	0.27%	+0.22 pp
Argentina	12.28%	14.10%	+1.82 pp
Asia	4.90%	12.19%	+7.29 pp
Asia Pacific (EI)	5.38%	13.81%	+8.43 pp
Australia	3.99%	14.98%	+10.99 pp
Austria	32.59%	40.08%	+7.49 pp
Azerbaijan	3.43%	2.32%	−1.11 pp
Bangladesh	1.63%	1.01%	−0.62 pp
Belarus	0.03%	1.10%	+1.06 pp
Belgium	0.43%	12.53%	+12.09 pp
Brazil	42.44%	50.33%	+7.89 pp
Bulgaria	3.58%	15.01%	+11.43 pp
CIS (EI)	6.96%	6.23%	−0.73 pp
Canada	29.77%	29.26%	−0.50 pp
Central America (EI)	25.20%	26.83%	+1.63 pp
Chile	19.78%	30.53%	+10.75 pp
China	5.66%	16.16%	+10.51 pp

Table 11. *Cont.*

Countries	2000	2023	Absolute Change
Colombia	29.51%	28.92%	−0.59 pp
Croatia	19.77%	31.57%	+11.80 pp
Czechia	1.60%	7.98%	+6.39 pp
Denmark	7.10%	42.73%	+35.64 pp
Eastern Africa (EI)	33.73%	36.21%	+2.47 pp
Ecuador	21.61%	28.98%	+7.36 pp
Egypt	7.42%	5.89%	−1.52 pp
Estonia	0.34%	15.52%	+15.18 pp
Europe	7.79%	17.93%	+10.15 pp
Europe (EI)	8.28%	22.91%	+14.63 pp
European Union (27)	6.84%	21.98%	+15.15 pp
Finland	19.82%	35.94%	+16.12 pp
France	6.72%	16.94%	+10.22 pp
Germany	2.89%	24.39%	+21.51 pp
Greece	3.28%	21.64%	+18.36 pp
High-income countries	6.78%	14.68%	+7.90 pp
Hong Kong		0.94%	
Hungary	0.26%	10.98%	+10.72 pp
Iceland			
India	6.40%	9.68%	+3.28 pp
Indonesia	3.73%	10.45%	+6.71 pp
Iran	0.81%	1.82%	+1.01 pp
Iraq			
Ireland	2.03%	22.30%	+20.27 pp
Israel	0.04%	7.07%	+7.03 pp
Italy	7.16%	19.28%	+12.12 pp
Japan	4.82%	12.58%	+7.77 pp
Kazakhstan	6.02%	4.52%	−1.50 pp
Latvia	22.12%	31.92%	+9.80 pp
Lithuania	1.28%	17.46%	+16.19 pp
Lower-middle-income countries	5.38%	8.50%	+3.12 pp
Luxembourg	1.37%	11.75%	+10.38 pp
Malaysia	3.68%	7.89%	+4.21 pp
Mexico	6.91%	8.61%	+1.70 pp
Middle Africa (EI)	35.76%	28.54%	−7.21 pp
Middle East (EI)	0.67%	1.60%	+0.93 pp
Morocco	1.97%	8.44%	+6.48 pp
Netherlands	0.93%	17.79%	+16.86 pp
New Zealand	36.38%	42.27%	+5.88 pp
Non-OECD (EI)	8.50%	13.42%	+4.93 pp
North America	7.05%	13.36%	+6.31 pp
North America (EI)	7.12%	13.54%	+6.42 pp
North Macedonia	11.22%	16.81%	+5.59 pp
Norway	72.07%	72.09%	+0.02 pp
OECD (EI)	7.33%	16.49%	+9.16 pp

Table 11. *Cont.*

Countries	2000	2023	Absolute Change
Oceania	8.83%	18.40%	+9.56 pp
Oman			
Pakistan	11.34%	12.16%	+0.81 pp
Peru	32.80%	26.35%	−6.45 pp
Philippines	18.22%	11.99%	−6.22 pp
Poland	0.68%	12.15%	+11.47 pp
Portugal	13.04%	36.04%	+23.00 pp
Romania	10.40%	21.85%	+11.46 pp
Russia	6.73%	6.31%	−0.42 pp
Saudi Arabia	0.00%	0.47%	+0.47 pp
Singapore			
Slovakia	6.25%	11.76%	+5.51 pp
Slovenia	14.73%	24.55%	+9.82 pp
South Africa	0.41%	3.94%	+3.53 pp
South America	33.88%	38.35%	+4.47 pp
South Korea	0.54%	4.78%	+4.24 pp
South and Central America (EI)	30.42%	35.39%	+4.97 pp
Spain	6.96%	24.92%	+17.95 pp
Sri Lanka			
Sweden	37.87%	53.89%	+16.02 pp
Switzerland	30.64%	38.33%	+7.69 pp
Taiwan	1.65%	5.26%	+3.61 pp
Thailand	2.58%	7.84%	+5.27 pp
Trinidad and Tobago		0.01%	
Turkey	10.67%	18.70%	+8.03 pp
Turkmenistan			
USSR			
Ukraine	2.10%	8.79%	+6.68 pp
United Kingdom	1.13%	20.52%	+19.39 pp
United States	4.03%	11.66%	+7.63 pp
Upper-middle-income countries	9.43%	15.66%	+6.23 pp
Uzbekistan	2.92%	3.25%	+0.33 pp
Venezuela	24.09%	24.24%	+0.15 pp
Vietnam	20.09%	22.75%	+2.66 pp
Western Africa (EI)	13.10%	8.79%	−4.30 pp
World	7.82%	14.56%	+6.75 pp

CIS—the Commonwealth of Independent States; OECD—the Organisation for Economic Co-operation and Development; EI—Education International. Source: Adapted from Our World in Data (2025f)—Energy Institute—Statistical Review of World Energy (2025)—with major processing by Our World in Data.

Table 12 shows the changes in electricity generation from renewables (TWh). Some countries experienced a significant increase in electricity generation from renewable energy sources from 2000 to 2023. The change from 2022 to 2023 in Africa was +143; in Brazil, +314; in China, +3163; in Germany, +239; in India, +327; in Japan, +136; in South America, +439; in Spain, +126; in Turkey, +124; in the United Kingdom, +135; in the United States, +706; and in Vietnam, +121.

Table 12. Electricity generation from renewables (TWh).

Countries	2000	2023	Absolute Change
ASEAN (Ember)	73	357	+284
Afghanistan	0	1	+1
Africa	78	221	+143
Africa (EI)	78	218	+141
Africa (Ember)	78	240	+162
Albania	5	9	+4
Algeria	0	1	+1
American Samoa	0	0	+0
Angola	1	14	+13
Antigua and Barbuda	0	0	+0
Argentina	29	47	+18
Armenia	1	3	+1
Aruba	0	0	+0
Asia	612	4253	+3642
Asia (Ember)	572	4670	+4098
Asia Pacific (EI)	570	4142	+3572
Australia	18	99	+82
Austria	43	68	+25
Azerbaijan	2	4	+2
Bahamas	0	0	+0
Bahrain	0	0	+0
Bangladesh	1	2	+1
Barbados	0	0	+0
Belarus	0	1	+1
Belgium	1	27	+26
Belize	0	0	+0
Benin	0	0	+0
Bermuda	0	0	+0
Bhutan	2	11	+9
Bolivia	2	5	+3
Bosnia and Herzegovina	5	6	+0
Botswana	0	0	+0
Brazil	312	654	+341
British Virgin Islands	0	0	+0
Brunei	0	0	+0
Bulgaria	3	12	+9
Burkina Faso	0	0	+0
Burundi	0	0	+0
CIS (EI)	209	269	+61
Cambodia	0	6	+6
Cameroon	3	5	+2
Canada	366	411	+45
Cape Verde	0	0	+0
Cayman Islands	0	0	+0
Central African Republic	0	0	+0
Central America (EI)	18	43	+24

Table 12. *Cont.*

Countries	2000	2023	Absolute Change
Chad	0	0	+0
Chile	20	62	+42
China	226	3388	+3163
Colombia	32	56	+24
Comoros	0	0	+0
Congo	0	1	+1
Cook Islands	0	0	+0
Costa Rica	7	12	+5
Cote d'Ivoire	2	3	+2
Croatia	6	11	+5
Cuba	1	1	−0
Cyprus	0	1	+1
Czechia	2	12	+10
Democratic Republic of Congo	6	16	+10
Denmark	6	31	+26
Djibouti	0	0	+0
Dominica	0	0	−0
Dominican Republic	1	5	+4
EU (Ember)	407	1303	+896
East Timor		0	
Eastern Africa (EI)	32	95	+63
Ecuador	8	24	+16
Egypt	14	27	+13
El Salvador	2	6	+4
Equatorial Guinea	0	0	+0
Eritrea	0	0	+0
Estonia	0	3	+3
Eswatini	1	1	−0
Ethiopia	2	18	+17
Europe	801	1827	+1026
Europe (EI)	681	1769	+1088
Europe (Ember)	832	2101	+1269
European Union (27)	407	1210	+804
Falkland Islands	0	0	+0
Faroe Islands	0	0	+0
Fiji	1	1	+0
Finland	23	46	+23
France	68	146	+79
French Guiana	0	1	+0
French Polynesia	0	0	+0
G20 (Ember)	2159	8371	+6212
G7 (Ember)	982	2401	+1419
Gabon	1	2	+1
Gambia	0	0	+0
Georgia	6	11	+6
Germany	35	274	+239

Table 12. *Cont.*

Countries	2000	2023	Absolute Change
Ghana	7	9	+3
Gibraltar	0	0	+0
Greece	4	28	+24
Greenland	0	0	+0
Grenada	0	0	+0
Guadeloupe	0	1	+0
Guam	0	0	+0
Guatemala	3	10	+7
Guinea	0	3	+3
Guinea-Bissau	0	0	+0
Guyana	0	0	+0
Haiti	0	0	−0
High-income countries	1674	3706	+2032
Honduras	2	7	+5
Hong Kong	0	0	+0
Hungary	0	12	+12
Iceland	8	20	+13
India	80	407	+327
Indonesia	20	65	+46
Iran	4	24	+20
Iraq	1	2	+1
Ireland	1	14	+13
Israel	0	8	+8
Italy	51	131	+80
Jamaica	0	1	+0
Japan	101	237	+136
Jordan	0	5	+5
Kazakhstan	8	18	+10
Kenya	2	12	+10
Kiribati	0	0	+0
Kosovo	0	0	+0
Kuwait	0	2	+2
Kyrgyzstan	14	14	+1
Laos	3	40	+37
Latin America and Caribbean (Ember)	605	1149	+544
Latvia	3	5	+2
Lebanon	0	2	+2
Lesotho	0	0	+0
Liberia	0	0	+0
Libya	0	0	+0
Lithuania	0	6	+6
Low-income countries	36	92	+56
Lower-middle-income countries	232	832	+601
Luxembourg	0	1	+1
Macao	0	0	+0
Madagascar	1	1	+0

Table 12. *Cont.*

Countries	2000	2023	Absolute Change
Malawi	1	2	+1
Malaysia	8	39	+31
Maldives	0	0	+0
Mali	0	2	+2
Malta	0	0	+0
Martinique	0	0	+0
Mauritania	0	0	+0
Mauritius	1	1	+0
Mexico	39	79	+40
Middle Africa (EI)	11	34	+23
Middle East (EI)	11	69	+58
Middle East (Ember)	8	79	+71
Moldova	0	1	+0
Mongolia	0	1	+1
Montenegro		2	
Montserrat	0	0	+0
Morocco	1	12	+11
Mozambique	10	16	+7
Myanmar	2	10	+8
Namibia	1	2	+0
Nauru	0	0	+0
Nepal	2	11	+9
Netherlands	3	62	+59
New Caledonia	0	1	+0
New Zealand	28	38	+10
Nicaragua	0	3	+2
Niger	0	0	+0
Nigeria	6	9	+4
Niue	0	0	+0
Non-OECD (EI)	1286	5312	+4026
North America	778	1514	+736
North America (EI)	751	1471	+720
North America (Ember)	717	1469	+752
North Korea	10	17	+7
North Macedonia	1	2	+1
Norway	142	154	+12
OECD (EI)	1578	3676	+2098
OECD (Ember)	1578	3901	+2323
Oceania	48	136	+88
Oceania (Ember)	48	140	+93
Oman	0	2	+2
Pakistan	17	61	+43
Palestine	0	0	+0
Panama	3	8	+5
Papua New Guinea	1	1	+0

Table 12. *Cont.*

Countries	2000	2023	Absolute Change
Paraguay	53	44	−9
Peru	16	38	+22
Philippines	19	27	+8
Poland	2	51	+48
Portugal	13	39	+27
Puerto Rico	0	1	+1
Qatar	0	0	+0
Reunion	1	1	+0
Romania	15	25	+10
Russia	164	220	+55
Rwanda	0	1	+1
Saint Helena	0	0	+0
Saint Kitts and Nevis	0	0	+0
Saint Lucia	0	0	+0
Saint Pierre and Miquelon	0	0	+0
Saint Vincent and the Grenadines	0	0	−0
Samoa	0	0	+0
Sao Tome and Principe	0	0	+0
Saudi Arabia	0	6	+6
Senegal	0	2	+2
Serbia	10	12	+2
Seychelles	0	0	+0
Sierra Leone	0	0	+0
Singapore	0	3	+2
Slovakia	5	7	+2
Slovenia	4	7	+3
Solomon Islands	0	0	+0
Somalia	0	0	+0
South Africa	2	32	+31
South America	544	983	+439
South Korea	4	60	+55
South Sudan		0	
South and Central America (EI)	565	1050	+485
Spain	34	160	+126
Sri Lanka	3	9	+6
Sudan	1	12	+10
Suriname	1	1	+0
Sweden	83	120	+37
Switzerland	38	53	+15
Syria	3	1	−2
Taiwan	6	31	+26
Tajikistan	14	20	+6
Tanzania	2	3	+1
Thailand	6	30	+23
Togo	0	0	+0
Tonga	0	0	+0

Table 12. *Cont.*

Countries	2000	2023	Absolute Change
Trinidad and Tobago	0	0	−0
Tunisia	0	1	+1
Turkey	31	156	+124
Turkmenistan	0	0	+0
Turks and Caicos Islands	0	0	+0
USSR			
Uganda	2	6	+4
Ukraine	11	20	+9
United Arab Emirates	0	14	+14
United Kingdom	10	145	+135
United States	351	1057	+706
United States Virgin Islands	0	0	+0
Upper-middle-income countries	917	4329	+3412
Uruguay	7	16	+9
Uzbekistan	4	7	+4
Vanuatu	0	0	+0
Venezuela	63	65	+2
Vietnam	15	135	+121
Western Africa (EI)	15	31	+16
Western Sahara	0		
World	2860	9848	+6988
Yemen	0	1	+1
Zambia	8	17	+10
Zimbabwe	3	6	+2

ASEAN—the Association of Southeast Asian Nations. Source: Adapted from Our World in Data (2026)—Ember (2026); Energy Institute—Statistical Review of World Energy—with major processing by Our World in Data.

Global energy supply is expected to increase by 2024, and fossil fuels still account for a significant share of total energy (86%). While energy demand is also increasing, there are some challenges in energy access. The Asia Pacific region accounted for 65% of energy demand. North America and Europe experienced the slowest growth. Investments in the zero-carbon energy transition became more visible after 2010. While the share of renewable energy was 3% globally in the 1990s, it increased significantly in the 2000s. Renewable energy is a good alternative for countries aiming to reduce energy imports to reduce energy dependency. Extraordinary events such as the COVID-19 pandemic, ongoing climate change, and the conflict in Ukraine have accelerated energy transitions in countries (Energy Institute, 2025).

4. Conclusions

A closer examination of green energy policies triggered by climate change reveals a focus on energy security. Energy dependence threatens the future of energy accessibility and the sustainability of energy to meet everyone's needs. Renewable energy sources, such as solar and wind, offer an opportunity for countries to break free from their externally dependent energy policies. Fossil-based energy stresses energy security and poses a problem in climate crisis. Renewable energy sources offer a better perspective for building a sustainable future. It can be argued that policies aimed at economic growth based on scarce reserves are unrealistic in the long term. One of the reasons for the recent acceleration in the transition to renewable energy in both developed and developing countries is the short time during which limited fossil fuel resources will be available. As a result, countries are increasingly choosing to invest in renewable energy rather than fossil fuels. The uncertainties created by the COVID-19 pandemic and wars have also triggered a green energy transformation. China leads in renewable energy investment in Asia. While the European Union aims to reach its goal of approaching 100% green energy transition, the African region is still lagging the 2030 target. Meanwhile, investments in green and renewable energy sources are increasing, and the share of renewable energy in primary energy is also increasing. Solar and wind energy investments are seen as leading investments.

Author Contributions: Conceptualisation, S.Y. and D.Ç.Y.; methodology, D.Ç.Y.; writing—original draft preparation, S.Y. and D.Ç.Y.; writing—review and editing, S.Y. and D.Ç.Y. All authors have read and agreed to the published version of the manuscript.

Funding: This research received no external funding.

Conflicts of Interest: The authors declare no conflicts of interest.

Author Names and Affiliations: Durmuş Çağrı Yıldırım, Department of Economics, Tekirdag Namık Kemal University, Tekirdag, Turkey; Seda Yıldırım, Department of Business Administration, Tekirdag Namık Kemal University, Tekirdag, Turkey.

Keywords: sustainable development; green energy transition; renewable energy investment; clean energy policies.

References

Badeeb, R. A., Lean, H. H., & Clark, J. (2017). The evolution of the natural resource curse thesis: A critical literature survey. *Resources Policy, 51*, 123–134. [CrossRef]

Beck, T. (2012). Chapter 5 Finance and oil: Is there a resource curse? In *Beyond the curse*. International Monetary Fund.

BloombergNEF. (2023). *Renewable energy investment hits record-breaking $358 billion in 1H 2023*. Available online: https://about.bnef.com/insights/finance/renewable-energy-investment-hits-record-breaking-358-billion-in-1h-2023/ (accessed on 12 July 2025).

ClientEarth Communications. (2025). *Fossil fuels and climate change: The facts*. Available online: https://www.clientearth.org/latest/news/fossil-fuels-and-climate-change-the-facts/ (accessed on 12 July 2025).

Cole, S. (2024). *13 compelling wind energy statistics & facts*. Available online: https://theroundup.org/wind-energy-statistics/ (accessed on 12 July 2025).

EIA. (2021). *The United States installed more wind turbine capacity in 2020 than in any other year*. Available online: https://www.eia.gov/todayinenergy/detail.php?id=50624 (accessed on 12 July 2025).

Energy Institute. (2025). *2024 regional overview—Access to energy and sustainability*. Available online: https://www.energyinst.org/statistical-review (accessed on 12 July 2025).

Fernández, L. (2024). *U.S. biomass energy—Statistics & facts*. Available online: https://www.statista.com/topics/1000/biomass-energy/#topicOverview (accessed on 12 July 2025).

Freeing Energy. (2021). *Energy fact—We only have a century of fossil and nuclear fuel reserves*. Available online: https://www.freeingenergy.com/facts/fossil-fuel-reserves-will-become-unviable-g120/ (accessed on 12 July 2025).

IEA. (2024a). *Bioenergy*. Available online: https://www.iea.org/energy-system/renewables/bioenergy (accessed on 12 July 2025).

IEA. (2024b). *Renewables 2024 analysis and forecast to 2030*. Available online: https://iea.blob.core.windows.net/assets/17033b62-07a5-4144-8dd0-651cdb6caa24/Renewables2024.pdf (accessed on 12 July 2025).

International Atomic Energy Agency—IAEA. (2005). *Energy indicators for sustainable development: Guidelines and methodologies*. IAEA. Available online: https://www.iaea.org/publications/7201/energy-indicators-for-sustainable-development-guidelines-and-methodologies (accessed on 12 July 2025).

Klein, C. (2024). *Chart: Clean energy set to attract double the investment spent on fossil fuels*. Available online: https://www.canarymedia.com/articles/climatetech-finance/-clean-energy-investment-2-trillion-fossil-fuels-record-high (accessed on 12 July 2025).

Meadows, D. H., Meadows, D. L., Randers, J., & Behren, W. W., III. (1972). *The limits to growth, A report for the club of Rome's project on the predicament of mankind*. Available online: https://www.donellameadows.org/wp-content/userfiles/Limits-to-Growth-digital-scan-version.pdf (accessed on 12 July 2025).

Munasinghe, M. (2002). The sustainomics trans-disciplinary meta-framework for making development more sustainable: Applications to energy issues. *International Journal of Sustainable Development*, *4*(2), 6–54. [CrossRef]

NASA (National Aeronautics and Space Administration). (n.d.). *Evidence*. Available online: https://science.nasa.gov/climate-change/evidence/ (accessed on 12 July 2025).

Our World in Data. (2025a). Annual change in hydropower consumption—Using the substitution method. In *Energy Institute—Statistical review of world energy (2025)—with major processing by Our World in Data*. Our World in Data. Available online: https://ourworldindata.org/grapher/annual-change-hydro?tab=table&time=2000..latest&tableFilter=continents (accessed on 27 July 2025).

Our World in Data. (2025b). Annual change in low-carbon energy consumption—Using the substitution method. In *Energy Institute—Statistical review of world energy (2025)— With major processing by Our World in Data*. Our World in Data. Available online: https://ourworldindata.org/grapher/annual-change-renewables?tab=table&time=2000..latest&tableFilter=continents (accessed on 27 July 2025).

Our World in Data. (2025c). Annual change in solar power consumption—Using the substitution method. In *Energy Institute—Statistical review of world energy (2025)—With major processing by Our World in Data*. Our World in Data. Available online: https://ourworldindata.org/grapher/annual-change-solar?tab=table&time=2000..latest&tableFilter=continents (accessed on 27 July 2025).

Our World in Data. (2025d). Annual change in wind power consumption—Using the substitution method. In *Energy Institute—Statistical review of world energy (2025)—With major processing by Our World in Data.* Our World in Data. Available online: https://ourworldindata.org/grapher/annual-change-wind?tab=table&time=2000..latest&tableFilter=continents (accessed on 27 July 2025).
Our World in Data. (2025e). Annual percentage change in hydropower consumption. In *Energy Institute—Statistical review of world energy (2025)—With major processing by Our World in Data.* Our World in Data. Available online: https://ourworldindata.org/grapher/annual-percentage-change-hydro?tab=table&time=2000..latest&tableFilter=continents (accessed on 27 July 2025).
Our World in Data. (2025f). Share of primary energy consumption that comes from renewables—Using the substitution method. In *Energy Institute—Statistical review of world energy (2025)—With major processing by Our World in Data.* Our World in Data. Available online: https://ourworldindata.org/grapher/renewable-share-energy?tab=table&time=2000..latest (accessed on 27 July 2025).
Our World in Data. (2025g). Years of fossil fuel reserves left, 2020. In *Energy Institute—Statistical review of world energy (2025)—With major processing by Our World in Data.* Our World in Data. Available online: https://ourworldindata.org/grapher/years-of-fossil-fuel-reserves-left (accessed on 27 July 2025).
Our World in Data. (2026). Electricity generation from renewables. In *Ember (2026); Energy Institute—Statistical review of world energy (2025)—With major processing by Our World in Data.* Our World in Data. Available online: https://ourworldindata.org/grapher/electricity-renewables?tab=table&time=2000..latest (accessed on 26 January 2026).
Pearce, D., Markandya, A., & Barbier, E. (1989). *Blueprint for a green economy.* Available online: https://www.iied.org/5008iied (accessed on 12 July 2025).
Reglobal. (2022). *Top countries for renewable energy investment.* Available online: https://reglobal.org/top-countries-for-renewable-energy-investment/ (accessed on 12 July 2025).
SolarPower Europe. (2025). *New report: World installed 600 GW of solar in 2024, could be installing 1 TW per year by 2030.* Available online: https://www.solarpowereurope.org/press-releases/new-report-world-installed-600-gw-of-solar-in-2024-could-be-installing-1-tw-per-year-by-2030 (accessed on 12 July 2025).
Spherical Insights. (2023). *Global wind energy market size to hit USD 151.47 billion by 2030 | CAGR of 8.4%.* Available online: https://www.sphericalinsights.com/press-release/wind-energy-market (accessed on 12 July 2025).
Statista Research Department. (2024). *Bioenergy worldwide—Statistics & facts.* Available online: https://www.statista.com/topics/6753/bioenergy/#topicOverview (accessed on 12 July 2025).
Stockholm50. (2022). *Stockholm+50: A healthy planet for the prosperity of all—Our responsibility, our opportunity.* Available online: https://www.stockholm50.global/ (accessed on 12 July 2025).

The Business Research Company. (2025). *Renewable energy investment global market report 2025—By type (solar energy, wind energy, hydro energy, biomass energy, ocean energy), by offerings (services, platform), by organization type (private equity firm, banking institution, energy company, asset manager, other organization types), by application (commercial, industry, residential)—Market size, trends, and global forecast 2025–2034*. Available online: https://www.thebusinessresearchcompany.com/report/renewable-energy-investment-global-market-report (accessed on 12 July 2025).

UN. (1973). *Report of the united nations conference on the human environment, Stockholm, 5–16 June 1972*. United Nations Publications. Available online: https://docs.un.org/en/A/CONF.48/14/Rev.1 (accessed on 12 July 2025).

UN. (1987). *Report of the world commission on environment and development, our common future*. Available online: https://www.brundtland.co.za/other-publication/brundtland-report-1987-our-common-future/ (accessed on 12 July 2025).

UN. (1993). *Report of the united nations conference on environment and development, Rio de Janeiro, 3–14 June 1992*. Volume I resolutions adopted by the conference. United Nations Publications. Available online: https://docs.un.org/en/A/CONF.151/26/Rev.1(vol.I) (accessed on 12 July 2025).

UN. (2002). *Report of the world summit on sustainable development, Johannesburg, South Africa, 26 August 4 September 2002*. Available online: https://docs.un.org/en/A/CONF.199/20 (accessed on 12 July 2025).

UN. (2008). *High-level event on the millennium development goals 25 September 2008*. Available online: https://www.un.org/millenniumgoals/2008highlevel/pdf/commiting.pdf (accessed on 12 July 2025).

UN. (2012). *Report of the united nations conference on sustainable development, Rio de Janeiro, Brazil, 20–22 June 2012*. Available online: https://docs.un.org/en/A/CONF.216/16 (accessed on 12 July 2025).

UN General Assembly. (1997). *Special session of general assembly on implementation of agenda 21 concludes at headquarters, 23–27 June, press release, GA/9276, ENV/DEV/442*. Available online: https://press.un.org/en/1997/19970627.ga9276.html (accessed on 12 July 2025).

UN General Assembly. (2005). *Resolution adopted by the general assembly on 16 September 2005, 60/1. 2005 world summit outcome*. Available online: https://docs.un.org/en/A/RES/60/1 (accessed on 12 July 2025).

UN General Assembly. (2010). *Resolution adopted by the general assembly on 22 September 2010*. Available online: https://docs.un.org/en/A/RES/65/1 (accessed on 12 July 2025).

UN General Assembly. (2015). *Transforming our world: The 2030 Agenda for sustainable development, resolution adopted by the general assembly on 25 September 2015*. Available online: https://docs.un.org/en/A/RES/70/1 (accessed on 12 July 2025).

WindEurope. (2020). *Wind energy in Europe in 2019—Trends and statistics*. Available online: https://windeurope.org/intelligence-platform/product/wind-energy-in-europe-in-2019-trends-and-statistics/ (accessed on 12 July 2025).

WindEurope. (2024). *Wind energy in Europe: 2023 statistics and the outlook for 2024–2030*. Available online: https://windeurope.org/intelligence-platform/product/wind-energy-in-europe-2023-statistics-and-the-outlook-for-2024-2030/ (accessed on 12 July 2025).

WWEA. (2024). *WWEA annual report 2023: Record year for windpower.* Available online: https://wwindea.org/AnnualReport2023 (accessed on 12 July 2025).

Yildirim, S. (2022a). The consumer role for sustainable development: How consumers contribute to sustainable development goals. In Institute of Management Association (Ed.), *Research anthology on measuring and achieving sustainable development goals* (pp. 872–888). IGI Global Scientific Publishing. [CrossRef]

Yildirim, S. (2022b). 3R principle in household energy consumption patterns: A case of turkish households. In Institute of Management Association (Ed.), *Research anthology on measuring and achieving sustainable development goals* (pp. 666–685). IGI Global Scientific Publishing. [CrossRef]

Yildirim, S., Kaplan, M., & Yildirim, D. C. (2023). Climate change and the ocean economy: A review on OECD's ocean economy. In A. Pego (Ed.), *Handbook of research on bioeconomy and economic ecosystems* (pp. 212–232). IGI Global. [CrossRef]

Yildirim, S., & Yildirim, D. C. (2020). Achieving sustainable development through a green economy approach. In S. Patti, & G. Trizzino (Eds.), *Advanced integrated approaches to environmental economics and policy: Emerging research and opportunities* (pp. 1–22). IGI Global.

Yildirim, S., Yildirim, D. C., Bostancı, S. H., & Tarı, E. N. (2022). Winner or loser? The asymmetric role of natural resource rents on financial development among resource-rich countries. *Sustainable Development*, *30*(6), 1921–1933. [CrossRef]

Yildirim, S., Yildirim, D. C., & Erdogan, S. (2024). Energy security dilemma in OECD countries: The COVID-19 pandemic, Russia-Ukraine war, and energy issues. In R. Castanho (Ed.), *Green economy and renewable energy transitions for sustainable development* (pp. 83–105). IGI Global Scientific Publishing. [CrossRef]

The Pressure of Climate Change on the Tourism Economy and the Role of Public Expenditure in Responding to This Situation

Kerem Özen

Abstract: Climate change can be defined as the artificial alteration of the climate beyond its natural variability, resulting from human activities that push the ecological limits of the environment. The increasing greenhouse gas effect, particularly due to the use of fossil fuels, is the primary cause of climate change and poses significant threats to all living beings, countries, and economies. Therefore, in recent years, both scientific circles and political authorities have placed greater emphasis on studies aimed at determining the current and potential effects of climate change. As a result of climate change, the gradual warming of the atmosphere has led to an increase in the number and frequency of extreme weather events, which in turn have had serious effects on economic activities. These effects are particularly evident in the rise in public spending and the field of international trade. Various studies are being conducted to counteract climate change and its effects on public expenditures. This study was undertaken to theoretically examine the effects of climate change on the tourism economy and public expenditures. In this context, it can be seen that climate change has a direct impact on tourism and public expenditure.

1. Introduction

At the beginning of the 20th century, especially after World War II, the rapid growth of countries brought the increasing need for energy and raw materials to the forefront. During this period, energy needs were met with fossil fuels such as coal and oil, while raw materials were obtained from nature at the expense of its reckless use. Along with rapid population growth, various environmental problems, such as water and air pollution, also emerged. Initially, environmental problems observed at the regional or national level only attracted the attention of a limited segment of society. This situation was influenced by the perception of nature as a free commodity with no price tag, as well as the belief that technological developments would solve environmental problems. Additionally, the fact that environmental problems were not yet felt on a global scale during this period was another reason why the environment was not given sufficient importance.

Global warming and the resulting climate change are considered serious problems that directly affect all countries in the world in terms of their effects and consequences. The main cause of global warming is the concentration of greenhouse gases released into the atmosphere because of economic activities exceeding the required level. As the atmosphere continues to warm due to climate change, glaciers are melting, sea levels are rising, local and regional rainfall patterns are changing, and extreme weather events are increasing in both number and frequency. In this context, it is anticipated that this could lead to the extinction of certain plant and animal species due to ecosystem degradation, as well as an increase in natural disasters such as floods, storms, hurricanes, and droughts.

The main sectors affected by climate change include agriculture, food production, fishing, livestock farming, forestry, foreign trade, tourism, health, air conditioning, construction, logistics, and finance and insurance. The tourism sector is of great importance due to the significant contribution of both domestic and international travel to the country's economy. There are several sectors directly related to climate, and one of them is the tourism sector. In tourism, natural attractions are offered thanks to climatic conditions, and various tourism activities can be carried out thanks to suitable weather conditions. For example, skiing cannot be done without sufficient snow; similarly, glaciers, which are presented as natural beauties, cannot survive without snow. People from many regions and countries that do not have suitable climate conditions for vacation travel to regions that are favourable in terms of climate for relaxation. The tourism sector is of considerable importance in terms of its economic size.

Considering that external environmental and natural factors have a significant impact on tourism movements and tourist preferences, it is inevitable that climate change will affect the tourism sector. Today, climate change has begun to affect the tourism sector; coastal and winter tourism has been negatively affected by this change. Due to rising temperatures, beaches are experiencing algae blooms and jellyfish infestations, while ski resorts are either closing early or unable to open at all due to insufficient snowfall.

2. Climate Change

Climate is, by its very nature, a dynamic system shaped by slow processes and changing over long periods of time. These natural processes, occurring entirely within the Earth's own cycles without human intervention, are defined as 'climate variability'. In contrast, "climate change" refers to changes caused by human activities that directly or indirectly affect the composition of the atmosphere, in addition to the natural variability observed in the climate over a specific period. Within this fundamental distinction, while natural factors were the primary cause of past climatic transformations, anthropogenic (human-caused) activities are the main culprits behind the changes we are witnessing today. Indeed, the Intergovernmental Panel on Climate Change (IPCC) has statistically established with 95% confidence that climate change is caused by human activities (Başoğlu, 2014).

While the Mediterranean climate prevails in the western and southern regions of Turkey, continental climate conditions dominate in the eastern and inland regions. Climate change, in the simplest terms, means the transformation of these climate types. In other words, summers in the western and southern parts of Turkey will become hotter and drier than their current hot and dry nature, while winters will evolve from cool and rainy weather to milder and less rainy conditions. In the eastern regions, temperatures and aridity will increase further in the summer months, while winters will transition from cold and snowy weather to a milder and rainier climate. Such changes do not occur overnight like daily weather events. However, when examining the measurements of climate-determining factors such as temperature and precipitation recorded over the years, these changes can be seen by analysing averages and extreme values. For example, while there used to be heavy snowfall in

Istanbul during the winter months in the days of our grandparents, in recent years, there has been a significant decrease in snowfall. Summer temperatures, on the other hand, are rising so rapidly that the average temperatures measured are almost always higher than those in the previous year. Climate change is occurring in every region of the world. While these changes have led to cooler and wetter climate conditions in some regions, the general trend in countries like Turkey, which are located around the Mediterranean, is toward a warmer and drier climate (Kurnaz, 2021).

This is not the first climate change in world history; the climate has changed many times in the past. However, the level of change we are facing today is unprecedented in at least the last 25 million years. Previous changes occurred over hundreds of thousands of years, not in short periods of 100–150 years like today, so nature and living beings had sufficient time to adapt to these transformations.

Causes of Climate Change

The natural greenhouse effect caused by the sun's rays provides an average temperature level on Earth that allows humans, animals, and plants to live, thanks to greenhouse gases acting like a blanket in the atmosphere; this temperature is around 15 °C. If there were no greenhouse gases in the atmosphere, the average temperature on Earth would be approximately 18 °C. With the Industrial Revolution, the concentration of greenhouse gases in the atmosphere began to increase from the 18th century onwards, with carbon dioxide levels rising by 40%. According to data from the European Union's Copernicus Climate Change Service, the average temperature measured in the Northern Hemisphere during the summer of 2023 reached record levels globally, and this period was recorded as one of the hottest three-month periods in world history.

According to the 6th Assessment Report of the Intergovernmental Panel on Climate Change published in August 2021, the main cause of climate change is greenhouse gases emitted into the atmosphere by humans. Gases such as carbon dioxide, methane, and nitrous oxide are called greenhouse gases. These gases envelop the Earth like a blanket, preventing heat from escaping into space, which causes the climate to change. Global climate change is occurring because the levels of greenhouse gases in the atmosphere have risen to levels not seen in millions of years. Energy from the Sun heats the Earth's surface. When the Earth re-emits this energy into space, meaning when the incoming and outgoing energy are in balance, the Earth's average temperature remains constant. However, if this balance is disrupted, meaning if the amounts of incoming and outgoing energy differ, the temperature also changes. Today, greenhouse gases prevent some of this energy from escaping into space, causing the Earth's average temperature to rise. If these gases did not exist, our planet would be too cold to live on. Therefore, the amount of greenhouse gases in the atmosphere is in a very delicate balance. As long as this balance is maintained, the average temperature remains constant. However, with the increase in industrialisation, especially in the last century, this balance has been disrupted, and global temperatures have begun to rise (Kurnaz, 2021).

3. The Impact of Climate on Tourism

Climate change is seriously affecting the tourism sector for many reasons, primarily extreme weather events and natural disasters. Among the factors that can contribute to climate change in tourism, vehicles are at the forefront. In this regard, prioritising environmentally friendly fuels in transportation, reducing the carbon footprint, and preventing waste of water, energy, and food will yield significant benefits. Additionally, the importance of tourism facilities constructed with climate sensitivity in mind is also quite significant. The tourism sector is not only affected by climate change, but also contributes to this change (Demiralp, 2022). Due to the negative effects of climate change on tourism, public authorities need to identify and address these effects (Ahmed & Helhel, 2022).

Although the effects of climate and climate change on travel and tourism throughout history are of great importance, it is observed that these effects are not sufficiently utilised in tourism education. The excessive focus on technological developments, economic development, and socio-cultural habits has overshadowed the role of transformations related to the natural environment—especially climate change—in shaping the history of tourism (Weir, 2017). Adverse weather conditions caused by climate change can cause serious damage to tourist destinations and facilities, leading to major damage to facilities and changes in tourist expectations. Recent studies show that the issue of climate change is becoming increasingly important and that various measures can be taken in this area. The tourism sector is influenced by many external factors, such as economic, social, political, and demographic factors. While some sudden developments can quickly affect the sector, climate change has a slower and more gradual impact (Aygün Oğur, 2022).

Transportation is a critical area in terms of tourism's impact on the climate. Therefore, this sector needs to take steps toward transitioning to electric and modern vehicles. Renewable energy sources, however, have not yet been fully adopted in the tourism sector (Özekici & Silik, 2017).

For this reason, some tourism businesses are seen to be ignoring these effects and failing to develop strategic plans. With changes in climate conditions, the identification of new tourism destinations has become important in terms of the quality of services offered to visitors (Yalçın, 2022). Nature tourism is also affected by climate change, and because of the resulting negative effects, some regions are losing their appeal to tourists. Irregular rainfall causes problems in air transportation and makes access to tourist areas difficult. Extreme temperatures also have negative effects on both tourists and tourism workers (Dube & Nhamo, 2020).

Compared to other sectors such as energy and manufacturing, the tourism sector contributes to carbon dioxide (CO_2) and other greenhouse gas emissions to a limited extent. Therefore, there are relatively few studies examining the impact of this sector on climate change (Becken, 2005). In a study conducted by Becken et al. (2003) in the Fiji Islands, the effects of transportation and accommodation activities on energy use were analysed. Through interviews, fieldwork, and surveys, the study determined that the tourism sector's priority is energy conservation and cost reduction rather than emission levels, and that a common approach to climate change adaptation has not yet been developed within the sector. Danielopol et al. (2003) found that coastal tourism can have significant negative impacts on water resources. Two different case studies conducted by Lordkipanidze et al. (2005) and Williams and Ponsford (2009) showed that joint action in the tourism sector could be effective in sustainably managing the relationship between tourism and climate.

Various studies have reached a consensus that transportation, one of the sub-sectors of tourism, contributes significantly to CO_2 and other greenhouse gas emissions (Gössling & Michael Hall, 2008). Transportation activities, particularly the aviation sector, have been found to harm the environment despite their significant contributions to economic development (Daley, 2009). These studies address strategies and policies aimed at reducing the impact of transportation on climate change while also analysing the effects of these policies on tourism demand and economic benefits. Although the tourism sector's impact on climate change is milder than that of other industries, it is important to take the necessary measures to effectively manage the process and ensure the sustainability of tourism activities. Another important finding from the research is that it would be more effective to develop specific strategies that consider regional conditions, activity types, and sub-sectors rather than generalised solutions.

Climate change not only carries risks that could trigger many natural disasters but also has the potential to directly affect the experiences of tourism businesses and tourists. Temperature, as one of the basic elements of climate, plays a decisive role in the selection of holiday destinations. Sudden and severe changes in the climate system, or, in other words, "unforeseen circumstances," present various challenges for the tourism sector, decision-makers, and planners. On the other hand, the effects of short-lived greenhouse gases such as methane and black carbon are not considered in this assessment (Becken & Hay, 2007).

4. The Impact of Climate on Public Expenditure

Following the Second World War, with the adoption of the concept of the welfare state, the duties and responsibilities of the state increased significantly. The state no longer limited itself to providing national security and justice services but also took on a more active role in the economy to achieve various economic and social goals. In particular, the inadequacy of market mechanisms in providing certain goods and services and eliminating externalities has made state intervention inevitable. One of the fundamental goals of states is to ensure the country's development and raise the level of social welfare. These goals are directly related to increased production and investment. However, some businesses operating in the production process often do not include the external costs they cause in their cost calculations. To internalise such externalities, the state must intervene to remind businesses of this responsibility and take the necessary regulatory measures (Aydoğan, 2019).

In a free market economy, firms only consider their production costs when determining production quantities and sell their goods at market prices. However, in cases where negative externalities are present, firms do not bear the costs of the damage they cause to the environment; they only consider inputs such as labour, capital, energy, and transportation as cost items. Although this situation may appear to represent the optimal level of production from the firm's perspective, it does not ensure the efficient use of resources from the perspective of society. As a result, the existence of negative externalities leads to overproduction.

The negative effects of economic activities on ecological balance and the world have necessitated serious measures at both the national and international levels. In this context, the concept of economic development has been questioned, and the view that it needs to be redefined in terms of content has gained widespread acceptance. In line with this thinking, the concept of "Sustainable Development" has emerged as a development model that meets the needs of the present generation without compromising the ability of future generations to meet their own needs. This concept does not advocate abandoning economic development to avoid harming the environment; rather, it aims to ensure the sustainability of the current situation by preventing negative externalities that may arise during the development process and to establish a balance between ecological, economic, and social sustainability (Özçağ & Hotunluoğlu, 2015).

In today's contemporary understanding of the state, the sole reason compelling the state to spend is not the necessity of providing public services. Public expenditures are one of the most important financial tools in achieving economic and social goals such as ensuring economic growth and development, maintaining macroeconomic stability, distributing resources efficiently, and sharing national income fairly. In situations where negative externalities exist, the market price of goods and services does not fully reflect their marginal social costs. This situation leads to a loss of efficiency in resource allocation and the imposition of costs on society. With the development of the free market system, the increase in firms' production activities has led to an increase in negative externalities from an environmental perspective, causing production levels to reach a point that is inefficient for society. The fact that the firms causing these externalities do not take any responsibility for rectifying the situation has made state intervention necessary. In the context of combating global climate change, one of the most significant examples of negative externalities, states are undertaking various initiatives at both the national and international levels (Aydoğan, 2019).

Two fundamental principles stand out in the public economy in the context of efforts to combat climate change. The first is the "polluter pays" principle, which is based on the idea that all or part of the damage caused to the environment should be borne by the producers or consumers who caused the damage. The second is the "joint financing" principle, which involves public spending and tax incentives to reduce environmental damage in cases where the first principle cannot be applied. One of the most important tools for implementing the "polluter pays" principle is the carbon tax. Although the carbon tax is an effective financial instrument in the fight against global climate change, it cannot be fully implemented due to factors such as the tax being a source of revenue based on the state's sovereignty and the lack of sufficient tax awareness in developing countries (Yalçın & Gök, 2015).

5. Literature Review

Aybarç et al. (2019) aimed to measure the technical efficiency levels of provinces in Turkey in the tourism sector by examining the effects of public incentive policies implemented from 2005 to 2015 using the Data Envelopment Analysis (DEA) method. The input variables used in the analysis are the number of tourism investment incentive certificates at the provincial level, fixed capital investments financed by these incentives, employment rates, individual loans used for tourism purposes, expenditures for public services and the number of facilities, and rooms and beds with tourism certificates. The output variables were determined by the total number of visitors and the number of overnight stays. The findings showed that provinces located in the Mediterranean and Aegean regions have higher technical efficiency in the field of tourism compared to the Eastern provinces.

In Şen's (2022) study, the economic value of thermal resources in Kütahya province and the status of thermal tourism activities were evaluated using the survey method. The data obtained revealed that the expenditures of tourists coming to the region make positive contributions to local development. In addition, the study shows that if the plans for tourism in Kütahya are carried out at both micro and macro scales, the benefits that the region will gain from tourism can increase. The role of thermal tourism in revitalising the local economy is clearly emphasised.

According to Kahraman and Gültekin Tarla's (2022) study, the tourism sector has become one of the important areas contributing to economic growth with direct foreign investments. In this process, the expenditure of these tourists, as well as the increase in the number of tourists, play a decisive role in terms of economic efficiency. To increase this contribution, countries must determine their tourism targets in a sustainable and value-added-oriented structure. To create appropriate policy sets, the interaction between FDI and economic growth should be carefully analysed. In this context, the panel causality test applied for the period 2005–2020, specific to OECD countries, was used to evaluate the effectiveness of tourism policies. The findings obtained show that focusing only on the number of visitors in tourism is insufficient, and the main priority is to focus on tourists that have high spending capacity and contribute to sustainable tourism. Therefore, it is a critical necessity that tourism policies to be developed are built on environmentally friendly and technological foundations. According to Ahmed and Helhel (2022), the mutual relationship between tourism and climate change has become more noticeable with the growth of global environmental problems. In this context, existing studies aim to reveal the effects of climate change on regional tourism by providing examples, especially from tourism destinations in Europe and the Mediterranean basin. The reports and institutional collaborations in the relevant literature were evaluated; the effects of climate-related factors on tourism supply and demand were examined in the light of secondary data. Promotion strategies, seasonality, and natural disaster risks were among the prominent issues in this context. In addition, discussions on sustainability revealed how important the preservation of environmental balance is for long-term development in the tourism sector. As a result, it was stated that sustainable tourism practices should be developed in line with the prepared reports and meeting outputs. Steps such as climate-friendly infrastructures, environmentally friendly transportation options, and energy efficiency were evaluated among the basic headings that should be at the centre of tourism policies in the future.

In a study by Bayazıt (2018), climate change is shown to be an important environmental factor that can directly affect the nature-based tourism sector in a multidimensional way. In this context, sensitivity to climate events should be considered in the development of tourism projects; greenhouse gas emissions caused by sectoral activities should be controlled, and damage to natural sink areas should be prevented. Studies conducted specifically on Turkey analyse how domestic tourism interacts with climate change with existing data and estimation methods. The increase in tourism revenues is evaluated simultaneously with the increase in greenhouse gas emissions, thus shedding light on opportunities and threats in the context of climate change. The policy and implementation recommendations developed within this scope are structured with an approach that prioritises the environmental sustainability of the sector. It is emphasised that climate-friendly and nature-sensitive steps should be prioritised in tourism planning. In the study of Başoğlu (2014), climate change is defined as the artificial transformation of the climate outside of its natural variability because of human-induced activities straining the environmental balance. The increasing greenhouse gas effect due to fossil fuel use poses serious risks for all living things, countries, and economic systems. In recent years, scientific and political initiatives aimed at revealing both the current and potential effects of climate change have intensified. In particular, the negative effects on productivity, employment and economic growth in sectors directly dependent on the climate, such as agriculture, tourism and energy, are noteworthy. In this study, the aim was to outline the risks that climate change may create in terms of the sectors and economic indicators in question. The evaluations obtained indicate the necessity of developing preventive policies against environmental threats with a sustainable development perspective.

Aygün Oğur (2022) aims to determine the opportunities and threats that the tourism sector may face in line with the climate change scenarios predicted for Turkey and to develop suggestions that can form the basis of future tourism planning. For this purpose, a comprehensive literature review was conducted, and the obtained data were evaluated using the SWOT analysis method. The research makes an important contribution in terms of revealing the current and future situation of Turkish tourism in the face of climate change and offering suggestions in this direction.

Yalçın (2022) addresses climate and tourism issues and examines the literature sources of previous periods. Researchers have frequently focused on the relationship between climate and tourism in literature. In this context, climate indices, climate changes, the effects of climate on tourism, and the effects of tourism on climate and climate change have been discussed in detail. As a result of the literature review, it was seen that the results of the studies conducted were largely similar to each other. It was determined that Güçlü's study, like Aydelikenol's research, reached a common conclusion that choosing tourism types suitable for changing climate conditions based on climate change will provide success for tourism businesses.

Demiralp (2022) evaluated the relationship between the tourism sector and climate change by conducting a literature review. Within the scope of the research, it was concluded that to ensure the sustainability of the tourism sector and its resilience to climate change, adaptation actions should be implemented as soon as possible to reduce greenhouse gas emissions and minimise the negative effects of climate change on the sector. In addition, it was stated in the study that the measures to be taken within the framework of the interaction between climate change and the tourism sector are also important in terms of achieving the goals of the United Nations 2030 Agenda and Sustainable Development Goals and the Paris Climate Agreement, to which Turkey is a party. Dube and Nhamo (2020) examined the evidence and potential impacts of climate variability and change on nature-based tourism activities in Kariba resort, Zimbabwe. A case study approach was used where primary and secondary data were analysed using ArcGIS 10.3. Content and thematic analysis and Mann–Kendall trend analysis were also conducted. The study found that nature-based tourism in Kariba is under threat from increasing and intense droughts, likely resulting from climate change. Extreme temperatures and droughts are critical threats to biodiversity and water levels in Lake Kariba, undermining both specific tourist activities and destination attractiveness.

6. Conclusions

In the early days of tourism, individuals' reasons for participating in tourism were primarily limited to travel, faith, entertainment, and cultural experiences. However, today, a wide range of different motivations have come to the forefront, including sea tourism, conference tourism, health tourism, golf, gastronomy, and winter tourism. Despite this diversification, climate and weather conditions such as temperature, rainfall, and humidity, as well as the natural environment, continue to be fundamental determinants for the sustainability of tourism activities. Tourism activities are carried out in different forms across various geographies worldwide and constitute a significant economic sector globally in terms of Gross Domestic Product (GDP).

This study, in line with the findings in the literature, reveals that climate change has direct and significant impacts on tourism activities and public spending. However, one of the main contributions of the study is that it clearly shows this relationship varies significantly across regions. Tourism activities are more vibrant in regions with more favourable geographical and climatic conditions, and it is observed that the climate-related pressures on public spending in these regions are relatively more limited. In contrast, tourism revenues are declining in areas more susceptible to extreme weather events and experiencing more intense environmental degradation; in parallel, public spending is increasing in areas such as infrastructure repairs, disaster management, and environmental protection.

These interregional differences also indicate a clear divergence in the policy approaches being pursued. Climate-advantaged regions can focus more on maintaining competitiveness in tourism, diversifying products, and implementing preventive policies to protect natural and cultural assets. In contrast, public policies in regions more vulnerable to climate change often take on a reactive nature; emergency response, adaptation investments, and the restructuring of tourism activities become priorities. This situation not only creates additional burdens on public finances but also contributes to the deepening of interregional economic disparities.

The displacement of tourism regions caused by climate change, the destruction of natural areas, and the damage to cultural heritage present a picture that extends beyond the tourism sector, leading to global human and economic consequences. However, the capacity of regions to adapt to these effects is not equal. While some regions can manage climate shocks relatively easily due to strong institutional structures and financial capacity, others are entering a more fragile economic cycle due to declining tourism revenues and increased public spending.

In conclusion, this study demonstrates a direct causal relationship between climate change, tourism, and public spending and shows that this relationship varies significantly depending on regional climate conditions. Therefore, tourism and climate policies need to be addressed not with a uniform approach, but with differentiated policy frameworks that take into account the climatic, economic, and institutional characteristics of each region. Otherwise, the negative impacts of climate change on tourism and the resulting pressure on public spending will seriously threaten both the sector's sustainability and regional development goals in the long run.

Funding: This research received no external funding.

Conflicts of Interest: The author declares no conflicts of interest.

Author Name and Affiliation: Kerem Özen, Department of Economics, Van Yüzüncü Yıl University, Van, Turkey.

Keywords: climate change; tourism; public expenditures.

References

Ahmed, Y., & Helhel, Y. (2022). Relationship between climate change and tourism: Possible adaptation and solution suggestions. *Journal of Tourism Research Institute, 3*(2), 101–122.

Aybarç, S., Selim, S., & Kızıngöl, Ö. A. (2019). Effectiveness analysis of provinces within the framework of public incentive policies for tourism in Türkiye. *Journal of Economics and Administrative Sciences, 14*(1), 129–148.

Aydoğan, S. (2019). The role and importance of public expenditures as a financial tool in combating global climate change in Turkey. *Tax Report, 243*, 209–220.

Başoğlu, A. (2014). *Economic impacts of global climate change* [Ph.D. thesis, Black Sea Technical University].

Bayazıt, S. (2018). Investigation of the relationship between climate change and tourism in terms of domestic tourism in Turkey, Anatolia. *Journal of Tourism Research, 29*(2), 221–231.

Becken, S. (2005). Harmonizing climate change adaptation and mitigation: The case of tourist resorts in Fiji. *Global Environmental Change, 15*(4), 381–393. [CrossRef] [PubMed]

Becken, S., & Hay, J. E. (2007). Tourism and climate change: Risks and opportunities. Channel View Publications, Clevedon choices. *Tourism Management, 24*(3), 267–277.

Becken, S., Simmons, D. G., & Frampton, C. (2003). Energy use associated with different travel. *Tourism Management, 24*(3), 267–277. [CrossRef]

Daley, B. (2009). Is air transport an effective tool for sustainable development? *Sustainable Development, 17*(4), 210–219. [CrossRef]

Danielopol, D. L., Griebler, C., Gunatilaka, A., & Notenboom, J. (2003). Present state and prospects for groundwater ecosystems. *Environmental Conservation, 30*(2), 104–130. [CrossRef]

Demiralp, M. (2022). The impact of climate change on tourism. *Journal of Environment, City and Climate, 1*(2), 251–272.

Dube, K., & Nhamo, G. (2020). Vulnerability of nature-based tourism to climate variability and change: Case of Karibare sort town, Zimbabwe. *Journal of Outdoor Recreation and Tourism, 29*, 100281. [CrossRef]

Gössling, S., & Michael Hall, C. (2008). Swedish tourism and climate change mitigation: An emerging conflict? *Scandinavian Journal of Hospitality and Tourism, 8*(2), 141–158. [CrossRef]

Kahraman, N., & Gültekin Tarla, E. (2022). Examination of the causal relationship between tourism expenditures, economic growth, and foreign direct investment and policy recommendations: The case of OECD countries. *Journal of Tourism and Gastronomy Studies, 10*(3), 2339–2357.

Kurnaz, M. L. (2021). Küresel iklim krizi. *Bilim ve Teknik*, (648), 12–21. Available online: https://bilimteknik.tubitak.gov.tr/wp-content/uploads/sites/154/2025/09/c8ce2391-d632-4a04-9f81-a6f745e4f230-1.pdf (accessed on 5 March 2026).

Lordkipanidze, M., Brezet, H., & Backman, M. (2005). Entrepreneurship is a factor in sustainable tourism development. *Journal of Cleaner Production, 13*(8), 787–798. [CrossRef]

Oğur, A. (2022). Climate change sensitive tourism planning: Opportunities and threats for Turkey. *Journal of Environment, City and Climate, 1*(1), 80–104.

Özçağ, M., & Hotunluoğlu, H. (2015). A new dimension in development understanding: Green economy. *Manisa Celal Bayar University Journal of Social Sciences, 13*(2), 303–324.

Özekici, Y. K., & Silik, C. E. (2017). The place of the tourism sector in climate change plans and policies in Turkey. *Gazi University Tourism Faculty Journal*, *2*, 58–79.
Şen, G. (2022). Effects of tourist expenditures on regional economy: Kütahya example. *Journal of Social Sciences*, *74*, 97–112. [CrossRef]
Weir, B. (2017). Climate change and tourism—Are we forgetting lessons from the past? *Journal of Hospitality and Tourism Management*, *32*, 108–114. [CrossRef]
Williams, P. W., & Ponsford, I. F. (2009). Confronting tourism's environmental paradox: Transitioning to sustainable tourism. *Futures*, *41*(6), 396–404. [CrossRef]
Yalçın, A. Z. (2022). The effects of climate change on tourism. *Selçuk Journal of Tourism and Informatics Research*, *1*(1), 32–37.
Yalçın, A. Z., & Gök, M. (2015). Analysis of public environmental protection expenditures in the European Union and Turkey. *International Journal of Management Economics and Business*, *11*(25), 67.

Climate Risk and Corporate Accountability: The Role of Business in Mitigation

Christian Pirker

Abstract: Climate risk is currently the most pressing challenge facing our society. This article addresses the question of how companies can achieve real and effective accountability in business to better manage climate risk. The method involves a mixture of proven theories, empirical studies, and best practices. An interdisciplinary approach is pursued, examining various topics and aspects from different perspectives. It becomes clear that existing governance models mostly have limitations or are completely inappropriate approaches. Conversely, it becomes clear that systemic management, ambidexterity, organisational transformation, and transformative learning are essential for meeting the challenges of our time. It is about responsibility within companies and management, and ultimately about genuine and effective corporate accountability as a viable system. A paradigm shift in dealing with the climate crisis, away from external paternalism and toward internal responsibility and sustainable accountability, is therefore necessary. Thus, companies and management are increasingly becoming key actors in sustainable development and in dealing with the climate crisis.

1. Introduction

Climate risk is one of the major issues of our time. The topic dominates discussions in politics, society, and business. The past two decades have been increasingly shaped by this central topic. The problem has been and remains that the analyses, problem definitions, and proposed solutions are mostly of subpar quality and do not lead to any real solutions.

Corporate accountability is a term that has been a topic in politics, society and the economy for some time now. In Europe, this is fraught with the problem that there has been and still is an asymmetry between politics and business. Politics tries to dominate business and push it in a certain direction through laws, regulations, and guidelines. A key word here is the European Union's Green Deal. Business has been fundamentally too passive in this regard and has withdrawn into a passive role, partly out of fear and insecurity or dependence on politics. This negative development has been criticised behind closed doors and in private conversations. In public and public statements, the Green Deal was approved and received as a good thing. No one dared to say, to paraphrase Hans Christian Andersen, that the emperor is naked!

The role of business in mitigation needs to be rethought. This paper explores various aspects of why this is the case and how it can be achieved in corporate practice. One thing is already clear: this can only be achieved with the active participation of enterprises and management. Management must be aware of its role and importance. Management, by definition, must be able to deal with uncertainty and incomplete information, think, make good decisions, and ultimately act consistently. This can only be achieved with a high degree of trust and responsibility. This ultimately means true accountability.

First, this contribution will focus on concrete approaches to the core topics of climate risk and corporate responsibility. It will then present initial critical approaches to addressing these topics in practice. Finally, it will introduce a new perspective on the topic of "The Role of Business in Mitigation". This will initially focus on new self-confidence and consistent personal responsibility in management. This chapter will then address the question of which approaches from management theory and practices we can build on to redesign companies as ones that are viable and truly sustainable.

At the end of the contribution, there is a framework for dealing with this challenge, as well as concrete recommendations for the management practice of the sustainable enterprise.

We will see that this is about the question of what constitutes correct and good management. Theoretical and empirical findings will be presented here. Then, the question is how to master the challenges of our time. This includes, but is not limited to, climate risk. We will see that a clear awareness of the structural distinction between operational, strategic, and normative management within companies is essential to enable sustainable corporate development. This is then about ambidexterity, transformation, and ultimately effectiveness and viability as a system.

This contribution addresses the question of how we can achieve real and effective accountability in business to better manage climate risk. The method involves a mixture of proven theories, empirical studies and best practices.

2. Selected Theoretical Foundations

2.1. The Basic Concepts and Central Approaches

Climate risks are among the greatest challenges of our time. They concern ecological sustainability, economic stability, and social resilience—but not only that. They also involve risks arising from the consequences of climate change. These include physical risks such as extreme weather events but also risks associated with the transition to a low-carbon economy. Finally, there are liability risks (TCFD, 2017). These diverse risk dimensions are increasingly impacting decision-making processes in politics, the financial system, and the economy and require new concepts and instruments for risk analysis, assessment, and management, both in a theoretical–analytical and application-related context.

In recent years, the topic of climate risk has developed from a peripheral field of discourse to a central subject of strategic risk analysis. Research by the Task Force on Climate-related Financial Disclosures (TCFD) shows that climate risk is a long-term challenge. Thus, it involves a far-reaching and structural transformation with corresponding impacts on business models, supply chains, capital flows, and the stability of the financial system (TCFD, 2017; Bolton et al., 2020; Kölbel et al., 2020).

Against this background, this article addresses the question of how climate risk can be conceptualised, systematically structured, and addressed across sectors. This involves an interdisciplinary approach that combines economic, political, and ecological perspectives. This should then enable a correspondingly deeper understanding of the dynamics, mechanisms of action, and control logic of climate-related risks.

The topic of corporate accountability has become important in academia, politics, and even the public sphere. This raises the question of who companies are truly accountable to and how this accountability can be established accordingly. Corporate accountability is therefore more than just legal liability or financial transparency. It also requires a comprehensive understanding of corporate accountability to various stakeholders (Crane et al., 2019).

In academic discourse, corporate accountability has established itself as an interdisciplinary field of research that brings together perspectives from law, business ethics, business, and social sciences. While traditional models of corporate governance primarily address the relationship between owner interests and company management, more recent research emphasises the multidimensional responsibility of companies towards society, the environment, and future generations (Gray et al., 2014). This is especially true for countries in the Global South, with weak government regulation, where corporate governance becomes an essential element of corporate responsiveness—but not only that (Scherer & Palazzo, 2011; Malik, 2012).

This raises the following questions: Which institutional, economic, and cultural mechanisms promote or inhibit corporate responsibility? How can responsibility be effectively institutionalised within cross-border value chains? And to what extent do changing social expectations influence the governance structures and normative commitments of companies?

This contribution explores these questions and locates corporate accountability as a dynamic concept in the field of tension between corporate autonomy, public interest, and global power asymmetries. The aim is to combine theoretical perspectives with empirical findings to critically analyse and further develop the conditions and challenges of effective accountability systems.

In this context, this contribution is also about the interplay between science, politics, and society. It is about boundary work (Gieryn, 1999), Mode 2 (Nowotny et al., 2001), and, in some cases, new forms of learning (Gelbmann & Pirker, 2023). The themes are closely related to each other or are consciously linked repeatedly. Ulrike Gelbmann and Christian Pirker work on and combine topics such as Education for Sustainable Development (ESD), Transdisciplinary, Mode-2-Learning, Transformative Learning, Service Learning, Third Mission, and Social Engagement.

In recent years, the climate crisis has increasingly intensified calls for profound systemic change. Governments, civil society, and now also the private sector are key actors in various climate protection efforts. Companies are considered major contributors to greenhouse gas emissions, but also sites of potential solutions through technological innovations or appropriate capital investment (Rockström et al., 2017).

The UNEP believes that climate protection, in the sense of reducing greenhouse gas emissions, should no longer be driven by environmental regulations or government initiatives. It is encouraging that companies are increasingly integrating corresponding climate strategies into their business models (UNEP, 2021). The academic literature describes the ambivalent role of stakeholders within companies and warns against pure greenwashing. There is a call for robust governance mechanisms to ensure accountability, transparency, and substantial impact (Wright & Nyberg, 2015).

2.2. *Responsibility and Accountability*

In business practice, responsibility is being talked about increasingly often. This is not only happening in a systemic context. There is also the concept of accountability, which is like the concept of responsibility, but it is not congruent. In the context of managing complex systems, the question ultimately arises as to how accountability can be effective (Drucker, 2002).

There are different approaches to accountability in different disciplines. In many cases, it is a form of external control. But how can it become a form of self-control? How can we use the possibilities of managing complex systems in accountability? What is the significance of self-organisation here? What about attitude and real responsibility? Am I and are we prepared to bear the consequences of my and our actions? Can I and we live responsibility in such a way that I and we can also response critical questions?

Responsibility and accountability are discussed in different contexts. For example, they are present in the issue of responsible innovation (Stilgoe et al., 2013). Stilgoe et al. (2013) note that dissatisfaction with the previous focus on liability and risk-based regulation has led to a greater focus on future-oriented dimensions of responsibility such as care and responsiveness. These approaches make it easier to deal with uncertainties (Drucker, 1980) and promote reflection on the goals and values of science and innovation (Stilgoe et al., 2013). Chhotray and Stoker (2009) describe the challenge of democracy and accountability. They emphasise that in the context of modern governance, the classic understanding of personal political liability is increasingly reaching its limits, as political responsibility in complex networks and diverse constellations of actors is difficult to assign. While some authors emphasise that new forms of governance also require democratic accountability and that the state should continue to act as a guarantor of public interest, experience shows that state control in modern, network-based structures remains problematic. The concept of accountability could therefore be rethought instead of demanding individual accountability, attention should be paid to the systemic characteristics of governance—namely how power is shared, how learning processes are enabled, and how concentration of power is prevented. In this way, accountability can also be understood as a systemic characteristic that can be realised through shared responsibility and reflexivity in complex decision-making structures (Chhotray & Stoker, 2009). Fridlund (2020) works on the topic of post-truth politics, performatives, and the force. Ultimately, he emphasises the importance of function and effectiveness (Drucker, 2002). He writes a significant sentence at the end of the abstract: "This evokes serious questions about accountability and responsibility and also about human action and freedom" (Fridlund, 2020). Patrik Fridlund also brings the terms resonance and response into play. In any case, we will take with us the central concepts of accountability, responsibility, human action, and freedom, as well as resonance and response.

These tools enable companies to present their responsibilities in detail and record their interrelationships to analyse and improve their social and sustainable accountability. If Responsible Research and Innovation (RRI) is understood as a meta-responsibility, its investigation in the industrial sector requires a clear definition of responsibility. This term, which has a long tradition in philosophy and law, has recently gained importance as a cultural framework for risk, complexity, and uncertainty (Drucker, 1980). In the corporate context, such as Corporate Social Responsibility (CSR), responsibility is seen as an alternative to decreasing state control in the face of growing corporate power. The understanding of responsibility also encompasses the relationship between research, innovation, and society, particularly in the RRI discourse. CSR and RRI demand economic, social, and ecological responsibility towards all stakeholders. Access to information is essential for responsible action and accountability. Sustainability reporting clarifies how well organisations meet the requirements of (un)sustainability. Auditing and reporting control information flows for internal decisions and external stakeholders, such as NGOs. Performance monitoring supports CSR and RRI by highlighting potential for improvement and risks. Social and sustainability reporting is therefore central to the increased sense of responsibility (Timmermans et al., 2017).

The added value of the concept of responsibility in the context of Responsible Research and Innovation (RRI) compared to Corporate Social Responsibility (CSR) and sustainability reporting lies in the fact that a broader spectrum of relevant stakeholders is addressed. While CSR and reporting usually focus on the responsibility of organisations, companies, or their management, RRI also includes individuals or groups within these organisations, such as researchers, innovators, and political decision-makers. This more precise understanding of individual responsibility is not only important for RRI but also strengthens the accountability of companies and supports reporting and management processes by showing what knowledge and information individual organisational members can contribute to social and ecological tasks (Timmermans et al., 2017).

In addition to the three elements of the basic model and the standard, the temporal dimension is also important. Responsibility can relate to future objects, such as when a researcher is liable to users for the reliability of a product, but also to past actions, such as when an innovative artefact is defective. Since research and innovation are characterised by uncertainty, a forward-looking view of responsibility is more appropriate for Responsible Research and Innovation (RRI). Retrospective responsibilities, such as liability and accountability, rely too heavily on the predictability of consequences. Therefore, our study focuses on forward-looking responsibility (Timmermans et al., 2017).

In addition to the links to Corporate Social Responsibility (CSR), RRI is particularly important as it also influences sustainability reporting. As an innovation in the governance of research and innovation, RRI expands social accountability through new or expanded responsibilities for innovative companies. Sustainability often becomes the subject or norm of these responsibilities. In this way, RRI can promote sustainability reporting and strengthen responsibility for sustainable performance. At the same time, sustainability reporting and accounting offer effective means of implementing RRI in companies. This article deals only briefly with these relationships, which is why further research is needed—especially on the role of sustainability reporting and its significance for RRI, for example, in the financial sector (Timmermans et al., 2017).

To better understand the interactions between Responsible Research and Innovation (RRI) and sustainability reporting, the issue of how responsibilities are linked to specific information requirements and the collection of certain information should be investigated. In addition, further studies should shed light on possible conflicts and risks within responsibility networks and develop strategies for dealing with them. For a clearer picture of networks across different cultures and organisational types, the qualitative methodology of such a study should be complemented by quantitative approaches that capture data from different industries, company sizes and locations. RRI has the ambitious goal of making research and innovation more social and ethical, but there is still a great need to bridge the gap between theory, policy, and practice, especially in non-academic sectors such as industry. The concept of RRI as a meta-responsibility that governs existing responsibility networks offers a promising and grounded approach with its new approach to untangling complex responsibility relationships (Timmermans et al., 2017).

2.3. Selected Critical Approaches

In the context of the climate problem, Grunwald (2012) has already asked whether previous solutions were failing. Since the Industrial Revolution, humanity has increasingly intervened in the climate system. This is particularly the case through CO_2 emissions from fossil fuels, methane from agriculture, and other greenhouse gases. These changes were unplanned and are closely linked to economic growth, technological progress, consumption, and intensive land use. The solution lies in reducing emissions through more efficient technologies, the use of renewable energies, and a generally sustainable lifestyle. However, this path is very difficult. Global climate policy with a focus on mitigation is showing little success, while emissions continue to rise, mainly due to strong population and economic growth in emerging and developing countries such as China, India, and Brazil (Grunwald, 2012).

As it is becoming increasingly clear that measures to mitigate climate change alone will probably not be enough, the focus has also been adapted over the years. This is less about simply stopping climate change than about developing appropriate strategies to cope with the coming changes. This includes appropriate precautionary measures that prevent major disasters and ensure decent living conditions even in the event of more severe climate change. However, adaptation strategies reach their limits when climate change exceeds certain proportions. In this context, new technological options have been gaining importance for some years now—technological futures of a different kind than mitigation or adaptation (Grunwald, 2012).

The situation described could mean a revival of the "principle of responsibility" formulated by Jonas (1979). Jonas emphasises that "the whole"—i.e., the continued existence of human life on Earth—must not be put at risk or subjected to a risky experiment. It would therefore first have to be examined whether the risks of climate engineering involve scenarios that endanger this "whole". If this is the case, according to Jonas, its use would not be justifiable. On the other hand, it can also be argued that, if measures to mitigate (mitigation) and adapt (adaptation) to climate change are insufficient, climate engineering could, according to Paul Crutzen, be the "ultima ratio" to still save the "whole". In this sense, it would be our duty to research these technologies and make them ready for use. The precautionary principle does not provide any clear answers to this dilemma. The situation shows that a deeper ethical consideration is necessary, in which positive arguments must be taken into account alongside the risks (Grunwald, 2012).

Armin Grunwald has analysed the problem very well from the perspective of the future of technology. What is still missing, however, is a look at the possibilities and necessities of management in this context. This is what this article aims to do.

The Austrian magazine *Der Pragmaticus* features the headline "Protecting the climate, but please do it right!" in its July 2025 issue (Issue 6). At first glance, this title suggests that current climate efforts are falling short. In his editorial, Editor-in-Chief Andreas Schnauder emphasises the magazine's goal of speaking plainly. In the second sentence, he asserts that climate policy has failed and proceeds to explain why. Andreas Schnauder argues that a major mistake has been the failure to involve industry as a partner. Instead, industry is being pushed out, along with economic prosperity. He therefore calls for a smarter approach to climate policy. The issue goes on to advocate for greater pragmatism and realism: a co-evolution of climate policy and the economy, more effective measures, and practical solutions that are compatible with people's needs. Ultimately, the focus is on "saving the world 2.0", that is, climate protection grounded in pragmatism rather than unattainable ideals. Above all, they insist that Eurocentrism must be abandoned in favour of a more global perspective (Der Pragmaticus, 2025).

Doing the right thing to protect the climate is closely linked to the issue of correct and good management.

3. Sustainable Enterprise, Systemic Management, and Effective Learning

3.1. Sustainable Enterprise

Brundtland (1987), the former Norwegian Prime Minister and Chair of the UN Commission on Environment and Development, defined sustainability as development that meets the needs of the present without compromising the ability of future generations to meet their own needs. Ben-Eli (2012), founder of the Sustainability Lab in New York, defines sustainability as a dynamic balance between a population and the carrying capacity of its environment, allowing the population to develop fully without causing irreversible damage to the environment on which it depends. Meanwhile, the ecological focus has been supplemented by Sachs (2015) by the goal of socially inclusive and ecologically sustainable economic growth (Schwaninger, 2000).

The following Figure 1 shows the three dimensions of sustainability. All three dimensions are important and must be adhered to.

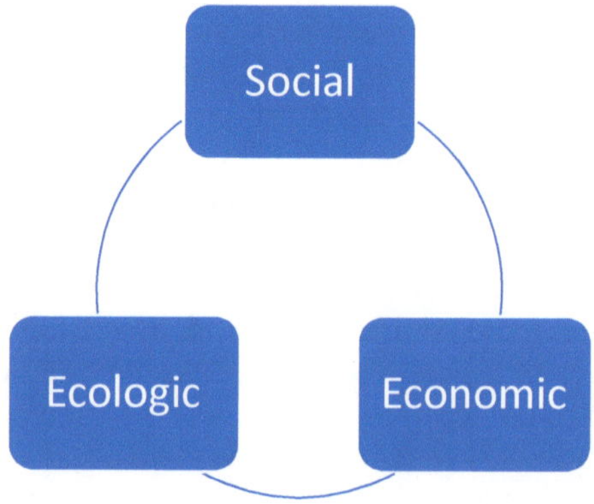

Figure 1. Three dimensions of sustainability. Source: Figure by author.

Sustainable enterprise is a topic that is becoming increasingly popular in theory and practice. In theory, the first approaches can be found that focus on the sustainable enterprise from a holistic perspective in the narrower sense (Pirker, 2021). In addition, there are already traditional approaches from management theory, strategic management, systemic management, and transformation management, which, thanks to their high quality, are still justified in 2025 and provide us with valuable insights and models for sustainable corporate development.

Closely related to this is the question of learning in and by organisations, learning organisation (Senge, 1990), and the question of effective learning (Pirker, 2019). This is always about the viability of the company as a system, as well as the development and transformation of companies in terms of sustainable corporate development.

Pirker (2021), in "Three Perspectives for the Development of Sustainable Enterprises," has already outlined how the development of sustainable businesses should be approached. This framework emphasises three key dimensions: effectiveness, raising awareness of sustainability, and building competencies. The basic ideas are also relevant to the issue of "Climate Risk and Corporate Accountability". Now that we have seen all the things that do not work and where politicians repeatedly fall short, it is probably the companies that we need to hold increasingly accountable. In corporate practice, however, this does not mean unthinkingly following political rules, but rather genuine corporate accountability in the sense of sustainable enterprise and companies as intelligent and viable systems.

Coping with complexity is a central challenge for management and leadership in today's dynamic environments. Drawing on a systems perspective, Markus Schwaninger argues that organisations require transdisciplinary approaches and models to manage this complexity more effectively than with traditional, single-discipline methods. He introduces a framework for "intelligent organisations" that incorporates the Model for Systemic Control (MSC), the Viable System Model (VSM), and the Team Syntegrity Model. The Viable System Model, developed by Stafford Beer (1926–2002), is especially relevant for understanding and implementing sustainability in organisations (Schwaninger, 2000).

The precise definition of a "sustainable enterprise" is still evolving. Fredmund Malik equates the concepts of viability and sustainability, suggesting that both refer to an organisation's enduring capability to survive and prosper. He criticises a sole focus on shareholder value, instead advocating for management approaches that emphasise organisational health, adaptability, and long-term survival. Markus Schwaninger supports this view, highlighting that while profitability ensures survival, a narrow focus on profit maximisation can undermine a company's capacity for adaptation and long-term success. Both authors consider organisational development and ongoing transformation as central to sustainability (Malik, 2012; Schwaninger, 2000).

Sustainability in practice requires organisations to focus on changing management, learning, and the continuous evolution of their internal culture. The MSC sets viability and ongoing development as fundamental management objectives, calling for organisations not only to maintain themselves but also to develop and adapt to ever-changing demands. This includes the willingness to renew and, if necessary, even transform their identity. Approaches by John Kotter, Peter Senge, and Jim Collins stress the importance of organisational learning, confronting uncomfortable truths, and refining strategies (Ansoff, 1985) in response to changing circumstances as critical to achieving sustainable success (Senge, 1990; Kotter, 1996; Collins, 2001; Pirker, 2019).

3.2. Systemic Management

In systemic management, the terms "systemic" and "cybernetic" are often used synonymously. This is fine because the foundations of systems theory lie in cybernetics, at least in terms of the history of ideas. It is a circular organisation that distinguishes cybernetic systems from other organised systems (von Foerster, 1993). Heinz von Foerster (1911–2002) made a significant contribution to the understanding of systems when he distinguished between "trivial machines" and "non-trivial machines". The term "machine" is initially confusing, but replacing it with "system" makes it easier to use in practice. The reason Heinz von Foerster speaks of "machines" lies in the example of Alan Turing (1912–1954), the inventor of the "Turing machine". Alan Turing called his logical–mathematical scheme a "machine". A trivial machine has a unique relationship between its input and its output (as a reaction or effect). Since the operation is unique, the same result always occurs (a deterministic system), making this a predictable system. Coffee machines are typical trivial machines. You insert a coin at the top, select the desired flavour, and the desired coffee comes out at the bottom. If it does not, then the machine is broken and needs to be repaired. A non-trivial machine is something completely different. It is determined by its previous operations. This means that the respective history or biography determines the current behaviour of the machine. Thus, the result is not (fully) analysable, making this non-trivial machine an unpredictable system. Humans are typically non-trivial machines, and so are all teachers and learners, as well as managers. All people, and therefore all managers, are autopoietic systems. This must always be considered in the context of management competence, management education, and management training. Self-organisation plays a major role in the systemic approach. This applies both to learning itself and to the organisation of learning. A special form of self-organisation is autopoiesis. Here, again, there is a close connection between the systemic approach and constructivism (von Foerster, 1993; von Glasersgeld, 1995; Pirker, 2019).

The works of Beer (1979) and Ulrich (2001) are considered major steps in the development of systemic management. In the 1960s, Hans Ulrich (1919–1997), together with his colleagues, began to question existing business studies and establish a systems-oriented management theory. This was later refined and further developed by his student Fredmund Malik and by Markus Schwaninger.

In a long-term empirical study (12 years), Christian Pirker explored the research question of what management is and how and where it is taught. Many existing theoretical approaches were confirmed. However, there were certainly new insights, especially ub terms of the empirical basis.

The term "management" originated in the USA and became increasingly used in postwar Europe. Wolfgang Staehle (1938–1992) pays tribute here to the 1948 German translation of the American bestseller *The Managerial Revolution* (Burnham, 1941) by James Burnham (1905–1987). From then on, it became common practice to "retain the original terms manager and management" (Staehle, 1990). We still do this very consistently, at least in German-speaking countries. In contrast to other cultures, the question of the difference between "management" and "leadership" is essentially never asked or is asked much less frequently (Pirker, 2019). Fredmund Malik assumes, at least in a very simplified way, that anyone who manages in the broadest sense is also a manager. Anyone who bears responsibility for the performance of others, anyone who can influence the performance of others, is a manager (Malik, 1992).

According to Hans Ulrich (1919–1997), two definitions of management dominate in practice-oriented management theory (Ulrich, 2001):

- The first is the countlessly reproduced definition: management = "getting things done through other people".
- The second is the enumerative definition: management = organising, planning, deciding, and leading people (or another list of "functions").

Fredmund Malik's definition of management, which generally defines management as the transformation of resources into benefits, is in line with the first paraphrase. For the knowledge society, he further refined the definition of management as the transformation of knowledge into benefits. According to Hans Ulrich, the purpose of management theory is "to provide knowledge for practical action; without the hope that its statements would be useful for people outside of science, there would be no management theory". Thus, the topics addressed by management theory must have a clear connection to the problems facing managers (Ulrich, 2001). Fredmund Malik criticises the fact that few managers have systematic management training. This is more remarkable because management is the most important mass profession in modern society. Fredmund Malik goes a step further: in no other profession is training as poor as in management (Malik, 2000). Managers who have attended universities possess knowledge in their respective academic subjects, but they are not trained to become managers there. Henry Mintzberg describes it similarly: so-called management training suffers from the fact that it is a business education that only distorts the reflection of a manager's tasks (Mintzberg, 2005). According to Malik (2000), there are only two organisations that truly systematically prepare their future managers and leaders for their management tasks:

- The military;
- The church.

Christian Pirker empirically investigated the question of management competence. He identified eight elements of management competence (Pirker, 2019). You can see the eight elements of management competence in Figure 2.

"System and control" are the first elements. This is no coincidence, because, on the one hand, they were mentioned repeatedly in the empirical study, and, on the other hand, they logically come first because, according to Hans Ulrich, management is about the management of institutions. This has been empirically confirmed.

Although management competence is more than just technical competence, the study made it clear that it cannot be achieved entirely without "technical" aspects. Thus, the "technical" element is a category of management competence.

Choosing the next term was not easy, but ultimately it became clear that "personality" is the right term. A manager's personality plays a decisive role in everyday life when it comes to work, motivation, performance, and goal achievement.

In modern organisations, "teams" are a recurring theme, and the interviewees addressed many aspects of teams and the importance of managing and developing teams.

"Interaction" is a category that determines whether an organisation or company can operate successfully. Interaction with other people, with managers, employees, and colleagues, with teams and the organisation, with customers, suppliers, and stakeholders in general, is probably a recurring theme in a manager's work.

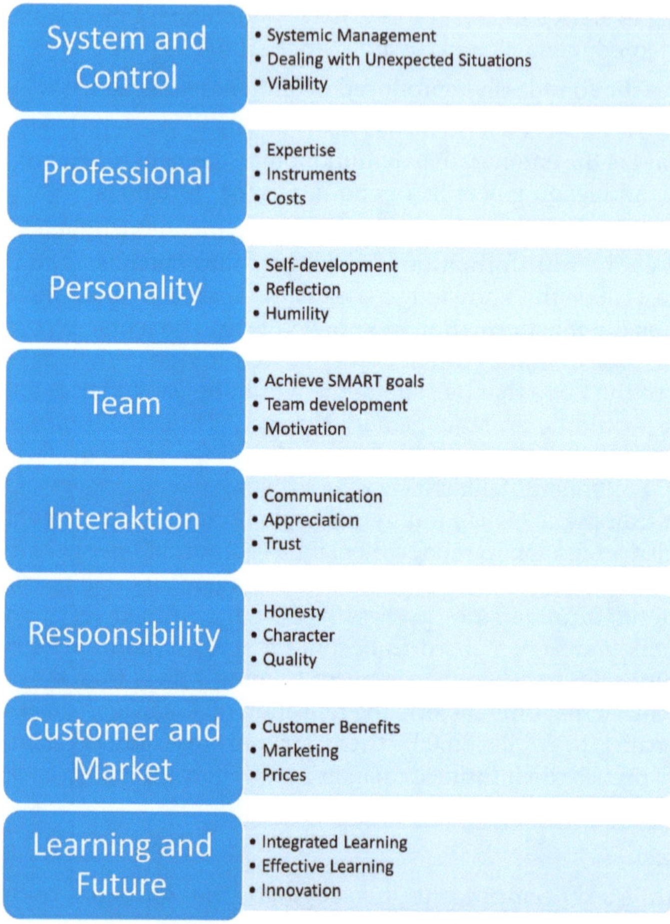

Figure 2. Management. Source: Figure by author.

You often read in newspapers how irresponsible managers are. But is it even possible to be successful as a manager in the long term without "responsibility"? If you read and listen to the news carefully, you will already realise that it is impossible without responsibility. The interviewees repeatedly mentioned the word "responsibility" and repeatedly emphasised how important responsibility is for managers.

The topic of "customer and market" was often ignored. Nevertheless, it has become a separate category because customers and the market are so often ignored or given too little attention. "The only thing that bothers me is the customer", and "customer threatens to cancel the order" are funny sayings in management seminars, but they are often bitter realities in everyday professional life. Managers must therefore be even more careful not to lose sight of the customer and the market.

"Learning and the future" is a combination that identifies cause and effect. "No future without learning" is the short version. The topics "learning" and "future" were addressed by interviewees in almost every interview. The importance of learning is clear to managers (Pirker, 2019).

In addition to the empirical knowledge of what management is, this work also reveals some things that are important for the contribution in this book. At its core, it is about systemic management. We can no longer ignore this in times of high dynamism. It is also about dealing with unexpected situations, namely the ability to cope with surprise. Finally, this field is about the viability of the company as a system. This model also reflects the personality of the manager. In recent years, there has been increasing criticism that personalities are lacking, especially in large companies. However, these personalities also require courage and poise, as well as a strong backbone. Then we have the essential point of responsibility. This is also closely linked to the personality of the manager. When I spent two days as a speaker and lecturer at the Military Academy 10 years ago, the staff officers explained to me at the end of the evening: "Responsibility means being able to answer questions and doing so." That is, at its core, what constitutes true responsibility. In German, this is called "Rechenschaft" (accountability). Finally, there is the topic of learning and the future. This involves actively shaping the company's future through ambidexterity, based on day-to-day business. This ultimately concerns the company's viability and sustainable development (sustainable enterprise).

4. The Role of Business Mitigation

4.1. Mastering the Dynaxity

Climate risk is a dynamic and highly complex issue. Referring to Hayek (1945), this cannot be solved with naive rationalism or centralised control. Rather, it is about recognising the high level of dynamism and complexity, the "Dynaxity" defined by Rieckmann (1997), and thinking and acting accordingly. It is therefore clear that a central aspect of problem-solving lies in corporate governance (Malik, 2012), the management of companies, and sustainable corporate development, or sustainable enterprises (Schwaninger, 2000; Pirker, 2021). The following section will paint an even clearer picture of this.

Markus Schwaninger tells us: "Management in systemic terms means to cope with complexity." (Schwaninger & Ott, 2023). It is therefore clear that in management, and specifically in systemic management, we should seek and find solutions to dynamic and complex problems of all kinds.

This is about mastering dynaxity. Here, we can build historically and systematically on the essential insights of systemic management (Beer, 1979; Ulrich, 2001; Malik, 1992; Schwaninger, 2000; Pirker, 2019, 2021), strategic management (Ansoff, 1985; Gälweiler, 2005), and normative management and organisational culture (Bleicher, 2001; Schein, 2017; Pirker, 2024.), as well as change management (Kotter, 1996), organisational transformation (Pirker, 2019), and the learning organisation (Senge, 1990; Rieckmann, 1997; Pirker, 2019) and organisations as viable systems (de Geus, 1997; Malik, 1992). In addition, we must utilise the new possibilities offered by the internet, new media, ever-increasing digital networking, and artificial intelligence. However, the latter are merely instruments. At its core, it is about people, the networking of people, and the collaboration of people (Pirker, 2019).

4.2. Variety Engineering

Schwaninger and Ott (2023) describe variety engineering with reference to the three dimensions of sustainability. Variety engineering describes processes in which interacting actors increase or reduce complexity. The goal is to demonstrate new approaches to managing complexity, illustrated by examples from ecological, social, and economic contexts.

The methods of variety engineering include reducing external (hetero-variety) and increasing internal variety (eigen-variety). What happens when a company operates in a complex market? The company has two options here:

1. Modelling, segmentation, new grouping methods, focusing on market segments or system realignment can be used to reduce market complexity.
2. Market intelligence, better information systems, a larger sales force, or stronger capabilities can be used to increase one's diversity. Reframing remains the central tool of variety engineering.

The most effective way to reduce external variety and strengthen internal variety is to redesign the context. Creating alternative realities creates new possibilities (strengthening) and a more focused, less complex context (mitigation). Attenuation and strengthening are closely linked. A company should examine whether its markets fit its identity or need to be redefined (attenuation) while simultaneously improving its structures and capabilities for long-term viability (strengthening).

The smaller levers of variety engineering influence perception and understanding rather than actions:

1. Reinforcing hetero-variety: If the market is immutable, factors of market complexity, such as individualisation, fragmentation, and specialisation, should be understood.
2. Weakening of eigen-varieties: It is important to recognise factors such as operational blindness, bureaucracy or rigid habits that reduce intrinsic diversity.

The authors present four case studies on variety engineering: ecological, social, and economic sustainability, as well as the integration of perspectives. Finally, residual variety is addressed, and conclusions are drawn (Schwaninger & Ott, 2023).

In the ecological dimension, Schwaninger and Ott describe the case of design for self-control. Here, it becomes clear that, for a long time, traditional legal and governmental interventions, based on the example of river pollution by factories, have only been of limited help (Schwaninger & Ott, 2023). An example from the author's own experience is as follows: In Styria, we learned in elementary school that the Mur (a river) is severely polluted from its confluence with the Pöls, where a large paper factory still stands today. By requiring the factory to extract water from below the factory and then pump it into the factory, the factory (as in numerous other cases), through self-organisation and self-control, took all necessary measures to ensure that only clean water leaves the factory.

In the social dimension, Schwaninger and Ott describe the case of unintended side effects and how to cope with them. This case illustrates how social dynamics during an economic crisis (2008/09) led to a loss of diversity in an organisation. A drop in sales leads to downsizing, which costs knowledge and skills. It also creates a culture of fear that triggers stress among the workforce. A destabilising loop develops stress and leads to burnouts and staff losses, which causes overload and more stress. A further loop emerges: stress reduces quality, which lowers sales. Staff reductions trigger social consequences that exacerbate the decline and threaten the company's existence (Schwaninger & Ott, 2023). The author himself had a similar experience during this crisis. As a board member of a know-how supplier to the automotive industry, I had a different opinion and vision about the crisis and how to deal with it than the owners. A conflict arose, and the result was that I left the company and waived all outstanding bonuses and premiums. This was because, on the one hand, I did not want to lay people off during the crisis, and, on the other, I was convinced that we would need all employees and managers again after the crisis to be able to operate successfully. It was a difficult step for me, and, although I did not want them to, several outstanding second-level managers followed me. The result was a massive drop in sales for the company, much greater than the crisis would have indicated. Two years later, the owner's representatives approached me and asked if I would like to return to the company. I said no, thank you.

In the economic dimension, Schwaninger and Ott describe the case of designing business systems. Designing a business system requires many decisions and a high degree of complexity. A heuristic tool for this is the generic structure of business systems, in which variables are logically linked to form a loop. The diagram shows a generic structure, as the dimensions and variables are recognisable in any business system. The specific design varies from individual to individual. The diversity in the design spectrum results from m design dimensions (e.g., m = 5) and n variants per dimension (4). A rough estimate of VH is 1.024. $VH = n^m$. $VH = 4^5 = 1.024$. With n = 4 and m = 5, there are 1024 possible system states, which demonstrates the complexity of the business. Since the variables can hardly be reduced, a complementary, intuitive approach to reducing variability is needed. Such a method is known as morphology. In business practice, the values are then exorbitantly higher. After exponential growth, the diversity of the business system encompasses, for example, over four million states that would only be effective if the company could manage them. However, an "everything for everyone" approach fails. By reducing dimensions such as price level, distribution channels, region, and competition to one variant, diversity could be reduced by a factor of 256–16,384, which improves manageability. Nevertheless, this could be insufficient or later impractical. This is where morphology helps. An analytical explanation is not possible here; an intuitive approach defines profiles of combinations across the dimensions (Schwaninger & Ott, 2023). In management consulting practice, this is precisely the approach taken in sustainable corporate development.

In the context of integral governance and control of organisations, Schwaninger and Ott describe the case of corporate governance and management. Experts recommend holistic approaches to governance and management that take all three dimensions of sustainability—ecological, social, and economic—into account in a comprehensive manner. The management of organisations aims at achieving viability, sustainability, and further development. Two cybernetic models support this: the viable system for structural design and the systemic control model for governance and management. The model of systemic control is divided into operational, strategic, and normative management levels. Operational management focuses on short-term success and value creation. Strategic management secures long-term value potential for the future. Normative management defines identity, values, and guiding principles with a virtually timeless horizon. Complexity increases from the bottom up, and integral governance requires simultaneous control of all three levels despite potential contradictions.

1. Operational level: Efficiency improvements, increased marketing budget, sales reinforcement, logistics optimisation.
2. Strategic level: Investments in R&D, business system redesign, and new sales strategy.
3. Normative level: Commitment to sustainability, focus on customer lifestyles.

The total variety (VEt) in the three management levels is the product of their subvarieties. Change in one dimension affects the total variety linearly, while changes in multiple dimensions lead to disproportionate increases or decreases (Schwaninger & Ott, 2023).

Finally, Schwaninger and Ott describe the concept of residual variety. There are three interconnected entities for managing complexity: the environment, organisation, and management. Each absorbs complexity through self-organisation, leaving residual complexity. This is absorbed by the organisation for the environment and by management for the organisation.

Variety engineering is an unorthodox approach to managing complexity. It can guide decisions in conflict situations, promote innovation, and redesign complex systems. It also strengthens resilience to uncertainty and holds great potential for transformation (Schwaninger & Ott, 2023).

4.3. Transformation, Viability, and Sustainability Through Successful Ambidexterity

The challenge for management in sustainable corporate development lies in the successful ambidexterity of day-to-day business and innovation. In business practice, both are important. However, it is by no means a given that this integration and synthesis of the two areas will succeed. There are too many contradictions, polarities, and ambiguities for that to happen. Sustainable corporate development is only possible when ambidexterity is achieved (Figure 3).

Ambidexterity has already been addressed by Igor Ansoff (1918–2002). He wrote a separate chapter on it entitled "Assuring Coexistence of Competitive and Entrepreneurial Activities". Competitive activities are what we call daily business. Entrepreneurial activities are what we call innovative businesses. Igor Ansoff then writes that certain industrial companies had to begin developing a so-called "dual capability" as early as the 1960s. This involves the "effective coexistence" of the two dimensions (Ansoff, 1985), i.e., what we now call ambidexterity. It is striking that Igor Ansoff and Aloys Gälweiler (1922–1984) use similar ideas and language in this context, without explicitly quoting each other. These groundbreaking ideas were in the air in strategic management at the time. In any case, this was an initial reaction to the rising dynasticity of the post-war period.

For this, it is important to refer to Markus Schwaninger's logical levels of management. It makes a difference whether we are in daily business, i.e., operational management, or in innovative business, i.e., strategic management. We owe this essential distinction to the brilliant management practitioner and management theorist Aloys Gälweiler. Added to this is the conscious approach to normative management. This is a relevant complement to strategic management. In times of major challenges, such as climate change, sustainable corporate development is no longer possible without considering all three dimensions.

It is about clear and networked thinking, well-founded and good decisions, and consistent implementation.

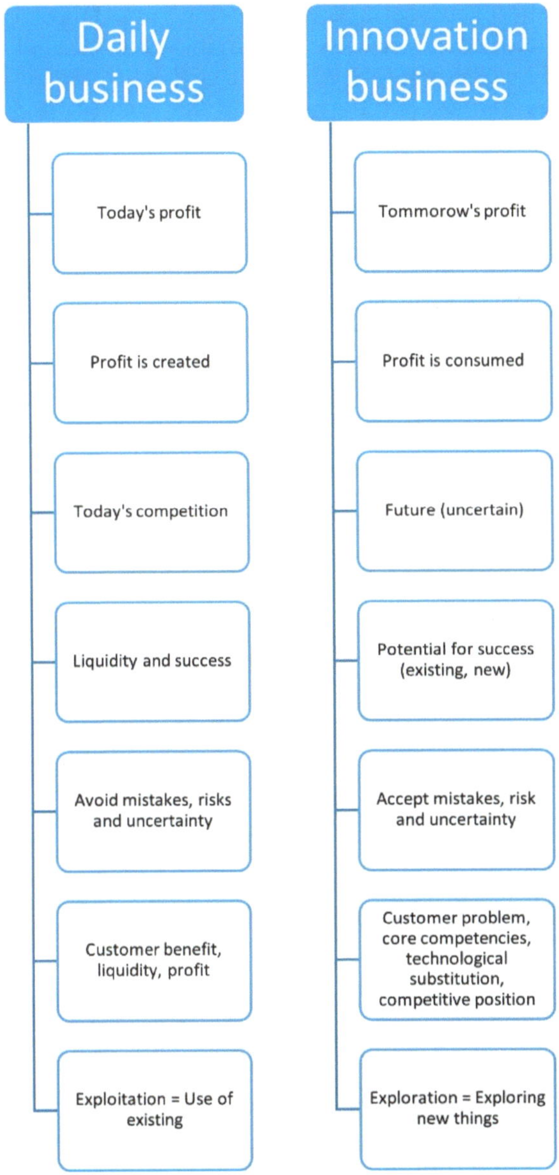

Figure 3. The ambidexterity of daily business and innovation business. Source: Figure by author.

5. Conclusions

The role of business in mitigation can be described in its foundation and application as attempted in this book contribution. The presentation is relatively simple within the linear nature of a book, even though it deals with a highly dynamic and complex topic. Its practical application, however, presents its own unique and specific challenge. We are dealing with dynamic and complex systems. The people within these systems are, in turn, complex systems. Added to this are the many teams and other challenges.

This contribution demonstrates the growing importance of climate protection measures in various areas. Companies are playing an increasingly central role in the development and implementation of climate strategies. However, the question of responsibility always arises. On the one hand, companies are driving innovations and sustainable business models, but on the other hand, there is always the risk of greenwashing and a lack of transparency. This demonstrates how important the approaches and measures presented are for sustainable development in the economy and society to truly succeed.

We cannot avoid a corresponding awareness of proper and good management. We must accept that we all share responsibility. This applies especially to management, but not only to them. True corporate accountability can make the decisive difference when dealing with climate risk. Furthermore, it is beneficial for companies to address the ambidexterity of their daily business and innovative business and to engage in profound transformation processes. Ultimately, it is about sustainable corporate development and the viability of the company. Only in this way can we overcome the challenges of climate change.

Ambidexterity and organisational change are real and significant challenges. Therefore, companies should engage experienced transformation consultants to support them throughout the transformation process. This greatly increases the likelihood of a successful outcome.

Funding: This research received no external funding.

Conflicts of Interest: The author declare no conflicts of interest.

Author Name and Affiliation: Christian Pirker, Christian Pirker KG, Management Consulting, Klagenfurt, Carinthia, Austria.

Keywords: climate risk management; corporate accountability; sustainable governance; organisational transformation.

References

Ansoff, I. (1985). *Corporate strategy* (Revised ed.). Penguin Books.

Beer, S. (1979). *The heart of enterprise*. Wiley.

Ben-Eli, M. U. (2012). The cybernetics of sustainability: Definition and underlying principles. In J. Murray, G. Cawthorne, C. Dey, & C. Andrew (Eds.), *Enough for all forever: A handbook for learning about sustainability* (pp. 255–268). Common Ground Publishing, University of Illinois.

Bleicher, K. (2001). *Das konzept integriertes management, visionen-missionen-programme* (6th ed.). Campus Fachbuch.

Bolton, P., Després, M., Pereira da Silva, L. A., Samama, F., & Svartzman, R. (2020). *The green swan: Central banking and financial stability in the age of climate change*. Bank for International Settlements.

Brundtland, G. H. (1987). *Our common future: The world commission on environment and development*. Oxford University Press.

Burnham, J. (1941). *The managerial revolution: What is happening in the world?* John Day.

Chhotray, V., & Stoker, G. (2009). *Governance theory and practice: A cross-disciplinary approach.* Palgrave Macmillan.
Collins, J. C. (2001). *Good to great. Why some companies leap... and others don't.* Harper Business.
Crane, A., Matten, D., Glozer, S., & Spence, L. J. (2019). *Business ethics: Managing corporate citizenship and sustainability in the age of globalisation* (5th ed.). Oxford University Press.
de Geus, A. (1997). The living company. *Harvard Business Review, 75*(2), 51–59. [PubMed]
Der Pragmaticus. (2025). *Klima schützen, aber bitte richtig!* Available online: https://www.derpragmaticus.com/wp-content/uploads/2025/06/inahalt-vorschauheft-06-2025.pdf (accessed on 13 February 2026).
Drucker, P. F. (1980). *Managing in turbulent times.* Heinemann.
Drucker, P. F. (2002). *The effective executive.* Harper Business.
Fridlund, P. (2020). Post-truth politics, performatives and the force. *Jus Cogens, 2,* 215–235. [CrossRef]
Gälweiler, A. (2005). *Strategische unternehmensführung* (3rd ed.). Campus Verlag GmbH.
Gelbmann, U., & Pirker, C. (2023). Interdisciplinary practical training as a contribution of higher education to raising sustainability awareness among the public. In S. Hummel, P. Assinger, C. Bauer, T. Brudermann, A. Jany, M. Jury, R. Rauter, & M. van Poppel (Eds.), *Shaping tomorrow today—SDGs from multiple perspectives* (pp. 235–255). Springer VS.
Gieryn, T. F. (1999). *Cultural boundaries of science: Credibility on the line.* University of Chicago Press.
Gray, R., Owen, D., & Adams, C. (2014). *Accountability, social responsibility and sustainability: Accounting for society and the environment.* Pearson Education Limited.
Grunwald, A. (2012). *Technikzukünfte als medium von zukunftsdebatten und technikgestaltung.* KIT Scientific Publishing.
Hayek, F. A. (1945). The use of knowledge in society. *The American Economic Review, 35*(4), 519–530.
Jonas, H. (1979). *Das prinzip verantwortung: Versuch einer ethik für die technologische zivilisation.* Suhrkamp.
Kotter, J. P. (1996). *Leading change.* Harvard Business School Press.
Kölbel, J. F., Heeb, F., Paetzold, F., & Busch, T. (2020). Can sustainable investing save the world? Reviewing the mechanisms of investor impact. *Organisation & Environment, 33*(4), 554–574.
Malik, F. (1992). *Strategie des managements komplexer systeme. Ein beitrag zur management-kybernetik evolutionärer systeme* (4th ed.). Haupt.
Malik, F. (2000). *Führen, leisten, leben. Wirksames management für eine neue zeit* (8th ed.). Deutsche Verlags-Anstalt.
Malik, F. (2012). *The right corporate governance. Effective top management for mastering complexity.* Campus Verlag.
Mintzberg, H. (2005). *Manager, not MBAs. A hard look at the soft practice of managing and management development.* Berrett-Koehler.
Nowotny, H., Scott, P., & Gibbons, M. (2001). *Re-thinking science. Knowledge and the public in an age of uncertainty.* Wiley.
Pirker, C. (2019). *Effektives lernen im management: Wie sie die digitale transformation mit einem menschenorientierten ansatz, den eckpfeilern des change-managements und entsprechender managementkompetenz sowie effektiver managementpädagogik erfolgreich meistern.* Arbeitsbereich Schulpädagogik und Historische Bildungsforschung.

Pirker, C. (2021). Three perspectives for the development of sustainable enterprises. In M. Ince-Yenilmez, & B. Darici (Eds.), *Engines of economic prosperity: Creating innovation and economic opportunities through entrepreneurship* (pp. 291–301). Palgrave Macmillan.
Pirker, C. (2024). Identity and consumer behaviour. In M. Uzunöz Altan, M. İnce Yenilmez, O. Altınkoz, & S. Bağçe (Eds.), *Identity economics: Multidisciplinary insights into decision-making behaviour* (pp. 48–69). Routledge.
Rieckmann, H. (1997). *Managen und führen am rande des 3. Jahrtausenden*. Lang.
Rockström, J., Gaffney, O., Rogelj, J., Meinshausen, M., Nakicenovic, N., & Schellnhuber, H. J. (2017). A roadmap for rapid decarbonization. *Science, 355*(6331), 1269–1271. [CrossRef] [PubMed]
Sachs, J. D. (2015). *The age of sustainable development*. Columbia University Press.
Schein, E. H. (2017). *Organisational culture and leadership* (5th ed.). John Wiley & Sons.
Scherer, A. G., & Palazzo, G. (2011). The new political role of business in a globalised world: A review of a new perspective on CSR and its implications for the firm, governance, and democracy. *Journal of Management Studies, 48*(4), 899–931. [CrossRef]
Schwaninger, M. (2000). Managing complexity—The path toward intelligent organisations. *Systemic Practice and Action Research, 13*(2), 207–241. [CrossRef]
Schwaninger, M., & Ott, S. (2023). What is variety engineering, and why do we need it? *Systems Research and Behavioural Science, 41*(2), 235–246. [CrossRef]
Senge, P. (1990). *The fifth discipline. Art & practice of the learning organisation*. Currency Doubleday.
Staehle, W. (1990). *Management* (5th ed.). Vahlen.
Stilgoe, J., Owen, R., & Macnaghten, P. (2013). Developing a framework for responsible innovation. *Research Policy, 42*(9), 1568–1580. [CrossRef]
Task Force on Climate-Related Financial Disclosures. (2017). *Recommendations of the task force on climate-related financial disclosures*. Available online: https://www.fsb-tcfd.org/recommendations/ (accessed on 13 February 2026).
Timmermans, J., Yaghmaei, E., Stahl, B., & Brem, A. (2017). Research and innovation processes revisited: Networked responsibility in industry. *Sustainability Accounting, Management and Policy Journal, 8*(3), 307–334. [CrossRef]
Ulrich, H. (2001). *Systemorientiertes management. Das werk von hans ulrich, studienausgabe*. Haupt.
United Nations Environment Programme (UNEP). (2021). *Emissions gap report 2021: The heat is on—A world of climate promises not yet delivered*. UNEP.
von Foerster, H. (1993). *Wissen und gewissen, versuch einer brücke*. Suhrkamp.
von Glasersgeld, E. (1995). *Radical constructivism. A way of knowing and learning*. The Falmer Press.
Wright, C., & Nyberg, D. (2015). *Climate change, capitalism, and corporations: Processes of creative self-destruction*. Cambridge University Press.

Energy Uncertainty Index and Energy Sector Performance: An Empirical Study on the MSCI World Energy Index

Hakan Yıldırım and Kenan Aydın

Abstract: Energy resources play a key role in the industrial sector, its subsidiary sectors, and national economies, making developments in the energy sector of interest to many. The significant increase in demand for oil, electricity, natural gas, and renewable energy sources strengthens the energy sector's position in the global economy and can have crucial impacts on variables such as financial markets and economic growth. Meanwhile, the concepts of green transformation and sustainability, which have recently gained increasing importance, have become a focal point for the financial sector. This is considered a significant factor in increasing investments in renewable energy and sustainability. In this study, we test the effect of changes in the energy uncertainty index (EUI) on the price movements of the MSCI World Energy Index (MSCI), which is considered an important indicator for the global energy sector and includes companies engaged in the production of wind, solar, and other renewable energy sources, in addition to fossil fuels. In the study, the Johansen cointegration test, Vector Error Correction Model (VECM), and FMOLS and DOLS estimators were applied using monthly data for the period between January 2005 and October 2022. The applied analyses revealed a statistically significant and long-term connection between the EUI and the MSCI World Energy Index, and it was determined that increases in the EUI have negative effects on the MSCI World Energy Index. On the other hand, the short-term relationship between the EUI and the MSCI World Energy Index was found to be statistically insignificant.

1. Introduction

Before the 2008 global crisis, pricing in securities markets was shaped by macroeconomic news and by microeconomic news. However, recently, it has also been shaped by news related to policymakers' announcements on budgets, reforms, and rescue packages, which can be a cause of potential volatility in the markets (Gürsoy & Zeren, 2022, p. 355).

In this context, the global crisis and the subsequent European debt crisis have accelerated research on the concept of uncertainty. On the other hand, while a lot of research indicating the effect of uncertainties on economic events and financial markets has been conducted, it is observed that this has become an important issue for policymakers and market actors in managing various processes and making financial decisions under uncertainty conditions (Şencan, 2024, p. 821). However, as a result of the integration between globalisation and markets and the accelerating mutual interaction, the need for investors to consider many variables when making investment decisions has emerged, and in recent times, various uncertainty indices have become important indicators, especially for stock market investors (Yıldırım et al., 2023, p. 242).

Especially when evaluating the pressure of uncertainties in the field of energy on financial markets, the fluctuation of energy prices can significantly influence the costs and profitability of companies, while from an investor's perspective, it can create significant obstacles in managing investment processes in the stock market (Karhan & Aydın, 2018; Özkan et al., 2025).

In this context, particularly when examining studies that test the impact on stock price movements and stock market indices through oil prices, works such as those by Kling (1985), Park and Ratti (2008), Miller and Ratti (2009), Aloui et al. (2012), Ramos and Veiga (2013), Cevik et al. (2020), Ajala et al. (2021), and Jingjian et al. (2023) are encountered.

It has been found that the potential effects are usually tested through fluctuations in oil prices, even though there are numerous studies in the literature examining how energy uncertainty affects different stock exchanges. However, it was discovered that there are not many studies examining how the energy uncertainty index affects stock markets (Saka Ilgın, 2024, p. 35).

Using commonly used techniques from the literature, including the Johansen cointegration test, VECM, FMOLS, and DOLS, the study seeks to understand how uncertainty of energy affects the prices of the MSCI World Energy Index, a global indicator.

The EUI, improved by Dang et al. (2023) and included in the analysis, indicates market uncertainties and shocks based on 28 different countries. The index is constructed through an algorithmic structure composed of various keywords obtained from the monthly reports of the Economist Intelligence Unit (Kamışlı, 2023, p. 383).

Another variable, the MSCI World Energy Index, encompasses medium and large-scale companies within the energy sector class across 23 different developed country markets. The country weights of the index are 61.95%—United States; 15.04%—Canada; 11.08%—United Kingdom; 4.78%—France; 1.75%—Australia; and 5.41%—others (MSCI Inc., 2025).

This study is anticipated to make three distinct contributions to the literature. The first is that, in contrast to other studies of a similar nature, it uses global indicators rather than energy prices and national stock indices. In addition, the impact of energy uncertainty on the global energy share market can be tested, and its predictive power can be determined, thus creating an early warning system for both investors' investment processes and policymakers' measures against price fluctuations.

The investigation is divided into five sections in this context. The first section is the introduction, which includes theoretical information about energy uncertainty, while the second section, the literature review, contains empirical studies that have been conducted. In the third section, information is provided about the variables used and the time series analyses applied, while the fourth section, the findings, presents the analysis results and interpretations. In the final part, the findings are compared with the existing literature, and various recommendations are made based on the interpretation of the findings.

2. Literature Review

When previous research was evaluated, different studies that analyse the influence of energy uncertainty on the market share were found. Even though these investigations examine the influence of energy prices on different types of stock markets, studies testing the impact of the EUI on the share market appear to be limited. This section includes studies that test the influence of energy uncertainty, which is the subject of this study, on share market price movements through energy prices and energy uncertainty indicators.

In Kling's (1985) study, which is among the important studies, the Granger causality test revealed that the relationship between crude oil and S&P 500 prices was significant and negative. In the study by Park and Ratti (2008), the effect of volatility and shocks in oil prices on stock returns in 13 different European countries, along with the United States, was tested. When the outcomes of the VAR analysis were examined, it was found that there was a negative effect on stock returns owing to oil prices in 9 of the 14 selected countries.

Miller and Ratti (2009) found a long-term inverse relationship between Brent oil price fluctuations and stock market returns in OECD countries, based on VECM and Johansen cointegration tests. The findings of the causality and cointegration tests applied in the study of Güler et al. (2011) indicate that oil prices influence the BIST energy sector index. There was an investigation conducted by Aloui et al. (2012) to determine how shocks to oil prices impacted the share returns of 25 developing countries. According to the findings of long-term correlation studies and the conditional multifactor pricing model, the effects of oil prices on share markets are asymmetric and statistically significant. A study conducted by Ramos and Veiga (2013) investigated the asymmetric impact that changes in the oil price have on the share markets of nations that import and export oil. The data suggests that the influence of oil prices on the share markets of oil-importing economies is not evenly distributed across countries. Furthermore, the research reveals that share markets in oil-exporting economies benefit from oil price fluctuations, while share markets in oil-importing countries are negatively affected by these fluctuations. In their study, Aktaş and Akdağ (2013) used Granger causality tests and regression analyses to test the influence of oil price fluctuations on the BIST100 index. Using different macroeconomic indicators, the findings of the study suggest that there is no connection between the two variables.

Cevik et al. (2020) investigated how much the crude oil price fluctuated and how that affected returns on the Turkish share market. The EGARCH analysis indicates that share market returns are impacted by the crude oil price.

Elder's (2020) study investigated the impacts of energy uncertainty on employment across sectors and in general, but it did not examine how energy uncertainty directly affected the stock index. The results of the employed VAR and GARCH models show that an increase in uncertainty has a statistically significant and adverse influence on employment figures. In this case, it can be said that uncertainty has a negative impact on the share market when viewed from the viewpoint of companies whose shares are traded on the stock exchange.

Ajala et al. (2021) looked at how changes in oil prices affected share prices and exchange rates. According to NARDL analysis, movements in oil prices had an uneven effect on the Nigerian share market index and exchange rate over the short and long terms.

Kamışlı (2023) examined the connection between the EUI and the returns of the energy sector indexes of 37 different nations. The Toda–Yamamoto causality test, which employs the fractional frequency flexible Fourier form, demonstrated a significant causal link between the uncertainty index and the returns of the selected countries' energy sectors.

Jingjian et al. (2023) tested the asymmetric influence of oil price shocks on energy company stocks. VAR-PVAR findings demonstrate that oil prices have an influence on energy share prices depending on investor interest. Wang et al. (2024) evaluated the influence of the GEUI, the EUI for the US and China, and macroeconomic indicators on Chinese stock market index prices. The findings suggest that global and country-based indices of energy uncertainty have stronger effects on Chinese stock market index price movements than economic variables.

A summary of empirical studies testing the impact of energy prices and uncertainty on the share market is also presented in Table 1.

Table 1. Summary of the literature.

Study	Method	Country	Data	Result
Dursun and Özcan (2019)	Panel cointegration analysis with multiple structural breaks	25 OECD countries	Quarterly natural gas, oil, and electricity prices on stock market indices between 2005 and 2017	There is a cointegration relationship in the long run
Balcilar et al. (2019)	Time-varying parameter panel data stochastic volatility model	28 European countries	Energy uncertainty and energy transition for the period 1990–2015	There is an impact from uncertainty in fossil fuels towards renewable energy
Salisu et al. (2024)	GARCH-MIDAS	28 developed and developing economies	EUI and daily stock market return volatility for the period 1996:01–2022:10	EUI has an impact on markets
Saka Ilgın (2024)	ARDL model	ABD and Türkiye	Monthly data for CPUI, EUI, S&P500, BIST100 for the period 2014:12–2022:10	CPUI and EUI have an impact on the S&P 500 index
Zhang (2024)	sPCA, PLS, PCA technique	28 Country	EUI and 28 Country stock market index for the period 1996:4–2021:12	EUI has predictive power on stock market returns

OECD—the Organisation for Economic Co-operation and Development; EUI—Energy-Related Uncertainty Index; GARCH-MIDAS—Generalized Autoregressive Conditional Heteroskedasticity—Mixed Data Sampling; CPUI—Commodity Price Uncertainty Index; ARDL—Autoregressive Distributed Lag; ABD—Average Bubble Duration; sPCA—Sparse Principal Component Analysis; PLS—Partial Least Squares. PCA—Principal Component Analysis; Source: Table by authors.

3. Data and Methodology

In this study, the MSCI World Energy Index and energy uncertainty index variables developed in the study of Dang et al. (2023) were used. While trying to determine the long-term connection between the variables using the Johansen cointegration test, the long-term equilibrium model was established and analysed using the VECM, and the direction of the long-term effect, the existence of the short-run connection, and the functioning of the error correction mechanism were revealed. Furthermore, FMOLS and DOLS cointegration coefficient estimators were used to understand the direction of the connection. To test whether the series was stationary or not, the KPSS test developed by Kwiatkowski et al. (1992) was used. Data regarding the EUI variable was obtained from www.policyuncertainty.com, while data for the MSCI variable were obtained from www.policyuncertainty.com. Detailed information about the data used in the study is shown in Table 2.

Table 2. Information on variables.

Variable	Description	Period	Frequency
EUI	Energy-Related Uncertainty Index	January 2005–October 2022	Monthly
MSCI	MSCI World Energy Index	January 2005–October 2022	Monthly

Source: Table by authors.

Cointegration analysis is utilised to understand the long-run connection between time series (Gujarati & Porter, 2012). For the application of cointegration analysis, the series must include a unit root at the level and be cointegrated at the same level. In other words, to discuss cointegration between the series, it is required that the error terms of the series be stationary (Dikmen, 2012). In this context, the series was initially subjected to the KPSS test.

The established hypothesis is the reason why the applied KPSS test is different from other conventional unit root tests. In other words, the null hypothesis suggests that the series is stationary, and the alternative hypothesis in the KPSS test suggests that the series is non-stationary (Sevüktekin & Nargeleçekenler, 2007).

First, it is concluded that the single equation cointegration analysis developed in the study by Engle and Granger (1987) was later improved with a multi-equation approach in studies by Johansen (1988) and by Johansen and Juselius (1990). It is widely accepted that Johansen cointegration analysis based on VAR analysis is advantageous in determining whether there are multiple cointegrating vectors among the series when there are multiple explanatory variables (Doğan & Değer, 2016, p. 334).

The formula for the VAR model, which forms the basis of the Johansen cointegration test, can be explained as follows (Greene, 2012, p. 1006):

$$y_t = \Gamma_1 y_{t-1} + \Gamma_2 y_{t-2} + \cdots + \Gamma_p y_{t-p} + \varepsilon_t \quad (1)$$

In the detection of cointegration between series, trace statistics are used, and the null hypothesis is established that there is a cointegration vector at the maximum "r"

level based on this statistical value. The process related to the trace statistic can be indicated as follows (Greene, 2012, p. 1007):

$$\gamma_{tr} = -T \sum_{i=r+1}^{M} \ln\left[1 - (r_i{}^*)^2\right] \quad (2)$$

To prevent potential issues arising from a long-term relationship, the FMOLS method was developed in the study by Hansen and Phillips (1988), which used a semi-parametric correction. The FMOLS method, which allows for the Wald test and is asymptotically independent, enables the variables used to be rearranged (Khan et al., 2019, p. 9).

By including lagged first differences in the model, the DOLS approach, which was created by Saikkonen (1991) and Stock and Watson (1993), eliminates the cause of the autocorrelation issue. The following equations explain the FMOLS and DOLS estimators (Breitung & Pesaran, 2008, p. 31; Narayan & Wong, 2009, p. 2774):

$$y_t = \hat{\beta} x_t + \sum_{k=-\infty}^{\infty} \hat{\gamma}_k \Delta x_{t-k} + \mu_t \quad (3)$$

$$y_t = \alpha_{it} + \beta x_t + \varepsilon_t \quad (4)$$

$$x_t = x_{t-1} + \varepsilon_t \quad (5)$$

y_t is the dependent variable, x_t is the independent variable, μ is the error term, and β is the cointegration vector.

The traditional ECM model can be said to use the equation below. The VECM model can be used to identify both short- and long-term dynamics, provided that the series are cointegrated at I(1) rather than stationary at the level (Engle & Granger, 1987).

$$\Delta y_t = \beta_0 + \sum_{i=1}^{n} \beta_i \Delta y_{t-i} + \sum_{i=1}^{n} \delta_i \Delta x_{t-i} + \varphi z_{t-1} + \mu_t \quad (6)$$

The equation below shows the OLS residuals from the long run cointegration regression, while "z" in the equation refers to the error correction term.

$$y_t = \beta_0 + \beta_1 x_t + \varepsilon_t \quad (7)$$

The equation mentioned above can be defined as follows:

$$z_t = ECT_{t-1} = y_{t-1} - \beta_0 - \beta_i x_{t-1} \quad (8)$$

After the change in x, the ECT coefficient, which measures the speed at which y reaches equilibrium, is expressed as the adjustment rate.

When the speed adjustment parameter in VECM remains constant at zero, it can be said that there is no long-range equilibrium relationship, and the model does not have error correction properties. In this context, it is expected that the coefficient of the lagged error term is different from zero (Charemza & Deadman, 1997).

4. Findings

In this section, graphs and descriptive statistics related to the variables used are presented first.

When the Figure 1 is examined, it is observed that the changes in the time series are high, and it is particularly noticeable that the changes in the MSCI are higher compared to those in the EUI. Descriptive statistics for the variables are demonstrated in the table.

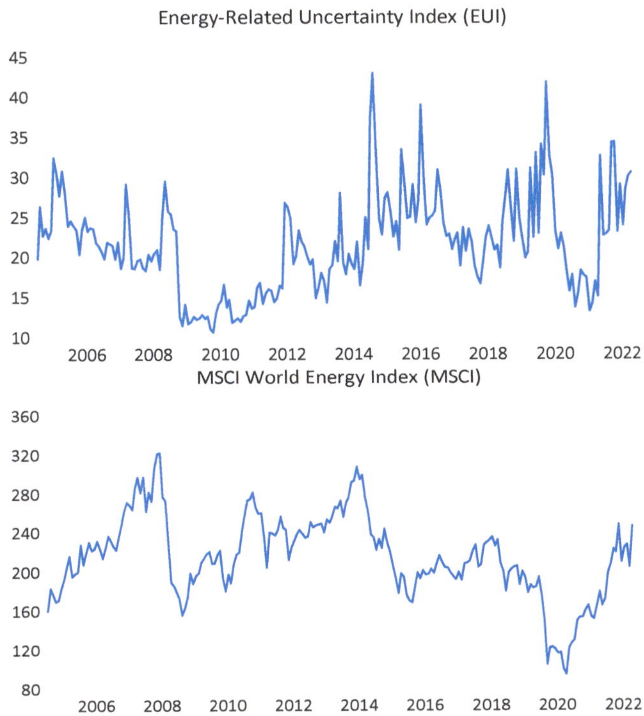

Figure 1. Time series data. Source: Authors' compilation based on data from Economic Policy Uncertainty (n.d.) (the price series for the EUI variable) and Investing.com (n.d.) (the price series for the MSCI variable).

It is evident from looking at Table 3 that the MSCI variable's standard deviation (42.74648) is greater than the EUI variable's standard deviation (6.106531). In this case, the MSCI is more volatile than the EUI. The KPSS test was used to determine whether the variables contained a unit root, and the findings can be found in Table 4.

Table 3. Descriptive statistics.

Variables	Mean	Maximum	Minimum	Std. Dev.	Skewness	Kurtosis
EUI	21.97707	43.25689	10.94266	6.106531	0.558523	3.446021
MSCI	217.9486	324.6700	97.28000	42.74648	−0.165111	3.238286

Source: Table by authors.

Table 4. KPSS results.

Variables	KPSS	
	Constant	Constant and Trend
MSCI	0.5419 **	0.1529 **
ΔMSCI	0.0734	0.0676
EUI	0.4129 *	0.1678 **
ΔEUI	0.0694	0.0510

**, *: significance at 5%, and 10%, respectively. Note: null hypothesis: the variable is stationary. KPSS—Kwiatkowski–Phillips–Schmidt–Shin Test. Source: Table by authors.

While the findings obtained from the KPSS test indicated that there was no stationarity at the level for both time series, it was concluded that stationarity became statistically significant at the first difference. It was observed that the variables were integrated at the same level, and the Johansen cointegration test was applied.

The Johansen cointegration test results in Table 5 indicates that there is a statistically significant long-run interrelation between the EUI and the MSCI. In this context, it can be said that the EUI has a long-term effect on the MSCI. Table 6 presents the findings of the long-run equilibrium model and the VECM, which were developed to ascertain the direction of the long-run effect of the EUI on the MSCI stock index, as well as to test for the presence of a short-run connection and the effectiveness of the error correction mechanism.

Table 5. Johansen cointegration test results.

$\mathbf{MSCI{=}\alpha{+}\beta EUI}_{t-i}{+}\varepsilon_t$			
H0	**H1**	**Trace Statistics**	**Maximum Eigenvalue Statistics**
$r = 0$	$r \geq 1$	124.0214 **	81.47804 **
$r \leq 1$	$r \geq 2$	42.54337 **	42.54337 **

** denotes a 5% significance level. Note: The lag length was determined according to the Akaike Information Criterion (AIC) and was 3. Source: Table by authors.

An analysis of the findings reveals a negative long-term link between the EUI and the MSCI variable. In this case, increasing uncertainty for the energy market could lead to a decline in the MSCI stock index.

On the other hand, the findings of the long-run equilibrium model and the VECM model show that the lagged error term coefficient for the MSCI is negative and significant, confirming the operation of the error correction mechanism. Furthermore, it demonstrates that any deviation from the long-run equilibrium between variables may be reversed in the next period and approach the equilibrium value. When the relevant deviation value is examined (1/0.0731 = 13.67), the deviations reach long-term equilibrium again after 13.67 periods. When the short-run connection between the EUI and MSCI is tested, it is determined that there is no statistically significant connection between the variables in the short term. Following the VECM model, FMOLS and DOLS tests were applied to the time series, and the findings are presented in Table 7.

Table 6. Long-run equilibrium and VECM model for MSCI variables.

MSCI Long-Run Equilibrium Model			
Variables	**Coefficients**	**Standard Error**	**t Statistic**
EUI	26.18367 ***	2.63227	9.94720
C	−0.965540		
	MSCI = 0.965540 − 26.18367 × Energy		
	MSCI VECM Model		
Variables	**Coefficients**	**Standard Error**	**t Statistic**
ECM	−0.073184 ***	0.00748	−9.78196
ΔEUI(−1)	−0.327974	0.61461	−0.53363
ΔEUI(−2)	0.213111	0.45871	0.46459
ΔEUI(−3)	−0.095483	0.27317	−0.34954
ΔMSCI(−1)	0.033713 **	0.01941	2.41363
ΔMSCI(−2)	0.033713	0.02259	1.49266
ΔMSCI(−3)	0.015442	0.01831	0.84357
C	0.132390	1.10789	0.11950

***, **: significance at 1% and 5%, respectively. VECM—Vector Error Correction Model; ECM—Error Correction Model; C—Constant (Intercept Term). Source: Table by authors.

Table 7. FMOLS/DOLS findings for the MSCI World Energy Index.

	FMOLS Results	
	Coefficient	**t-Statistics**
EUI	−2.022813	−2.073376 **
	DOLS Results	
	Coefficient	**t-Statistics**
EUI	−2.602232	−2.164577 **

**, Significance of 5%. FMOLS—Fully Modified Ordinary Least Squares; DOLS—Dynamic Ordinary Least Squares. Source: Table by authors.

The findings of both tests show that the EUI variable has a significant and negative effect on the MSCI variable, according to an analysis of the FMOLS and DOLS test results shown in Table 7.

5. Conclusion and Recommendations

Risk and uncertainty, which are extremely important for the decisions that stock investors and policymakers will make, can have serious effects on long-term decisions. In this context, the risks and uncertainties that may arise can lead to the differentiation of strategies, especially in the private sector and public policies, while causing stock investors to avoid risks due to potential changes in their risk perceptions (Keskin, 2025, p. 114).

In this context, this investigation observed the relationship between the EUI and the MSCI and concluded that there is a long-term connection between the variables. Furthermore, the findings demonstrate that the EUI has a negative impact on the selected share index. An examination of the short-run link between the variables reveals that it is not significant. The findings obtained in this context support similar studies, such as Balcilar et al. (2019), Kamışlı (2023), Wang et al. (2024), Salisu et al. (2024), Saka Ilgın (2024), and Zhang (2024). However, unlike similar studies in the literature, the findings demonstrate that the variables show a negative relationship.

In this case, when energy uncertainty increases, the reasons for the long-term decline in the MSCI World Energy Index can be attributed to the negative impacts of increased uncertainty on energy production and exports, as well as the rising costs faced by companies operating in the energy sector. Another important reason is that, especially in the face of long-term uncertainty, stock investors tend to avoid risk, leading to a decrease in energy stock purchases and consequently a decline in the prices of energy stocks.

Among the reasons why energy uncertainty does not have an impact on the energy index in the short term may be the pricing of stock price movements, more within the framework of speculative movements, and investors considering the uncertainties that may arise in the short term as short-term shocks.

According to these results, the potential energy uncertainty is expected to have negative impacts on stock market investors who invest in energy stocks, the energy sector, and policymakers in the long term. In this case, the EUI can be expressed as an indicator for stock investors, policymakers, and actors in the energy sector. In this context, the EUI can be recommended for use when making investment decisions, monitoring developments in the energy sector, and in the policy-making process. In future similar studies, the impact of the energy uncertainty index and related similar uncertainty indicators on the MSCI World Energy Index, as well as on energy sector stock indices of developed and emerging economies, can be examined. In this way, the extended effects of energy uncertainty in both global and national contexts could be examined.

Author Contributions: These authors contributed equally to this work. All authors have read and agreed to the published version of the manuscript.

Funding: This research received no external funding.

Conflicts of Interest: The authors declare no conflicts of interest.

Author Names and Affiliations: Hakan Yıldırım, Department of Logistics Management, Istanbul Gelisim University, Istanbul, Turkey; Kenan Aydın, Istanbul Gelisim University, Istanbul, Turkey.

Keywords: energy; energy uncertainty index; MSCI world energy index; cointegration analysis; FMOLS and DOLS.

References

Ajala, K., Sakanko, M. A., & Adeniji, S. O. (2021). The asymmetric effect of oil price on the exchange rate and stock price in Nigeria. *International Journal of Energy Economics and Policy*, *11*(4), 202–208. [CrossRef]

Aktaş, M., & Akdağ, S. (2013). Türkiye'de ekonomik faktörlerin hisse senedi fiyatlari ile ilişkilerinin araştirilmasi. *International Journal of Social Science Research*, *2*(1), 50–67.

Aloui, C., Nguyen, D. K., & Njeh, H. (2012). Assessing the impacts of oil price fluctuations on stock returns in emerging markets. *Economic Modelling, 29*(6), 2686–2695. [CrossRef]

Balcilar, M., Roubaud, D., & Shahbaz, M. (2019). The impact of energy market uncertainty shocks on energy transition in Europe. *The Energy Journal, 40*, 55–80. [CrossRef]

Breitung, J., & Pesaran, M. H. (2008). Unit roots and cointegration in panels. In *The econometrics of panel data: Fundamentals and recent developments in theory and practice* (pp. 279–322). Springer. [CrossRef]

Cevik, N. K., Cevik, E. I., & Dibooglu, S. (2020). Oil prices, stock market returns and volatility spillovers: Evidence from Turkey. *Journal of Policy Modeling, 42*(3), 597–614. [CrossRef]

Charemza, W. W., & Deadman, D. F. (1997). *New directions in econometric practice*. Number 1139. Edward Elgar Publishing.

Dang, T. H. N., Nguyen, C. P., Lee, G. S., Nguyen, B. Q., & Le, T. T. (2023). Measuring the energy-related uncertainty index. *Energy Economics, 124*, 106817. [CrossRef]

Dikmen, N. (2012). *Ekonometri: Temel kavramlar ve uygulamalar*. Dora Basım Yayım Dağ. Ltd. Şti.

Doğan, B., & Değer, O. (2016). Enerji tüketimi, finansal gelişme ve ekonomik büyüme ilişkisi: Hindistan örneklemi. *Yaşar Üniversitesi E-Dergisi, 11*(44), 326–338. [CrossRef]

Dursun, A., & Özcan, M. (2019). Enerji fiyat değişimleri ile borsa endeksleri arasındaki ilişki: OECD ülkeleri üzerine bir uygulama. *Muhasebe ve Finansman Dergisi, (82)*, 177–198. [CrossRef]

Economic Policy Uncertainty. (n.d.). *Energy-related uncertainty indexes*. Available online: https://www.policyuncertainty.com/energy_uncertainty.html (accessed on 13 January 2025).

Elder, J. (2020). Employment and energy uncertainty. *The Journal of Economic Asymmetries, 21*, e00159. [CrossRef]

Engle, R. F., & Granger, C. W. (1987). Co-integration and error correction: Representation, estimation, and testing. *Econometrica: Journal of the Econometric Society, 55*, 251–276. [CrossRef]

Greene, W. (2012). *Econometric analysis* (7th ed.). Pearson Education Limited.

Gujarati, D. N., & Porter, D. C. (2012). *Temel ekonometri* (Ü. Şenesen, & G. Günlük-Şenesen, Trans.). Literatür Yayıncılık.

Güler, S., Tunç, R., & Orçun, Ç. (2011). Petrol fiyat riski ve hisse senedi fiyatlari arasindaki ilişkinin belirlenmesi: Türkiye'de enerji sektörü üzerinde bir uygulama. *Atatürk Üniversitesi İktisadi ve İdari Bilimler Dergisi, 24*(4), 297–315.

Gürsoy, S., & Zeren, F. (2022). Ekonomik politika belirsizliği ve borsa ilişkisi: G7 ve BRIC ülkeleri örneği. *Erciyes Üniversitesi İktisadi ve İdari Bilimler Fakültesi Dergisi, (61)*, 353–368. [CrossRef]

Hansen, B. E., & Phillips, P. C. (1988). *Estimation and inference in models of cointegration: A simulation study*. Available online: https://elischolar.library.yale.edu/cowles-discussion-paper-series/1125 (accessed on 15 January 2025).

Investing.com. (n.d.). *MSCI world energy*. Available online: https://www.investing.com/indices/msci-world-energy (accessed on 13 January 2025).

Jingjian, S., Xiangyun, G., Jinsheng, Z., Anjian, W., Xiaotian, S., Yiran, Z., & Hongyu, W. (2023). The impact of oil price shocks on energy stocks from the perspective of investor attention. *Energy, 278*, 127987. [CrossRef]

Johansen, S. (1988). Statistical analysis of cointegration vectors. *Journal of Economic Dynamics and Control, 12*(2–3), 231–254. [CrossRef]

Johansen, S., & Juselius, K. (1990). Maximum likelihood estimation and inference on cointegration—With appucations to the demand for money. *Oxford Bulletin of Economics and Statistics, 52*(2), 169–210. [CrossRef]

Kamışlı, M. (2023). Enerji belirsizliği ve enerji sektörü getirileri ilişkisi. In M. F. Buğan, & İ. Tuna (Eds.), *Finansal piyasalarin evrimi IV*. Özgür Yayınları. [CrossRef]

Karhan, G., & Aydın, H. İ. (2018). Petrol fiyatlari, kur ve hisse senedi getirileri üzerine bir araştirma. *Akademik Araştırmalar ve Çalışmalar Dergisi (AKAD), 10*(19), 405–413. [CrossRef]

Keskin, Ö. (2025). Petrol fiyatlarindaki belirsizlik, jeopolitik risk ve BİST GUBRF arasindaki etkileşim: Frekans alanda zamanla değişen bootstrap nedensellik testi. *EKOIST Journal of Econometrics and Statistics, (42)*, 114–128. [CrossRef]

Khan, M. W. A., Panigrahi, S. K., Almuniri, K. S. N., Soomro, M. I., Mirjat, N. H., & Alqaydi, E. S. (2019). Investigating the dynamic impact of CO_2 emissions and economic growth on renewable energy production: Evidence from FMOLS and DOLS tests. *Processes, 7*(8), 496. [CrossRef]

Kling, J. L. (1985). Oil price shocks and stock market behavior. *The Journal of Portfolio Management, 12*(1), 34–39. [CrossRef]

Kwiatkowski, D., Phillips, P. C., Schmidt, P., & Shin, Y. (1992). Testing the null hypothesis of stationarity against the alternative of a unit root: How sure are we that economic time series have a unit root? *Journal of Econometrics, 54*(1–3), 159–178. [CrossRef]

Miller, J. I., & Ratti, R. A. (2009). Crude oil and stock markets: Stability, instability, and bubbles. *Energy Economics, 31*(4), 559–568. [CrossRef]

MSCI Inc. (2025). *MSCI world energy index (USD): Cumulative index performance*. Available online: https://www.msci.com/www/index-factsheets/msci-world-energy-index/09405823 (accessed on 18 June 2025).

Narayan, P. K., & Wong, P. (2009). A panel data analysis of the determinants of oil consumption: The case of Australia. *Applied Energy, 86*(12), 2771–2775. [CrossRef]

Özkan, O., Köseoğlu, O., & Bilkan, T. (2025). Enerji belirsizliklerinin borsa ve döviz piyasasına etkisi: Türkiye'den ampirik kanıtlar. *Afyon Kocatepe Üniversitesi İktisadi ve İdari Bilimler Fakültesi Dergisi, 27*(1), 78–89. [CrossRef]

Park, J., & Ratti, R. A. (2008). Oil price shocks and stock markets in the US and 13 European countries. *Energy Economics, 30*(5), 2587–2608. [CrossRef]

Ramos, S. B., & Veiga, H. (2013). Oil price asymmetric effects: Answering the puzzle in international stock markets. *Energy Economics, 38*, 136–145. [CrossRef]

Saikkonen, P. (1991). Asymptotically efficient estimation of cointegration regressions. *Econometric Theory, 7*(1), 1–21. [CrossRef]

Saka Ilgın, K. (2024). Analysis of the impact of climate policy and energy uncertainties on the stock exchange: The case of Turkiye and America. *PressAcademia Procedia (PAP), 20*, 34–40. [CrossRef]

Salisu, A. A., Ogbonna, A. E., Gupta, R., & Bouri, E. (2024). Energy-related uncertainty and international stock market volatility. *The Quarterly Review of Economics and Finance, 95*, 280–293. [CrossRef]

Sevüktekin, M., & Nargeleçekenler, M. (2007). *Ekonometrik zaman serileri analizi: EViews uygulamalı*. Nobel Yayın Dağıtım.

Stock, J. H., & Watson, M. W. (1993). A simple estimator of cointegrating vectors in higher order integrated systems. *Econometrica: Journal of the Econometric Society, 61*, 783–820. [CrossRef]

Şencan, İ. (2024). GEPU endeksinin borsa endeksleri volatilitesi üzerindeki etkisi: MIST ülkeleri üzerine bir çalişma. *Ömer Halisdemir Üniversitesi İktisadi ve İdari Bilimler Fakültesi Dergisi, 17*(4), 821–833. [CrossRef]

Wang, Y., Huang, X., & Huang, Z. (2024). Energy-related uncertainty and Chinese stock market returns. *Finance Research Letters, 62*, 105215. [CrossRef]

Yıldırım, H., Akdağ, S., & Kaya, İ. G. (2023). ABD para politikaları belirsizliğinin pay senedi getirileri üzerine etkisi: BIST100 örneği. *Maliye ve Finans Yazıları, (120)*, 231–246. [CrossRef]

Zhang, X. (2024). Country-level energy-related uncertainties and stock market returns: Insights from the US and China. *Technological Forecasting and Social Change, 204*, 123437. [CrossRef]

Climate-Resilient Supply Chains: Adapting Business Models in a Warming World

Zekeriya Şahin

Abstract: Global climate change is a multifaceted crisis that necessitates the restructuring of economic systems and supply chains. This book chapter discusses how businesses can adapt their business models to increase their resilience to climate change, exploring climate-resilient supply chain approaches and the role of green financing instruments. The development of green bonds is introduced within the framework of the Green Bond Principles published by ICMA, and the impact of these financing instruments on energy, transportation, and infrastructure projects is assessed. ESG criteria, social bonds, and thematic investment practices are explained within the scope of sustainable investment strategies, and the contributions of actors such as the World Bank, EBRD, and BIST are illustrated. The final section discusses market challenges such as greenwashing, transparency, and standards and presents future perspectives. The findings suggest that businesses should view climate action not only as an environmental imperative but also as a strategic and financial imperative. In this context, green bonds and sustainable investment practices are among the key tools for directing capital in the transition to a low-carbon economy.

1. Introduction

Climate change is considered one of the most complex, multifaceted, and long-term risks facing businesses today. Scientific research shows that greenhouse gas concentrations in the atmosphere are rapidly increasing, resulting in an increase in average temperatures of 1.1 °C compared to the pre-industrial era (Craighead et al., 2020). This increase is causing serious disruptions to the global climate system; extreme weather events, droughts, floods, forest fires, and sea level rise directly and indirectly affect businesses across all sectors. This has become a serious threat to the sustainability of supply chains, especially for companies operating within a globalised economic structure (Ketchen & Craighead, 2020).

Supply chains are complex, multi-actor systems that organise the flow of products or services from raw materials to end users. These systems depend on natural resources, logistics infrastructure, production facilities, and human resources. The impacts of climate change create risks for each of these components (Haraguchi & Lall, 2015). For example, extreme temperatures and droughts reduce agricultural yields, heavy rainfall and floods damage transportation infrastructure, energy outages disrupt production processes, and natural disasters threaten the security of human resources (Sarkis, 2020). This situation causes both supply disruptions and cost increases in supply chains, negatively impacting critical indicators such as customer satisfaction, brand reputation, and financial sustainability (Le & Phi Tran, 2025).

The COVID-19 pandemic has exposed the fragility of global supply chains, and this fragility has revealed the system's unpreparedness for potential shocks from the climate crisis (Ivanov, 2021). Logistics delays, raw material shortages, and price fluctuations experienced during the pandemic have led businesses to seek alternative suppliers, localise production, and digitise. This experience has triggered similar strategic thinking in the context of climate change. Businesses must not only manage current risks but also adapt to future climate scenarios (Ivanov et al., 2023). In this context, the concept of "climate-resilient supply chains" is emerging not only to ensure environmental sustainability but also to ensure operational continuity, manage risks, reduce adaptation costs, and gain a competitive advantage (Al-Harthy, 2025). A climate-resilient supply chain should be built with structures that are flexible, diversified, digitalised, low-carbon, and minimise environmental impacts. Furthermore, the quality of relationships businesses establishes with suppliers, selection mechanisms based on sustainability criteria, and transparent reporting practices also play a critical role (Al Habsi & Al Kalbani, 2023).

This book chapter will systematically examine the impacts of climate change on supply chains, then detail the strategies, models, and technological approaches businesses can use to build climate-resilient supply chains. It will also evaluate regulations, international standards, and policy instruments, and offer concrete recommendations for businesses and policymakers. This will contribute to the development of new business models that prioritise both environmental and economic sustainability in a warming world.

2. The Effects of Climate Change on Supply Chains

Climate change stands out as a multifaceted environmental crisis that creates direct and indirect impacts on all stages of supply chain management. Supply chains are highly vulnerable to sudden changes in climate conditions and extreme weather events, and the sustainability of these systems is increasingly threatened by climate-related physical and transition risks (Dasaklis & Pappis, 2013). Physical risks refer to direct impacts such as floods, droughts, storms, extreme temperatures, and fires, while transition risks encompass indirect processes such as carbon taxes, regulations, customer preferences, and financial pressures (Ghadge et al., 2020).

Extreme weather events can cause serious disruptions in raw material supplies, particularly in the first link of the supply chain. For example, temperature increases and changes in precipitation patterns in agricultural production processes reduce product yields, leading to disruptions in supply times and increased costs (Wenz & Willner, 2022). On the other hand, sudden natural events such as floods or hurricanes directly impact the physical infrastructure of production facilities, causing temporary or permanent shutdowns. This affects not only manufacturers but also all supply chain links, extending to the end consumer (Pankratz & Schiller, 2024).

Climate risks also manifest themselves in logistics processes. Weather-related delays in maritime transport, infrastructure damage in road transport, and cancellations in air transport extend delivery times and reduce customer satisfaction (Osborne & Berroa, 2023). Furthermore, such logistical disruptions can lead to cascading problems, including increased inventory costs, the need for rescheduling, and order cancellations. In this context, businesses need to assess climate risks not only from a natural disaster perspective but also within a broader framework, such as operational efficiency, scheduling, cost, and reputation management (Steenbergen

& Saurav, 2023). However, transition risks stemming from climate change are also increasing pressure to restructure supply chains. Carbon taxes, border carbon adjustments, and regulations regarding sustainable sourcing principles are causing businesses to reexamine their production processes, supplier selection criteria, and product lifecycles (Twarakavi et al., 2022). In particular, the "Border Carbon Adjustment Mechanism (CBAM)", which the European Union plans to implement by 2026, is creating significant transformation pressure for carbon-intensive sectors. In this context, climate-friendly supply chains have become not only an environmental responsibility but also a prerequisite for gaining competitive advantage in global markets (Bellora & Fontagné, 2023).

The "Supply Chain Due Diligence Act" (Lieferkettengesetz), which entered into force in Germany in 2021, mandates large-scale companies to identify environmental and social risks in their supply chains and act. This regulation aims to ensure that all actors in the supply chain assume responsibility and make environmental awareness a corporate standard (Kolev & Neligan, 2022). The emergence of similar regulations in many developed economies, especially in European countries, demonstrates that regulatory compliance in climate risk management is also a strategic priority (Mittwoch & Bremenkamp, 2023).

On the other hand, the global nature of supply chains demonstrates that climate risks are not limited to regional impacts (Berg et al., 2025). The major flood disaster in Thailand in 2011 caused serious production disruptions in the electronics and automotive sectors worldwide, and the production processes of multinational companies operating in countries such as Japan, Germany, and the USA came to a halt (Haraguchi & Lall, 2015). This situation constitutes an important example as it demonstrates that climatic events are not limited to one country but can also affect global value chains (Twarakavi et al., 2022).

Climate change is ushering into a new era in which traditional approaches to supply chain management are proving inadequate. Businesses must address climate risks not only as an environmental threat but also as a multifaceted management area for protecting business continuity, financial stability, regulatory compliance, and corporate reputation (Dasaklis & Pappis, 2013). In this context, establishing climate-resilient supply chains is considered not only an environmental responsibility but also a strategic imperative (Yun & Ülkü, 2023).

3. Climate-Resistant Supply Chain Models

To manage the impacts of climate change and maintain uninterrupted supply chains, businesses must adopt not only reactive but also proactive and adaptive strategies (Christopher & Peck, 2004). In this regard, developing climate-resilient supply chain models facilitates businesses' preparedness for climate-related threats and the achievement of long-term sustainability goals. The concept of resilience provides a fundamental framework here: it is the capacity of a system to maintain its functionality when exposed to shocks and to recover quickly when necessary (Pettit et al., 2010).

The first fundamental characteristic of climate-resilient supply chains is based on the principle of flexibility. Such structures are not dependent on a single source; they ensure the system's survivability in times of crisis through methods such as the use of multiple suppliers, alternative logistics routes, and modular production (Ponis & Koronis, 2012). For example, if a manufacturing company sources certain raw materials from only one region, climatic events such as floods, droughts, or fires in that region could halt the entire production process. However, a structure that supplies multiple geographies minimises such impacts by dispersing risks (Shishodia et al., 2023).

Secondly, the localisation strategy is gaining importance. With global supply chains becoming increasingly vulnerable due to climate change, it is recommended that production and distribution processes be carried out as close to consumption as possible (Ehrenhuber et al., 2015). This contributes to reducing carbon footprints, shortening delivery times, and reducing logistics costs. Local sourcing, particularly in the agriculture, food, and fast-moving consumer goods sectors, offers a critical advantage in mitigating the negative impacts of climate uncertainty (Dolgui et al., 2020).

Another approach is the integration of digital technologies into supply chain management. Technologies such as cloud-based systems, IoT (Internet of Things), artificial intelligence, data analytics, and blockchain increase chain visibility and enable precautions against potential climate risks through early warning systems, performance monitoring, and scenario analysis (Dolgui & Ivanov, 2022). For example, advanced sensor systems enable maritime transport to detect adverse weather conditions in advance and make route changes, ensuring delivery continuity (Genovese et al., 2017). Additionally, integrating circular economy models into supply chains is among the climate-friendly solutions. Strategies such as product reuse, recycling, and repair reduce resource use and limit environmental impacts. This approach extends the supply chain not only from production to consumption but also to the post-consumption recovery process (Chua et al., 2022).

Climate-resilient models must align with sustainability principles and be structured according to international standards. Environmental management systems such as ISO 14001 help businesses organise their processes to minimise environmental risks, while reporting mechanisms such as TCFD (Task Force on Climate-related Financial Disclosures) encourage transparent assessment of climate-related risks and opportunities (Xhindole et al., 2025). The success of all these models is directly linked not only to technological and operational changes, but also to organisational culture, leadership, and employee engagement. Building a climate-resilient supply chain requires a holistic and strategic transformation process (Rana et al., 2016).

4. Adaptation Strategies in Business Models

In the face of the increasingly severe impacts of climate change, traditional business models are falling short in terms of sustainability, resilience, and adaptability. Therefore, it has become essential for businesses to restructure not only operationally but also strategically during their climate-focused transformation processes (Bocken et al., 2014). In this context, redesigning business models in the context of climate change is crucial for effectively managing both environmental and economic risks (Braasch & Velte, 2023).

First, climate risk-based scenario analyses should become an integral part of businesses' strategic planning processes. Businesses can assess long-term risks by analysing how their business models will be affected under different temperature increase scenarios (e.g., 1.5 °C, 2 °C, 3 °C) (Whelan & Fink, 2016). These analyses should be comprehensive, including factors such as supply chain disruptions, raw material price fluctuations, and carbon taxes. Such an approach increases business model resilience and allows for proactive future planning (Sharma et al., 2021).

Secondly, reshaping value propositions enables businesses to become more sustainable by considering their environmental responsibilities and customer expectations. Consumer preferences are no longer solely determined by price and quality; factors such as carbon footprint, ethical production, and recyclability are also key factors (Lüdeke-Freund et al., 2018). In response to these changing dynamics, businesses are turning to environmentally friendly innovations in product and service designs, thereby increasing brand value and complying with regulations (Schroedel, 2023). Another important strategy is setting and monitoring carbon reduction targets throughout the value chain. Businesses that measure their Corporate Carbon Footprint (Scope 1, 2, and 3) develop a sustainability approach that encompasses all actors, from suppliers to customers (Remer, 2021). Such measurement systems not only reduce environmental impact but also provide transparency and reliability in financial markets. Indeed, many investors are turning to green financial instruments by choosing companies with high sustainability performance (Reuter et al., 2010).

Transforming supplier management and collaboration structures also plays a key role in business model adaptations. By establishing climate-sensitive supplier selection criteria, businesses are moving away from suppliers operating in risky regions or those that fail to comply with environmental standards, instead opting to collaborate with actors who demonstrate low carbon emissions, energy efficiency, and environmental certifications (Land et al., 2022). Furthermore, platform-based models that increase knowledge sharing and technological collaborations with suppliers offer effective tools for increasing resilience (Flammer, 2021).

Adopting climate-compatible financial strategies supports business model transformation in terms of financial sustainability. Access to capital can be provided through tools such as green bonds, sustainable development loans, and ESG ratings, and these resources can be used for low-carbon projects. Integrating financial resources with climate goals in this way creates both a confidence boost for investors and a long-term competitive advantage for businesses (Franke & Katzer, 2024). In summary, businesses seeking to adapt to climate change need to restructure their business models holistically, including their vision, structure, processes, and partnerships. This transformation should not only be considered a defence mechanism against the climate crisis, but also an innovative, flexible, and responsible growth strategy (Ghadge et al., 2020).

5. Policy, Regulation, and Standards

Policies and regulations developed to combat climate change are forcing a radical transformation in businesses' supply chain management approach. The various legal and administrative frameworks put in place by governments, international organisations, and financial regulators to combat the climate crisis are creating not only environmental but also economic and strategic adaptation processes (Tsalis & Nikolaou, 2017). In this context, it has become imperative for businesses to closely monitor these regulations and revise their business models accordingly to adapt their supply chains to climate change (Dröge, 2016).

Firstly, one of the most effective frameworks at the international level is the Paris Agreement. This agreement, which entered into force in 2015, aims to limit global temperatures to below 2 °C and preferably to 1.5 °C (Bertoldi et al., 2018). To achieve this goal, countries are committed to reducing carbon emissions, and the private sector is also expected to participate in this process. This guidance, introduced by the Paris Agreement, increases pressure on companies operating in carbon-intensive sectors to decarbonise their supply chains (Pan & Liu, 2024).

The European Union's Carbon Border Adjustment Mechanism (CBAM), scheduled to enter into force in 2026, is also a critical regulation for businesses (Leal-Arcas et al., 2022). This mechanism aims to prevent carbon leakage by pricing the carbon content of products imported from outside the EU. In this context, businesses trading with the EU are required to transparently report their production processes and supply chains in terms of carbon emissions and ensure compliance (Rühl, 2022).

At the national level, many countries have implemented legal regulations that increase supply chain accountability. For example, Germany's Supply Chain Due Diligence Act (Lieferkettengesetz), adopted in 2021, imposes a responsibility on large companies to monitor and prevent environmental and human rights risks not only in their areas of activity but also in their direct and indirect supply chains (Rühmkorf, 2023). Such regulations mandate not only a technical but also a governance and ethical approach to climate risks in their supply chains (Demers et al., 2024). Furthermore, one of the most important frameworks encouraging businesses to systematically analyse climate risks is the reporting system developed by the Task Force on Climate-related Financial Disclosures (TCFD). The TCFD recommends that companies provide transparent reports on how they manage climate-related risks and opportunities. This system facilitates investors and financial actors' ability to measure climate-related performance by conducting an assessment under the headings of governance, strategy, risk management, and measurement-metrics (Bravi et al., 2020).

Other important tools that play a role in structuring supply chains according to environmental sustainability criteria are various international standards. The ISO 14001 Environmental Management System Standard provides a management framework that helps businesses systematically reduce their environmental impact. This standard guides businesses towards sustainable management with a comprehensive checklist that includes elements such as risk analysis, environmentally friendly production, energy management, and legal compliance (Köroğlu Göğüş & Yaman, 2024). Furthermore, platforms such as CDP (Carbon Disclosure Project), SBTi (Science-Based Targets initiative), and GRI (Global Reporting Initiative) support corporate climate action by providing tools that ensure transparency, measurability, and comparability in the supply chain. Through these platforms, businesses can both measure their carbon footprint and communicate sustainability-based strategies with global investors (Mora et al., 2025).

All these regulations and standards transform climate action from a voluntary practice into a strategic, operational, and legal imperative. It is critical for businesses to consider these developments not as a cost driver but as a long-term value-creation strategy to achieve competitive advantage (Ibn-Mohammed et al., 2021).

Climate change is increasingly impacting global economic structures and business models, forcing businesses to reassess their existing systems. Supply chains, by their nature, are multi-actor, multi-geographic, and dynamic, and are directly affected by the physical and transition risks created by climate change. In this context, establishing climate-resilient supply chains has become a strategic necessity not only for environmental sustainability but also for maintaining competitiveness, ensuring operational continuity, and mitigating financial risk (Petricevic & Teece, 2019).

This book demonstrates that a series of strategic steps must be implemented at both the internal and external levels of businesses to establish climate-resilient supply chains. First, it is crucial for businesses to systematically analyse climate risks and develop strategic adaptation capabilities under different climate scenarios. Furthermore, operational strategies such as digitalisation, localisation, multi-supplier use, and circular economy practices should increase resilience and reduce environmental vulnerabilities (Agwu & Bessant, 2021).

Restructuring business models in line with climate change is a fundamental component of this process. Value propositions must be aligned with environmentally friendly principles, carbon footprint reduction targets must be set, sustainability-based collaborations with suppliers must be established, and climate risks must be integrated into financial planning. This transformation entails not only operational but also cultural changes, requiring the active contribution of leadership, employee engagement, and stakeholder management (Kardish et al., 2021).

Furthermore, operating within the framework of policies, regulations, and international standards is a cornerstone of climate-compatible supply chain management. Regulatory structures such as the Paris Agreement, CBAM, TCFD, and ISO 14001 guide businesses and make climate action a legal obligation. Within this framework, businesses must not only ensure regulatory compliance but also utilise these standards to create a competitive advantage (Abdelkafi & Täuscher, 2016).

In this regard, policymakers, sectoral associations, and public authorities also have important responsibilities. Incentive mechanisms, technology investments, financial support programs, and capacity-building projects that support businesses' transition to low-carbon supply chains should be increased. Furthermore, legal regulations ensuring transparent reporting of climate risks will contribute to the establishment of sectoral reference frameworks (Franke & Katzer, 2024).

In conclusion, climate-resilient supply chain structures are not only a necessity but also a prerequisite for success in the sustainable business world of the future. In this process, businesses must act proactively, transparently, collaboratively, and with a long-term perspective. Reengineering supply chains requires considering environmental, economic, and social sustainability together. In this context, holistic strategies developed will both reduce risks at the business level and strengthen the collective fight against climate crisis on a global scale.

6. Green Bond and Sustainable Investment: Mobilising Capital for Climate Action

Effectively combating climate change is possible not only through policy and operational transformations, but also through the mobilisation of large-scale financial resources. In this context, capital markets play a vital role in achieving sustainable development goals (Petreski et al., 2025). Green bonds and sustainable investment strategies have become increasingly preferred instruments for financing environmentally friendly projects undertaken by both the public and private sectors (Agliardi & Agliardi, 2019).

Green bonds are debt instruments that stipulate that the issued financing proceeds be used only for projects that support environmental sustainability. Prominent among these projects are areas such as renewable energy production, energy efficiency, low-carbon transportation systems, water and waste management, and climate-resilient infrastructure (Bonanno & Brunelli, 2020). First issued by the European Investment Bank in 2007, green bonds have seen record growth since the

2020s and have gained a significant presence in global bond markets (Deschryver & De Mariz, 2020). According to data from the Climate Bonds Initiative, the total volume of green bonds issued globally reached USD 2.5 trillion by the end of 2023 (Mertens & Thiemann, 2023).

The most fundamental function of green bonds is to help meet the substantial capital needs required for climate action. In developing countries, in particular, the viability of low-carbon development projects depends largely on affordable financing. In this regard, green bonds increase the private sector's share of climate finance while also responding to investors' search for long-term stability combined with environmental responsibility (Sultana et al., 2018).

Sustainable investing, on the other hand, means structuring investment decisions by considering environmental, social, and governance (ESG) criteria. Unlike traditional investment approaches, sustainable investment strategies consider social and environmental impact in addition to financial returns. These strategies encompass different models, such as negative screening (excluding harmful sectors), positive selection (favouring sustainability leaders), thematic investing (e.g., climate funds), and impact investing (Ziolo et al., 2019).

In recent years, investors have been turning to companies that act responsibly against climate change, while companies that ignore carbon risks face difficulties accessing capital. This requires companies to transparently present not only financial reporting but also environmental performance indicators such as carbon footprint, water usage, and energy efficiency. Platforms such as TCFD and CDP standardise this process, making it easier for investors to conduct sustainability-based assessments (Syed, 2017). Furthermore, the proliferation of sustainable financial products is accelerating the restructuring of supply chains. Establishing low-carbon supply networks for businesses, in turn, increases their access to sustainable funds. ESG compliance and green financing strategies create competitive advantage, particularly for companies aiming to integrate with international markets (Shishlov et al., 2016). On the other hand, certain structural prerequisites must be met for the healthy development of the green bond market. Transparency, impact assessment, third-party verification, and independent certification processes are critical elements for investor confidence. Furthermore, combating mislabelling, also known as greenwashing, and monitoring whether issued bonds truly deliver environmental benefits are crucial (Deschryver & De Mariz, 2020).

Green bonds and sustainable investment strategies are among the most important tools for effectively allocating capital to combat climate change. Public policies, regulatory frameworks, and investor preferences are accelerating this transformation, establishing a strong link between environmental and financial sustainability. The role of these financial instruments in building climate-responsive economic structures will become even more critical in the coming years (Bhutta et al., 2022).

7. The Emergence and Development of Green Bonds

In the fight against climate change, the involvement of the private sector in areas where public resources are insufficient and the diversification of financing for climate-friendly projects have become essential. In this context, green bonds stand out as a specialised debt instrument designed for investments that prioritise environmental sustainability. A green bond is a type of security that provides capital to the issuer from investors in exchange for a set interest rate, but with the requirement that the funds be directed solely to environmentally friendly projects (Ibrić et al., 2024).

The concept of green bonds was first materialised in 2007 with the "Climate Awareness Bond" issued by the European Investment Bank (EIB). The purpose of this bond was to provide funding for renewable energy and energy efficiency projects (Gabr & Elbannan, 2024). Following the EIB, the World Bank issued its first official green bond in 2008. This bond emerged at the request of several Swedish institutional investors and became a significant milestone in integrating the concept of sustainability into capital markets (Partridge, 2019).

Initially issued exclusively by development finance institutions, green bonds quickly attracted the attention of corporations and municipalities. In 2013, the French energy company EDF issued the first corporate green bond in Europe, followed by major companies such as Apple, Toyota, and Starbucks. With these developments, the green bond market has experienced rapid growth on a global scale, becoming an important financing tool in both developed and developing countries (Rachello, 2019).

One of the key factors contributing to the increasing appeal of green bonds is that investors are increasingly considering environmental, social, and governance (ESG) criteria in their investment decisions. Large institutional investors and pension funds tend to gravitate towards investments that consider not only financial returns but also environmental impact. This trend has strengthened the demand for the green bond market (Ziolo et al., 2019). Another critical development occurred with the publication of the Green Bond Principles (GBPs) by the International Capital Markets Association (ICMA) in 2014. These principles established market trust and standardisation by defining the definition of green bonds, appropriate project criteria, revenue allocation, transparency, and reporting standards. This step by ICMA significantly contributed to the institutionalisation of the market and encouraged the development of third-party verification mechanisms (Manasses et al., 2022).

Today, the green bond market has moved beyond being a mere financial instrument; it has become a strategic tool for financing climate action. For both public and private actors, green bond issuances offer a significant opportunity to fulfil environmental commitments and establish the financial infrastructure for the transition to a low-carbon economy (Nanayakkara & Colombage, 2022).

8. ICMA Green Bond Principles

The rapid growth of green bonds as a market instrument has brought with it certain risks and structural issues. A fundamental element necessary for the healthy functioning of this market is ensuring that bonds issued are truly used in projects that comply with environmental sustainability principles. In response to this need, the International Capital Markets Association (ICMA) published the Green Bond Principles (GBPs) in 2014, providing a voluntary framework for the green bond market (Gatti & Florio, 2018).

The Green Bond Principles consist of four key components: (1) Eligible Project Categories (Use of Proceeds), (2) Project Evaluation and Selection Process, (3) Management of Proceeds, and (4) Reporting. These principles guide both issuers and investors, increasing the reliability and transparency of green bonds (De Assis et al., 2022).

The first component, "Eligible Project Categories", defines the types of projects that green bond proceeds can be used for. These are typical areas that provide environmental benefits, such as renewable energy, energy efficiency, sustainable transportation, wastewater treatment, biodiversity conservation, and climate-resilient infrastructure projects. These definitions require that projects serve measurable environmental objectives, such as carbon emission reduction or climate change adaptation (Nanayakkara & Colombage, 2022).

The second component, the "Project Selection and Evaluation Process", requires the issuer to transparently define its environmental objectives, project selection methodology, and sustainability policies. This process is expected to answer questions such as how environmental risks are addressed and why the selected projects are deemed suitable. This structure allows investors to evaluate not only the bond itself but also the underlying corporate governance and environmental strategy (Agostini, 2023).

The third element, "Revenue Management", requires that bond proceeds be held in separate accounts or through a properly traceable system and directed only to appropriate projects. This prevents funds from being diverted to other areas, thus increasing investor confidence. Independent auditing organisations often monitor this process, and annual reports are encouraged (Logutov, 2023). Finally, the "Reporting" principle requires the issuer to publish impact and usage reports to investors at least annually. These reports should include quantitative and qualitative information on the funds allocated to projects, the progress of expenditures, and environmental impacts (e.g., CO_2 emission reductions, energy savings). Transparency is key in this regard (Mishra et al., 2023).

GBPs also encourage independent review and third-party assessment processes. Services such as second-party opinion (SPO), sustainability consulting, green certification, and sustainability ratings have become widespread as tools to support the environmental credibility of green bonds. These verification mechanisms also play a significant role in protecting the market from the risk of "greenwashing" (Deschryver & De Mariz, 2020). Consequently, the Green Bond Principles developed by ICMA have institutionalised trust, transparency, and accountability in the green bond market, establishing an internationally recognised framework for both issuers and investors. This framework addresses the lack of standards in the market and increases the effectiveness and traceability of green financing (Fatica & Panzica, 2021).

9. The Contribution of Green Bonds to Climate Action

The economic, social, and environmental impacts of climate change are forcing restructuring across all sectors (Bašić et al., 2023). In this transformation process, where traditional financial instruments are limited, private financing models directed towards climate-friendly projects have gained significant importance (Ahmed et al., 2024). Green bonds, foremost among these models, stand out not only as an investment instrument with environmental responsibilities but also as a critical capital mobilisation tool for achieving sustainable development goals (Alamgir & Cheng, 2023).

The contribution of green bonds to climate action is concentrated in four main areas: reducing carbon emissions, energy transition, greening transportation systems, and establishing climate-resilient infrastructure (Lin & Hong, 2021).

9.1. *Reducing Carbon Emissions*

More than 75% of global carbon emissions originate from energy production, transportation, and industrial activities (Ahmed et al., 2024). In this context, green bonds are used to reduce carbon-intensive practices in these sectors and finance cleaner production methods. Solar and wind power plants, energy-efficient building renovations, LED lighting systems, and low-emission manufacturing facilities are among the primary projects financed by these bonds (Alamgir & Cheng, 2023).

Approximately 60% of the USD 110 billion in green bonds issued in China in 2021 was allocated to projects that directly reduce carbon emissions. Similarly, in Europe, many countries, particularly Germany and the Netherlands, are positioning green bonds as an important policy tool to achieve net-zero emissions targets in the energy sector (Tolliver et al., 2020).

9.2. *Renewable Energy Financing*

The energy sector is the area with the largest allocation of funds in the green bond market. In 2023, 40% of green bonds issued were directed to renewable energy projects (Azhgaliyeva et al., 2020). These projects not only generate environmental benefits but also support energy supply security and cost efficiency (Fu & Ng, 2021).

In countries such as India, South Africa, and Brazil, projects such as solar farms, wind turbine parks, and biomass power plants have been implemented through public–private partnerships using green bond financing (Nayak et al., 2024). The National Bank of India (IREDA)'s USD 500 million green bond issuance in 2022 provided funding for projects that will increase solar energy generation capacity by 15% (De Assis et al., 2022).

9.3. *Sustainable Transportation Systems*

The transportation sector accounts for approximately one-quarter of greenhouse gas emissions. The transition from fossil fuel-based transportation to electric, hybrid, and public transport-focused systems plays a key role in combating climate change. Green bonds offer a critical financing source for this transformation (Baranova & Efimovskii, 2023).

High-speed rail projects financed by green bonds issued by France's SNCF railway company are saving approximately 1 million tons of CO_2 annually (Kozera et al., 2024). Similarly, in Poland, the Warsaw Municipality has renewed its electric bus fleet with green bonds, significantly reducing both air pollution and carbon emissions (Glemarec, 2023).

9.4. *Climate-Resilient Infrastructure Investments*

The physical impacts of climate change (extreme weather events, sea level rise, drought, etc.) directly threaten infrastructure systems. Therefore, city infrastructures must be strengthened to adapt to climate change (Am et al., 2017). Such investments are considered within the scope of "adaptation finance" and are increasingly being used in green bonds (Al Habsi & Al Kalbani, 2023).

In this context, flood risk fortifications, natural drainage systems, green roof applications, coastal protection projects, and regulations to reduce the urban heat island effect are financed with green bond proceeds. Infrastructure strengthening projects in low-lying areas in the Netherlands have been carried out with green bonds supported by the European Bank for Reconstruction and Development (EBRD) (Meyer & Schwarze, 2019).

9.5. Impact Measurement and Quantification of Carbon Impact

Impact measurement criteria and methodologies are evolving to measure the environmental impact of green bonds. In line with frameworks proposed by ICMA and the Climate Bonds Initiative, indicators such as CO_2 reduction, energy savings, and water use improvements achieved by projects supported by bond proceeds are reported at least annually (Bazbauers, 2022).

These reports help meet investors' expectations for not only financial but also environmental returns and increase the accountability of green financing instruments (Maltais & Nykvist, 2020).

10. Sustainable Investment Instruments and Strategies

Climate change is deepening the impact of environmental risks on the financial system while also radically transforming investor behaviour. Now, not only financial returns but also environmental and social impact play a decisive role in investment decisions. Sustainable investment strategies developed in this direction integrate environmental, social, and governance (ESG) factors into investment decision-making processes with a holistic perspective (Jonsdottir et al., 2021).

10.1. ESG Investment Approach

The ESG approach is based on evaluating companies for investment based on criteria such as their environmental impact (e.g., carbon footprint, natural resource use), level of social responsibility (employee rights, social contribution, diversity), and governance quality (transparency, board structure, ethical standards). ESG-based investments are particularly adopted by institutional investors to create long-term value and mitigate systemic risks (Joshi et al., 2024).

Global indicators such as the MSCI ESG Index, FTSE4 Good, and the Dow Jones Sustainability Index allow investors to filter companies based on their ESG scores. These indicators ensure that sustainable investment decisions are supported by objective criteria (Çetin, 2022).

10.2. Social Bonds

While social bonds share a similar structure to green bonds, they differ in that funds are allocated to projects that aim to create social rather than environmental impact. These projects include low-income housing, healthcare, education infrastructure, and women's employment. The Social Bond Principles (SBPs), published by ICMA, define appropriate project categories, revenue allocation, impact reporting, and transparency principles for social bonds (Ahmed et al., 2024).

Social bond issuance has increased rapidly following the COVID-19 pandemic. Institutions such as the World Bank, the Asian Development Bank, and the European Investment Bank have issued billions of dollars in social bonds to respond to the economic and health impacts of the pandemic. Social bonds are considered an important tool that directly contributes to the "social justice" dimension of the Sustainable Development Goals (Azhgaliyeva et al., 2020).

10.3. Sustainable Bonds and Hybrid Models

In recent years, sustainability bonds, hybrid bond types encompassing both environmental and social impacts, have gained prominence. These bonds enable the simultaneous allocation of resources to green and social projects. For example, the proceeds from a sustainable bond could be used to build a solar power plant and provide vocational training to disadvantaged communities in the region where the plant is located (Ahmed et al., 2024).

The most significant advantage of sustainable bonds is their potential to create a multidimensional impact. They also offer investors a wider portfolio diversity. As of 2022, the sustainable bond market has surpassed USD 300 billion in volume and continues to increase its share of the global bond market (Maltais & Nykvist, 2020).

10.4. Thematic Investment Strategies

Thematic investment refers to investing focused on a specific sustainability theme (e.g., combating climate change, clean water, a circular economy, or gender equality). This strategy allows investors to focus on specific social or environmental goals. Examples of this strategy include "green energy funds", "climate adaptation funds", or "women's leadership-themed ETFs" (Dhar et al., 2025).

Thematic investments are also accessible to individual investors, offering value-based investment with financial returns. They can also act as insurance against ESG risks in investors' portfolios (Kwok, 2022).

10.5. Green Indices and Performance Indicators

Indicators that guide investment decisions based on sustainability play a major role in the widespread adoption of green investment strategies. The BIST Sustainability Index is a leading indicator that tracks the ESG performance of companies operating on the Borsa Istanbul in Turkey. This index allows investors to identify companies sensitive to sustainability and make investment decisions accordingly (Ahmed et al., 2024).

Internationally, indices such as the MSCI ESG Leaders Index and the Bloomberg Barclays MSCI Green Bond Index guide investors by monitoring both green bond performance and stock performance that align with ESG criteria (Gülay & Ergun, 2024).

11. Global and Turkish Examples: World Bank, EBRD, BIST Sustainability Index

Successful practices in green finance are developing not only under the leadership of corporate firms but also international financial institutions and countries. Multilateral development banks such as the World Bank and the European Bank for Reconstruction and Development (EBRD) play a significant role in deepening and building confidence in green bond markets. In Turkey, the BIST Sustainability Index, established within Borsa Istanbul, contributes to the development of ESG-based investment strategies (Rumpf, 2019).

11.1. The World Bank Example

The institutional foundations for green bonds were first laid in 2008 with the World Bank's USD 400 million green bond issuance, launched at the request of Swedish institutional investors. This issuance was a landmark initiative demonstrating how environmental projects could be financed through capital markets (Deschryver &

De Mariz, 2020). Since then, the World Bank has issued more than USD 18 billion in green bonds in more than 40 currencies (Talbot, 2017).

Funds have been channelled into projects such as energy efficiency, renewable energy, sustainable agriculture, climate change adaptation, and combating deforestation. The World Bank has been one of the institutions that shaped the fundamental principles of the green bond market, such as transparency, impact reporting, and third-party verification (Gibon et al., 2020). It also publishes an annual Green Bond Impact Report, reporting to investors on indicators such as the environmental impact of projects financed with bond proceeds and CO_2 reductions achieved. This approach builds confidence for sustainable investors (Vinokurov et al., 2023).

11.2. The Example of the European Bank for Reconstruction and Development (EBRD)

The EBRD provides financing for projects that promote environmental sustainability across a wide geography, including Eastern Europe, Central Asia, the Mediterranean, and Turkey. Having begun issuing green bonds in the 2010s, the EBRD invests in low-carbon and resource-efficient projects within its Green Economy Transition (GET) framework (Gedikli & Balaban, 2018).

The EBRD's green bonds address a wide range of areas, including the development of climate-compatible urban infrastructure, sustainable transportation systems, and energy-efficient building renovations. In Turkey, transportation infrastructure and waste management projects in cities such as Konya, Gaziantep, and Izmir have been supported by EBRD financing and green bond proceeds (Reichelt et al., 2023). As of 2022, the EBRD allocated more than 50% of its total portfolio to climate action projects and issued more than EUR 6 billion in green bonds in this regard (Güzyurdu & Yaman, 2024).

11.3. The Turkish Example: BIST Sustainability Index

One of the most important steps taken towards the institutionalisation of sustainable finance in Turkey is the creation of the BIST Sustainability Index. Established by Borsa Istanbul in 2014, this index guides investors by identifying companies that meet ESG criteria among the BIST 100 (Yavuz et al., 2025).

The index scores companies based on their environmental impact (waste management, energy efficiency, carbon management), social responsibility policies (employee rights, occupational health and safety, supply chain management), and governance practices (ethical rules, transparency, stakeholder relations). This structure enables investors to make sustainability-based decisions and encourages companies to improve their ESG performance (Türkay et al., 2023). Additionally, Borsa Istanbul's publication of the "Green and Sustainable Bond Guide" and its support for companies to pursue green bond issuance have contributed to the development of the green finance ecosystem in Turkey. The first CMB-approved green bond issuances in Turkey began in 2022, spearheaded by banks and energy companies. These bonds financed renewable energy projects, sustainable infrastructure systems, and environmentally friendly housing (Bhagat, 2024).

12. Challenges and Future Perspectives: Greenwashing, Transparency and Standard Issues

The green bond market has grown rapidly in recent years, becoming a cornerstone of the global sustainable finance system. However, this growth has also brought with it some structural problems and risks of undermining trust in the market. The most frequently discussed problems are greenwashing, lack of transparency, and the lack of maturity of international standards. Resolving these issues is critical to ensuring the future growth of the green bond market in a reliable, effective, and scalable manner (Demirci, 2021).

12.1. Greenwashing Risk

Greenwashing is the presentation of projects that do not create environmental benefits or have very limited impacts on investors as "green". This misleads investors and undermines trust in the green bond market. Some issuers proceed directly to projects with questionable environmental impacts; for example, they label controversial projects, such as fossil fuel-based production facilities that claim to be energy efficient, as "green" (Veral, 2022).

The risk of greenwashing is most common in issuances where independent third-party assessments are lacking or reporting is inadequate. Therefore, it is recommended that verification mechanisms such as second-party opinion (SPO), verifiers, and certifiers be strengthened in the market. The Climate Bonds Initiative and ICMA contribute to the standardisation process by publishing impact classifications and reporting guidelines for specific project types (Shishlov et al., 2016).

12.2. Transparency and Traceability Issues

Another fundamental challenge of the green bond market is the lack of transparency and traceability. Bond issuers often fail to provide sufficient data on the environmental impacts of projects or limit reporting to financial reporting. In cases where impact reporting is absent or only provided with general information, investors cannot objectively assess whether bonds are truly green (Teixeira, 2025).

In response to these issues, organisations such as ICMA and EU Taxonomy have defined impact measurement criteria, including quantitative indicators such as annual CO_2 emission reductions, energy efficiency coefficients, or water savings among mandatory reporting elements. However, such data infrastructure remains inadequate, particularly in developing countries, and market practices vary widely (Maragopoulos, 2023).

12.3. International Standard Issues and Taxonomy Discrepancies

The green bond market has not yet reached a single standard worldwide. While ICMA's Green Bond Principles guidelines are widely used, this framework is voluntary. The EU Green Bond Standard, launched by the European Union in 2023, is the first major initiative to introduce legally binding green bonds (Pyka, 2023). However, there are significant differences between the EU's classification system and those of other countries or regions (e.g., China's Green Bond Indications). While some controversial projects in China, such as "efficient coal", can still be classified as green, the EU excludes such activities. Such taxonomy discrepancies make global comparisons difficult for investors and threaten market integrity (Deschryver & De Mariz, 2020).

12.4. Future Perspectives and Strategic Recommendations

To ensure that the green bond market grows on a more solid foundation in the future, the following key strategies are recommended:

- Mandatory impact reporting and external auditing practices should be expanded; independent approval and monitoring processes should be standardised for all issuances.
- Global taxonomy harmonisation should be ensured, and the integration of different countries' green project definitions into the international framework should be encouraged.
- Transparency should be increased, and project-based proceeds from issued bonds and environmental impact reports should be made publicly available and auditable.
- Strengthening sanctions against greenwashing will serve as a deterrent mechanism that will increase market confidence.
- Technical support and reporting capacity should be provided to developing countries, facilitating their access to green bond markets (Sartzetakis, 2021).

The green bond market is a powerful financial tool for achieving global climate goals; however, realising this potential requires not only financial size but also reliability, transparency, and compliance with standards. The sustainable finance architecture of the future will be shaped around solving these problems.

Climate change, one of the greatest challenges of our time, is creating far-reaching impacts not only on environmentally but also at economic, social, and governance levels. In this context, it has become imperative that not only policymakers but also the private sector, investors, and financial institutions take responsibility for achieving sustainable development goals. Businesses can only become resilient to climate risks by developing climate-sensitive business models and a strong financial infrastructure to support them.

Green bonds, discussed in this book chapter, stand out as one of the most dynamic and effective examples of sustainable investment instruments. By financing high-impact projects such as renewable energy, low-carbon transportation, energy efficiency, and climate-resilient infrastructure, green bonds directly mobilise the financial dimension of climate action. In this respect, they both drive private sector investment and increase the effectiveness of public policies. For businesses seeking to build climate-resilient supply chains, green bonds offer not only a financing source but also a strategic competitive advantage. Companies with high ESG (environmental, social, and governance) performance become more attractive to investors and, by increasing their brand value, gain a stronger position in global markets. However, for this potential to be realised sustainably, several significant structural issues in the market must be resolved. Preventing greenwashing, ensuring transparency and traceability of impact reporting, harmonising global taxonomies, and increasing capacity, particularly in developing countries, are critical to the future of green finance.

From Turkey's perspective, while steps such as the establishment of the BIST Sustainability Index, the CMB's green and sustainable bond guidelines, and the first private sector bond issuances are positive, there are still many steps to be taken towards deepening markets, increasing institutional capacity, and achieving full compliance with standards.

As a result, green bonds and sustainable investment strategies stand out as indispensable tools for businesses to adapt their business models in a warming world, build resilience to climate risks, and create sustainable value. Success in this process is only possible with a holistic, transparent, and accountable financial ecosystem. The effective use of green bonds represents a strategic turning point for both the future of the planet and the sustainability of the economic system.

Funding: This research received no external funding.

Conflicts of Interest: The author declares no conflicts of interest.

Author Name and Affiliation: Zekeriya Şahin, Faculty of Business and Management Sciences, Istanbul Esenyurt University, Istanbul, Turkey.

Keywords: climate-resilient supply chains; green bonds; sustainable fnance; ESG investment strategies.

References

Abdelkafi, N., & Täuscher, K. (2016). Business models for sustainability from a system dynamics perspective. *Organisation & Environment*, *29*(1), 74–96.

Agliardi, E., & Agliardi, R. (2019). Financing environmentally sustainable projects with green bonds. *Environment and Development Economics*, *24*(6), 608–623. [CrossRef]

Agostini, F. (2023). From "green bond principles" to "green bond clauses": Mitigating greenwashing through contract law. In *Quo vadis Commercial Contract? Reflections on sustainability, ethics and technology in the emerging law and practice of global commerce* (pp. 151–177). Springer International Publishing.

Agwu, U. J., & Bessant, J. (2021). Sustainable business models: A systematic review of approaches and challenges in manufacturing. *Revista de Administração Contemporânea*, *25*, e200202. [CrossRef]

Ahmed, R., Yusuf, F., & Ishaque, M. (2024). Green bonds as a bridge to the UN sustainable development goals on environment: A climate change empirical investigation. *International Journal of Finance & Economics*, *29*(2), 2428–2451.

Alamgir, M., & Cheng, M. C. (2023). Do green bonds play a role in achieving sustainability? *Sustainability*, *15*(13), 10177. [CrossRef]

Al Habsi, J., & Al Kalbani, A. (2023). Building climate-resilient supply chains in Oman: Challenges, strategies, and best practices. *Journal of Engineering Research*, 1–25.

Al-Harthy, L. S. (2025). Enhancing supply chain resilience to climate change in Oman: Challenges and solutions. *Ayden Multidisciplinary Research Journal*, *13*(3), 1–15. [CrossRef]

Am, A. O. K., Pryke, J., & Wurf, H. (2017). *Strengthening the Asian development bank in 21st century Asia*. LOWY Institute.

Azhgaliyeva, D., Kapoor, A., & Liu, Y. (2020). Green bonds for financing renewable energy and energy efficiency in South-East Asia: A review of policies. *Journal of Sustainable Finance & Investment*, *10*(2), 113–140.

Baranova, A., & Efimovskii, E. (2023). *Railway sustainability: Sustainability of railways in Finland and other European countries* (pp. 1–80). LAB University of Applied Sciences Bachelor of Business Administration, International Business.

Bašić, M., Kovše, Š., Opačić, A., Pecarević, M., & Obrecht, M. (2023). Supply chain management mitigation to climate change in three selected industrial sectors. *Logist Supply Chain Sustain Glob Challenges, 14*(1), 1–13. [CrossRef]

Bazbauers, A. R. (2022). Sustainable, green, and climate-resilient cities: An analysis of multilateral development banks. *Climate and Development, 14*(8), 689–704. [CrossRef]

Bellora, C., & Fontagné, L. (2023). EU in search of a carbon border adjustment mechanism. *Energy Economics, 123*, 106673. [CrossRef]

Berg, C., Bettarelli, L., Furceri, D., Ganslmeier, M., Grover, A., Lang, M., & Schiffbauer, M. (2025). *Firm-level climate change adaptation*. World Bank.

Bertoldi, P., Kona, A., Rivas, S., & Dallemand, J. F. (2018). Towards a global comprehensive and transparent framework for cities and local governments enabling an effective contribution to the Paris climate agreement. *Current Opinion in Environmental Sustainability, 30*, 67–74. [CrossRef]

Bhagat, C. (2024). Greenwashing vs. genuine efforts: The role of transparent communication in building corporate credibility. *Journal of Law For Future Security, 1*(2), 51–62.

Bhutta, U. S., Tariq, A., Farrukh, M., Raza, A., & Iqbal, M. K. (2022). Green bonds for sustainable development: Review of literature on development and impact of green bonds. *Technological Forecasting and Social Change, 175*, 121378. [CrossRef]

Bocken, N. M., Short, S. W., Rana, P., & Evans, S. (2014). A literature and practice review to develop sustainable business model archetypes. *Journal of Cleaner Production, 65*, 42–56. [CrossRef]

Bonanno, T., & Brunelli, S. (2020). *Green bonds: European taxonomy alignment and correlation with pricing*. Polytechnic of Milan.

Braasch, A., & Velte, P. (2023). Climate reporting quality following the recommendations of the task force on climate-related financial disclosures: A Focus on the German capital market. *Sustainable Development, 31*(2), 926–940.

Bravi, L., Santos, G., Pagano, A., & Murmura, F. (2020). Environmental management system according to ISO 14001: 2015 as a driver to sustainable development. *Corporate Social Responsibility and Environmental Management, 27*(6), 2599–2614.

Christopher, M., & Peck, H. (2004). Building the resilient supply chain. *International Journal of Logistics Management, 15*(2), 1–13. [CrossRef]

Chua, W. F., James, R., King, A., Lee, E., & Soderstrom, N. (2022). Task force on climate-related financial disclosures (TCFD) implementation: An overview and insights from the australian accounting standards board dialogue series. *Australian Accounting Review, 32*(3), 396–405. [CrossRef]

Craighead, C. W., Ketchen, D. J., Jr., & Darby, J. L. (2020). Pandemics and supply chain management research: Toward a theoretical toolbox. *Decision Sciences, 51*(4), 838–866. [CrossRef]

Çetin, D. T. (2022). Green bonds in climate finance and forecasting of corporate green bond index value with artificial intelligence. *Journal of Research in Business, 7*(1), 138–157. [CrossRef]

Dasaklis, T. K., & Pappis, C. P. (2013). Supply chain management in view of climate change: An overview of possible impacts and the road ahead. *Journal of Industrial Engineering and Management (JIEM), 6*(4), 1139–1161. [CrossRef]

De Assis, T. F., Ricci, L. M., Monteiro, T. G. M., de Abreu, V. H. S., D'Agosto, M. D. A., & Santos, A. S. (2022). Sustainable transport indicators and mitigation actions applied to the green bond principles. In *Carbon footprints of manufacturing and transportation industries* (pp. 139–169). Springer Nature.

Demers, E., Hendrikse, J., & Metzner, M. (2024). *TCFD reporting: Early evidence related to the future of global climate-related disclosures*. Working Paper. TCFD.

Demirci, K. (2021). Sürdürülebilir geleceğin önündeki tehdit: Yeşil boyama (greenwashing) Türkiye kentleri üzerinden bir değerlendirme. *Kent ve Çevre Araştırmaları Dergisi, 3*(2), 34–55. [CrossRef]

Deschryver, P., & De Mariz, F. (2020). What future for the green bond market? How can policymakers, companies, and investors unlock the potential of the green bond market? *Journal of risk and Financial Management, 13*(3), 61. [CrossRef]

Dhar, B. K., Roshid, M. M., Dissanayake, S., Chawla, U., & Faheem, M. (2025). Leveraging FinTech and GreenTech for long-term sustainability in South Asia: Strategic pathways toward Agenda 2050. *Green Technologies and Sustainability, 4*(1), 100263.

Dolgui, A., & Ivanov, D. (2022). 5G in digital supply chain and operations management: Fostering flexibility, end-to-end connectivity and real-time visibility through internet-of-everything. *International Journal of Production Research, 60*(2), 442–451. [CrossRef]

Dolgui, A., Ivanov, D., & Sokolov, B. (2020). Reconfigurable supply chain: The X-network. *International Journal of Production Research, 58*(13), 4138–4163. [CrossRef]

Dröge, S. (2016). *The Paris agreement 2015: Turning point for the international climate regime*. No. RP 4/2016. SWP Research.

Ehrenhuber, I., Treiblmaier, H., Engelhardt-Nowitzki, C., & Gerschberger, M. (2015). Toward a framework for supply chain resilience. *International Journal of Supply Chain and Operations Resilience, 1*(4), 339–350. [CrossRef]

Fatica, S., & Panzica, R. (2021). Green bonds as a tool against climate change? *Business Strategy and the Environment, 30*(5), 2688–2701. [CrossRef]

Flammer, C. (2021). Corporate green bonds. *Journal of Financial Economics, 142*(2), 499–516. [CrossRef]

Franke, B., & Katzer, D. (2024). *Climate change exposure and corporate green bonds*. Available online: https://papers.ssrn.com/sol3/papers.cfm?abstract_id=4913842 (accessed on 15 July 2025).

Fu, J., & Ng, A. W. (2021). Scaling up renewable energy assets: Issuing green bond via structured public-private collaboration for managing risk in an emerging economy. *Energies, 14*(11), 3076. [CrossRef]

Gabr, D. H., & Elbannan, M. A. (2024). Green finance insights: Evolution of the green bonds market. *Management & Sustainability: An Arab Review, 3*(3), 274–297.

Gatti, S., & Florio, A. (2018). Issue spread determinants in the green bond market: The role of second party reviews and of the Green Bond Principles. In *Research handbook of finance and sustainability* (pp. 206–224). Edward Elgar Publishing.

Gedikli, B., & Balaban, O. (2018). An evaluation of local policies and actions that address climate change in Turkish metropolitan cities. *European Planning Studies, 26*(3), 458–479. [CrossRef]

Genovese, A., Acquaye, A. A., Figueroa, A., & Koh, S. L. (2017). Sustainable supply chain management and the transition towards a circular economy: Evidence and some applications. *Omega, 66*, 344–357. [CrossRef]

Ghadge, A., Wurtmann, H., & Seuring, S. (2020). Managing climate change risks in global supply chains: A review and research agenda. *International Journal of Production Research, 58*(1), 44–64. [CrossRef]

Gibon, T., Popescu, I. Ş., Hitaj, C., Petucco, C., & Benetto, E. (2020). Shades of green: Life cycle assessment of renewable energy projects financed through green bonds. *Environmental Research Letters, 15*(10), 104045. [CrossRef]

Glemarec, Y. (2023). Financing green and climate resilient infrastructure in ASEAN countries. *Environmental Progress & Sustainable Energy, 42*(4), e14097. [CrossRef]

Gülay, G., & Ergun, K. (2024). The role of green bonds in achieving SDG 13: The case of Türkiye. In *Pursuing sustainable development goals: The performance of Türkiye in the centennial of the republic* (p. 597). Istanbul University Press.

Güzyurdu, F., & Yaman, S. (2024). Exploring the Impacts of financial failure risk on sustainable growth policies: Evidence from the BIST sustainability index companies. *Ekonomi Politika ve Finans Araştırmaları Dergisi, 9*(2), 230–253. [CrossRef]

Haraguchi, M., & Lall, U. (2015). Flood risks and impacts: A case study of Thailand's floods in 2011 and research questions for supply chain decision making. *International Journal of Disaster Risk Reduction, 14*, 256–272. [CrossRef]

Ibn-Mohammed, T., Mustapha, K. B., Godsell, J., Adamu, Z., Babatunde, K. A., Akintade, D. D., Acquaye, A., Fujii, H., Ndiaye, M. M., Yamoah, F. A., & Koh, S. C. L. (2021). A critical analysis of the impacts of COVID-19 on the global economy and ecosystems and opportunities for circular economy strategies. *Resources, Conservation and Recycling, 164*, 105169. [CrossRef]

Ibrić, M., Kozarević, E., & Mešković, A. (2024). The rise of green bonds: Global context and european insights. *Journal of Economics, Law, and Society, 1*(1), 55–71.

Ivanov, D. (2021). Supply chain viability and the COVID-19 pandemic: A conceptual and formal generalisation of four major adaptation strategies. *International Journal of Production Research, 59*(12), 3535–3552. [CrossRef]

Ivanov, D., Dolgui, A., Blackhurst, J. V., & Choi, T. M. (2023). Toward supply chain viability theory: From lessons learned through COVID-19 pandemic to viable ecosystems. *International Journal of Production Research, 61*(8), 2402–2415. [CrossRef]

Jonsdottir, G. E., Sigurjonsson, T. O., Alavi, A. R., & Mitchell, J. (2021). Applying responsible ownership to advance SDGs and the ESG framework, resulting in the issuance of green bonds. *Sustainability, 13*(13), 7331. [CrossRef]

Joshi, D., Paul, S., Singh, P., Mane, N. S., & Yadav, M. (2024). Sustainable finance: The role of green bonds in driving ESG investments. *Library of Progress-Library Science, Information Technology & Computer, 44*(3), 11449.

Kardish, C., Li, L., & Hellmich-Adelphi, M. (2021). The EU carbon border adjustment mechanism (CBAM) and China. In *Unpacking options on policy design, potential responses, and possible impacts*. The Adelphi.

Ketchen, D. J., Jr., & Craighead, C. W. (2020). Research at the intersection of entrepreneurship, supply chain management, and strategic management: Opportunities highlighted by COVID-19. *Journal of Management*, *46*(8), 1330–1341. [CrossRef]

Kolev, G. V., & Neligan, A. (2022). *Effects of a supply chain regulation: Survey-based results on the expected effects of the German Supply Chains Act*. No. 8/2022. IW-Report.

Kozera, A., Satoła, Ł., & Standar, A. (2024). European Union co-funded investments in low-emission and green energy in urban public transport in Poland. *Renewable and Sustainable Energy Reviews*, *200*, 114530.

Köroğlu Göğüş, M., & Yaman, E. S. (2024). *CDP climate change and water report 2023/Türkiye edition*. CDP.

Kwok, K. (2022). ESG Data, Ratings, and Indexes. In *Responsible investment in fixed income markets* (pp. 363–383). Routledge.

Land, A., Gruchmann, T., Siems, E., & Beske-Janssen, P. (2022). Dynamic capabilities theory. In *handbook of theories for purchasing, supply chain and management research* (pp. 378–398). Edward Elgar Publishing.

Le, M. H., & Phi Tran, P. (2025). Managing supply chain resilience in climate and disaster-prone environments: A bibliometric analysis. *Competitiveness Review: An International Business Journal*, *36*(2), 299–320. [CrossRef]

Leal-Arcas, R., Faktaufon, M., & Kyprianou, A. (2022). A legal exploration of the European Union's carbon border adjustment mechanism. *European Energy and Environmental Law Review*, *31*(4), 223–240. [CrossRef]

Lin, L., & Hong, Y. (2021). Developing a green bonds market: The case of China. *European Business Organization Law Review*, 1–40. [CrossRef]

Logutov, A. V. (2023). Global "Green Bond" market analysis and perspective of its development. In *Smart green innovations in industry 4.0 for climate change risk management* (pp. 625–631). Springer International Publishing.

Lüdeke-Freund, F., Carroux, S., Joyce, A., Massa, L., & Breuer, H. (2018). The sustainable business model pattern taxonomy—45 patterns to support sustainability-oriented business model innovation. *Sustainable Production and Consumption*, *15*, 145–162. [CrossRef]

Maltais, A., & Nykvist, B. (2020). Understanding the role of green bonds in advancing sustainability. *Journal of Sustainable Finance & Investment*, *11*(3), 233–252. [CrossRef]

Manasses, G., Paulik, E., & Tapaszti, A. (2022). Green bond impact report as an essential next step in market development. *Financial and Economic Review*, *21*(4), 180–204. [CrossRef]

Maragopoulos, N. (2023). Toward a European green bond standard: A European initiative to promote sustainable finance. In *Greening the bond market: A European perspective* (pp. 21–50). Springer International Publishing.

Mertens, D., & Thiemann, M. (2023). The European investment bank: The EU's climate bank? In *Handbook on European Union climate change policy and politics* (pp. 68–82). Edward Elgar Publishing.

Meyer, P. B., & Schwarze, R. (2019). Financing climate-resilient infrastructure: Determining risk, reward, and return on investment. *Frontiers of Engineering Management*, *6*(1), 117–127. [CrossRef]

Mishra, S. P., Kumar, R., & Rout, J. (2023). An overview of green, social, sustainability, and sustainability-linked (GSSS) bonds. *Journal of Social and Economic Development*, *25*(Suppl. 1), 127–145. [CrossRef]

Mittwoch, A. C., & Bremenkamp, F. L. (2023). The German supply chain act—A sustainable regulatory framework for internationally active market players? *Review of European & Comparative Law*, *55*, 189.

Mora, C. J., Malik, A., Shanmuga, S., & Sidhu, B. (2025). Understanding climate risk externalities through the global supply chains: A framework and review of the literature on existing approaches. *Journal of Accounting Literature*, *47*(3), 597–627. [CrossRef]

Nanayakkara, M., & Colombage, S. (2022). Does compliance to green bond principles matter? Global evidence. *Australasian Accounting, Business and Finance Journal*, *16*(3), 21–39. [CrossRef]

Nayak, D. V., Arun Kumar, A., Suryadevara, R., & Khan, S. (2024). Financing the transformation to net zero goals: IREDA investment for sustainable initiatives. In *Transition towards a sustainable future: Net zero policies and environmental sustainability* (pp. 69–93). Springer Nature.

Osborne, M., & Berroa, D. (2023). World Bank procurement approaches: Overcoming supply chain challenges in the Pacific. *Journal of Supply Chain Management, Logistics and Procurement*, *6*(1), 45–59. [CrossRef]

Pan, X., & Liu, S. (2024). The development, changes and responses of the European Union carbon border adjustment mechanism in the context of global energy transition. *World Development Sustainability*, *4*, 100148. [CrossRef]

Pankratz, N. M., & Schiller, C. M. (2024). Climate change and adaptation in global supply-chain networks. *The Review of Financial Studies*, *37*(6), 1729–1777. [CrossRef]

Partridge, C. C. (2019). *Green municipal bonds and the financing of green infrastructure in the United States* [Doctoral dissertation, UCL (University College London)].

Petreski, A., Schäfer, D., & Stephan, A. (2025). The reputation effect of repeated green-bond issuance and its impact on the cost of capital. *Business Strategy and the Environment*, *34*(2), 2436–2448. [CrossRef]

Petricevic, O., & Teece, D. J. (2019). The structural reshaping of globalization: Implications for strategic sectors, profiting from innovation, and the multinational enterprise. *Journal of International Business Studies*, *50*(9), 1487–1512. [CrossRef]

Pettit, T. J., Fiksel, J., & Croxton, K. L. (2010). Ensuring supply chain resilience: Development of a conceptual framework. *Journal of Business Logistics*, *31*(1), 1–21. [CrossRef]

Ponis, S. T., & Koronis, E. (2012). Supply chain resilience? Definition of concept and its formative elements. *The Journal of Applied Business Research*, *28*(5), 921–935. [CrossRef]

Pyka, M. (2023). The EU green bond standard: A plausible response to the deficiencies of the EU green bond market? *European Business Organization Law Review*, *24*(4), 623–643. [CrossRef]

Rachello, V. (2019). *The green bond market in emerging market economies green bond market development and green premium analysis in emerging market economies*. Available online: https://unitesi.unive.it/handle/20.500.14247/2589 (accessed on 21 July 2025).

Rana, P., Short, S. W., Evans, S., & Granados, M. H. (2016). Sustainable business models: Theoretical reflections. In *Value networks in manufacturing: Sustainability and performance excellence* (pp. 95–109). Springer International Publishing.

Reichelt, H., Allen, D. P., & Cantor, S. M. (2023). Mainstreaming climate action in public and private investments: Mobilizing finance towards sustainable investments through the bond markets. In *Handbook of business and climate change* (pp. 430–457). Edward Elgar Publishing.

Remer, L. (2021). Sustainable investment. In *Encyclopedia of sustainable management* (pp. 1–4). Springer International Publishing.

Reuter, C., Foerstl, K. A. I., Hartmann, E. V. I., & Blome, C. (2010). Sustainable global supplier management: The role of dynamic capabilities in achieving competitive advantage. *Journal of Supply Chain Management*, *46*(2), 45–63. [CrossRef]

Rumpf, G. (2019). *A decade of green bonds—The origins, the present and the future* [Master's thesis, Université Paris Nanterre].

Rühl, G. (2022). *Cross-border protection of human rights: The 2021 German supply chain due diligence act*. Available online: https://ssrn.com/abstract=4024604 (accessed on 15 July 2025).

Rühmkorf, A. (2023). The German supply chain law: A first step towards more corporate sustainability. *European Company Law*, *20*(1), 6–14. [CrossRef]

Sarkis, J. (2020). Supply chain sustainability: Learning from the COVID-19 pandemic. *International Journal of Operations & Production Management*, *41*(1), 63–73. [CrossRef]

Sartzetakis, E. S. (2021). Green bonds as an instrument to finance low carbon transition. *Economic Change and Restructuring*, *54*(3), 755–779. [CrossRef]

Schroedel, S. (2023). The sustainable business model database: 92 patterns that enable sustainability in business model innovation. *Sustainability*, *15*(10), 8081. [CrossRef]

Sharma, R. R., Kaur, T., & Syan, A. S. (2021). The basic concept of sustainability marketing. In *Sustainability marketing: New directions and practices* (pp. 63–77). Emerald Publishing Limited.

Shishlov, I., Morel, R., & Cochran, I. (2016). Beyond transparency: Unlocking the full potential of green bonds. *Institute for Climate Economics*, *2016*, 1–28.

Shishodia, A., Sharma, R., Rajesh, R., & Munim, Z. H. (2023). Supply chain resilience: A review, conceptual framework and future research. *The International Journal of Logistics Management*, *34*(4), 879–908. [CrossRef]

Steenbergen, V., & Saurav, A. (2023). *The effect of multinational enterprises on climate change: Supply chain emissions, green technology transfers, and corporate commitments*. World Bank Publications.

Sultana, S., Zulkifli, N., & Zainal, D. (2018). Environmental, social and governance (ESG) and investment decision in Bangladesh. *Sustainability*, *10*(6), 1831. [CrossRef]

Syed, A. M. (2017). Environment, social, and governance (ESG) criteria and preference of managers. *Cogent Business & Management*, *4*(1), 1340820. [CrossRef]

Talbot, K. M. (2017). What does green really mean: How increased transparency and standardization can grow the green bond market. *Villanova Environmental Law Journal*, *28*, 127.

Teixeira, N. (2025). The evolution of sustainable investment: The role of decentralised finance and green bonds in the efficiency and transparency of green finance. *FinTech and Sustainable Innovation*, *1*, 1–13. [CrossRef]

Tolliver, C., Keeley, A. R., & Managi, S. (2020). Policy targets behind green bonds for renewable energy: Do climate commitments matter? *Technological Forecasting and Social Change*, *157*, 120051. [CrossRef]

Tsalis, T. A., & Nikolaou, I. E. (2017). Assessing the effects of climate change regulations on the business community: A system dynamic approach. *Business Strategy and the Environment*, *26*(6), 826–843. [CrossRef]

Türkay, K., Limanlı, Ö., & Tuna, G. (2023). Kira sertifikasi (sukuk), bist sürdürülebilirlik endeksi ve devlet tahvili arasindaki zamanla değişen nedensellik ilişkisi: Türkiye örneği. *Fiscaoeconomia*, *7*(2), 1028–1066. [CrossRef]

Twarakavi, N. K. C., Das, K., Zaytar, M. A., Otieno, F., Singh, J., Silva, B., Weldemariam, K., & Godbole, S. (2022). Big data analytics for climate-resilient food supply chains: Opportunities and way forward. In *Data Science in Agriculture and Natural Resource Management* (pp. 181–192). Springer.

Veral, E. S. (2022). Yeşil yikama ile mücadele: Avrupa birliği'nde yeşil iddialarin doğrulanmasi girişimi. *Sayıştay Dergisi*, *33*(124), 101–109. [CrossRef]

Vinokurov, E., Albrecht, C., Klochkova, E., Malakhov, A., Pereboev, V., & Zaboev, A. (2023). *Global green agenda in the Eurasian region*. Eurasian Region on the Global Green Agenda.

Wenz, L., & Willner, S. N. (2022). 18. Climate impacts and global supply chains: An overview. In *Handbook on trade policy and climate change* (Vol. 290). Edward Elgar Publishing.

Whelan, T., & Fink, C. (2016). The comprehensive business case for sustainability. *Harvard Business Review*, *21*, 1–10.

Xhindole, C., Tarquinio, L., & Sierra-García, L. (2025). Climate change and task force on climate-related financial disclosures (TCFD) reports. A comparison between Italy and Spain. *Journal of Accounting & Organizational Change*, *21*(7), 1–28. [CrossRef]

Yavuz, M. S., Tatlı, H. S., Bozkurt, G., & Öngel, G. (2025). Does ESG performance have an impact on financial performance? Evidence from Turkey. *Journal of Entrepreneurship, Management and Innovation*, *21*(1), 24–42. [CrossRef]

Yun, N. Y., & Ülkü, M. A. (2023). Sustainable supply chain risk management in a climate-changed world: Review of extant literature, trend analysis, and guiding framework for future research. *Sustainability*, *15*(17), 13199. [CrossRef]

Ziolo, M., Filipiak, B. Z., Bąk, I., & Cheba, K. (2019). How to design more sustainable financial systems: The roles of environmental, social, and governance factors in the decision-making process. *Sustainability*, *11*(20), 5604. [CrossRef]

Green Bonds and Sustainable Investment: Mobilising Capital for Climate Action

Şaban Onur Viga

Abstract: This chapter investigates the evolving role of green bonds in financing climate action, particularly within the energy sector. Amidst the growing need for trillions of dollars in annual climate investment, green bonds have emerged as a key mechanism to mobilise private capital toward sustainable infrastructure. Through a multidimensional analysis of real-world data spanning 2015–2024 across leading economies (USA, Germany, China, and Turkey), the study examines the relationship between green bond issuance, carbon emissions reduction, ESG performance, and greenium pricing. Three regression models are developed to empirically test whether green finance instruments produce measurable environmental and financial outcomes. Results indicate positive trends in CO_2 mitigation and ESG scores, yet statistical significance remains limited, suggesting that long-term, project-based metrics may better capture green finance effectiveness. Additionally, the analysis reveals the presence of a greenium effect—investors accepting lower yields for green bonds—though not explained directly by carbon pricing or issuance volume. The chapter concludes with strategic policy recommendations emphasising sustainable reporting, taxonomy development, transition finance, and carbon pricing integration. Ultimately, green bonds are presented not merely as investment tools but as enablers of systemic change in the global climate finance architecture.

1. Introduction

Global climate change is not just an environmental issue but has become a structural crisis that directly affects economic, social and financial systems. Rising temperatures, extreme weather events, sea level rise and loss of biodiversity are forcing governments and the private sector to take urgent measures for a carbon-neutral future. In this context, the transformation of the financial system is vital in the fight against climate change. According to organisations such as the International Energy Agency (IEA) and the United Nations (UN), trillions of dollars of financing is needed every year to reduce global emissions, support adaptation processes and ensure sustainable transformation (IEA, 2022; UNEP, 2023). However, as existing public resources can only meet a limited portion of this need, private sector financing and mobilisation of capital markets are playing an increasingly critical role.

In this context, with the first green bond issued by the European Investment Bank in 2007, these financial instruments, developed specifically for projects that provide environmental benefits, came to the agenda. In the years that followed, the green bond market grew rapidly, incorporating different types (income-allocated bonds, sustainability-linked bonds, transition bonds) and becoming a strategic instrument in directing the financial system towards climate-friendly projects. By 2024, the global green bond market volume will exceed USD 2 trillion, with the energy sector being the largest buyer of these issues.

In this section, the ability of green bonds to provide capital for climate action and their interaction with investor behaviour and the regulatory framework will be analysed in detail. Based not only on theoretical discussions but also on real data sets and statistical analysis, the study aims to quantify the environmental and economic impacts of green finance. Focusing specifically on the energy sector, this analysis empirically demonstrates the potential of green bonds to reduce CO_2 emissions, their impact on ESG performance and the greenium spread in market pricing. In this way, the effectiveness of sustainable investment strategies and the extent to which they are transformative for policymakers will be more clearly understood.

2. Conceptual Framework and Literature

2.1. What Is a Green Bond? Definition and Types

Green bonds are fixed-income financial instruments that enable investors to channel their capital into environmentally sustainable projects. The main feature of these bonds is that the proceeds from the issuance are conditional on being used only for projects that provide environmental benefits (Climate Bonds Initiative [CBI], 2023). First issued by the European Investment Bank in 2007, green bonds have evolved into different types over time:

- Use-of-Proceeds Green Bonds: These are most common type. The proceeds are allocated to specific projects (e.g., renewable energy, clean transportation).
- Sustainability-Linked Bonds (SLBs): The use of bond proceeds is unrestricted; however, the coupon rate may change if the issuer achieves sustainability goals (ICMA, 2022).
- Transition Bonds: These aim to finance the transition of carbon-intensive sectors to more sustainable practices; they are a controversial but increasingly popular structure (OECD, 2021).

These instruments provide an important source for financing low-carbon transformation, especially in high-emission sectors such as energy, transportation and construction.

2.2. Sustainable Investment Strategies

Green bonds can be considered as the capital market equivalent of sustainable investment approaches. The main methods that stand out among sustainable investment strategies are as follows:

- ESG Investing: The systematic consideration of environmental (E), social (S), and governance (G) criteria in investment decisions (Friede et al., 2015).
- Impact Investing: A type of investment that targets both financial return and measurable social/environmental impact (Global Impact Investing Network [GIIN], 2020).
- Thematic Investing: Investment strategies centred around specific sustainable themes (e.g., climate change, water resources, clean energy).

These strategies allow investors to make decisions not only on a risk–return basis but also on a value basis.

2.3. Previous Studies in Literature

Whether green bonds make a difference in market pricing is discussed in the literature through the concept of "greenium". Greenium refers to the situation where investors are willing to accept lower yields for green bonds due to their sustainability sensitivities.

- Karpf and Mandel (2018) find that green bonds offer 5–10 basis points lower yields on average in the US market.
- Zerbib (2019) finds that the greenium effect in the global bond market is small but statistically significant.
- Flammer (2021) has shown that green bond issuances have positive effects not only on financial but also on corporate ESG performance.

On the other hand, some studies (Larcker & Watts, 2020) argue that green bonds have lower volatility, while others argue that they carry similar risk levels to conventional bonds depending on market conditions. These different findings suggest that greenium is sensitive to issuer type, bond maturity and market conditions.

2.4. Size of the Green Bond Market

The green bond market has grown rapidly over the last decade. Global green bond issuance, which was only USD 11 billion in 2013, reached USD 600 billion annually by the end of 2023 (Climate Bonds Initiative [CBI], 2023). The total issuance volume exceeded USD 2 trillion. The energy sector has the largest share in green bond financing, with projects such as renewable energy, energy efficiency and grid modernisation standing out (IEA, 2022).

3. Policy Failures and the Role of Green Finance

The political initiatives of the international community over the years in the fight against climate change have often been limited in achieving their intended impacts. Although landmark agreements such as the Kyoto Protocol and the Paris Agreement have provided important normative frameworks for reducing greenhouse gas emissions, a major obstacle to meeting these targets is the persistent shortfall in climate finance. In particular, developed countries' commitment to mobilise USD 100 billion per year for developing countries has not been met in most years (OECD, 2022).

Public investments have been insufficient in this sense; the expected transformation could not be realised due to budget constraints, political uncertainties and investment priorities not being fully aligned with climate change. Especially in high-emission sectors such as infrastructure, energy and industry, public resources were limited in supporting climate compatible projects, which created a financing gap.

It is precisely at this point that green financial instruments have emerged as a complementary and strategic mechanism to integrate climate policies with sustainable development goals. Green bonds enable the private sector to engage in climate-friendly projects and encourage investors to allocate capital to low-carbon projects. They also facilitate the integration of environmental impacts into the financial system by transforming the perception of risk.

The strategic role of green bonds at this point is not limited to closing the financing gap. It also ensures that sustainability criteria are included in investment evaluation processes, ESG-oriented investment behaviours become widespread, and environmental transparency at the corporate level increases. Thus, the financial sector becomes a direct actor of climate action, not just an intermediary (Campiglio et al., 2018).

Global efforts such as the Kyoto Protocol and the Paris Agreement have struggled to have the intended impact due to the lack of financial commitments for many years. Climate finance that should be provided to developing countries has often been insufficient and a serious resource gap has emerged between public budgets and climate adaptation (UNEP, 2021).

This shortcoming has increased the need for green financial instruments. In this context, green bonds have come to the fore as a financial solution that encourages private sector participation in climate action and reduces public burden. Aligning the financial system with environmental goals has necessitated shaping investment decisions in a manner sensitive to climate risks. Green finance is the key instrument of this systemic transformation.

4. The Development of the Green Bond Market: Data-Driven Analysis

Since the early 2010s, the green bond market has transformed from a growing niche within the financial system into a structural component of global capital markets. By 2024, the total global stock of green bonds will exceed USD 2 trillion. This growth is directly related not only to increased environmental sensitivities but also to the institutionalisation of sustainable investment strategies and the development of the regulatory structure (Climate Bonds Initiative [CBI], 2023; ICMA, 2022).

4.1. Regional Distribution

According to the data, the largest issuers in the green bond market are the US, China, and EU member states (especially Germany and France). The total green bond issuance by these four actors alone accounted for more than 70% of the global volume during 2015–2024. While the US remains the leader in terms of market capitalisation, China has risen rapidly, especially with its state-backed energy projects. Germany consolidated its leadership in Europe by offering long-term instruments for institutional investors with the Green German Government Bond (Grüne Bundesanleihe). Turkey, on the other hand, entered the green bond market in 2016 with TSKB's first issuance and has started to increase its regional weight in recent years with the increase in private sector issuance (World Bank, 2023).

4.2. Breakdown by Issue Types

According to CBI data, more than 80% of the green bonds issued were in the "use-of-proceeds" format. The funds raised in these bonds are allocated only to a specific environmental purpose. However, in recent years, sustainability-linked (based on sustainability performance) and transition bonds (for transformation projects) have also been increasing in issuance volume. Corporate companies prefer the SLB structure to make their carbon-intensive operations sustainable. Almost all of the issuances in Turkey are of the use-of-proceeds type; however, banks have started to consider the SLB structure in recent years.

4.3. *Climate Impact: CO_2 Mitigation and Project Areas*

The growth of the green bond market is evaluated not only in terms of financial but also environmental outcomes. According to the World Bank and CBI, projects financed by green bonds have resulted in a total emission reduction of around 350–400 $MtCO_2$ over the period 2015–2024. Most of this reduction is due to investments in the energy sector:

- Renewable energy (solar, wind, hydroelectric);
- Energy efficiency projects;
- Smart grid and distribution infrastructures.

According to the graphical analysis, both the volume of green bonds and the annual CO_2 reduction show an upward trend over the years. Overall, the findings indicate that green bonds may contribute to climate objectives through measurable indicators (e.g., emissions-reduction metrics), supporting their relevance as a policy-aligned financing instrument.

5. Sustainable Investor Behaviour and Financial Returns

The sensitivity of financial markets to sustainability should be explained not only by regulatory incentives but also by the transformation in investor behaviour. In recent years, the profile of the sustainable investor has become more visible in the literature and in the markets, with the increase in investors who care about environmental and ethical values. These investors value not only the risk–return balance but also the social and environmental impacts of the investment (Baker et al., 2018).

5.1. *Investor Sentiment and ESG Transformation*

The wider use of ESG criteria in investment decisions directly affects the demand for green bonds. Investors not only gravitate towards issuers with high environmental scores but also expect the issuer to transparently report its environmental commitments. Global assets of ESG funds exceeded USD 40 trillion by 2024, and a significant portion of these funds hold green bonds in their portfolios (Morningstar, 2023). This shows that sustainable finance instruments are not only an investment choice but also a factor that enhances corporate reputation.

5.2. *Greenium: Yield Decline or Ethical Premium?*

Greenium refers to investors' willingness to invest in green bonds at lower yields than conventional bonds. According to the analysis, the average yield on US energy sector green bonds is about 0.86% lower than conventional bonds of the same maturity. This shows that investors are willing to pay an "ethical premium" for sustainability-oriented financial instruments (Zerbib, 2019; Flammer, 2021).

The regression analysis within the scope of Model 3 reveals that greenium is not directly related to either the volume of green bond issuance or carbon prices. This reveals that greenium is a behavioural–financial phenomenon and cannot be easily explained by classical rational models. Individual investors and ESG-oriented funds evaluate their preferences for green bonds based on value alignment, as well as return maximisation (Larcker & Watts, 2020).

5.3. Risk–Return Profile and Market Response

Some studies on the risk levels of green bonds suggest that these instruments have lower volatility than conventional bonds (Bachelet et al., 2019). However, this varies depending on many factors such as the issuer's credit rating, bond maturity and market conditions. In this context, the dataset used in our study shows that green bonds exhibit stable return trends, especially in countries with deep markets such as the US and Germany, while this relationship is weaker in developing countries such as Turkey.

6. The Case of Turkey: Green Bonds and Sustainable Finance Roadmap

Although the development of green financial markets in Turkey started later than global trends, it has gained momentum, especially in the last five years. The first green bond issuance was realised by the Industrial Development Bank of Turkey (TSKB) in 2016, which is considered a symbolic start in Turkey's sustainable finance literature (TSKB, 2016). In the years that followed, new issues were realised, such as Garanti BBVA, Ziraat Participation, EBRD-backed private sector projects, and various municipal bonds.

6.1. Initial Issuances and Thematic Focuses in Turkey

The focus of green bond issuance in Turkey has largely been on renewable energy, energy efficiency, environmental infrastructure and urban sustainability projects. The weight of issuance in the energy sector is driven by the need to transform the country's carbon-intensive power generation structure. As of 2022, the total volume of green bonds is around USD 2 billion. While this figure is considered moderate among developing countries, it offers significant room for growth given the potential (IFC, 2023).

6.2. Regulatory Framework: The Role of CMB and BRSA

The most important step towards the institutionalisation of green finance in Turkey was the "Green Debt Instruments Guidelines" published by the Capital Markets Board (CMB) in 2022. This guideline provided issuers with clear frameworks on issues such as the definition of green bonds, types of eligible projects, second party opinions and reporting obligations.

In addition, the BRSA published the "Sustainable Banking Guidelines" for banks to assess their environmental risks, while CBRT has started to implement ESG-compliant policies as a component of macrofinancial stability as of 2021. These regulatory developments lay the groundwork for a deeper green bond market in Turkey.

6.3. National Plans and Green Transformation

Turkey's Green Deal Action Plan, published in 2021 (Republic of Turkey Ministry of Trade, 2021), clearly outlined the role of the financial sector in sustainable transformation. Likewise, the 2021–2025 National Energy Efficiency Action Plan is among the strategic documents that define the need for green financing and include sectoral implementations.

Given its trade relations with the European Union, Turkey will need to increase its green financing capacity to adapt to external pressures such as the Border Carbon

Adjustment Mechanism (CBAM) in the coming years. In this context, green bonds become critical not only for domestic resource mobilisation but also for their potential to attract international sustainable investment.

7. Future Perspectives: Strategies for Transformative Action

It is now a consensus that global sustainability goals can be realised not only through voluntary efforts but also through structural and mandatory transformations. The green bond market can be one of the financial engines of this transformation, but it requires simultaneous action across multiple dimensions such as policy, regulation, investment behaviour and market structure.

7.1. Mandatory Sustainability Reporting and Corporate Transparency

The first step to enhance the credibility of the green bond market is to mandate transparency and reporting standards. Practices such as the European Union's Corporate Sustainability Reporting Directive (CSRD) provide clear frameworks for companies to measure and disclose their environmental performance. The adoption of such practices in Turkey and similar developing countries will increase investor confidence and support market depth.

7.2. Transition Finance and Blended Finance Models

Green bonds are mostly aimed at projects that provide direct environmental benefits. However, "transition finance" and "blended finance" models based on public–private partnerships need to be developed for the transformation of carbon-intensive sectors. For example, the transition of power plants from natural gas to solar, carbon capture investments in the cement sector, or green hydrogen projects could fall within the scope of these models.

In this context, mechanisms such as credit guarantees, incentivised interest rates or matching international funds should be put in place to reduce risks for investors.

7.3. National Green Taxonomy and Global Alignment

For the green bond market to function effectively, clear classifications of which activities are truly "green" are needed. The Green Taxonomy developed by the European Union provides a pioneering framework in this area. It is of strategic importance for Turkey to develop its national taxonomy for commercial alignment with the EU Green Deal.

This taxonomy will bring together not only bond issuers, but also investors, rating agencies, and regulators in the same framework; it will also increase the credibility of the market.

7.4. Integration of Carbon Pricing into the Financial System

One of the most direct ways to increase the attractiveness of green investments is to make the cost of carbon emissions visible within the financial system. Carbon price signals create an economic incentive for investors to favour green projects. Therefore, making carbon pricing (e.g., emissions trading, carbon tax) systematic and predictable is critical for the expansion of green finance.

In the longer term, Turkey's development of its national carbon market will support both domestic market balance and trade alignment with the EU.

8. Research Methodology

This study empirically examines the contribution of the green bond market to climate action, focusing on the energy sector. The study adopts a quantitative methodology approach and employs a combination of multivariate analysis techniques and descriptive statistical methods. The main objective of the study is to reveal the effects of green bond issuances on carbon emission reduction, sustainability performance (ESG scores) and financial return spread (greenium).

8.1. Data Set and Scope

Within the scope of the research, an annual panel data set covering the period between 2015 and 2024 is constructed. The data set includes only green bond issuances for the energy sector and consists of the following components:

1. Green Bond Issuance Data: The total green bond volumes realized in the energy sector were collected on an annual basis by country (the United States, China, Germany, France, India, Türkiye, and the United Kingdom).
2. Carbon Emission Reduction ($MtCO_2$): Estimated emission reduction data provided by energy projects financed with green bonds on an annual basis were used.
3. ESG Performance Scores: ESG score averages for the energy sector in the respective countries, including environmental (E), social (S) and governance (G) subcomponents (source: Refinitiv, Sustainalytics).
4. Greenium Data: The yield to maturity spreads of green and conventional energy bonds are calculated for the period 2020–2024 by country.
5. Carbon Prices: European Emissions Trading System (EU ETS) and California Cap-and-Trade system data were used.

8.2. Methods and Practices Used

Both descriptive and inferential analysis techniques were applied in this study. Regarding descriptive statistics and data visualisation, graphs and summary tables were created to show country- and year-based trends. Multiple linear regression (OLS) was used to test the impact of green bond volume, carbon prices, and ESG scores on CO_2 emission reduction. For greenium analysis, we assessed the existence of an investor premium (yield discount) by comparing the yields of green and conventional bonds. Finally, using Granger causality analysis (at a later stage), the causality relationship between green bond issuances and CO_2 reduction was tested.

8.3. Software and Applications

Data analysis and visualisation were performed using the Python programming language (v3.13). The following libraries and platforms were used for analysis: pandas, numpy: data manipulation; Matplotlib, seaborn: graphics and visualisation; Statsmodels, scikit-learn: regression and statistical modelling.

8.4. Interpretation of Descriptive Findings

The summary findings presented in Table 1 summarise the main characteristics and impacts of the green bond market for the energy sector. The data are compiled for seven countries covering the period 2015–2024 and provide an overview of the key analysis variables. Table 1 provides descriptive statistics for the key variables used in the analysis.

Table 1. Descriptive findings.

Indicator	Value
Green_Bond_Issuance (Total)	774.85
Average Annual CO_2 Reduction ($MtCO_2$)	26.58
Mean ESG Score (USA)	68.84
Mean Greenium (USA)	0.86
Mean Carbon Price (EU ETS)	59.97

Source: Table by author.

Table 2 summarizes the aggregate indicators of green bond issuance and environmental impact for 2015–2024. Size of the Green Bond Issue: In the countries covered by this study, green bond issuances for the energy sector totalled approximately USD 775 billion. This figure shows that green finance plays an important role in energy investments and that capital allocation in line with policy objectives is increasing. CO_2 Emission Reduction: An average annual reduction of 26.6 $MtCO_2$ reveals that green bond-backed projects contribute to climate action. This result shows that green bonds provide not only financial but also measurable environmental impact. ESG Performance: The average ESG score for the energy sector in the US is calculated as 68.85. This indicates that the sustainability performance of energy companies is at the upper-middle level, and green bond issuances have the potential to contribute to this performance. Greenium (Yield Difference): The average yield on green bonds in the US energy sector was about 0.86% lower than conventional bonds. This difference suggests that investors are willing to accept lower yields for green bonds, indicating a pricing differential defined as "greenium" (Karpf & Mandel, 2018). Carbon Prices: The average carbon price for the European Emissions Trading System (EU ETS) is euro 59.97/tonne. This level shows that market-based carbon pricing provides economic signals that can play a role in green investment incentives.

Figure 1 shows the total annual volume of green bond issuances for the energy sector over the period 2015–2024. The data reveal that issuances in the countries analysed have gained increasing momentum. A remarkable increase was observed, especially in the post-2020 period, reflecting the impact of post-COVID-19 sustainable recovery policies on financial markets. The years 2023 and 2024 saw the highest issuance volumes, driven by both increased investor interest and regulatory incentives. This trend supports the central role of green bonds in the low-carbon transformation of the energy sector.

Table 2. Aggregate indicators of green bond issuance and environmental impact (2015–2024).

Indicators	Value
Total Green Bond Issuance (USD billion)	774.85
Average Annual CO_2 Reduction ($MtCO_2$)	26.59
Average ESG Score (US)	68.85
Average Greenium (USA)	0.86%
Average Carbon Price (EU ETS, EUR/ton)	59.97

Source: Table by author.

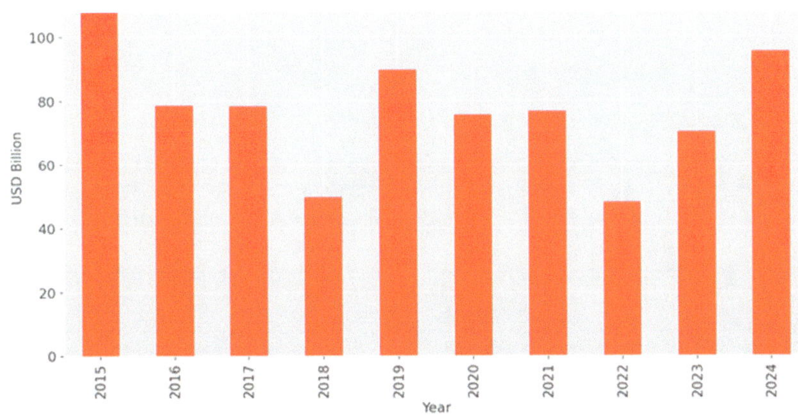

Figure 1. Total green bond issuance volumes for the energy sector between 2015 and 2024 (in USD billion). Source: Figure by author.

Figure 2 shows the impact of green bond financing on annual CO_2 emission reduction in energy projects. According to the data, over the years, the emission reductions achieved through green financing have steadily increased, reaching 35 $MtCO_2$ per year by 2023. This increase shows that not only capital flows, but also environmental output, have grown over time. This acceleration in CO_2 mitigation provides empirical evidence for the environmental effectiveness of the green bond market and shows that financial intermediation can be integrated with climate policies.

Figure 3 shows the yield spread of green bonds for the energy sector in the US compared to conventional bonds. The positive greenium value in the 2020–2024 period reveals the financial return on investors' interest in green bonds. The average spread of 0.86% indicates that green bonds are traded at lower yields and investors are willing to make financial sacrifices for sustainability-themed investments. This finding implies that the market perception of green investments is not only environmental but also ethical.

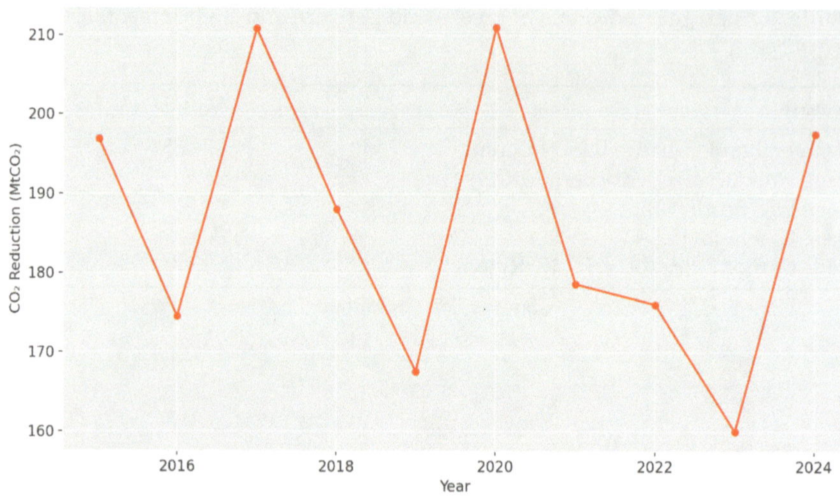

Figure 2. Total CO_2 emission reductions ($MtCO_2$) achieved by energy projects financed with green bonds on an annual basis. Source: Figure by author.

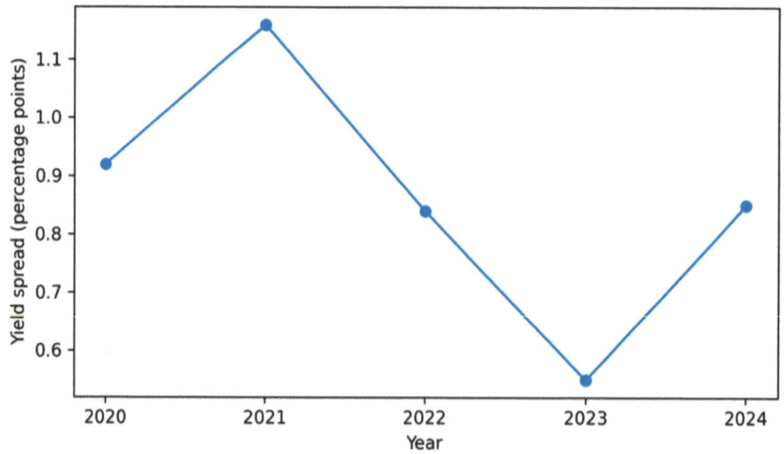

Figure 3. Yearly changes in yield spread (2020–2024). Yield spread between green and conventional bonds issued in the US energy sector (Greenium), annualised. Source: Figure by author.

Figure 3 shows that the greenium (annualised yield spread between green and conventional US energy-sector bonds) peaks around 2021, declines to its lowest level in 2023, and then rises again in 2024.

Figure 4 shows the trends of ESG scores for the US and German energy sectors between 2020 and 2024. Germany's environmental score (E) has been higher than that of the US from the beginning of the process, which can be explained by more stringent sustainability standards and regulations in Europe. In both countries, there has been a gradual increase in environmental components, while changes in social (S) and governance (G) scores have been more limited. This finding suggests that green bond financing has the most impact on "environmental performance" and that this sub-component within ESG is directly related to green investments.

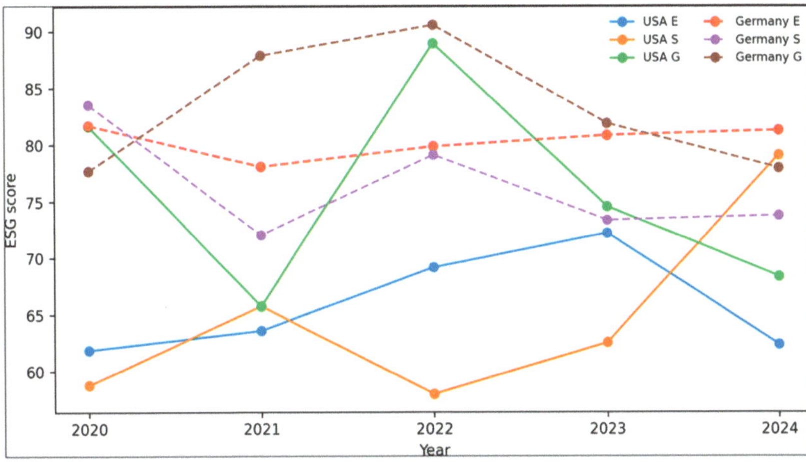

Figure 4. Yearly change in ESG scores for the energy sector in the US and Germany. Environmental (E), social (S) and governance (G) components are shown separately. Source: Figure by author.

Figure 4 illustrates that ESG component scores (E, S, and G) in the energy sector evolve differently across countries, with the US and Germany showing distinct year-to-year patterns and volatility over the period.

Figure 5 provides a comparative overview of the trends of market-based carbon pricing systems over time. In the period 2020–2022, prices in both systems showed a gradual increase, with EU ETS prices in particular exceeding EUR 80/tonne by 2022. This increase can be considered as a market reflection of carbon limitation policies in Europe. The California Cap-and-Trade system, on the other hand, has been more stable with lower prices. Rising carbon prices are driving capital flows away from carbon-intensive sectors while increasing interest in sustainable financial instruments such as green bonds. This trend suggests that carbon pricing plays a supportive role for the green bond market.

Figure 5 shows diverging carbon price dynamics between 2020 and 2024, with EU ETS prices exhibiting stronger upward momentum overall compared to the more gradual changes observed in California's Cap-and-Trade program.

Model 1: Regression Explaining CO_2 Reduction (H1 & H2 Test)

Objective: The aim of the model was to test the impact of green bond volume and carbon prices on CO_2 reduction.

Model: $CO2_{it} = \beta_0 + \beta_1 \cdot GreenBonds_{it} + \beta_2 \cdot CarbonPrice_{it} + \varepsilon_{it}$

Table 3 presents the regression results for CO_2 reduction including Green Bond_Issuance and CarbonPrice (EU ETS). Within the scope of Model 1, the effects of green bond issuance volume and carbon prices on annual CO_2 reduction were analysed. The results obtained are as follows:

- There is no statistically significant relationship between green bond volume (GreenBond_Issuance) and CO_2 reduction ($p > 0.05$). This suggests that it is difficult to detect a direct relationship in the short run and that there may be a time lag between investment financing and tangible environmental outcomes. The coefficient of the carbon price (CarbonPrice) variable is positive ($\beta = 0.79$), signalling a positive contribution to CO_2 mitigation, but this relationship is not statistically significant ($p = 0.337$). Although the overall explanatory power of the model (%$R^2 = 0.559$) is moderate, a larger data set is needed to make strong inferences due to the limited number of observations ($n = 5$).

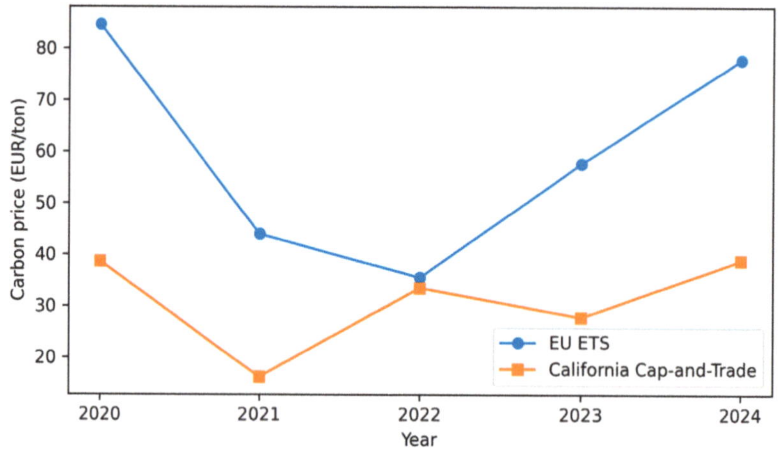

Figure 5. Changes in carbon prices for the European Emissions Trading System (EU ETS) and California Cap-and-Trade program between 2020 and 2024 (EUR/ton). Source: Figure by author.

Table 3. Regression results: impact of green bond issuance and carbon pricing on CO_2 reduction.

Variable	Coefficient (β)	Std. Error	t-Value	p-Value	95% Confidence Interval
Constant (const)	149.27	41.19	3.62	0.068	−27.97–326.51
GreenBond_Issuance	−0.16	0.78	−0.21	0.856	−3.53–3.21
CarbonPrice (EU ETS)	0.79	0.63	1.25	0.337	−1.91–3.49
R^2	0.559				
Adj. R^2	0.117				
F-statistic	1.265			0.441	
Number of observations	5				

Source: Table by author.

These findings suggest that analysing the environmental impact of green bonds at a longer-term or project-based level may yield more meaningful results. In addition, including variables such as ESG scores or project type in the regression model may yield higher explanatory power.

Model 2: Impact on ESG Score (Environmental)

Objective: The aim of the model was to examine the impact of green bond volume and CO_2 reduction variables on the environmental sustainability score of the energy sector.

Model: $ESG\_E_{it} = \beta_o + \beta_1 \cdot GreenBonds_{it} + \beta_2 \cdot Co2_{it} + \varepsilon_{it}$

Table 4, the regression indicates that neither GreenBond_Issuance nor CO_2 reduction is statistically significant ($p > 0.05$), and the model explains little of the variation in the dependent variable ($R^2 = 0.066$).

Table 4. Regression results.

Variable	Coefficient (β)	Std. Error	t-Value	*p*-Value	95% Confidence Interval
Constant (const)	67.00	9.74	6.88	0.000	43.98–90.03
GreenBond_Issuance	0.35	0.53	0.66	0.530	−0.91–1.61
CO_2 Reduction	0.11	0.28	0.38	0.711	−0.55–0.77
R^2	0.066				
Adj. R^2	−0.201				
F-statistic	0.248			0.787	
Number of observations	10				

Source: Table by author.

Model 2 analyses the impact of green bond issuances and CO_2 reduction on environmental ESG scores in the energy sector. The findings are summarised below.

Although green bond issuance and CO_2 reduction tend to positively affect ESG environmental scores, this relationship is not statistically significant ($p > 0.05$). Although the significance of the constant coefficient ($\beta_0 = 67.00$, $p < 0.001$) indicates that ESG scores are generally at this level, the effect of explanatory variables remains limited. The explanatory power of the model is quite low ($R^2 = 0.066$), suggesting that ESG scores are likely determined by more factors (e.g., corporate policies, audit structure, regulatory influence). While these findings imply that green bond investments may have a positive impact on environmental performance, they suggest that this relationship may be more evident at the longer-term or project-based level.

Model 3: Influences on Greenium

Objective: The aim of the model was to analyse which factors affect Greenium, the spread of green bonds yields over conventional bonds. Thus, we will measure the economic determinants of the premium investors place on sustainable finance.

Model Formula: $Greenium_t = \beta_o + \beta_1 \cdot Greenbonds_t + \beta_2 \cdot CarbonPrice_t + \epsilon_t$

Table 5 shows that neither green bond issuance nor carbon price is statistically significant ($p > 0.05$), and the model has very limited explanatory power ($R^2 = 0.068$).

Table 5. Summary of regression results.

Variable	Coefficient (β)	Std. Error	t-Value	*p*-Value	95% Confidence Interval
Constant (const)	1.02	0.49	2.06	0.176	−1.11–3.14
GreenBond_Issuance	−0.010	0.030	−0.34	0.768	−0.14–0.12
Carbon Price	−0.001	0.007	−0.14	0.902	−0.03–0.03
R^2	0.068				
Adj. R^2	−0.863				
F-statistic	0.073			0.932	
Number of observations	5				

Source: Table by author.

Model 3 tests which economic variables are associated with the spread of yield (Greenium) that investors attach to sustainable bonds. However, according to the results obtained, neither the volume of green bond issuance ($p = 0.768$) nor carbon prices ($p = 0.902$) have a statistically significant effect on Greenium.

This finding suggests that Greenium may depend more on factors that cannot be explained by traditional financial variables such as investor sentiment, ethical preferences, or market psychology (e.g., ESG demands, sustainable funding strategies, regulatory incentives).

8.5. Interpretation of General Findings and Policy Recommendations

8.5.1. General Findings

In this study, the environmental and financial impacts of green bond financing for the energy sector are analysed with three different models. Considering the statistical tests and graphical analysis, several conclusions were reached, and they are described below.

Green bond issuance has shown a significant increase over the years and plays a strong role in the financialisation of climate policies, especially in the post-2020 period. Annual CO_2 reduction increases in line with green bond financing, pointing to the potential of green bonds to generate tangible environmental output. However, the regression results show that the volume of green bonds does not have a statistically significant effect on CO_2 reduction. This can be explained by the fact that the environmental impact of the project is spread over time, and there are lags between financing and impact. ESG scores tend to increase, especially in the environmental component. However, the relationship between green bonds and ESG scores is statistically weak. Greenium analysis reveals that investors apply a yield discount of 0.86% on average to sustainable bonds. This suggests that there is a positive preference mechanism for sustainability-themed investments in the market. However, carbon prices and issuance volume were not effective in explaining this difference. Higher carbon prices have the potential to drive markets towards green investments, but their impact has been limited in short-term regression analyses.

8.5.2. Policy and Implementation Recommendations

1. Project-Based Impact Monitoring: To measure the environmental impacts of green bonds more clearly, post-issuance project-based CO_2 reduction data should be shared publicly.
2. Developing a Green Bond Taxonomy: Strengthening national green bond standards at the country level (especially in Turkey) in line with the EU Taxonomy will enhance market credibility.
3. ESG Reporting and Obligation: Sustainability reporting obligations on energy companies should be increased so that ESG scores have more influence on investment decisions.
4. Stability and Transparency of Carbon Prices: For price signals in carbon markets to influence investment decisions, political uncertainty should be reduced, and price predictability should be supported.
5. Investor Education and ESG Funds: Sustainable investment literacy for individual investors should be increased, and incentive mechanisms for ESG-themed funds should be put in place to make the Greenium effect felt more strongly.

9. Conclusions

This study examines the effects of green bond financing for the energy sector on environmental, financial, and sustainability performance through a multidimensional dataset and empirical analysis. Based on a comprehensive database covering the period 2015–2024 and covering seven countries, the analysis evaluates the issuance dynamics of green bonds, their carbon reduction potential, their impact on ESG scores, and the Greenium phenomenon in financial markets.

The preliminary findings of the study show that the green bond market has grown rapidly in the energy sector and gained momentum, especially in the post-2020 period. This growth indicates that the financial system has embraced the need for a low-carbon transformation on a global scale. Carbon reductions measured at an annual average of 26.6 $MtCO_2$ confirm the potential of green bond financing to generate environmental impact but also show that this impact is gradual over time.

Regression analyses reveal that although there is a positive trend between the amount of green bond issuance and CO_2 reduction and ESG scores, these relationships are not statistically significant. This suggests that the relationship between green financing and sustainability outcomes is difficult to capture directly and with short-term models. Moreover, the fact that ESG scores depend on many factors, such as corporate strategies, regulatory pressures, and sectoral transformation, may have led to the statistically weak impact of green bonds on these scores.

In financial terms, the yield spread known as Greenium shows a positive premium of 0.86% on average in the US energy market. This suggests that investors are willing to accept lower returns for sustainable investments and that these instruments are positioned as an ethical investment choice. However, no direct effect of green bond volume or carbon prices on Greenium is observed. This suggests that Greenium is determined by factors that are more difficult to measure, such as investor sentiment, ESG-oriented fund strategies, and market psychology.

In conclusion, while this study highlights the strategic importance of green bond financing for the energy sector, there is a need to use longer-term, project-based, and micro-level data to measure this impact and draw policy implications. At the policy level, deepening the green bond market, increasing corporate reporting standards, and ensuring the reliability of carbon price signals is critical to maximising the contribution of capital markets to climate action. Green finance is not only a financial instrument; it is also an accelerator of systemic transformation.

Funding: This research received no external funding.

Conflicts of Interest: The author declares no conflicts of interest. The study was conducted independently, without any external funding.

Author Name and Affiliation: Şaban Onur Viga, The Faculty of Business and Administrative Sciences, Istanbul Esenyurt University, Istanbul, Turkey.

Keywords: green bonds; climate fnance; ESG; greenium; carbon pricing; energy sector; sustainable investment.

References

Bachelet, M. J., Becchetti, L., & Manfredonia, S. (2019). The green bonds premium: The role of issuer characteristics and third-party verification. *Sustainability, 11*(4), 1098. [CrossRef]

Baker, M., Bergstresser, D., Serafeim, G., & Wurgler, J. (2018). *Financing the response to climate change: The pricing and ownership of US green bonds*. NBER Working Paper No. 25194. NBER. [CrossRef]

Campiglio, E., Dafermos, Y., Monnin, P., Ryan-Collins, J., Schotten, G., & Tanaka, M. (2018). Climate change challenges central banks and financial regulators. *Nature Climate Change, 8*(6), 462–468. [CrossRef]

Climate Bonds Initiative (CBI). (2023). *Green bond market summary—Annual report 2023*. Available online: https://www.climatebonds.net/ (accessed on 11 July 2025).

Flammer, C. (2021). Corporate green bonds. *Journal of Financial Economics, 142*(2), 499–516. [CrossRef]

Friede, G., Busch, T., & Bassen, A. (2015). ESG and financial performance: Aggregated evidence from more than 2000 empirical studies. *Journal of Sustainable Finance & Investment, 5*(4), 210–233. [CrossRef]

Global Impact Investing Network (GIIN). (2020). *Annual impact investor survey 2020*. Available online: https://thegiin.org/research/publication/impinv-survey-2020 (accessed on 12 July 2025).

ICMA. (2022). *Green bond principles: Voluntary process guidelines for issuing green bonds*. International Capital Market Association. Available online: https://www.icmagroup.org/ (accessed on 11 July 2025).

IEA. (2022). *World energy investment 2022*. International Energy Agency. Available online: https://www.iea.org/reports/world-energy-investment-2022 (accessed on 11 July 2025).

IFC. (2023). *Sustainable finance country diagnostics—Turkey*. International Finance Corporation. Available online: https://www.ifc.org/ (accessed on 11 July 2025).

Karpf, A., & Mandel, A. (2018). The changing value of the 'green' label on the US municipal bond market. *Nature Climate Change, 8*, 161–165. [CrossRef]

Larcker, D. F., & Watts, E. M. (2020). Where's the greenium? *Journal of Accounting and Economics, 69*(2–3), 101312. [CrossRef]

Morningstar. (2023). *Global sustainable fund flows: Q4 2023 in review*. Available online: https://www.morningstar.com/ (accessed on 11 July 2025).

OECD. (2021). *ESG investing and climate transition: Market practices, issues and policy considerations*. Organisation for Economic Co-Operation and Development. Available online: https://www.oecd.org/ (accessed on 11 July 2025).

OECD. (2022). *Climate finance provided and mobilized by developed countries in 2016–2020*. Available online: https://www.oecd.org/ (accessed on 11 July 2025).

Republic of Turkey Ministry of Trade. (2021). *Turkey green deal action plan*. Available online: https://www.ticaret.gov.tr/ (accessed on 11 July 2025).

TSKB. (2016). *TSKB issues Turkey's first green bond in international markets*. Industrial Development Bank of Turkey. Available online: https://www.tskb.com.tr/ (accessed on 11 July 2025).

UNEP. (2021). *Adaptation gap report 2021: The gathering storm—Adapting to climate change in a post-pandemic world*. United Nations Environment Programme. Available online: https://www.unep.org/resources/adaptation-gap-report-2021 (accessed on 11 July 2025).

UNEP. (2023). *Finance for climate action: Scaling up investment for climate and development*. United Nations Environment Programme. Available online: https://www.unep.org/ (accessed on 7 July 2025).
World Bank. (2023). *State and trends of carbon pricing 2023*. Available online: https://carbonpricingdashboard.worldbank.org/ (accessed on 7 July 2025).
Zerbib, O. D. (2019). The effect of pro-environmental preferences on bond prices: Evidence from green bonds. *Journal of Banking & Finance, 98*, 39–60. [CrossRef]

The Role of Central Banks in Climate Stabilisation

Gül Ş. Huyugüzel Kışla

Abstract: This study examines the evolving role of central banks in taking climate change into consideration within the financial system. The paper reviews existing climate change agreements and policies and analyses the transmission channels through which climate risks impact economies and the financial systems. It also discusses various central bank responses, including green monetary policies, climate stress testing, and regulatory measures aimed at promoting sustainable finance. While the traditional roles of central banks are important, it is emphasised that they have additional responsibilities when it comes to dealing with climate change. By reviewing the related literature, it is found that coordinated efforts for climate change are vital for all countries.

1. Introduction

Central banks differ from commercial banks in many ways due to their roles in the economy. In fact, their most important responsibilities can be listed as defining monetary policy, regulating the money in circulation, supervising the interbank market, establishing and operating systems, issuing regulations, and acting as the lender of last resort. Central banks perform all these tasks to ensure the stability of the financial system (i.e., price stability and financial stability). In general, central banks are important and independent institutions that may have several tools for their tasks. They can sell or buy government securities in the open market; they can set interest rates, and they can also set minimum reserves, which commercial banks should hold (required reserves). Beyond the main roles of the central banks within the economy, during economic, financial, or global crises, they step up as the first responders to the unexpected shocks or unprecedented situations respectively.

Considering the growing climate risks, financial systems may need to consider climate-related activities. The escalating climate crisis presents an existential threat to global financial stability. Climate change could disrupt production, destabilise markets, and impair asset valuations. It can also weaken the resilience of financial institutions. There is no consensus about the intervention of the central banks for climate change; failing to address such risks could threaten the primary objectives of stability and resilience of central banks (Schabel, 2020). Specifically, as the major players of the economies and financial systems, central banks began to expand their scope of responsibilities to deal with the climate-related risks (Tamez et al., 2024). The primary objective of this chapter is to examine the evolving role of central banks in climate stabilisation. In this respect, climate change and the financial system will be discussed at first sight, and then the role of central banks will be examined.

2. Climate Change and the Financial System

2.1. What Is Climate Change?

According to NASA, climate change can be defined as the large-scale, long-term changes in the average weather patterns and temperatures (NASA, 2025). These changes have a wide variety of observed effects associated with the term. These changes can be natural, but since the 19th century, climate change has mainly been driven by human activities, particularly the burning of fossil fuels (i.e., coal, oil and gas), which have increased from year to year. Before the Industrial Revolution, the average temperature across the world was almost 14 °C. Burning fossil fuels releases carbon dioxide (CO_2, methane and nitrous oxide (i.e., greenhouse gases) into the atmosphere. Unfortunately, these gases trap the Sun's heat and cause the Earth's average temperature to increase. This process is called "global warming". In addition to the use of fossil fuels, greenhouse gases may increase due to events such as deforestation and certain agricultural and industrial practices.

In Figure 1, it can be observed that after industrialisation in the 1950s, emissions have surged dramatically. There are regional differences to be observed. While industrialised countries were responsible for past emissions, developing countries like China and India have shown a steep upward trend and now dominate most of the global growth in emissions.

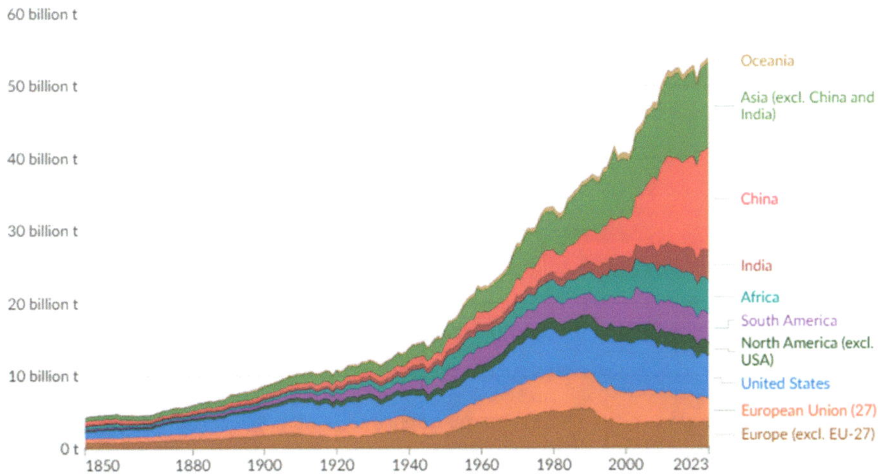

Figure 1. The evolution of greenhouse gas emissions by world region from 1859 to 2023. Source: Reprinted from Jones et al. (2025)—with major processing by Our World in Data.

Another fact about greenhouse gas emissions is their growth rate. Emissions grew from 1990 to 2021 by 51%. In 2021, most of the emissions came from the energy sector, at 75.7%; agriculture was the second sector, contributing 11.7%; industrial processes contributed 6.5%, waste contributed 3.4%, and land use, change, and forestry contributed 2.7%. Electricity and heat (29.7%) are the biggest shares of energy emissions; transportation (13.7%) is the second, manufacturing and construction (12.7%) are the third, and buildings (6.6%) are in fourth place (Ge et al., 2024).

In the context of climate change, temperatures are rising, glaciers and polar ice sheets are melting, and therefore sea levels are rising. Extreme weather conditions like floods, droughts, forest fires, and severe storms are being observed more frequently, and the marine ecosystem is deteriorating. Those events may affect humankind, listed as ecological migrations, changing agricultural patterns, flood tides, storm intensifications, and heat wave intensifications (United Nations, 2025). The balance of the Earth is changing irreversibly. However, governments and institutions are becoming more conscious about climate change compared to the past. In fact, the changing weather conditions and the balance of this ecosystem have brought about new initiatives and awareness. For example, in 1988, the Intergovernmental Panel on Climate Change (IPCC) was established by the United Nations Environment Programme (UNEP) and the World Meteorological Organisation (WMO). Its initial task was to prepare a comprehensive review and recommendation on climate change to support the governments. After its establishment, there were many assessment reports issued. As climate change is a global threat to all countries, important climate-related agreements and initiatives have been made. Table 1 presents a summary table of these initiatives and agreements.

Table 1. Selected agreements/initiatives.

Agreement/Initiative	Year	Purpose and Scope	Features and Participants
United Nations Framework Convention on Climate Change (UNFCCC)	1992	To stabilise greenhouse gas concentrations to prevent dangerous human interference with the climate system.	The convention has over 190 parties and establishes the framework of principles such as common but differentiated responsibilities.
Kyoto Protocol	1997	Legally binding targets for developed countries to reduce their greenhouse gas emissions.	It entered into force in 2005 and includes binding reduction commitments for Annex I countries, as well as an emissions trading scheme.
Paris Agreement	2015	Limit global warming to below 2 °C, with a target of 1.5 °C, whilst also pursuing sustainable development goals.	A legally binding treaty with over 190 parties and nationally determined contributions from all countries.
Montreal Protocol	1987	Regulates the production and consumption of nearly 100 man-made chemicals referred to as ozone-depleting substances (ODSs).	It is considered highly successful and includes 196 parties. It protects the ozone layer, which affects the climate.
European Green Deal	2019	Achieving net-zero greenhouse gas emissions by 2050.	A comprehensive EU plan that covers all sectors, including energy, transport and agriculture.

Source: Author's compilation based on data from UNFCCC (2025).

There is more effort, of course. In 2021, to strengthen Paris targets, the Glasgow Climate Pact (COP26) was adopted to aim at reducing unabated coal usage. At this event, 120 world leaders and over 40,000 registered participants were brought together. They all agreed on recognising the emergency of global warming, reducing the carbon dioxide emissions, moving away from fossil fuels, delivering on climate finance, and focusing on the loss and damage of especially developing countries. United Nations (UN) climate conferences continued every year in different countries (Egypt, United Arab Emirates, Azerbaijan, and soon Brazil).

2.2. How Does Climate Change Affect the Financial System?

Climate change affects humankind regardless of citizenship. The costs of climate change are common to all countries. The amounts of economic damage caused by natural disasters from 1990 to 2024 are presented in Figure 2.

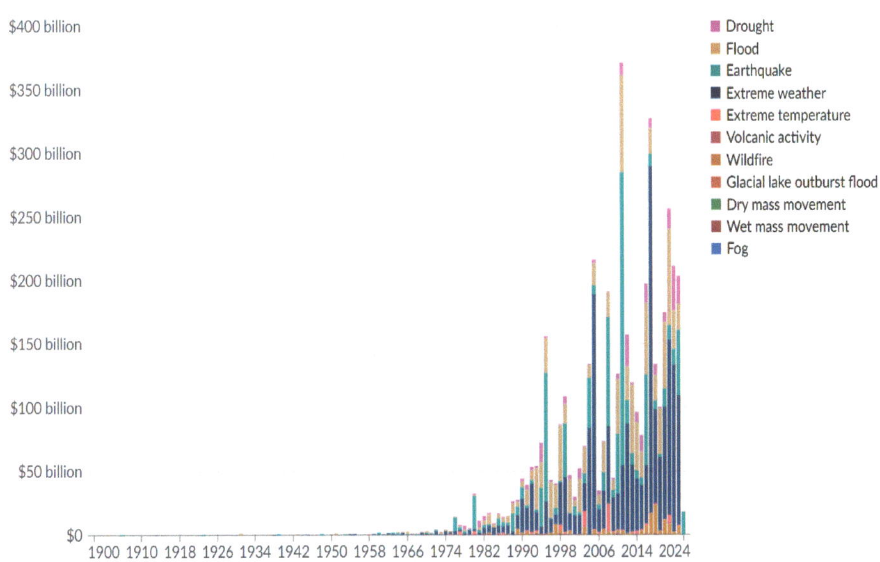

Figure 2. Economic damage by natural disaster type. Global economic damage from natural disasters, differentiated by disaster category and measured in USD per year. Source: Reprinted from EM-DAT, CRED/UCLouvain (2025)—with major processing by Our World in Data.

Figure 2 shows that major economic damages were observed after the 1970s and 1980s in line with globalisation. The highest economic losses from the disasters were seen in the years after 2000. The figure provides that the most significant contributors to losses are earthquakes, floods, extreme weather, and extreme temperatures. These disasters increased the vulnerability of countries in this respect.

It is important to note that disasters resulting directly or indirectly from climate change may also have impacts on the financial system. According to Zhou et al. (2023), climate change and natural disasters lower insurer profitability, stock and bond returns, and international lending. Basically, the financial system is affected by climate change through two main channels, namely physical risks and transition risks. In case of physical risks, hurricanes, floods, droughts, and forest fires interrupt the production process and damage the infrastructure and therefore lead to rising insurance costs. In other words, physical risks emanate from those potential damages to properties, infrastructures, and lands (Grippa et al., 2019). Market and credit risks resulting from physical risks could also become concentrated in certain sectors or regions of the real economy. This is another probability. For example, Bernstein et al. (2019) stated that the value of properties exposed to rising sea levels is lower than that of similar properties in other locations.

There is more evidence of the negative effects of climate change. In Thailand, floods led to a reduction in GDP of 30% in 2011. Climate change may also affect financial institutions or firms by disrupting their operations. In case of the transition risks, there might be risks which arise from the policy, regulatory, and technological changes that are required to adjust to a low-carbon economy. To achieve a low-carbon economy, the structure of the economy needs to be adjusted. In other words, the production processes of firms may need to change from using fossil fuels to renewable energy sources (FSB, 2020). Hence, the production costs of firms may increase due to the transition of the production process. Consumer behaviour may change from traditional firms to environmentally friendly companies, which may bring market and reputational risks. Figure 3 presents a summary of the transmission channels from climate risks to financial risks. Climate risks affect the economy from both the micro and macro perspectives and may pose several financial risks to the overall financial system.

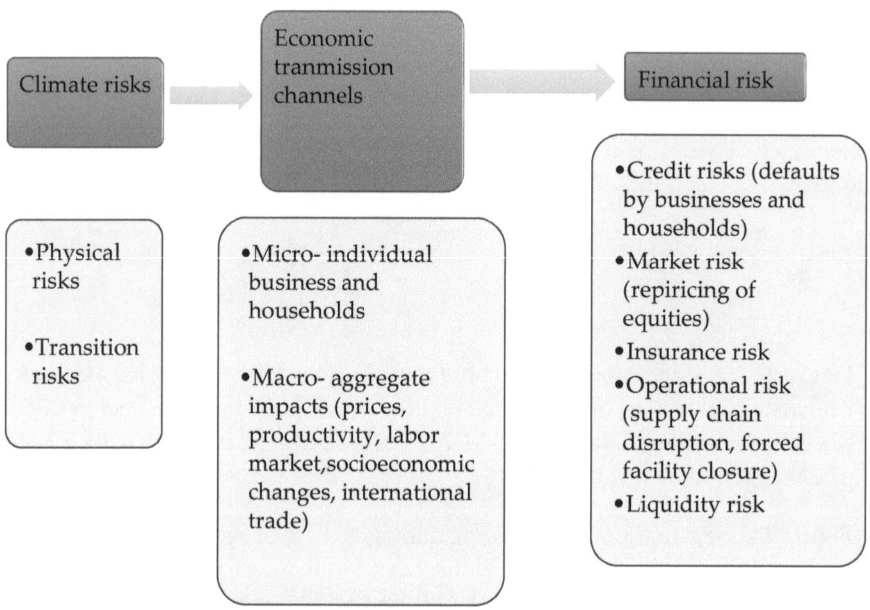

Figure 3. Transmission channels. Source: Reprinted from NGFS (2022).

3. The Role of Central Banks

Central banks have traditional roles such as maintaining price stability. In this respect, they use monetary policy instruments to achieve lower and stable inflation rates. They also promote financial stability by ensuring the smooth functioning of payment systems and safeguarding the banking sector. During times of crisis, they provide liquidity to the financial system.

Although these roles are important, they are not enough to tackle the long-term structural issues caused by climate change. In fact, central banks need to have the necessary tools and responsibilities to deal with climate change because it affects the financial stability of countries directly. As one of the important and oldest central banks, the Bank of England is, for example, aware of the risks that come with climate change, and it aims to keep the financial system stable as the UK economy evolves into a net-zero economy. They focus on important tasks such as building the resilience of UK banks and insurers to climate-related financial risks and supporting the coordination of the international approach to climate change. Indeed, the Bank of England was the first bank to propose "greening" its monetary portfolio and targets net-zero emissions from its own operations by 2050. The bank also helped to set up a network called the "Network for Greening the Financial System (NGFS)". This group was established to support the global response required to achieve the Paris Agreement goals, as well as to support the financial system in the context of sustainable development (NGFS, 2025).

When it comes to dealing with climate change, economists have also proposed different suggestions, such as green dual interest rates. These kinds of interest rates could be considered a form of incentive for banks to provide more loans to the specific sectors or green energy projects. Another option for climate change action could be to increase the interest rates for banks that invest in fossil fuels (Costa, 2025).

In addition, Green Quantitative Easing (QE) is another option for reducing the effects of climate change or global warming. Dafermos et al. (2018) mentioned that Green QE programmes, including the purchase of green corporate bonds, can indeed reduce global warming. Abiry et al. (2022) developed a model to analyse the effectiveness of green quantitative easing (QE) in supporting climate change mitigation policies. They consider the portfolio selection of the central banks and the fiscal policies involving the carbon tax. The results of the model show that the carbon tax is much more effective compared to green QE.

Climate stress tests are also conducted by major central banks. The European Central Bank (ECB), the United States Federal Reserve, Banque de France, the Dutch National Bank, and the Swiss FINMA are applying the climate stress tests to evaluate the financial institutions which may face financial risks posed by climate change (Battiston & Monasterolo, 2024).

Figure 4 shows the relationship between climate goals and the possible policy instruments for central banks and governments to address climate change. Carbon pricing can be defined as a policy that curbs greenhouse gas emissions by placing a fee on emissions and/or offering an incentive for emitting less. Green subsidies and incentives support clean energy sources while financial regulations ensure that funds flow towards sustainable production (Boneva et al., 2022).

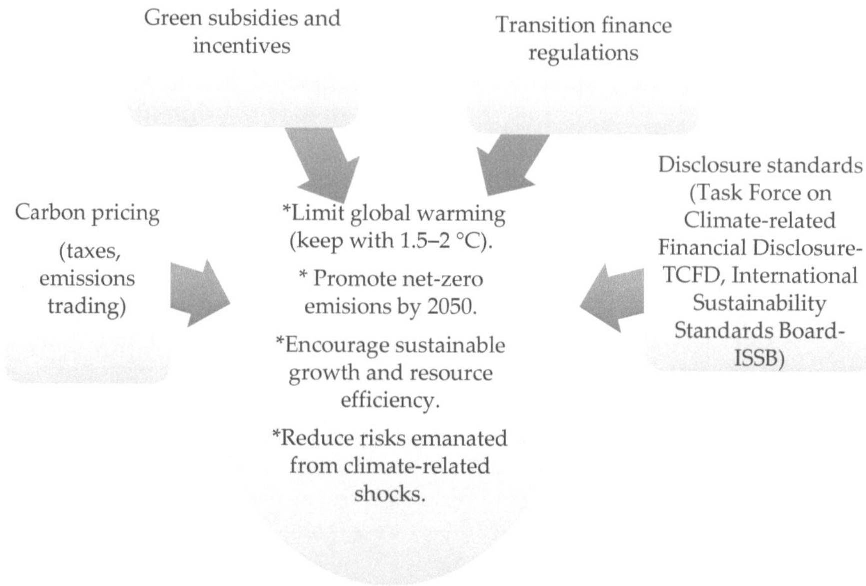

Figure 4. Possible climate policy instruments (rectangular shape) and the climate goals (round shape). Source: Figure by author.

4. Conclusions

The effects of climate change have become extremely severe and multidimensional today. Rising temperatures, more destructive storms, intensifying droughts, rising sea levels, loss of biodiversity, weakening food security, and increased health risks are the globally observed consequences of the climate crisis. However, climate change is not only an environmental threat, but also a process that deepens poverty and increases socioeconomic vulnerabilities. According to United Nations data, adapting to climate change is becoming much more difficult, especially for refugees and vulnerable populations; on average, an estimated 23.1 million people are becoming more vulnerable to poverty. However, these effects and the policy responses to them show significant differences across regions.

Interregional policy contrasts are particularly evident in terms of access to institutional capacity and financial instruments, especially in combating climate change. Advanced economies can integrate climate policies with long-term strategies thanks to stronger financial structures and institutional frameworks; central banks and regulatory institutions can more effectively integrate climate risks into financial supervision and monetary policy frameworks. In contrast, in developing and climate-vulnerable regions, limited fiscal space and institutional capacity constraints make it difficult to implement climate policies, leading to short-term economic priorities taking precedence over long-term climate goals.

In this context, while the primary responsibility for combating climate change lies with governments, central banks are also seen to play a complementary and supportive role (Diluiso et al., 2021). Central banks promote the formation of a sustainable financial system through financial regulation powers and monetary policy tools, indirectly contributing to climate stability. However, while monetary policy and regulatory frameworks are often designed with short-term goals in mind, climate targets require a long-term and structural perspective. This situation creates significant divergence, particularly in the degree of alignment between monetary policy and climate policies in different regions.

Difficulties in measuring climate risks, the complexity of climate impacts, and structural limitations in some economies can restrict the effectiveness of central bank interventions (Vyshnevskyi & Shon, 2025). While these constraints are felt relatively less in regions with strong data infrastructure and advanced financial markets, they further complicate the implementation of climate policies in fragile economies. Therefore, instead of a one-size-fits-all policy approach to combating climate change, flexible and differentiated policy frameworks are needed that take regional differences into account.

In conclusion, coordination between governments, central banks, financial institutions, the private sector, and civil society organisations has become a decisive factor in combating climate change. However, the success of this coordination varies depending on the economic structure, institutional capacity, and climate vulnerability levels of the regions. Designing climate policies in alignment with monetary policy, fiscal incentives, and regulatory tools is critically important, especially in fragile regions, to reduce the risk of climate-induced poverty. Ultimately, either decisive steps will be taken today to address the climate crisis, considering different regional realities, or much higher economic and social costs will be paid in the future.

Funding: This research received no external funding.

Conflicts of Interest: The author declares no conflict of interest.

Author Name and Affiliation: Gül Ş. Huyugüzel Kışla, Department of Economics, Ege University, Izmir, Turkey.

Keywords: central banks; climate risk; green monetary policy; sustainable finance.

References

Abiry, R., Ferdinandusse, M., & Alexandar Ludwig, C. N. (2022). *Climate change mitigation: How effective is green quantitative easing?* No. 2701. ECB. [CrossRef]

Battiston, S., & Monasterolo, I. (2024). *Enhanced scenarios for climate stress-tests*. Available online: https://eprints.lse.ac.uk/129129/ (accessed on 14 May 2025).

Bernstein, A., Gustafson, M. T., & Lewis, R. (2019). Disaster on the horizon: The price effect of sea level rise. *Journal of Financial Economics*, *134*(2), 253–272. [CrossRef]

Boneva, L., Ferruci, G., & Mongelli, F. P. (2022). Climate change and central banks: What role for monetary policy? *Climate Policy*, *22*(6), 770–787. [CrossRef]

Costa, M. (2025). Available online: https://greencentralbanking.com/2025/07/08/ecb-to-consider-climate-and-nature-in-monetary-policy/ (accessed on 24 May 2025).

Dafermos, Y., Nikolaidi, M., & Galanis, G. (2018). Can green quantitative easing (QE) reduce global warming? *Policy Brief*. Available online: https://research.gold.ac.uk/id/eprint/25412/ (accessed on 20 May 2025).

Diluiso, F., Annicchiarico, B., Kalkuhl, M., & Minx, J. C. (2021). Climate actions and macro-financial stability: The role of central banks. *Journal of Environmental Economics and Manaement, 110*, 102548. [CrossRef]

EM-DAT, CRED/UCLouvain. (2025). *With major processing by Our World in Data. "Economic damage by natural disaster type—EM-DAT" [dataset]. EM-DAT, "The International Disasters Database" [original data].* Available online: https://archive.ourworldindata.org/20260304-094028/grapher/economic-damage-from-natural-disasters.html (accessed on 10 July 2025).

FSB. (2020). *The implications of climate change for financial stability*. Available online: https://www.fsb.org/uploads/P231120.pdf (accessed on 18 June 2025).

Ge, M., Friedrich, J., & Leandro, V. (2024, December). *Where do emissions come from? 4 charts explain greenhouse gas emissions by sector*. Available online: https://www.wri.org/insights/4-charts-explain-greenhouse-gas-emissions-countries-and-sectors (accessed on 20 June 2025).

Grippa, P., Schimttmann, J., & Suntheim, F. (2019). Climate change and financial risk. *Finance and Development*, 26–29.

Jones, M. W., Peters, G. P., Gasser, T., Andrew, R. B., Schwingshackl, C., Gütschow, J., Houghton, R. A., Friedlingstein, P., Pongratz, J., & Le Quéré, C. (2025). *With major processing by Our World in Data. "Annual greenhouse gas emissions including land use" [dataset]. Jones et al., "National contributions to climate change 2025.1" [original data].* Available online: https://archive.ourworldindata.org/20260304-094028/grapher/ghg-emissions-by-world-region.html (accessed on 10 July 2025).

NASA. (2025). *What is climate change?* Available online: https://science.nasa.gov/climate-change/what-is-climate-change/#: :text=Climate%20change%20is%20a%20long,are%20synonymous%20with%20the%20term (accessed on 28 June 2025).

NGFS. (2022). *NGFS scenarios for central banks and supervisors*. Available online: https://www.ngfs.net/en/publications-and-statistics/publications/ngfs-climate-scenarios-central-banks-and-supervisors (accessed on 21 May 2025).

NGFS. (2025). Available online: https://www.ngfs.net/en/about-us (accessed on 4 May 2025).

Schabel, I. (2020). *When markets fail—The need for collective action in tackling climate change*. Available online: https://www.ecb.europa.eu/press/key/date/2020/html/ecb.sp200928_1 268b0b672f.en.html (accessed on 19 May 2025).

Tamez, M., Weenink, H., & Yoshinaga, A. (2024). *Central banks and climate change: Key legal issues*. Available online: https://papers.ssrn.com/sol3/papers.cfm?abstract_id=4960434 (accessed on 3 July 2025).

UNFCCC. (2025). Available online: https://unfccc.int/ (accessed on 1 July 2025).

United Nations. (2025). Available online: https://www.un.org/en/climatechange/science/causes-effects-climate-change#: :text=As%20greenhouse%20gas%20emissions%20blanket,the%20usual%20balance%20of%20nature (accessed on 3 July 2025).

Vyshnevskyi, I., & Shon, W. (2025). Central banks' support for climate action: A literature review and key issues. *Journal of Economic Survey*, *40*(1), 182–198. [CrossRef]
Zhou, F., Endendijk, T., & Botzen, W. (2023). A review of the financial sector impacts of risks associated with climate change. *Annual Review of Resource Economics*, *15*, 233–256. [CrossRef]

Climate Justice in Economics: Addressing Inequities in Green Transitions

Hakan Eygu

Abstract: Today, as countries pursue industrialisation to grow their economies, fossil fuel consumption is increasing, leading to adverse effects on climate variables. Within the framework of the Sustainable Development Goals (SDGs), identifying the variables that influence the green transformation process is considered critical, especially in alignment with the goals of poverty reduction (SDG 1) and climate action (SDG 13). This study aims to contribute to the existing literature by examining the factors that determine green growth in the context of the SDGs. Given its rapidly growing economy, large population, and increasing energy demand, India's environmental sustainability and green growth performance are addressed in this study. Annual data covering the period from 2010 to 2023 are used. The green growth index (GGI) is selected as the dependent variable, while energy productivity capacity (EPC), gross domestic product (GDP), income inequality (Gini), human development index (HDI), and renewable energy consumption (REC) are included as explanatory variables. To test stationarity and cointegration relationships, the Fourier KPSS and bootstrap Fourier–Shin tests are applied, and long-run coefficients are estimated using the Fully Modified Least Squares (FMOLS) method. The findings reveal that EPC, GDP, Gini, and HDI have statistically significant effects on the GGI; EPC and GDP have positive impacts, while HDI has a negative impact. The effect of REC is found to be limited. As a result, India's green growth is supported by energy efficiency and economic growth; however, policies need to be reconsidered to integrate income distribution equity and human development indicators with environmental goals.

1. Introduction

Climate change, as one of the most pressing global issues of our time, underscores the necessity of striking a balance between economic growth and environmental sustainability. The Kyoto Protocol and the subsequent Paris Agreement project that global temperatures could rise by approximately 2.5 °C. Therefore, the United Nations Sustainable Development Goals (SDGs), particularly SDG 13 (climate action) and SDG 1 (no poverty), promote the implementation of green transformation processes fairly and inclusively. Stern (2011) stated that the economic costs of climate change are not environmental. In addition, it has been determined that climate change can increase social inequalities, and it has been emphasised that green policies should be approached with a focus on justice. This highlights the importance of providing a justice-oriented approach to green economy policies in societies. Similarly, recent IPCC (2022) reports state that green growth in developing countries such as India is heavily influenced by socioeconomic dynamics such as income inequalities and levels of human development. Therefore, it was stated that justice should be given priority. Hallegatte (2016) argued that green transformations carry the risk of disadvantaging low-income groups and, therefore, policies should be sensitive to local dynamics. However, Barbier (2010) states that green growth policies in emerging economies should be linked to environmental factors such as energy efficiency and renewable energy consumption, as well as social indicators such as income distribution and human development. This is because, in the face of climate, which is a global problem, considering variables is the basis of producing fair solutions (Sultana, 2021). In this context, climate justice focuses on the nature of the measures to be taken regarding climate change, and which responsibilities should be shared in line with the principle of justice (Zahnow et al., 2025; Mohtat & Khirfan, 2021). This approach is critical to balancing India's rapid industrialisation with sustainable development, ensuring that marginalised communities are not disproportionately burdened by the costs of green transitions. The intersection of multiple inequalities needs to be considered (Zahnow et al., 2025). In areas such as income, trade, energy production, and social and political development, the unequal and unjust distribution of rights in the context of global warming has brought the concept of climate justice to the forefront (Resnik, 2022; Sengupta, 2023). In this regard, the Paris Agreement, which embraces a justice-based approach to climate, proposes that developed countries especially should act collectively within the scope of this agreement in response to the climate crisis and global warming (Bozoğlu, 2021; Ünsal, 2024). This is because the injustices caused by climate change have a particularly negative impact on individuals living in developing countries and on economically disadvantaged groups (Greer, 2023). In the existing literature, there is a limited number of studies that comprehensively examine the effects of the variables used in this study on green growth. In this context, the present study aims to contribute to the literature by empirically addressing climate justice and the handling of inequalities within green transition processes, with a specific focus on India.

This study focuses on the green economy and a just transition. While some studies in the literature imply assumptions about justice, they often do not engage in the topic through data-driven analysis. To investigate the factors influencing green transformation, an empirical analysis was conducted on India. The choice of India is primarily due to its highly unequal income distribution. Moreover, the country is particularly vulnerable to climate impacts, and those most affected are typically low-income and rural communities. Therefore, the concept of climate justice is directly applicable. Finally, although India has made significant commitments under the Paris Agreement, it faces challenges in balancing development needs with environmental goals. This raises the question of whether green growth is truly equitable. In this context, this study makes three important contributions to the green transition literature. First, to the best of our knowledge, there is no other empirical study that specifically analyses the impact of India's rapidly growing economy (GDP), energy productive capacities (EPC), income inequality (GINI), human development index (HDI), and renewable energy consumption (REC) on the green growth index (GGI) within the existing body of knowledge. From this perspective, this study offers researchers and policymakers an opportunity to evaluate the factors influencing green transitions in national economies from a new viewpoint.

Second, the environmental injustices brought about by global climate change compel governments to act collectively to eliminate political, economic, and social inequalities. In this context, ensuring that green transitions are carried out in a just manner and developing policies aligned with the Sustainable Development Goals (SDG 1 and SDG 13) have become imperative. Minimising the adverse effects of green transitions must be addressed in conjunction with local policy and planning processes. To the best of our knowledge, studies examining the relationship between green growth, climate justice, and economic growth remain limited in the existing literature. Moreover, no study to date has comprehensively examined the effects of these variables on green growth. Therefore, this study contributes to the literature by offering new findings through the analysis of key explanatory variables for green growth—namely, energy productive capacities, gross domestic product, income inequality, human development index, and renewable energy consumption.

Third, the Fourier KPSS and bootstrap Fourier–Shin tests were employed to examine stationarity and cointegration relationships, while long-run coefficients were estimated using the Fully Modified Least Squares (FMOLS) method. This approach is justified by the possibility of structural breaks in the series, as time series data may be exposed to shocks during certain periods. If structural breaks are ignored, they may lead to biased results; therefore, the Fourier unit root test was also employed alongside conventional unit root testing. Additionally, the use of the Fully Modified Least Squares (FMOLS) method to estimate long-run coefficients allows for a more robust and consistent identification of long-term relationships by accounting for nonlinear trends and structural breaks in time series analysis. This is critically important for accurately modelling complex economic and environmental dynamics, such as green growth, and for developing sound policy recommendations.

In line with the above discussions, the remainder of the study is structured as follows: Section 2 summarises and discusses the relevant empirical literature. Section 3 presents the materials and methodology used in the research. Section 4 provides an evaluation of the empirical findings and their implications for green growth. Finally, Section 5 outlines the main conclusions of the study and offers policy recommendations.

2. Literature Review

The injustices emerging alongside global climate change are compelling governments to collaborate to eliminate political, economic, and social inequalities. In this context, the literature review in this study is organised into two subsections: green growth and energy production and green growth and climate justice.

2.1. Energy Production and Green Growth

Energy production is one of the fundamental pillars of economic development and social welfare in modern societies. However, the environmental impact of traditional energy production methods, especially carbon emissions and depletion of natural resources, has brought the concept of sustainability to the forefront of the global agenda. In this context, green growth is an approach that aims to align economic development with the principles of environmental sustainability (Hickel & Kallis, 2020; Antal & Van Den Bergh, 2016). Green growth encourages the use of renewable energy sources. It also aims to support economic growth by promoting the use of renewable energy sources. The relationship between these two concepts plays a critical role in both reshaping energy policies and balancing long-term environmental and economic goals. For this reason, the interaction between sustainable energy production, and green growth has recently received more attention both in the academic literature and in policymaking processes (Barua, 2022). Adewuyi et al. (2020) promote a sustainable energy transition: they define it as an effective, efficient, and durable restructuring of the energy sector without jeopardising the social and environmental security of the current and future generations of society. Green growth poses special challenges for developing economies. These countries may be inefficient in terms of their energy production and face various obstacles in increasing green growth based on sustainable energy. These obstacles include a fragile economy, a level of development, and a lack of awareness of an inadequate environment (Razzaq et al., 2023).

A sufficient, sustainable, and reliable energy sector is among the fundamental conditions for both economic growth and social development. Studies on development and developing countries show that energy consumption and security will increase economic growth and an important production input besides capital (Stern, 2011; Azam, 2020; Bahl & Kumar, 2025). In this process, sustainable development and green transition depend on the use of environmentally friendly energy sources by countries. In this case, prioritising renewable energy in developed and developing countries and implementing various incentives is important for green growth and achieving SDG targets (Tawiah et al., 2021; Alam et al., 2024). According to the IEA (2023) and the UN (2024), achieving goals such as affordable and clean energy (SDG 7), climate action (SDG 13), and economic growth (SDG 8) requires enhancing efficiency, expanding the use of renewable energy sources, and fostering innovation. Khan et al. (2021) researched the relationship between energy consumption and sustainable economic growth for 38 International Energy Agency (IEA) economies between 1995 and 2015. As a result of the research, it was found that both energy transition and sustainable growth affect economic growth in the long and short periods. Taşkın et al. (2020) researched the interface between green GGI and REC for the OECD countries between 1990 and 2015. The study found a significant and positive relationship between these variables. In a study conducted on Asian countries, it was determined that renewable energy sources had a positive effect on green growth in the long term (Shang et al., 2023). A similar study conducted between 1991 and 2022 found a statistically significant and positive relationship between both carbon emissions and non-renewable energy consumption on economic growth in the short and long term (Imran et al., 2025; Daştan & Eygü, 2024). Similar findings suggest that in the long run, renewable energy, environmental stewardship, and technological innovation drive green growth, and that the benefits of the energy transition become more pronounced as supportive policies (Wang et al., 2023; Razzaq et al., 2023; Dzwigol et al., 2023). Moreover, a study by Eygu and Soğukpınar (2023) demonstrated that economic growth and energy consumption contribute to environmental degradation.

2.2. Climate Justice and Green Growth

Climate justice is a subcomponent of the understanding of environmental justice. In this context, it focuses on the effect of climate change, eliminating injustices in vulnerable communities, and on reducing exploitation and oppression (Schlosberg & Collins, 2014; Sultana, 2021). In a broader sense, the consequences of ecological destruction and climate change are not evenly distributed over societies; developed and developing countries have different levels of environmental damage and economic costs resulting from this crisis (Nesmith et al., 2021; Sultana, 2021; Schlosberg & Collins, 2014). Moreover, when structural inequalities such as gender, race, and class are included, it is seen that this injustice is even deeper (Fragkou, 2019; Deivanayagam et al., 2023). Today, climate justice is a powerful social and political force. It is included in the government laws of some countries, such as the US (Resnik, 2022). The connection between income inequality, often measured by the Gini index, and green growth is a hot topic in discussions about climate justice. Climate justice is all about ensuring that everyone gets a fair share of environmental benefits and responsibilities. However, income inequality significantly impacts how this plays out. A study conducted by Hallegatte (2016) pointed out that green transition policies could have negative impacts on low-income communities, which might result in climate injustice. A study in the literature discusses how economic inequality affects justice (Zimm et al., 2024). It has been shown that high Gini index values for developing countries will result in an unfair distribution of resources in green growth policies (Hallegatte, 2016). Similarly, research by Uzar and Eyuboglu (2023) suggested that the Gini coefficient, which measures income inequality, influences environmental degradation when it increases. In addition, tools like the Gini coefficient, Palma ratio, and Theil index are often utilised to evaluate income inequality (Volodzkiene & Streimikiene, 2023). These measures can also be important indicators when discussing climate justice.

Taking a closer look at the climate justice literature shows that researchers often rely on case studies and empirical research to gain a deeper understanding of specific phenomena (Alves & Mariano, 2018; Newell et al., 2021). There is a wealth of academic research that has woven together environmental concerns and discussions on climate justice, often using mixed-methods approaches (Hughes & Hoffmann, 2020; Eygu, 2026). Research conducted by Juhola et al. (2022) developed an index by considering the dimensions of justice with different forms of planning. They noted that this index is an appropriate tool for examining its effect on climate justice. Furlan and Mariano (2024) conducted a study using data from 2019 to explore how social inequality, democracy, and economic growth in 133 countries impact climate justice. The results revealed significant relationships among these variables. A study by Chakraborty (2024) used the Gini index for income inequality in developing countries between 1993 and 2020, analysing its relationship with renewable energy. To examine both short- and long-term effects, the panel ARDL method was employed. The results of the research revealed that a fair distribution of income can offer a green and sustainable future for economies. Lately, there has been a noticeable rise in the use of the Gini coefficient to assess how renewable energy is distributed, particularly in non-OECD and developing nations (Li et al., 2022; Xu et al., 2024). IPCC (2022) reports highlight that income inequality can hinder our ability to adapt to climate change. They stress the importance of ensuring that green growth policies are in harmony with social justice. In this context, the Gini index is recognised in the literature as an important indicator for understanding the relationship between climate justice and green growth.

3. Materials and Methodology

3.1. Data and Model

This study focuses on India over the period 2010–2023, utilising annual data to investigate the determinants of green growth. The dependent variable is the green growth index (GGI), while the explanatory variables include gross domestic product (GDP), energy productive capacities (EPC), income inequality (Gini index), human development (HDI), and renewable energy consumption (REC). The selection of this period is based on the availability of consistent and comparable data across the variables of interest. The model is outlined below.

This study employs annual data for India covering the period from 2010 to 2023 to examine the factors that determine green growth. The green growth index (GGI) is used as the dependent variable, with index scores ranging from 0 to 100. The explanatory variables consist of gross domestic product (GDP) to represent economic growth, energy productivity capacity (EPC), income inequality (Gini index), human development level (HDI), and renewable energy consumption (REC). This time period was selected due to the availability of consistent and comparable data for the relevant variables.

$$GGI_{it} = f(EPC_{it}, GDP_{it}, HDI_{it}, REC_{it}) \tag{1}$$

When Equation (1) is transformed into a log-linear form, it takes the form of Equation (2); this transformation allows for a clearer analysis of the elasticity relationships among the variables.

$$lnGGI_t = \alpha_0 + \beta_1 lnEPC_t + \beta_2 lnGDP_t + \beta_3 lnGINI_t + \beta_4 lnHDI_t + \beta_5 lnREC_t + \varepsilon_t \tag{2}$$

In Equation (2), *ln* denotes the natural logarithm; α_0 represents the constant term, while β_1, β_2, β_3, β_4, and β_5 indicate the coefficients of the independent variables. It denotes time and covers the period from 2010 to 2023. ε represents the error term in the model. Table 1 provides a detailed description of the study variables and their data sources.

Table 1. Description of variables.

Name	Abbreviations	Variable	Measurement	Source
Green growth index	GGI	Explained variable	Green growth index	GGI (2023)
Energy productive capacities	EPC	Independent variable	Productive capacity index	UNCTAD (2023)
Gross domestic product	GDP	Independent variable	2015, USD, per capita	WDI (2024)
Income inequality	GINI	Independent variable	Gini index	WDI (2024)
Human Development Index	HDI	Control	HDI index	UNDP (2023)
Renewable energy consumption	REC	Control	% of total final energy consumption	WDI (2024) and OECD (2024)

Source: Table by author.

Additionally, to avoid heteroscedasticity in the study, the logarithms of the variables were taken, and the coefficients were expressed as elasticities. These transformed variables were then included in the model estimation. Table 2 summarises the sources and descriptions of the selected variables.

Table 2. Summary statistics of variables.

Variables	Mean	Max	Min	Std. Dev.	Jarque-Bera
GGI	1.650	1.665	1.626	0.013	1.411
EPC	1.629	1.658	1.591	0.020	0.718
GDP	3.221	3.349	3.091	0.082	0.938
GINI	0.345	0.360	0.330	0.009	1.137
HDI	0.637	0.685	0.590	0.026	0.270
REC	1.539	1.578	1.511	0.019	0.688

Source: Table by author.

The average GGI in India is 1.650. When the maximum and minimum GGI values are perused, this narrow range suggests that India's green growth performance has been relatively stable during the period under review. Without a logarithmic transformation, the average GDP per capita in India is about USD 1700. It is observed that India allocates approximately 0.65% of its GDP to research and development (R&D) expenditures, a figure that is relatively low compared to the global average. A significant portion of this spending—about 36.4%—is contributed by the private sector (Statista, 2024). Although comprehensive data on annual environmentally friendly funding (EFF) investments remains limited, it is evident that India has made increasing efforts toward green innovation and sustainability.

3.2. Methodology

The results of the KPSS and Fourier KPSS stationarity tests are presented in Table 3. According to the KPSS test results, the null hypothesis, indicating that the series is stationary, was rejected at the 1% significance level for all variables. Similarly, based on the Fourier KPSS test results, the null hypothesis of stationarity was also rejected for all variables. The significance of the Fourier terms was tested using the F-test. According to the results of this test, the Fourier terms were statistically significant at the 1% significance level for all variables.

Following the stationarity test, the bootstrap Fourier–Shin cointegration test was applied using the bootstrap approach. The bootstrap method is frequently preferred because it incorporates factors such as sample size, initial conditions, and the distribution of errors into the analysis. Due to these characteristics, it can provide more accurate finite-sample results compared to procedures based on asymptotic approaches (Bertelli et al., 2022; Chang et al., 2006). The results obtained using this method were examined, and the bootstrap critical values are presented in Table 4.

Table 3. Results of the Fourier KPSS test.

Variables	ADF	KPSS		Fourier KPSS	
	ADF Test Stat. First Differences	LM Test Stat.	k	LM Test Stat.	$F_{\mu}(k)$
GGI	−3.3586 **	0.4581 *	1	0.1815 **	7.566 ***
EPC	−4.6228 ***	0.7823 **	1	0.4738 ***	8.368 ***
GDP	−3.2256 **	0.7705 **	1	0.3319 **	10.265 ***
GINI	−3.4641 **	0.5307 **	1	0.2544 **	9.499 ***
HDI	−3.5834 **	0.7537 **	1	0.3283	4.645 **
REC	−3.2949 **	0.2384 *	1	0.1987	24.256 ***

Note: ***, **, and * denote statistical significance at the 1%, 5%, and 10% levels. Critical values of the Fourier KPSS stationarity test are available in Becker et al. (2006). ADF—the Augmented Dickey–Fuller test; KPSS—Kwiatkowski–Phillips–Schmidt–Shin Test; LM—Lagrange Multiplier Test. Source: Table by author.

Table 4. Results of the bootstrap Fourier–Shin cointegration test.

Model		m = 0	m = 1	m = 0	m = 1
		CI_f^m		$F^m(k^*)$	
Test Stat.		0.0120 **	0.0104	18.9894	12.3078
Bootstrap kritik values	%1	0.0847 *	0.0464 **	9.3940	9.6349
	%5	0.0684 *	0.0395 **	6.4728	6.6748
	%10	0.0587 *	0.0360 **	5.1943	5.3206

Note: **, and * denote statistical significance at the 5%, and 10% levels. Source: Table by author.

The results indicate that there is a cointegration relationship between the dependent variable, GGI, and the independent variables. For both models, a long-term relationship was identified between GGI and the variables EPC, GDP, Gini, HDI, and REC. This finding suggests that the green growth index is associated with key environmental and economic variables such as energy productivity capacity, gross domestic product (economic growth), income inequality, human development index, and renewable energy consumption, and that these variables remain interconnected over time. According to the results of the F-test conducted to assess the significance of the Fourier terms in the model, the null hypothesis stating that the Fourier terms are statistically insignificant was rejected at the 1% significance level in all cases. Therefore, it can be concluded that the Fourier terms in the models are statistically significant. The significance of the Fourier terms in the estimated models indicates that the relationship between the dependent and independent variables exhibits nonlinear fluctuations over time. After detecting the cointegration relationship, the Fully Modified Least Squares (FMOLS) estimator developed by Phillips and Hansen (1990) was used to estimate the long-run parameters, and the results are presented in Table 5.

Table 5. FMOLS with Fourier term cointegration results.

Long-Run Results Dependent Variable: GGI				
Variables	Coeff.	Std. Err.	t-Stat.	*p*-Value
EPC	0.5376	0.2611	2.0587	0.0735 *
GDP	0.2732	0.1004	2.7196	0.0263 **
GINI	0.4801	0.1747	2.7474	0.0252 **
HDI	−0.6760	0.1693	−3.9912	0.0040 ***
REC	0.1026	0.0948	1.0818	0.3108

Note: ***, **, and * denote statistical significance at the 1%, 5%, and 10% levels. FMOLS—Fully Modified Ordinary Least Squares. Source: Table by author.

As shown in Table 5, the variables EPC, GDP, Gini, and HDI—which are considered to influence the green growth index in the long run—were found to be statistically significant. In India, a 1% increase in energy productivity capacity (EPC) leads to approximately a 0.54% increase in the green growth index, a 0.27% increase in economic growth (GDP), and a 0.48% increase in the Gini index, which reflects income inequality in the country. The inclusion of Fourier terms in the FMOLS model strengthens the analysis by accounting for nonlinear trends and structural breaks. The variables EPC, GDP, Gini, and HDI are found to be statistically significant at the 10%, 5%, and 1% levels, respectively. These findings indicate that India's green growth is supported by energy efficiency and economic growth; however, income inequality plays a complex role, and human development may have a counteractive effect. The limited contribution of renewable energy consumption suggests that policies in this area may need to be made more effective. These results highlight the importance of investing in energy infrastructure and promoting economic growth, while also indicating that income inequality requires strategic attention to ensure the fair distribution of green growth benefits. The negative impact of HDI underscores the necessity of integrating human development with environmental goals, whereas the limited effect of REC points to the need for a reassessment of renewable energy policies.

4. Discussion

Climate change stands out as one of the most critical issues adversely affecting human life on Earth. The main causes of this problem include increasing population, economic growth, industrial development, and technological advances. These causes lead to environmental degradation and play a critical role in setting sustainable policies. In this study, data from the period 2010 to 2023 are used to investigate ways to align economic growth in India with environmental sustainability and social indicators. The long-term positive and negative effects of variables such as energy productivity capacity (EPC), economic growth (GDP), income inequality (Gini index), human development index (HDI), and renewable energy consumption (REC) on the green growth index (GGI) have been estimated. In the analysis, two different control variables were used. Among these, renewable energy consumption has come to the fore as a striking factor in the green transformation. Long-term relationships were examined using cointegration techniques and the Fully Modified Least Squares (FMOLS) approach.

As a result of the unit root tests, it was determined that the variables in India were stationary. Our findings are consistent with the results obtained by B. Behera et al. (2023), Sharma and Rajpurohit (2022), Sahoo and Sethi (2020), and Shahbaz et al. (2017). The unit root behaviour of these series indicates that they are resistant to certain random shocks and tend to return to their previous levels in the long run. To the best of our knowledge, this result indicates that India can develop policies based on selected variables to boost its green growth. According to the results of bootstrap Fourier–Shin cointegration, the null hypothesis was rejected at different significant levels for many other variables, except for the renewable energy consumption series. This finding confirms that there is a long-term relationship between the green growth index and its determinants in India.

Afterwards, the long-term coefficients obtained through the FMOLS estimator were analysed. According to the findings, EPC, GDP, Gini, and HDI were found to be statistically significant. These results show that energy productivity capacity in India supports green growth. When the literature was reviewed, the results we found were supported by Bhardwaj and Chauhan (2025), Alola et al. (2023), and Elavarasan et al. (2020). Similarly, the positive and significant impact of GDP reveals the contribution of economic growth to sustainable development and is in line with studies such as Manigandan et al. (2024) and Roy (2024). The Gini index is found to have a positive and significant effect on the GGI. It can be said that income inequality is not always a factor hindering green growth. Especially in developing countries such as India, this result suggests that environmental investments may increase under the leadership of certain segments. In their study, Khan et al. (2023) stated that income inequality affects environmental quality through economic activities. However, Zou et al. (2024) found in their research that this effect is nonlinear. For example, an increase in income inequality reduces the green growth rate in BRICS economies in the long run while negatively affecting India and China. This result is consistent with our findings. This perspective is supported by Ritu and Kaur (2024) and Lamb and Rao (2015). A similar study stated that India is experiencing difficulties in terms of human development in the transition from economic growth to a green economy (Aaghaz et al., 2024). However, our findings contradict the positive effect of HDI on GGI in the studies of Ahmed and Wang (2019) and Wang et al. (2023). Finally, the effect of renewable energy consumption on GGI was found to be positive but statistically insignificant. This result can be said to limit the impact of India's energy sector, economic structure or environmental policies on this variable. This result differs from the findings of studies such as Bhardwaj and Chauhan (2025), P. Behera et al. (2024), and Bekun (2022).

5. Concluding Remarks and Policy Suggestions

The empirical findings obtained offer meaningful results in analysing the selected variables within the context of climate justice and green transformation, specifically for India. This study of green energy transition and environmental regulations, focused on climate justice, can guide global economies in developing long-term policies. Moreover, comprehensive efforts are required to achieve climate justice. Therefore, the energy transition and corresponding policies are critical for the long-term green transition. The findings support the need for countries to enhance their energy production capacities, ensure equity in income distribution, improve human development through educational policies, and invest in the development of green infrastructure.

In line with the demands for climate justice set out in the Paris Agreement, policies that promote energy efficiency in industry, production facilities, and homes should be developed. Governments should improve legal frameworks to strengthen their environmental governance systems. In this context, they should improve implementation and control mechanisms and encourage stakeholder participation in decision-making processes. Given the global nature of the energy transition, international cooperation is necessary to implement sustainable and equitable policies. Future research may comparatively examine the experiences of countries at different stages of development in terms of sustainable growth, energy transition, and environmental sustainability. Multi-threshold analytical approaches can reveal the differences between developed and developing economies from a climate justice perspective. This approach can offer more in-depth and inclusive insights into how green transition policies function across different socioeconomic contexts.

Funding: This research received no external funding.

Conflicts of Interest: The author declares no conflicts of interest.

Author Name and Affiliation: Hakan Eygu, Department of Econometrics, Ataturk University, Erzurum, Turkey.

Keywords: green growth; environmental pollution; Sustainable Development Goals (SDGs); energy productivity; India.

References

Aaghaz, Q. S., Khan, M. I., Gupta, P. K., & Faizi, M. N. (2024). The challenges of India's economy shift from economic growth to green growth. *Journal of Informatics Education and Research*, *4*(1), 168–183. [CrossRef]

Adewuyi, O. B., Kiptoo, M. K., Afolayan, A. F., Amara, T., Alawode, O. I., & Senjyu, T. (2020). Challenges and prospects of Nigeria's sustainable energy transition with lessons from other countries' experiences. *Energy Reports*, *6*, 993–1009. [CrossRef]

Ahmed, Z., & Wang, Z. (2019). Investigating the impact of human capital on the ecological footprint in India: An empirical analysis. *Environmental Science and Pollution Research*, *26*, 26782–26796. [CrossRef]

Alam, M. S., Dinçer, H., Kisswani, K. M., Khan, M. A. I., Yüksel, S., & Alsharif, M. (2024). Analysis of green energy-oriented sustainable development goals for emerging economies. *Journal of Open Innovation: Technology, Market, and Complexity*, *10*(3), 100368. [CrossRef]

Alola, A. A., Özkan, O., & Usman, O. (2023). Role of non-renewable energy efficiency and renewable energy in driving environmental sustainability in India: Evidence from the load capacity factor hypothesis. *Energies*, *16*(6), 2847. [CrossRef]

Alves, M. W. F. M., & Mariano, E. B. (2018). Climate justice and human development: A systematic literature review. *Journal of Cleaner Production*, *202*, 360–375. [CrossRef]

Antal, M., & Van Den Bergh, J. C. (2016). Green growth and climate change: Conceptual and empirical considerations. *Climate Policy*, *16*(2), 165–177. [CrossRef]

Azam, M. (2020). Gelişmekte olan Asya ekonomilerinde enerji ve ekonomik büyüme. *Asya Pasifik Ekonomisi Dergisi*, *25*, 447–471. [CrossRef]

Bahl, P., & Kumar, V. (2025). Electricity consumption and economic growth: Causal relationship in India. *Journal of Informatics Education and Research*, *5*(1), 712–720. [CrossRef]

Barbier, E. B. (2010). *A global green new deal: Rethinking the economic recovery*. Cambridge University Press.

Barua, S. (2022). Chapter 14—Green growth and energy transition: An assessment of selected emerging economies. In M. Shahbaz, A. K. Tiwari, & A. Sinha (Eds.), *Energy-growth nexus in an era of globalization* (pp. 323–352). Elsevier.

Becker, R., Enders, W., & Lee, J. (2006). A stationarity test in the presence of an unknown number of smooth breaks. *Journal of Time Series Analysis*, *27*(3), 381–409. [CrossRef]

Behera, B., Sucharita, S., Patra, B., & Sethi, N. (2023). A blend of renewable and non-renewable energy consumption on economic growth of India: The role of disaggregate energy sources. *Environmental Science and Pollution Research*, *31*(3), 3902–3916. [CrossRef]

Behera, P., Sethi, L., & Sethi, N. (2024). Balancing India's energy trilemma: Assessing the role of renewable energy and green technology innovation for sustainable development. *Energy*, *308*, 132842. [CrossRef]

Bekun, F. V. (2022). Mitigating emissions in India: Accounting for the role of real income, renewable energy consumption and investment in energy. *International Journal of Energy Economics and Policy*, *12*(1), 188–192. [CrossRef]

Bertelli, S., Vacca, G., & Zoia, M. (2022). Bootstrap cointegration tests in ARDL models. *Economic Modelling*, *116*, 105987. [CrossRef]

Bhardwaj, N., & Chauhan, N. (2025). Green growth in India: Nexus between renewable energy deployment and economic sustainability. *International Journal of Innovative Research in Engineering & Multidisciplinary Physical Sciences*, *13*(3), 1–7. [CrossRef]

Bozoğlu, B. (2021). *21. Yüzyilda iklim krizi, Paris anlaşmasi ve iklim değişikliğine uyum*. Dorion Yayınları, İstanbul.

Chakraborty, D. (2024). Does income inequality play a role in renewable energy consumption? A dynamic panel evidence of developing countries. *Review of Economics*, *75*(3), 233–248. [CrossRef]

Chang, Y., Park, J. Y., & Song, K. (2006). Bootstrapping cointegrating regressions. *Journal of Econometrics*, *133*(2), 703–739. [CrossRef]

Daştan, M., & Eygü, H. (2024). An empirical investigation of the link between economic growth, unemployment, and ecological footprint in Turkey: Bridging the EKC and EPC hypotheses. *Environment, Development and Sustainability*, *26*(7), 18957–18988. [CrossRef]

Deivanayagam, T., English, S., Hickel, J., Bonifacio, J., Guinto, R., Hill, K., Huq, M., Issa, R., Mulindwa, H., Nagginda, H., De Morais Sato, P., Selvarajah, S., Sharma, C., & Devakumar, D. (2023). Envisioning environmental equity: Climate change, health, and racial justice. *Lancet*, *402*, 64–78. [CrossRef]

Dzwigol, H., Kwilinski, A., Lyulyov, O., & Pimonenko, T. (2023). The role of environmental regulations, renewable energy, and energy efficiency in finding the path to green economic growth. *Energies*, *16*(7), 3090. [CrossRef]

Elavarasan, R. M., Shafiullah, G. M., Padmanaban, S., Kumar, N. M., Annam, A., Vetrichelvan, A. M., Mihet-Popa, L., & Holm-Nielsen, J. B. (2020). A comprehensive review on renewable energy development, challenges, and policies of leading Indian states with an international perspective. *IEEE Access, 8*, 74432–74457. [CrossRef]

Eygu, H. (2026). Balancing Biofuel Production and Food Security: The Case of OECD Countries. *Renewable Energy, 262*, 125367. [CrossRef]

Eygu, H., & Soğukpınar, F. (2023). Investigation of the relationship between renewable energy, natural gas, and coal consumption with economic growth in Turkey: Evidence from augmented ARDL approach. *Environmental Science and Pollution Research, 30*(20), 58213–58225. [CrossRef]

Fragkou, M. (2019). Environmental justice. Ecology, revised and expanded. In *Science and politics: An A-to-Z guide to issues and controversies*. CQ Press. [CrossRef]

Furlan, M., & Mariano, E. B. (2024). Effects of democracy, social inequality and economic growth on climate justice: An analysis with structural equation modelling. In *Natural resources forum* (Vol. 48, No. 2, pp. 435–467). Blackwell Publishing Ltd. [CrossRef]

GGI. (2023). *Green growth index*. Available online: https://ggindex-simtool.gggi.org (accessed on 18 April 2025).

Greer, F. (2023). Leveraging environmental assessment and environmental justice to deliver equitable, decarbonized built infrastructure. *Environmental Research: Infrastructure and Sustainability, 3*(4), 040401. [CrossRef]

Hallegatte, S. (2016). *Shock waves: Managing the impacts of climate change on poverty*. World Bank Publications.

Hickel, J., & Kallis, G. (2020). Is green growth possible? *New Political Economy, 25*(4), 469–486. [CrossRef]

Hughes, S., & Hoffmann, M. (2020). Just urban transitions: Toward a research agenda. *Wiley Interdisciplinary Reviews: Climate Change, 11*(3), e640. [CrossRef]

IEA. (2023). *Energy efficiency 2023*. Available online: https://www.iea.org/reports/energy-efficiency-2023 (accessed on 2 June 2025).

Imran, M., Alam, M. S., Jijian, Z., Ozturk, I., Wahab, S., & Doğan, M. (2025). From resource curse to green growth: Exploring the role of energy utilization and natural resource abundance in economic development. In *Natural resources forum* (Vol. 49, No. 2, pp. 2025–2047). Blackwell Publishing Ltd. [CrossRef]

IPCC. (2022). *Climate change 2022: Impacts, adaptation and vulnerability. Contribution of working group II to the sixth assessment report of the intergovernmental panel on climate change*. Available online: https://www.ipcc.ch/report/ar6/wg2/ (accessed on 25 May 2025).

Juhola, S., Heikkinen, M., Pietilä, T., Groundstroem, F., & Käyhkö, J. (2022). Connecting climate justice and adaptation planning: An adaptation justice index. *Environmental Science & Policy, 136*, 609–619. [CrossRef]

Khan, I., Han, L., Zhong, R., Bibi, R., & Khan, H. (2023). Income inequality, economic growth, renewable energy usage, and environmental degradation in the Belt and Road initiative countries: Dynamic panel estimation. *Environmental Science and Pollution Research, 30*(19), 57142–57154. [CrossRef]

Khan, I., Hou, F., Zakari, A., & Tawiah, V. K. (2021). The dynamic links among energy transitions, energy consumption, and sustainable economic growth: A novel framework for IEA countries. *Energy, 222*, 119935. [CrossRef]

Lamb, W. F., & Rao, N. D. (2015). Human development in a climate-constrained world: What the past says about the future. *Global Environmental Change, 33*, 14–22. [CrossRef]

Li, Z., Luan, R., & Lin, B. (2022). The trend and factors affecting renewable energy distribution and disparity across countries. *Energy, 254*, 124265. [CrossRef]

Manigandan, P., Alam, M. S., Murshed, M., Ozturk, I., Altuntas, S., & Alam, M. M. (2024). Promoting sustainable economic growth through natural resources management, green innovations, environmental policy deployment, and financial development: Fresh evidence from India. *Resources Policy, 90*, 104681. [CrossRef]

Mohtat, N., & Khirfan, L. (2021). The climate justice pillars vis-à-vis urban form adaptation to climate change: A review. *Urban Climate, 39*, 100951. [CrossRef]

Nesmith, A. A., Schmitz, C. L., Machado-Escudero, Y., Billiot, S., Forbes, R. A., Powers, M. C., Buckhoy, N., & Lawrence, L. A. (2021). Climate change, ecology, and justice. In *The intersection of environmental justice, climate change, community, and the ecology of life* (pp. 1–12). Springer. [CrossRef]

Newell, P., Srivastava, S., Naess, L. O., Torres Contreras, G. A., & Price, R. (2021). Toward transformative climate justice: An emerging research agenda. *Wiley Interdisciplinary Reviews: Climate Change, 12*(6), 1–17. [CrossRef]

Organisation for Economic Co-Operation and Development (OECD). (2024). Available online: https://data-explorer.oecd.org/ (accessed on 21 April 2025).

Phillips, P. C. B., & Hansen, B. E. (1990). Statistical inference in instrumental variables regression with I (1) processes. *Review of Economics Studies, 57*(1), 99–125. [CrossRef]

Razzaq, A., Sharif, A., Ozturk, I., & Afshan, S. (2023). Dynamic and threshold effects of energy transition and environmental governance on green growth in COP26 framework. *Renewable and Sustainable Energy Reviews, 179*, 113296. [CrossRef]

Resnik, D. B. (2022). Environmental justica and climate change policies. *Bioethics, 36*(7), 735–741. [CrossRef]

Ritu, R. K., & Kaur, A. (2024). Towards environmental sustainability: Nexus of ecological footprint, human capital, economic growth and energy consumption in India. *Management of Environmental Quality: An International Journal, 35*(1), 179–200. [CrossRef]

Roy, A. (2024). Green growth in India: Balancing economic development with environmental sustainability. *Journal of Sustainable Solutions, 15*(3), 24–34. [CrossRef]

Sahoo, M., & Sethi, N. (2020). Impact of industrialization, urbanization, and financial development on energy consumption: Empirical evidence from India. *Journal of Public Affairs, 20*(3), e2089. [CrossRef]

Schlosberg, D., & Collins, L. B. (2014). From environmental to climate justice: Climate change and the discourse of environmental justice. *Wiley Interdisciplinary Reviews: Climate Change, 5*(3), 359–374. [CrossRef]

Sengupta, S. (2023). Climate change, international justice and global order. *International Affair, 99*(1), 121–140. [CrossRef]

Shahbaz, M., Hoang, T., Kumar, M., & Roubaud, D. (2017). Energy consumption, financial development and economic growth in India: New evidence from a nonlinear and asymmetric analysis. *Energy Economics, 63*, 199–212. [CrossRef]

Shang, Y., Lian, Y., Chen, H., & Qian, F. (2023). The impacts of energy resource and tourism on green growth: Evidence from Asian economies. *Resources Policy, 81*, 103359. [CrossRef]

Sharma, R., & Rajpurohit, S. S. (2022). Nexus between income inequality and consumption of renewable energy in India: A nonlinear examination. *Economic Change and Restructuring, 55*(4), 2337–2358. [CrossRef]

Statista. (2024). Available online: https://www.statista.com/topics/12602/research-and-development-in-india/#topicOverview (accessed on 2 March 2025).

Stern, D. I. (2011). The role of energy in economic growth. *Annals of the New York Academy of Sciences, 1219*(1), 26–51. [CrossRef] [PubMed]

Sultana, F. (2021). Critical climate justica. *The Georaphical Journal, 188*(1), 1–148. [CrossRef]

Taşkın, D., Vardar, G., & Okan, B. (2020). Does renewable energy promote green economic growth in OECD countries? *Sustainability Accounting, Management and Policy Journal, 11*(4), 771–798. [CrossRef]

Tawiah, V., Zakari, A., & Adedoyin, F. (2021). Determinants of green growth in developed and developing countries. *Environmental Science and Pollution Research International, 28*, 39227–39242. [CrossRef]

UNCTAD. (2023). *UN trade and development*. Available online: https://unctadstat.unctad.org/datacentre/ (accessed on 10 May 2025).

UNDP. (2023). *Human development reports*. Available online: https://hdr.undp.org/content/human-development-and-sustainability?utm_source=chatgpt.com (accessed on 10 May 2025).

United Nations (UN). (2024). Available online: https://sdgs.un.org/goals (accessed on 2 June 2025).

Uzar, U., & Eyuboglu, K. (2023). Does income inequality increase the ecological footprint in the US: Evidence from FARDL test? *Environmental Science and Pollution Research, 30*(4), 9514–9529. [CrossRef]

Ünsal, R. B. (2024). İklim değişikliği ile mücadelede paris anlaşmasi ve iklim adaleti. *Ekonomi Yönetim Politika, 2*(2), 112–126.

Volodzkiene, L., & Streimikiene, D. (2023). Energy inequality indicators: A comprehensive review for exploring ways to reduce inequality. *Energies, 16*(16), 6075. [CrossRef]

Wang, H., Peng, G., Luo, Y., & Du, H. (2023). Asymmetric influence of renewable energy, ecological governance, and human development on green growth of BRICS countries. *Renewable Energy, 206*, 1007–1019. [CrossRef]

World Development Indicators (WDI). (2024). Available online: https://databank.worldbank.org/source/world-development-indicators (accessed on 21 April 2025).

Xu, C., Gao, Y., Qin, Z., Li, Z., Pan, S., & Qi, L. (2024). Historical characteristics and projection of global renewable energy consumption. *Renewable Energy, 234*, 121222. [CrossRef]

Zahnow, R., Yousefnia, A. R., Hassankhani, M., & Cheshmehzangi, A. (2025). Climate change inequalities: A systematic review of disparities in access to mitigation and adaptation measures. *Environmental Science & Policy, 165*, 104021. [CrossRef]

Zimm, C., Mintz-Woo, K., Brutschin, E., Hanger-Kopp, S., Hoffmann, R., Kikstra, J. S., Kuhn, M., Min, J., Muttarak, R., Pachauri, S., Patange, O., Riahi, K., & Schinko, T. (2024). Justice considerations in climate research. *Nature Climate Change, 14*(1), 22–30. [CrossRef]

Zou, X. Y., Peng, X. Y., Zhao, X. X., Ma, J., & Chang, C. P. (2024). Does income inequality affect green innovation? A non-linear evidence. *Technological and Economic Development of Economy, 30*(3), 578–602. [CrossRef]

The Business Case for the Circular Economy—Reducing Waste, Increasing Value: Promoting Sustainable Consumption and Production Patterns to Lessen the Impact on the Environment

Serdar Yay and Melih Kabayel

Abstract: The circular economy has gained significant momentum in recent years, becoming a central theme in both academic research and business practice. It emerges as a response to the inefficiencies of the linear "take–make–dispose" model, which has contributed to ecological degradation and rising economic costs. Unlike the linear approach, the circular model focuses on extending product lifecycles, reducing waste, and recovering resources to create long-term value. By emphasising efficiency and innovation, it offers an opportunity to align economic growth with environmental sustainability. This study investigates the value proposition that the circular economy provides for firms, particularly the relationship between waste reduction and the strengthening of value chains. It explores the feasibility of implementing sustainable consumption and production models, drawing insights from literature reviews and international frameworks. Special consideration is given to policy instruments such as the European Union's Circular Economy Action Plan, which illustrates how regulatory measures can support businesses in adopting circular strategies. The findings indicate that the circular economy should be seen not only as an environmental necessity but also as a strategic opportunity. By embedding circular principles into their operations, businesses can enhance competitiveness, foster resilience, and contribute to sustainable development.

1. Introduction

Since the Industrial Revolution, the linear economic model has dominated global production and consumption systems, built upon the assumption of unlimited resource availability. This model has facilitated rapid industrialisation and economic growth, yet it has also produced severe environmental externalities such as excessive extraction of raw materials, increased waste generation, greenhouse gas emissions, and biodiversity loss. Today, with natural resources becoming scarcer and climate change posing existential threats, the limitations of the linear "take–make–dispose" paradigm have become increasingly evident, leading scholars and policymakers to call for alternative frameworks (Geissdoerfer et al., 2017).

The circular economy has emerged as one of the most comprehensive and promising responses to these challenges. Unlike the linear approach, circularity aims to redefine product life cycles through practices such as recycling and remanufacturing, thereby increasing material cycles and reducing waste, and keeping resources within the system for as long as possible (Kirchherr et al., 2017). This transition reflects a systemic change in how economies are structured, moving from volume-driven growth towards value-oriented, sustainable strategies.

Importantly, the circular economy is not limited to environmental considerations; it also represents a significant business case. By integrating circular principles, firms can reduce costs, increase resource efficiency, improve supply chain resilience, and strengthen their competitive position in global markets. Moreover, international initiatives such as the European Union's Circular Economy Action Plan emphasise that regulatory frameworks, innovation incentives, and sustainable design requirements are instrumental in facilitating this shift (European Commission, 2020). These measures highlight the potential for the circular economy to serve as both an ecological necessity and an economic opportunity.

Against this backdrop, the purpose of this study is to explore how the circular economy creates tangible value for businesses. Specifically, it examines the relationship between waste reduction and value creation, and it assesses the applicability of sustainable production and consumption models in fostering long-term competitiveness. By combining insights from the academic literature with international policy frameworks, this study seeks to demonstrate that the circular economy should be understood as a strategic paradigm capable of reshaping both business models and economic systems in pursuit of sustainable development.

2. Literature Review

The circular economy is mostly examined in the literature through three fundamental principles: reduce, reuse, and recycle (3R) (Ellen MacArthur Foundation, 2019). However, in recent years, this framework has expanded to encompass areas such as innovative business models, industrial symbiosis, the sharing economy, and product–service systems (Lewandowski, 2016).

According to reports by the Ellen MacArthur Foundation, the circular economy has the potential to add approximately EUR 1.8 trillion in value to the European economy by 2030 (Ellen MacArthur Foundation, 2019). This presents a significant opportunity not only in terms of environmental sustainability but also in terms of economic growth and employment.

Studies conducted in the Turkish context show that the revaluation of waste, particularly in industrial areas, and industrial symbiosis applications are still in their infancy (Albayrak, 2025). Therefore, both strengthening legal regulations and raising awareness among businesses are considered critical. Table 1 summarises the current situation within the context of the literature, thereby contributing to the understanding of the conceptual framework (Kirchherr et al., 2017; Geissdoerfer et al., 2017; Lewandowski, 2016; Stahel, 2016; Ellen MacArthur Foundation, 2019; OECD, 2020; Albayrak, 2025).

Table 1. Circular economy studies in a theoretical and conceptual framework

Author(s) and Year	Scope of the Study	Key Findings	Contribution
Kirchherr et al. (2017)	Conceptual analysis of the circular economy through 114 definitions	The concept of the circular economy is fragmented and has different perspectives.	Highlighting the need for conceptual clarity.
Geissdoerfer et al. (2017)	The relationship between circular economy and sustainability	The circular economy as a new sustainability paradigm.	Making a significant contribution to the theoretical framework.
Lewandowski (2016)	Designing circular business models	Business models need to be restructured for the circular economy.	Providing a framework applicable to the business world.
Stahel (2016)	The innovation dimension of the circular economy	Resource efficiency with service-oriented business models.	Highlighting strategic opportunities for businesses.
Ellen MacArthur Foundation (2019)	Policy report	The economic and environmental contribution potential of the circular economy.	Providing a roadmap for policymakers.
OECD (2020)	Circular economy in cities and regions	Promoting circular practices at the local level.	Highlighting the policy/local government dimension.
(Albayrak, 2025)	Industrial symbiosis in the Turkish context	Limited applications in Turkey.	Highlighting policy deficiencies at the local level.

Source: Authors' compilation based on data from Kirchherr et al. (2017), Geissdoerfer et al. (2017), Lewandowski (2016), Stahel (2016), Ellen MacArthur Foundation (2019), OECD (2020) and Albayrak (2025).

After the circular economy has been addressed conceptually, it is important to examine how its practical applications are shaped and how it is integrated into business processes. In this context, we can classify circular economy examples into five application approaches. These are as follows:

- Product-as-a-Service (PaaS): In this model, businesses offer customers the right to use a product through leasing or subscription systems rather than selling the product itself. This means the product remains the property of the manufacturer, and maintenance and recycling processes are simplified. Philips' "Lighting-as-a-Service" application is a typical example of this "service-based business" model; the company reduces resource consumption by offering lighting services instead of selling light bulbs (Stahel, 2016).
- Sharing Economy: This model is based on the shared use of resources rather than individual ownership. Examples include car-sharing platforms, office space sharing, and home sharing. This approach offers cost advantages and reduces waste in the production–consumption cycle (Botsman & Rogers, 2010).
- Product Life Extension: This model focuses on extending the useful life of products and includes maintenance, repair, and remanufacturing processes.

Renault has achieved cost savings and reduced waste by remanufacturing automotive parts at its facilities in France (OECD, 2020).

- Resource Recovery: In this model, waste is transformed into a new production input. For example, producing biofuel from coffee waste or converting waste fabric into new yarns in the textile industry fall under this category. Industrial symbiosis applications similarly create a waste–resource cycle between businesses (Ellen MacArthur Foundation, 2019).
- Circular Supply Chains: The integration of renewable, biological, or recycled inputs into the supply chain forms the basis of this business model. Patagonia incorporates recycled polyester and organic cotton into its products, thereby including them in the circular value chain (Lewandowski, 2016).

3. Methods and Findings

This study was prepared using a qualitative research approach. Firstly, the circular economy literature was reviewed, followed by an examination of reports from organisations such as the European Union, the OECD, and the World Bank. The study conducts a conceptual analysis based on secondary data and supports the theoretical framework through case studies.

The circular economy offers companies not only environmental compliance but also the opportunity to develop new business models. Product–service systems, leasing and sharing models increase businesses' long-term revenue streams (Lewandowski, 2016). Furthermore, thanks to resource efficiency, businesses reduce their energy and raw material costs, which in turn increases their global competitiveness.

According to European Union data, companies that transition to circular business models can reduce their costs by an average of 20% (OECD, 2020). Furthermore, companies that adopt environmentally friendly practices see a significant increase in their brand value.

The idea that waste is not merely a burden to be disposed of, but also a source of new value creation, forms the basis of the circular economy. For example, in the automotive sector, recycling practices and the remanufacturing of used parts both reduce environmental impacts and provide cost advantages to businesses (Stahel, 2016).

The Figure 1, titled "Ecological Cost of the Linear Economy (1970–2020)", illustrates the environmental costs of the linear economic model from a temporal perspective. The composite index (100), based on data from 1970, reveals a continuous upward trend in ecological costs reflecting greenhouse gas emissions, natural resource use, waste production, and biodiversity loss (IPCC, 2022; OECD, 2020; UNEP, 2019). Following the year 1990, the curve steepens with globalisation, dependence on fossil fuels, and accelerating industrialisation, while after 2000, costs rise dramatically. Had the circular economy been adopted earlier, these costs would not only have reduced environmental losses but also accelerated economic growth and development through sustainable investments. Thus, the delayed implementation of the circular approach has not only harmed the environment but also meant missed economic opportunities (Ellen MacArthur Foundation, 2019; Stahel, 2016).

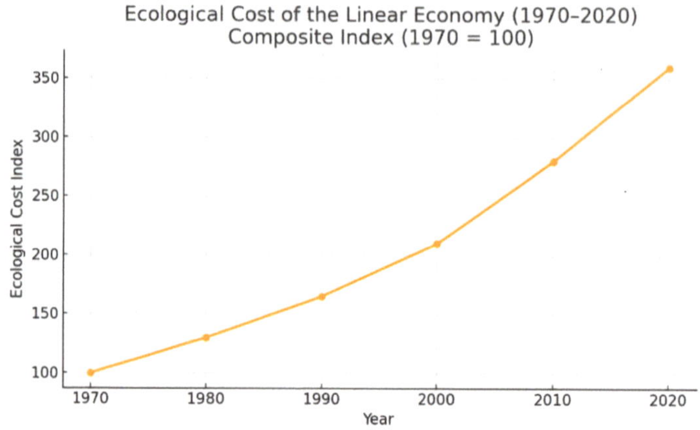

Figure 1. Ecological cost of the linear economy (1970–2020). Source: Authors' compilation based on data from IPCC (2022), OECD (2020) and UNEP (2019).

Therefore, the Figure 1 demonstrates that the costs of the linear economy are increasing uncontrollably; it also clearly indicates the potential of circular economy strategies to reduce future costs and promote investment-based development. In this context, Figure 2 visually illustrates the difference in ecological costs between linear and circular economies (IPCC, 2022; OECD, 2020; UNEP, 2019).

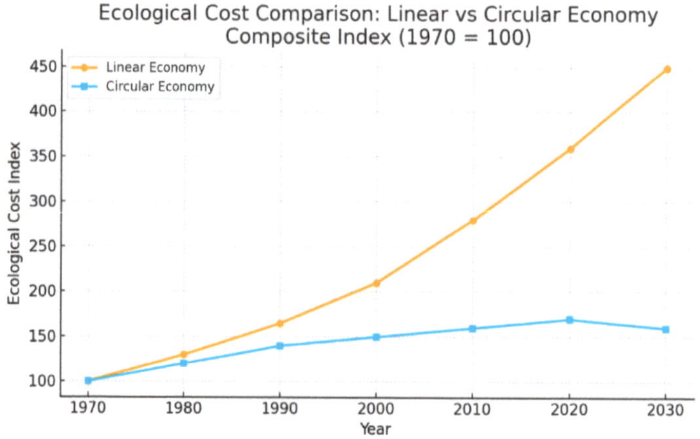

Figure 2. Ecological cost comparison: linear vs. circular economy (1970–2030). Source: Authors' compilation based on data from IPCC (2022), OECD (2020) and UNEP (2019).

The Figure 2 above, "Ecological Cost Comparison: Linear vs. Circular Economy (1970–2030)", highlights the ecological cost difference between linear and circular economy models. The composite index (100), based on 1970, represents greenhouse gas emissions, waste production, natural resource use, and biodiversity loss.

As clearly shown in the graph, the linear economic model continuously increases ecological costs over time. After 2000, the curve rose sharply, and the 2030 forecast shows that costs have reached dramatic levels. In contrast, the circular economy model has significantly slowed the rate of increase in costs and shows that costs began to stabilise after 2020 (IPCC, 2022; OECD, 2020; UNEP, 2019). Had the circular economy been adopted earlier, this would have led to stronger growth and development effects driven by investment, alongside a reduction in ecological costs. Therefore, the circular economy is not only an approach that reduces environmental damage, but also a strategic tool that will accelerate long-term economic development (Ellen MacArthur Foundation, 2019; Stahel, 2016).

Industrial symbiosis applications transform one company's waste into another company's raw material. Pilot projects launched in the İzmir Atatürk Organised Industrial Zone in Turkey demonstrate that this approach is particularly applicable in the chemical and metal sectors (Albayrak, 2025).

The success of the circular economy lies not only with producers but also in transforming consumer behaviour. The demand from younger generations for environmentally friendly products is driving businesses to develop green product design, eco-labelling, and products with a low carbon footprint (UNEP, 2019).

Consumers' new consumption habits, which focus on "using" rather than "owning", are strengthening the sharing economy and accelerating circular business models. For example, car sharing instead of car ownership or renting white goods instead of buying them is becoming increasingly common.

The literature on the circular economy increasingly emphasises the role of international organisations and policy frameworks in shaping both academic discourse and business practices. A pivotal reference in this regard is the European Union's Circular Economy Action Plan, which provides a comprehensive policy framework for promoting waste reduction, resource efficiency, and sustainable growth across member states. The plan outlines specific measures ranging from eco-design requirements and extended producer responsibility schemes to incentives for green innovation, thereby offering a blueprint for firms to integrate circular strategies into their operations (European Commission, 2020). Complementing this regional initiative, global institutions have also contributed significantly to the conceptual and practical development of the circular economy. The Ellen MacArthur Foundation (2019) has produced influential reports linking circular practices to climate change mitigation, arguing that a systemic transition could reduce global greenhouse gas emissions and enhance competitiveness. Similarly, the OECD (2020) highlights the importance of embedding circular principles in cities and regions, stressing the role of local governance, institutional capacity, and financial mechanisms in scaling up circular solutions. From a broader perspective, UNEP's (2019) Global Resources Outlook underscores the unsustainable trajectory of global resource use and emphasises the necessity of decoupling economic growth from environmental degradation. These insights are further reinforced by the IPCC (2022), which links the adoption of circular models with pathways to climate resilience and carbon neutrality. Collectively, these reports demonstrate that the circular economy is not merely a theoretical concept but a policy-driven transformation with far-reaching implications for sustainability. The convergence of international policy frameworks and organisational initiatives indicates a growing consensus that circularity is essential to addressing both ecological limits and economic challenges. This body of literature illustrates how regulatory measures, policy incentives, and global cooperation can accelerate the mainstreaming of the circular economy, while also providing businesses with strategic opportunities for innovation, resilience, and long-term value creation.

Policy makers' incentives play a decisive role in the widespread adoption of the circular economy. The European Union's Circular Economy Action Plan sets standards across a wide range of areas, from waste management to product design, and provides a roadmap for member states (European Commission, 2020). In Turkey, however, a comprehensive strategy has yet to be developed, and the fragmented nature of the legislation is slowing down the transformation of businesses.

4. Results

Based on the literature review and methodological framework, several key findings have emerged from the analysis:

Rising Ecological Costs under the Linear Economy

- The composite ecological cost index demonstrates a steady increase from 1970 to 2020.
- Major drivers include greenhouse gas emissions, accelerated natural resource use, waste generation, and biodiversity decline (IPCC, 2022; OECD, 2020).

Acceleration after 2000

- Globalisation and intensified industrial production after 2000 led to a steep upward trend in ecological costs.
- Fossil fuel dependency and insufficient regulatory frameworks amplified this escalation (UNEP, 2019).

Mitigation Potential of the Circular Economy

- Comparative projections indicate that adopting circular models can flatten and eventually reduce ecological costs.
- Practices such as product life extension, remanufacturing, and resource recovery demonstrate measurable reductions (Stahel, 2016).

Business Value Creation

- Circular models provide not only environmental benefits but also tangible economic advantages.
- Case examples (Philips, Renault, Patagonia) show that cost savings, resource efficiency, and brand value are enhanced through circular practices (OECD, 2020; Lewandowski, 2016).

Missed Opportunities

- Delayed adoption of circular strategies resulted in lost opportunities for sustainable growth.
- An earlier transition could have reduced ecological damage and simultaneously boosted long-term investment and development (Ellen MacArthur Foundation, 2019).

Role of Policy and Institutions

- Literature and empirical review underline the importance of policy instruments such as tax incentives, green financing, and awareness campaigns.
- Stronger institutional capacity is necessary to mainstream circular practices into industrial and urban systems (OECD, 2020).

5. Discussion

The findings of this research confirm that the persistence of a linear economic paradigm has contributed significantly to mounting ecological costs, while the gradual adoption of circular strategies has shown potential to mitigate such impacts. The linear trajectory, as illustrated in the ecological cost index, underscores how unsustainable production and consumption patterns have accelerated environmental degradation since the 1970s (IPCC, 2022). The steep increase after 2000 reflects the combined pressures of industrial expansion, resource extraction, and inadequate policy responses.

Simultaneously, the comparative projection between linear and circular models offers a critical perspective. Circular practices, although still unevenly applied, demonstrate a pathway towards flattening and eventually reducing ecological costs. This reinforces arguments in the literature that circularity can function not only as a waste management strategy but as a systemic transformation of value creation (Ellen MacArthur Foundation, 2019; Stahel, 2016). The discussion must therefore shift from viewing the circular economy as an environmental initiative to recognising it as an economic imperative.

Another crucial dimension is the business case. Evidence from companies such as Philips and Renault illustrates that circular strategies—ranging from product-as-a-service to remanufacturing—can simultaneously reduce environmental footprints and generate cost savings (OECD, 2020). This suggests that circularity is not a trade-off between profitability and sustainability but rather a convergence of both goals. Nevertheless, challenges persist: financing constraints, lack of regulatory coherence, and gaps in consumer awareness continue to hinder widespread implementation (Lewandowski, 2016).

Finally, the missed opportunities must be acknowledged. Had circular approaches been embraced earlier, both ecological costs and economic inefficiencies could have been avoided. This highlights the importance of proactive policy instruments such as tax incentives, green financing, and stricter regulations, alongside education and awareness-raising to shift consumer behaviour (UNEP, 2019).

Overall, the discussion demonstrates that the transition to a circular economy is not merely desirable but necessary. It requires collaboration between policymakers, businesses, and societies to transform structural barriers into opportunities for innovation and resilience.

6. Conclusions

The evidence presented throughout this study highlights the growing urgency of transitioning from a linear to a circular economic model. The analysis of ecological cost trends demonstrates that the "take–make–dispose" paradigm of the linear economy has resulted in continuously rising environmental externalities since the 1970s, including higher greenhouse gas emissions, escalating waste, and accelerated biodiversity loss. The steep trajectory of these costs after 2000 reveals the unsustainability of linear practices, particularly in the context of rapid globalisation and fossil fuel dependency.

By contrast, the circular economy offers a credible pathway to decoupling growth from resource consumption. Comparative projections show that ecological costs could be stabilised and even reduced if circular models such as product-as-a-service, sharing systems, resource recovery, and lifecycle extension are embraced. These models not only mitigate ecological damage but also generate opportunities for innovation, resilience, and competitiveness. The business cases of firms like Philips and Renault illustrate that circular practices can simultaneously lower costs and increase long-term value creation.

Crucially, the results also imply that had circular strategies been adopted earlier, ecological costs would have been significantly lower, while investments in sustainable production could have fostered stronger growth and development outcomes. This missed opportunity underscores the importance of timely policy interventions, regulatory frameworks, and financial incentives to accelerate circular adoption. Moreover, the growing demand for sustainable products among younger generations suggests that consumer behaviour can reinforce and amplify this transition.

In conclusion, the circular economy should not be perceived solely as an environmental necessity but as a strategic economic model capable of reshaping value creation. By aligning ecological sustainability with economic opportunity, circular practices offer a dual dividend: protecting planetary boundaries while fostering long-term prosperity. For policymakers, businesses, and societies alike, embracing circularity is no longer optional—it is a prerequisite for resilient and sustainable development in the twenty-first century.

The circular economy not only ensures environmental sustainability but also offers a strategic business model for companies. In this context,

- Businesses can gain both cost advantages and strengthen their brand value by adopting circular business models.
- The government should accelerate the transformation of the private sector by strengthening regulatory frameworks and incentive mechanisms.
- Awareness campaigns should be organised, and pilot projects should be rolled out through collaboration between academia, the private sector and the public sector.

Ultimately, the circular economy should be seen as more than just an environmental policy; it is a fundamental tool for sustainable development and a competitive economy.

Author Contributions: Conceptualisation: S.Y.; methodology: S.Y. and M.K.; validation: S.Y.; formal analysis: S.Y. and M.K.; investigation: S.Y. and M.K.; resources: S.Y. and M.K.; data curation: S.Y. and M.K.; writing—original draft preparation: S.Y.; writing—review and editing: S.Y.; visualisation: S.Y.; supervision: S.Y.; project administration: S.Y.; funding acquisition: S.Y. and M.K. All authors have read and agreed to the published version of the manuscript.

Funding: This research received no external funding.

Conflicts of Interest: The authors declare no conflicts of interest.

Author Names and Affiliations: Serdar Yay, Department of Public Finance, Faculty of Economics and Administrative Sciences, Izmir Democracy University, Izmir, Turkey; Melih Kabayel, Izmir Democracy University, Izmir, Turkey.

Keywords: circular economy; sustainable production and consumption; waste reduction; value chain resilience.

References

Albayrak, A. (2025). The transformation of industrial policies in Turkey within the framework of industrial ecology and circular economy. *Journal of Design for Resilience in Architecture and Planning*, *6*(3), 476–490. [CrossRef]

Botsman, R., & Rogers, R. (2010). *What's mine is yours: The rise of collaborative consumption*. Harper Business.

Ellen MacArthur Foundation. (2019). *Completing the picture: How the circular economy tackles climate change*. Ellen MacArthur Foundation. Available online: https://ellenmacarthurfoundation.org (accessed on 15 September 2025).

European Commission. (2020). *A new circular economy action plan: For a cleaner and more competitive Europe*. European Commission. Available online: https://eur-lex.europa.eu/legal-content/EN/TXT/?uri=CELEX:52020DC0098 (accessed on 3 September 2025).

Geissdoerfer, M., Savaget, P., Bocken, N. M., & Hultink, E. J. (2017). The circular economy—A new sustainability paradigm? *Journal of Cleaner Production*, *143*, 757–768. [CrossRef]

Intergovernmental Panel on Climate Change (IPCC). (2022). *Climate change 2022: Mitigation of climate change*. Cambridge University Press. [CrossRef]

Kirchherr, J., Reike, D., & Hekkert, M. (2017). Conceptualising the circular economy: An analysis of 114 definitions. *Resources, Conservation and Recycling*, *127*, 221–232. [CrossRef]

Lewandowski, M. (2016). Designing the business models for circular economy—Towards the conceptual framework. *Sustainability*, *8*(1), 43. [CrossRef]

Organisation for Economic Co-Operation and Development (OECD). (2020). *Circular economy in cities and regions: Synthesis report*. OECD Publishing. [CrossRef]

Stahel, W. R. (2016). The circular economy. *Nature*, *531*(7595), 435–438. [CrossRef] [PubMed]

United Nations Environment Programme (UNEP). (2019). *Global resources outlook 2019: Natural resources for the future we want*. United Nations Environment Programme. Available online: https://www.resourcepanel.org/reports/global-resources-outlook (accessed on 2 September 2025).

Public–Private Partnerships: Using Cooperation to Address Climate Change

Sonja Đuričin, Isidora Ljumović and Isidora Beraha

Abstract: Addressing climate change requires transformative action across all sectors, including the micro, small, and medium enterprise (MSME) sector, which often lacks the institutional capacity and financial means to pursue sustainable practices. Public–private partnerships (PPPs) are increasingly recognised as a mechanism to close this gap by mobilising private sector expertise and resources in support of public sustainability objectives. The process of green transition presents a complex challenge for MSMEs, requiring multifaceted and coordinated institutional responses. This study aims to map the areas where the application of PPP models could help to overcome the main barriers that MSMEs face in adopting sustainable practices in Serbia. Based on a structured questionnaire applied as part of a broader research initiative, the study identifies financial constraints, regulatory complexity, and limited access to technical and advisory services as the most pressing obstacles. In response, the research proposes the application of the Build–Operate–Transfer (BOT) PPP model as a targeted mechanism to support MSMEs through the development of shared green infrastructure. The proposed solution enables indirect financial support by engaging private actors in designing, financing, and managing infrastructure projects that benefit multiple enterprises while preserving public ownership and strategic oversight. The findings demonstrate that the PPP framework can effectively address structural limitations of MSMEs by integrating public and private resources toward common sustainability goals.

1. Introduction

Climate change is one of the most complex challenges of our time, with profound and multi-layered consequences for natural systems, economic dynamics, social cohesion, and institutional structures (Malerba, 2022; Savić et al., 2021; Somanathan et al., 2021; Orlov et al., 2024; Chae et al., 2020; Đuričin et al., 2016). It is a phenomenon that threatens biodiversity and ecological stability while undermining the foundations of economic growth by reducing resource availability, weakening the resilience of infrastructure, and destabilising market conditions (Hristov et al., 2023; Silvast et al., 2021; Campiglio et al., 2022). The cumulative effects of climate change led to complex challenges that affect all aspects of society, from the formulation and implementation of public policies to the stability of economic systems and the protection of citizens and their property.

Climate change poses a challenge to innovative governance approaches, as it requires integrated cooperation across different sectors and levels of government, with the active involvement of business and citizens to ensure both the effectiveness and legitimacy of institutional action. For this reason, the international community and national governments have committed to implementing ambitious climate change targets, notably through the Paris Agreement (2015) and the European Green Deal (2019) (UNFCCC, 2015; European Commission, 2019). These overarching documents set out commitments to reduce greenhouse gas emissions, increase energy efficiency, introduce renewable energy sources, strengthen the circular economy and conserve natural resources and biodiversity. Achieving these goals depends on the legal framework and requires a profound change in socioeconomic models, infrastructure systems, educational paradigms, and consumer habits.

In the contemporary literature, public–private partnerships (PPPs) are increasingly recognised as a relevant instrument for the implementation of sustainable development and climate change goals (Brinkerhoff & Brinkerhoff, 2011). Research indicates that the effective implementation of PPP models requires clearly defined legal frameworks, institutional stability, and the active participation of local stakeholders (Yuan et al., 2010; Amović, 2019). However, relatively few studies address the role of PPPs in supporting micro, small, and medium-sized enterprises (MSMEs) in the green transition process, particularly in the context of developing and emerging economies. Research on the MSME sector often addresses individual barriers such as access to finance (Farhan et al., 2024) and regulatory compliance (Wilson et al., 2011; Toromade & Chiekezie, 2024), while its synergy with the public sector remains under-researched. This gap in the literature justifies the need to explore the potential of PPP models in supporting the MSME sector in Serbia, which faces specific challenges and institutional constraints.

Previous research indicates that an effective transition to a climate-neutral economy depends on a combination of institutional stability (Fu et al., 2023), access to finance (Rusydiana, 2024; Scott, 2023), and innovative mechanisms of collaboration between the public and private sectors (Semieniuk et al., 2020). For precisely these reasons, the key challenge of today's climate policy lies in its operationalisation, i.e., the translation of global goals into concrete measures that have an impact at the local and sectoral level. In this process, it is essential to involve all stakeholders, especially government institutions, civil society organisations, and the business sector. Within the business sector, MSMEs play a special role, as they form the backbone of economic development in most countries (Đuričin & Beraha, 2024; Stevanović et al., 2019). MSMEs generate a significant share of gross domestic product, employ a considerable proportion of the workforce, and have the potential to serve as key sources of innovation, structural change and industrial renewal (Đuričin et al., 2022; Đuričin & Beraha, 2021b). At the same time, MSMEs are often the most vulnerable to climate risks due to their limited capacity to implement transformative strategies (Gannon et al., 2022; Neise et al., 2019; Asensio et al., 2021; Thongoh et al., 2021; Ljumović et al., 2015; Ljumović & Jakšić, 2015), further emphasising the need for systematic and targeted support for their transition to sustainability.

Despite the growing interest in the role of PPPs in achieving sustainable development goals, the existing literature rarely addresses the specific aspect of their application in supporting the MSME sector in the green transition process. Most studies focus on large infrastructure projects or public services in urban areas (Zhang et al., 2022; Himmel & Siemiatycki, 2017; Alghamdi et al., 2022), while micro, small, and medium-sized enterprises are often overlooked in PPP-related analyses. Furthermore, papers dealing with MSMEs in the context of climate change primarily address access to finance, regulatory barriers and technological capacity (Sibiya et al., 2023) but rarely explore institutional mechanisms of collaboration with the public sector as a potential tool to overcome these challenges (Fatemi et al., 2020). This gap is particularly pronounced in developing and emerging economies, where the MSME sector is both most vulnerable and most important for implementing sustainable solutions at the local level (Ahmadov et al., 2024; Kawane et al., 2023).

This research contributes to the existing theoretical foundations by providing empirical evidence generated in Serbia, with a particular focus on the specific needs and constraints of the MSME sector in key areas relevant to climate change implementation. These areas include energy efficiency, waste management, environmental protection. and adaptation to the relevant regulations in this field. In this context, the PPP concept is gaining importance as a potential mechanism to integrate government and market interests, enabling more efficient risk sharing, resource mobilisation, and capacity building for the implementation of green policies.

In the current context of implementing climate and sustainability policies, the PPP concept is increasingly recognised as an instrument that enables synergies between the public interest and market mechanisms in the pursuit of development priorities (Vassileva, 2022). A PPP is perceived as a long-term agreement between a government entity and a private party in the fulfilment of initiatives on a national and international level that solve socioeconomic problems, provide public assets or services, and promote sustainable development of the economies and civil societies (WB, 2017). In the context of climate policy, PPPs play a key role in achieving a variety of objectives. PPPs facilitate the development of infrastructure for the use of renewable energy sources (Ugwu et al., 2024) and contribute to the establishment of efficient waste management systems (Afful et al., 2023). In addition, PPPs enable the implementation of measures to increase energy efficiency (Balcılar et al., 2023), improve sustainable mobility (Vasyliev et al., 2019), and protect the environment (Naumov et al., 2022). Such integration of multiple aspects of sustainable development through PPPs can significantly contribute to reducing the negative impacts of climate change and promoting ecological balance.

PPPs can compensate for the limitations of budget financing and contribute to a more efficient and stable implementation of strategic projects in the context of the green transition (Wen et al., 2022). In addition, partnerships with the private sector stimulate innovation that supports decarbonisation and increases the economy's resilience to climate-related challenges (Joseph et al., 2025). In transition countries, the institutional and regulatory framework for the application of PPP mechanisms to support climate and green transformation is still in the early stages of development (Amović et al., 2020). Practice to date shows that PPPs have been used most frequently in traditional sectors such as transport infrastructure or public utilities (Amović, 2019), while their application in specific areas of sustainability and environmental protection remains relatively limited (Gajinov et al., 2022). As a result, there is a notable lack of a strategic approach that would systematically link public investment with the needs of MSMEs in the green transformation processes.

The aim of this study is to map the areas where the application of appropriate public–private partnership models could contribute to overcoming the challenges faced by MSMEs in the process of green transition in Serbia. Accordingly, the research hypothesis is as follows:

H: MSMEs in Serbia, in the process of green transition, face challenges that identify areas with high potential for the application of specific public–private partnership (PPP) models.

Empirical data collected in 2024 as part of a project entitled "Roadmap for the Implementation of the Green Agenda for MSMEs in the Republic of Serbia" was used to achieve the research objective. The project was carried out by the Institute of Economic Sciences in Belgrade with financial support from the Deutsche Gesellschaft für Internationale Zusammenarbeit (GIZ). The results of the analysis will show in which areas MSMEs in Serbia see the greatest obstacles to the implementation of the green transition and to what extent these areas offer potential for the application of various public–private partnership models. Based on these findings, recommendations will be formulated on how PPP instruments can be better adapted to the specific needs of the MSME sector to support the shift towards sustainable and resilient business practices.

2. Materials and Methods

Both secondary and primary data were used for the study. The secondary data was obtained by using desk research methods. The desk research was conducted to provide an analytical contextualisation of the problem, identify the regulatory and institutional framework for the green transition, and examine the existing knowledge on the role of PPPs in this area (Đuričin & Beraha, 2021a). Secondary data sources included relevant scientific articles, international studies, official reports and policy documents, documents from international organisations, and national strategic and legal documents. The desk analysis made it possible to identify general trends, obstacles and potentials for the application of PPP models and thus created the basis for defining the scope of the research and interpreting the results of the primary research.

The primary data comes from a survey conducted as part of the project "Roadmap for the Implementation of the Green Agenda for MSMEs in the Republic of Serbia", which was carried out in 2024 by the Institute of Economic Sciences in Belgrade with financial support from the Deutsche Gesellschaft für Internationale Zusammenarbeit (GIZ). The questionnaire was designed as a quantitative research tool to investigate existing sustainability practices, perceptions of barriers and needs related to the green transition, and awareness of available support mechanisms. The instrument comprised a total of 35 closed and semi-open-ended questions organised into five interlinked thematic units: general characteristics of the company and the respondent; sustainability and green transition practices; identification of barriers and needs; legal framework and institutional support; and green financing and availability of incentives. The study covered 353 micro, small, and medium-sized enterprises in four sectors: manufacturing rubber and plastic products, wood processing, paper and paper products, manufacturing metal products and machinery, manufacturing of food and beverages, and tourism. The collected data were analysed in Microsoft Excel (Microsoft 365) using descriptive statistics.

The survey results were analysed to map challenges and identify potential areas where PPP models could contribute to overcoming obstacles in the green transformation process of MSMEs in Serbia. A descriptive analysis of the frequency and distribution of responses was carried out, together with a comparative interpretation of the results across thematic areas defined by the previous analysis of secondary sources (Beraha & Đuričin, 2020). In this way, a basis for the thematic grouping of potential areas for PPP interventions was created, which serves as a basis for the discussion of the research findings.

The data used in this study are part of a broader corpus of evidence collected as part of the above-mentioned project. Only the results that are relevant to the topic of this paper are presented. The full-raw dataset is not publicly available due to contractual and ethical restrictions.

3. Results

The structure of the sample shows that the survey focused primarily on small and medium-sized enterprises, which form the backbone of the Serbian economy. Small enterprises made up the largest share of respondents, at 37%. This result underlines the significant role of small businesses in the broader economic context, given their importance within the economic structure of Serbia. Medium-sized enterprises, which are the main contributors to the output of the MSME sector, accounted for 34% of the sample, while micro and large enterprises were represented by 26% and 3%, respectively. The most strongly represented sector in the sample was tourism, with 28% of participants. This was followed by the manufacture of metal products and machinery (21%), the manufacture of rubber and plastic products (18%), and the manufacture of food and beverages, at 17% of the total sample. Finally, the wood processing, paper, and paper product sector represented 16% of the total.

The structure of the sample enabled the identification of the main barriers and needs within the MSME sector in relation to the implementation of sustainable practices and the transition to green business models. In line with the research objective, emphasis was placed on understanding the factors that hinder the implementation of sustainable solutions and identifying the forms of support that would be most beneficial to businesses in this process.

Understanding the challenges faced by MSMEs in adopting sustainable practices is essential for designing appropriate support tools and public policies. Identifying these challenges allows for a more accurate mapping of systemic weaknesses that hinder the green transition and the tailoring of support measures to the specific characteristics of each sector and their varying degrees of readiness to adopt sustainable practices. The most common challenges to implementing sustainable practices are shown in Figure 1. Lack of financial resources (25%) and high initial costs (13%) are the main challenges to implementing sustainable practices in the MSME sector. These results confirm that financial viability is a fundamental prerequisite for the transition to green business models. The third most cited challenge is the complexity of administrative procedures (15%), indicating the need to simplify bureaucratic obstacles and improve public administration in the green transition. Legal challenges are also strongly represented (11%), indicating the existence of inconsistencies or ambiguities within the legal framework for the green transition. Problems with human resources are another important category of challenges: 10% of responses refer to difficulties in finding qualified personnel, and 9% refer to a lack of knowledge and expertise within the enterprises themselves. Difficulties in identifying suitable technical and technological solutions account for 6% of all responses, indicating the need for additional technical support and the development of an innovative infrastructure. Limited market demand was mentioned in 4% of responses, while low profitability and lack of major challenges were each mentioned in 3% of responses.

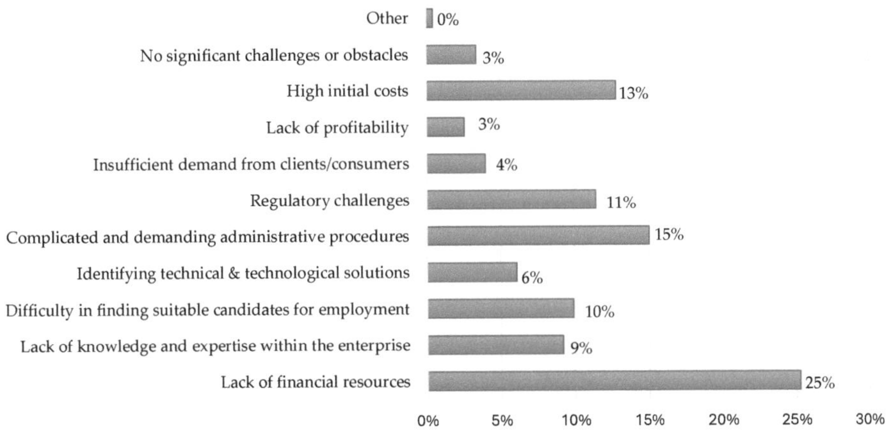

Figure 1. Challenges enterprises are facing in implementing sustainable practices. Source: Figure by authors.

Responses to the question about the types of support that would be most beneficial for the implementation of sustainable initiatives are shown in Figure 2 and reflect the clearly articulated expectations of small and medium-sized enterprises. MSMEs in Serbia cite financial incentives, including grants and favourable loans (23%), as the most important form of support for the successful implementation of sustainable practices. This result confirms previous findings on the limited financial capacity of the sector and underlines the need to develop targeted financing mechanisms to facilitate the green transition. Reducing administrative burdens and providing technical and advisory support are the second most important, each accounting for 14% of total responses. This points to the perceived complexity of the regulations and the technical requirements of the transition process, which can be a particular barrier for micro and small businesses that lack the internal resources to manage complex procedures and implement specific technical solutions. The second most frequently identified need is education and training (11%), further confirming the importance of strengthening internal skills and staff capacity to understand and apply sustainable business models. Improving access to information and establishing a green technology fund were each mentioned by 9% of respondents, underscoring the importance of access to knowledge, tools and resources for MSMEs looking to engage in the green economy. A moderate but not insignificant number of respondents also highlighted the importance of interpretation of regulations and guidelines (7%), as well as opportunities to network with other green businesses (6%) and improving infrastructure (6%). These results suggest that effective support for MSMEs needs to be multi-dimensional, encompassing regulatory, organisational and physical aspects of the business environment.

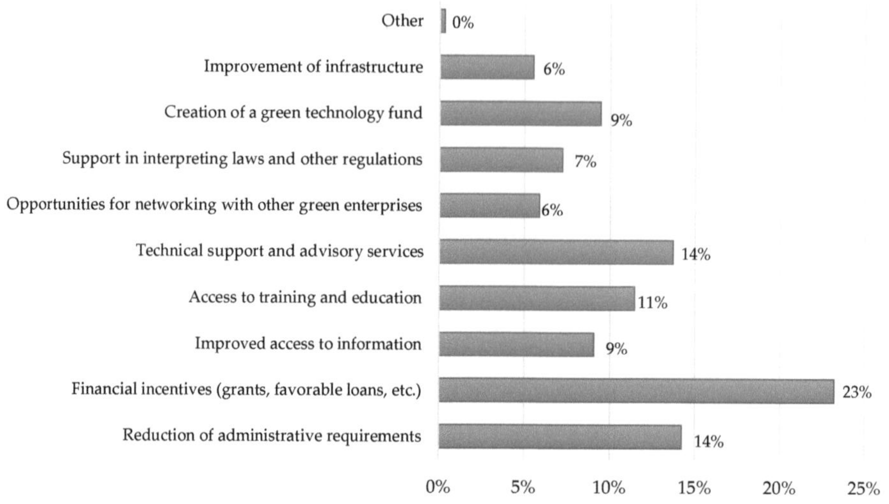

Figure 2. Most useful types of support for enterprises in the implementation of sustainable practices. Source: Figure by authors.

The challenges identified and the clearly expressed expectations of enterprises highlight the need for integrated and functionally coordinated support instruments that would enable the structural barriers to the green transition of the MSME sector to be overcome more effectively. In this context, the public–private partnership proves to be a suitable model for consolidating institutional capacities and resources with a clearly defined distribution of responsibilities and powers that can contribute to a sustainable and long-term adoption of green business practices.

4. Discussion

The research findings indicate that the process of green transition within the MSME sector in Serbia is complex, as the identified barriers go beyond financial constraints and include regulatory inconsistencies, limited technical and human resources, and underdeveloped internal capacities for planning and implementing sustainable business practices. Accordingly, enterprises not only see a need for financial support, but also cite the reduction of administrative burdens, the availability of advisory and technical services, and training and education programs as priority forms of support. These priorities directly reflect the multidimensional nature of the challenges identified. This constellation of needs shows that the green transition requires the simultaneous overcoming of several types of barriers, where a single measure is not sufficient without a coordinated institutional response. This means that an integrated approach is needed that combines regulatory reforms with capacity building and the availability of financial and technical resources.

This pattern should be placed in the context of previous research showing that limited institutional capacity, fragmented support and insufficient coordination between stakeholders further complicate the transformation process towards sustainable business models. Institutional fragmentation undermines local innovation due to a lack of coherence and alignment with broader government goals, which is further evidence of the inherent barriers created by insufficient institutional capacity (Tran et al., 2022). Similarly, Hatipoğlu et al. argue that structured collaboration is necessary to effectively implement sustainable projects and manage the complexity of stakeholder participation (Hatipoğlu et al., 2016). Effective coordination among stakeholders through policies is crucial for promoting sustainability practices and reflects the impact of institutional capacity on green transformations (Y. Li & Li, 2019). Furthermore, Droege et al. emphasise that overcoming public sector challenges in implementing circular economy assessments requires coordinated efforts between different stakeholders. Their research shows that without adequate communication and collaboration, the potential benefits of transitioning to sustainable practices may not be fully realised (Droege et al., 2021). This confirms the idea that effective coordination is essential for promoting sustainability across all sectors.

In this context, there is a clear need for strategic mechanisms that integrate public and private resources and align them towards common sustainable development goals. Public–private partnerships are increasingly recognised in the literature as an effective framework for mobilising various resources and capacities, including financial resources, expertise and advanced technologies, institutional support through the adaptation and implementation of regulatory measures and the deployment of adequate human resources, with the aim of effectively supporting the MSME sector. First, PPPs facilitate the mobilisation of financial resources, which is crucial for the sustainability of SMEs. Research shows that these partnerships enable cooperative financing mechanisms that alleviate the financing difficulties that SMEs often face. The PPP framework facilitates the provision of resources from both the public and private sectors, creating opportunities for SMEs to access financial support and innovative technologies. The involvement of private enterprises in PPPs can significantly improve the quality and efficiency of services by integrating innovative management methods into public services, which is essential for the growth of SMEs (Nikonova et al., 2019). In addition, studies show how PPPs create links that improve the financial sustainability of SMEs. Chumba's research discusses the potential of partnerships between universities, the government and private entities to mobilise funding and demonstrates a model where SMEs can thrive through collaborative efforts that go beyond mere funding (Chumba, 2020). This is in line with the findings of Popa, who points out that PPPs offer benefits such as overcoming financial constraints faced by SMEs, thus helping to strengthen their resources in competitive markets (Popa, 2018). In particular, the role of legal frameworks and institutional support is central to enabling these partnerships (C. Li et al., 2021). Second, PPP investments in technology and innovation are central to achieving environmental sustainability (Khan et al., 2020). This is consistent with the findings that such partnerships help mobilise technological innovation to respond to pressing climate issues (Lee et al., 2021). Third, PPPs have proven to be a crucial mechanism for facilitating the implementation of regulatory measures in the SME sector. The findings of Oksana et al. suggest that the effectiveness of PPP models in implementing public policies correlates directly with the involvement of the private sector in the policy-making process (Zakharina et al., 2020). The cooperative nature of PPPs ensures that the interests of private entities are taken into account, which not only increases compliance but also improves the overall business environment for SMEs. Finally, PPPs are increasingly recognised as an effective mechanism for improving human capital through the development of skills aligned with market needs. The joint engagement of the public and private sectors, supported by development actors, can contribute significantly to improving employability and boosting economic activity, especially in the manufacturing sector (Moll & Stucki, 2021). The advantage of the PPP model lies in its ability to facilitate the development of targeted and sustainable solutions through cooperation agreements, especially in cases where market mechanisms or traditional public measures are not sufficient to tackle complex challenges.

In line with the defined research objective, the areas for the application of PPP models were mapped. Given the large number of areas identified and to further pursue the objective of research in terms of proposing a specific PPP model, the focus will be on financial support, which has been identified as the most important factor for the successful implementation of sustainable business practices by MSMEs. To address the biggest obstacle for MSMEs in the context of green transition, a mechanism of indirect financial support through the development of a common green infrastructure is proposed. This mechanism can best be implemented through the BOT PPP model, which enables the use of private sector resources and expertise while safeguarding the public interest and the strategic objectives of sustainable development. Rather than providing direct budget support to MSMEs, which is often limited by public sector capacity and can lead to inefficient allocation of resources, the public sector can offer a more effective form of support by investing in the development of common green infrastructure (e.g., recycling centers, renewable energy systems, waste processing facilities). In this way, MSMEs gain access to important resources for implementing sustainable practices without having to bear high investment costs themselves, thus facilitating the transition to a green economy. Under the BOT model, the private partner (a financial institution, an investment fund or a domestic or foreign company specialising in green infrastructure) assumes responsibility for raising the initial capital, preparing the technical documentation, carrying out the construction work and managing the infrastructure facility during the agreed contract period (Hu et al., 2022). On the other hand, the public partner, usually a local government unit, a public utility company, or the responsible ministry, retains regulatory oversight of the project and acquires ownership of the constructed infrastructure after the concession expires (Dolla et al., 2022). The BOT model as a form of public–private partnership involves a high degree of privatisation and contractual autonomy, whereby the private sector is responsible for financing, building and operating public infrastructure before transferring ownership back to the government, while also bearing greater social responsibility due to the scale and complexity of such projects (Hu et al., 2022). Such an agreement enables the sharing of risks and benefits by leveraging the expertise and financial strength of the private sector, while the public sector ensures that the infrastructure projects are in line with the public interest and the strategic objectives of sustainable development. However, it should be noted that the successful implementation of the BOT model also depends on overcoming operational challenges, particularly in the selection of contractors, where structured decision support systems can help ensure efficiency and best value for the public sector (Krishnaraj et al., 2024). Further research confirms that the fair distribution of benefits and risks is not only a prerequisite for effective cooperation between the public and private sectors under the BOT model, but also a key factor in determining the concession period (Xue et al., 2019). The private partner's income during the operating period can be generated, for example, through user fees, energy sales or the provision of waste treatment services. This gives MSMEs access to advanced infrastructure solutions (e.g., energy efficiency systems, wastewater treatment plants, renewable energy facilities and recycling centres) without having to make direct capital investments, which reduces the investment risk and promotes their participation in the green transformation. The BOT model is particularly suitable for situations where there is a predictable income stream and a need for substantial capital investment (Yan et al., 2011; Mohammad, 2020). Its main advantages include the reduction of pressure on the public budget, the acceleration of implementation and the greater efficiency that the private sector brings in terms of management and innovation. The application of the BOT model provides MSMEs with indirect access to green infrastructure and promotes the integration of sustainable technological solutions that contribute to responsible business practices related to climate change. A performance measurement system specifically tailored to BOT projects has been developed to improve the delivery and outcomes of green infrastructure initiatives, demonstrating how such frameworks can improve the management of resources in environmental projects (Okudan et al., 2020). However, it should be noted that although the BOT model is widely used in public–private partnerships, it entails many specific risks that need to be systematically identified and managed throughout the project lifecycle, especially because the most critical risks are often assigned to the SPV, whose careful selection is crucial for project success (Akhtar et al., 2023; Ahmad et al., 2021).

5. Conclusions

Based on the conducted analysis, it can be concluded that the research objective has been achieved, as the areas with potential for the application of public—private partnership models in the green transition process of MSMEs in Serbia have been successfully mapped out, and the possibility of implementing a specific PPP model in one of these areas has been demonstrated. Accordingly, the hypothesis that MSMEs in Serbia face challenges in the process of green transition is accepted. These challenges indicate areas with high potential for the application of specific public–private partnership (PPP) models. The results show that the main barriers to implementing sustainable practices are the lack of financial resources, the complexity of administrative procedures, and the high initial costs, confirming previous findings from the literature on the challenges for micro and small enterprises in accessing sustainability. In this context, public–private partnerships emerge as a key mechanism that can facilitate MSMEs' transition to sustainable development. Models such as BOT enable the construction of the necessary infrastructure and the provision of services without placing a heavy financial burden on companies, thus promoting the implementation of environmentally friendly measures and strengthening innovation capacity. This model not only facilitates the mobilisation of resources from the private sector but also provides MSMEs with access to key technologies and expertise that are critical to their transition to sustainable practices.

Furthermore, this study clearly underlines the need for an integrated approach that requires better coordination between the public and private sectors. The development of specific institutional frameworks that support the interaction of these actors and the creation of conditions that facilitate access to financial resources are key issues for a successful green transition. Furthermore, it is necessary to develop integrated models that contribute to reducing administrative burdens, strengthening innovation capacities and empowering MSMEs through education and training. The research findings are relevant and offer concrete policy recommendations that could further promote the green transition process in Serbia. The proposed approach must be tailored to the specific needs of each sector and consider the complexity of the challenges faced by MSMEs. In addition, a stable institutional framework that supports the participation of all relevant stakeholders is considered essential for ensuring the long-term sustainability and resilience of the economy.

Ultimately, this study contributes to a better understanding of the role of PPPs as a tool to strengthen the sustainability of MSMEs, while opening the door for further analysis examining the long-term effects of such partnerships and their impact on different sectors of the economy. Understanding the dynamics of PPPs and applying specific models in other mapped sectors can significantly contribute to creating more sustainable and resilient economies, thus laying the foundation for future development and prosperity in Serbia.

Author Contributions: Conceptualisation: S.Đ.; Methodology: S.Đ.; Validation: S.Đ.; Formal Analysis: S.Đ. and I.L.; Investigation: S.Đ. and I.B.; Resources: S.Đ. and I.L.; Data Curation: S.Đ. and I.L.; Writing—Original Draft Preparation: S.Đ.; Writing—Review & Editing: S.Đ.; Visualisation: S.Đ.; Supervision: S.Đ.; Project Administration: S.Đ.; Funding Acquisition: S.Đ. and I.L. All authors have read and agreed to the published version of the manuscript.

Funding: This research was funded by Ministry of Science, Technological Development and Innovation of the Republic of Serbia grant number 451-03-33/2026-03.

Acknowledgments: The study is based on empirical data collected in 2024 as part of the project "Roadmap for the Implementation of the Green Agenda for MSMEs in the Republic of Serbia", implemented by the Institute of Economic Sciences in Belgrade with financial support from the Deutsche Gesellschaft für Internationale Zusammenarbeit (GIZ).

Conflicts of Interest: The authors declare no conflicts of interest.

Author Names and Affiliations: Sonja Đuričin, Innovation Economics Department, Institute of Economic Sciences, Belgrade, Republic of Serbia; Isidora Ljumović, Macroeconomics Department, Institute of Economic Sciences, Belgrade, Republic of Serbia; Isidora Beraha, Innovation Economics Department, Institute of Economic Sciences, Belgrade, Republic of Serbia.

Keywords: climate change mitigation; public–private partnerships (PPPs); MSME sustainability; green transition.

References

Afful, B. E. B., Addaney, M., Anaafo, D., Akudugu, J. A., Borkor, F. K., Yeboah, E. O., & Sampana, J. (2023). Public-private partnership in municipal solid waste management in the Sunyani municipality of Ghana. *Journal of Property, Planning and Environmental Law, 16*(3), 201–217. [CrossRef]

Ahmad, U., Akram, K., Fatima, E., & Muhammad, H. (2021). Risk management in the Malaysian build operate transfer projects. *iRASD Journal of Economics, 3*(3), 368–375. [CrossRef]

Ahmadov, T., Ulp, S., & Gerstlberger, W. (2024). Role of stakeholder engagement in sustainable development in Estonian small and medium-sized enterprises. *Green and Low-Carbon Economy, 2*(4), 277–286. [CrossRef]

Akhtar, M., Mufti, N. A., Mubin, S., Saleem, M. Q., Zahoor, S., & Ullah, S. (2023). Identification of various execution modes and their respective risks for public–private partnership (PPP) infrastructure projects. *Buildings, 13*(8), 1889. [CrossRef]

Alghamdi, F., Tatari, O., & Alghamdi, L. (2022). Enhancing the decision-making process for public-private partnerships infrastructure projects: A socio-economic system dynamic approach. *Journal of Engineering and Applied Science, 69*(1), 117. [CrossRef]

Amović, G. (2019). Public-private partnership: A new role of public sector in financing public investments. *Ekonomija: Teorija i Praksa, 12*(2), 25–44. [CrossRef]

Amović, G., Maksimović, R., & Bunčić, S. (2020). Critical success factors for sustainable public-private partnership (PPP) in transition conditions: An empirical study in Bosnia and Herzegovina. *Sustainability, 12*(17), 7121. [CrossRef]

Asensio, J. C., Kato, T., & Shin, H. (2021). *Lessons on engaging with the private sector to strengthen climate resilience in Guatemala, the Philippines and Senegal.* OECD development co-operation working papers. OECD. [CrossRef]

Balcılar, M., Uzuner, G., Nwani, C., & Bekun, F. V. (2023). Boosting energy efficiency in Turkey: The role of public–private partnership investment. *Sustainability, 15*(3), 2273. [CrossRef]

Beraha, I., & Đuričin, S. (2020). Survey on women's innovative entrepreneurship in Serbia. *Ekonomika, 66*(1), 93–104. [CrossRef]

Brinkerhoff, D. W., & Brinkerhoff, J. M. (2011). Public–private partnerships: Perspectives on purposes, publicness, and good governance. *Public Administration & Development, 31*(1), 2–14. [CrossRef]

Campiglio, E., Daumas, L., Monnin, P., & Jagow, A. V. (2022). Climate-related risks in financial assets. *Journal of Economic Surveys, 37*(3), 950–992. [CrossRef]

Chae, Y., Choi, S. H., & Kim, Y. J. (2020). Climate change policy implications of sustainable development pathways in Korea at sub-national scale. *Sustainability, 12*(10), 4310. [CrossRef]

Chumba, J. (2020). Beyond enterprise: The effect of linkages and partnerships resource mobilisation structure on the financial sustainability of universities in Kenya. *Journal of Economics and Sustainable Development, 65*, 16. [CrossRef]

Dolla, T., Delhi, V. S. K., & Laishram, B. (2022). Making BOT model great again: Revisiting the BOT standard concessions and exploring the expectations. *IOP Conference Series: Earth and Environmental Science, 1101*(5), 052018. [CrossRef]

Droege, H., Raggi, A., & Ramos, T. B. (2021). Overcoming current challenges for circular economy assessment implementation in public sector organisations. *Sustainability, 13*(3), 1182. [CrossRef]

Đuričin, S., & Beraha, I. (2021a). Assessment of the innovation capacity of business entities in the Republic of Serbia. In *Finance, innovation and technology: New models and structures* (pp. 179–198). Institute of Economics—Ss. Cyril & Methodius University. Available online: http://ebooks.ien.bg.ac.rs/id/eprint/1595 (accessed on 14 February 2026).

Đuričin, S., & Beraha, I. (2021b). Identifying medium-sized agricultural enterprises with the greatest potential for innovation development. *Ekonomika Poljoprivrede, 68*(1), 213–227. [CrossRef]

Đuričin, S., & Beraha, I. (2024). Promoting economic inclusivity in Serbia—Recommendations for enhancing national and local policies in women's entrepreneurship. *Journal of Women's Entrepreneurship and Education, 3–4*(2024), 138–159.

Đuričin, S., Beraha, I., Jovanović, O., Mosurović Ružičić, M., Lazarević-Moravčević, M., & Paunović, M. (2022). The efficiency of national innovation policy programs: The case of Serbia. *Sustainability, 14*(14), 8483. [CrossRef]

Đuričin, S., Savić, S., Bodroža, D., Cvijanović, G., & Đorđević, S. (2016). Climate change impacts on agricultural water management: Challenge for increasing crop productivity in Serbia. *Ekonomika Poljoprivrede, 63*(4), 1333–1346. [CrossRef]

European Commission. (2019). *The European Green Deal (COM(2019) 640 final).* Available online: https://eur-lex.europa.eu/legal-content/EN/TXT/?uri=CELEX:52019DC0640 (accessed on 14 February 2026).

Farhan, D., Haritsar, Y., & Kurniawan, D. (2024). The role of accountant competencies in improving financial statement quality in small and medium enterprises (SMEs): A case study analysis. *Global International Journal of Innovative Research, 2*(10), 2502–2512. [CrossRef]

Fatemi, M. N., Okyere, S. A., Diko, S. K., & Kita, M. (2020). Multi-level climate governance in Bangladesh via climate change mainstreaming: Lessons for local climate action in Dhaka City. *Urban Science, 4*(2), 24. [CrossRef]

Fu, C., Lü, L., & Pirabi, M. (2023). Advancing green finance: A review of sustainable development. *Digital Economy and Sustainable Development, 1*(1), 20. [CrossRef]

Gajinov, T., Uzelac, O., & Mijatović, M. (2022). Pravni aspekti svetlosnog zagađenja. *Ecologica, 29*(108), 617–626. [CrossRef]

Gannon, K. E., Castellano, E., Eskander, S., Agol, D., Diop, M., Conway, D., & Sprout, E. (2022). The triple differential vulnerability of female entrepreneurs to climate risk in Sub-Saharan Africa: Gendered barriers and enablers to private sector adaptation. *WIREs Climate Change, 13*(5), e793. [CrossRef]

Hatipoğlu, B., Álvarez, M. D., & Ertuna, B. (2016). Barriers to stakeholder involvement in the planning of sustainable tourism: The case of the Thrace Region in Turkey. *Journal of Cleaner Production, 111*, 306–317. [CrossRef]

Himmel, M. E., & Siemiatycki, M. (2017). Infrastructure public–private partnerships as drivers of innovation? Lessons from Ontario, Canada. *Environment and Planning C: Politics and Space, 35*(5), 746–764. [CrossRef]

Hristov, J., Domínguez, I. P., Fellmann, T., & Elleby, C. (2023). Economic impacts of climate change on EU agriculture: Will the farmers benefit from global climate change? *Environmental Research Letters, 19*(1), 014027. [CrossRef]

Hu, Y., Chiu, Y., Yen, G., & Ken, Y. (2022). Incorporation of the DEMATEL into evaluations of CSR performance in BOT projects. *Systems Research and Behavioral Science, 40*(1), 266–281. [CrossRef]

Joseph, E., Shyamala, M., & Nadig, R. (2025). Understanding public-private partnerships in the modern era. In *Public private partnership dynamics for economic development* (pp. 1–26). IGI Global. [CrossRef]

Kawane, T., Zhao, R., Ozaki, Y., Otaki, T., Mazumder, S., & Shaw, R. (2023). Local production, consumption, and innovation: Enhancing sustainability through SMEs in Japan. *Rural and Regional Development*, *1*(2), 10008. [CrossRef]

Khan, Z., Muhsin, A., Kırıkkaleli, D., Wahab, S., & Jiao, Z. (2020). The impact of technological innovation and public-private partnership investment on sustainable environment in China: Consumption-based carbon emissions analysis. *Sustainable Development*, *28*(5), 1317–1330. [CrossRef]

Krishnaraj, R., Anandakumar, S., Viswanathan, R., & Velusamy, S. (2024). Analyzing key success factors in public-private partnership BOT projects: An empirical study on financing influences, insights, and analysis in construction management. *Matéria (Rio de Janeiro)*, *29*(2), e20240140. [CrossRef]

Lee, W., Juskenaite, I., & Mwebaza, R. (2021). Public–private partnerships for climate technology transfer and innovation: Lessons from the climate technology centre and network. *Sustainability*, *13*(6), 3185. [CrossRef]

Li, C., Memon, J. A., Le, T. T., Ali, M., & Kırıkkaleli, D. (2021). The impact of public-private partnership investment in energy and technological innovation on ecological footprint: The case of Pakistan. *Sustainability*, *13*(18), 10085. [CrossRef]

Li, Y., & Li, H. (2019). Institutional analysis on stakeholder participation in China's environmental impact assessment: A state–attribution–motivation–interaction–reengineering framework. *Integrated Environmental Assessment and Management*, *15*(4), 607–620. [CrossRef] [PubMed]

Ljumović, I., & Jakšić, K. (2015). Dostupnost finansijskih resursa preduzećima na severu Kosova. In *Zbornik matice srpske za društvene nauke* (pp. 557–569). Matica srpska.

Ljumović, I., Viduka, B., & Cvijanović, J. M. (2015). Access to finance for organic producers in Serbia: Demand side. *Ekonomika Poljoprivrede*, *62*(4), 989–1002. [CrossRef]

Malerba, D. (2022). The effects of social protection and social cohesion on the acceptability of climate change mitigation policies: What do we (not) know in the context of low- and middle-income countries? *The European Journal of Development Research*, *34*(3), 1358–1382. [CrossRef]

Mohammad, O. I. O. (2020). Build-Operate-Transfer model and its role in developing railways transport section in Sudan. *American Journal of Transportation and Logistics*, *3*, 17. [CrossRef]

Moll, J., & Stucki, V. (2021). From pilot to scale—A framework for development practitioners for market driven vocational training. *International Journal of Business and Society*, *22*(2), 653–674. [CrossRef]

Naumov, V., Radchenko, E., Sedikh, V., & Vdovina, A. (2022). Public-private partnership in the field of waste management, not related to municipal solid waste. *IOP Conference Series: Earth and Environmental Science*, *981*(4), 042078. [CrossRef]

Neise, T., Sambodo, M. T., & Diez, J. R. (2019). Are micro-, small- and medium-sized enterprises willing to contribute to collective flood risk reduction? Scenario-based field experiments from Jakarta and Semarang, Indonesia. *Organization & Environment*, *34*(2), 219–242. [CrossRef]

Nikonova, E., Chursina, A. V., Sindeev, A., & Letunovskiy, A. (2019). Construction of CHP using public-private partnership. *E3S Web of Conferences*, *110*, 02078. [CrossRef]

Okudan, O., Budayan, C., & Dikmen, İ. (2020). Development of a conceptual life cycle performance measurement system for build–operate–transfer (BOT) projects. *Engineering, Construction and Architectural Management, 28*(6), 1635–1656. [CrossRef]

Orlov, A., Schleypen, J. R., Aunan, K., Sillmann, J., Gasparrini, A., & Mistry, M. (2024). A better integration of health and economic impact assessments of climate change. *Environmental Research Letters, 19*(3), 031004. [CrossRef]

Popa, F. (2018). About the advantages of public-private partnerships and its organizational forms. *Studies and Scientific Researches. Economics Edition*, (27). [CrossRef]

Rusydiana, A. S. (2024). Bibliometric analysis of Scopus-indexed climate finance studies. *Text Analytics in Economics, 1*(1). [CrossRef]

Savić, S., Czekus, B., Gregorić, E., Đuričin, S., & Matović, G. (2021). Production of Puno and Titicaca quinoa cultivars: Cost benefit analysis. *Romanian Biotechnological Letters, 26*(5), 2953–2963. [CrossRef]

Scott, C. (2023). Climate finance and its role in climate policy. *Journal of Climate Policy, 2*(1), 54–66. [CrossRef]

Semieniuk, G., Campiglio, E., Mercure, J., Volz, U., & Edwards, N. R. (2020). Low-carbon transition risks for finance. *WIREs Climate Change, 12*(1), e678. [CrossRef]

Sibiya, N. P., Das, D. K., Vogel, C., Mazinyo, S. P., Zhou, L., Kalumba, A. M., & Simatele, M. D. (2023). Overcoming bureaucratic resistance: An analysis of barriers to climate change adaptation in South Africa. *Climate, 11*(7), 145. [CrossRef]

Silvast, A., Kongsager, R., Lehtonen, T., Lundgren, M., & Virtanen, M. J. (2021). Critical infrastructure vulnerability: A research note on adaptation to climate change in the Nordic countries. *Geografisk Tidsskrift-Danish Journal of Geography, 121*(1), 79–90. [CrossRef]

Somanathan, E., Somanathan, R., Sudarshan, A., & Tewari, M. (2021). The impact of temperature on productivity and labor supply: Evidence from Indian manufacturing. *Journal of Political Economy, 129*(6), 1797–1827. [CrossRef]

Stevanović, S., Minovic, J., & Ljumovic, I. (2019). Liquidity profitability trade-off: Evidence from medium enterprises. *Management: Journal of Sustainable Business and Management Solutions in Emerging Economies, 24*(3), 71–81. [CrossRef]

Thongoh, M. W., Mutembei, H., Mburu, J., & Kathambi, B. (2021). An assessment of integration of MSMEs and CSA into livestock red meat value chain: A case study of Kajiado County, Kenya. *International Journal of Environment and Climate Change, 11*(4), 1–17. [CrossRef]

Toromade, A. S., & Chiekezie, N. R. (2024). Driving sustainable business practices in SMEs: Innovative approaches for environmental and economic synergy. *International Journal of Management & Entrepreneurship Research, 6*(8), 2637–2647. [CrossRef]

Tran, T. T., Bush, S. R., & van Leeuwen, J. (2022). Enhancing institutional capacity in a centralized state: The case of industrial water use efficiency in Vietnam. *Journal of Industrial Ecology, 27*(1), 210–222. [CrossRef]

Ugwu, M. C., Adewusi, A. O., & Nwokolo, N. E. (2024). The role of public-private partnerships in building clean energy infrastructure in the United States and Nigeria. *International Journal of Management & Entrepreneurship Research, 6*(4), 1049–1068. [CrossRef]

United Nations Framework Convention on Climate Change. (2015). *Paris agreement*. Available online: https://unfccc.int/sites/default/files/english_paris_agreement.pdf (accessed on 14 February 2026).

Vassileva, A. (2022). Green public-private partnerships (PPPs) as an instrument for sustainable development. *Journal of World Economy: Transformations & Transitions*, *2*(5), 2. [CrossRef]

Vasyliev, O., Волохов, В. А., Волохова, І. В., Лук'янова, О. М., & Zhovtiak, H. (2019). Priority-partnership approach as a mechanism for encouraging investment activities at the railway transport. *SHS Web of Conferences*, *67*, 04014. [CrossRef]

Wen, Y., Qu, C., Gao, C., Song, P., & Yang, D. (2022). The effect of public–private partnership investment, financial development, and renewable energy consumption on the ecological footprint in South Asia and the Pacific region. *Frontiers in Environmental Science*, *10*, 1022046. [CrossRef]

Wilson, C. D., Williams, I., & Kemp, S. (2011). An evaluation of the impact and effectiveness of environmental legislation in small and medium-sized enterprises: Experiences from the UK. *Business Strategy and the Environment*, *21*(3), 141–156. [CrossRef]

World Bank. (2017). *Public-private partnerships: Reference guide (version 3.0)*. World Bank. Available online: https://ppp.worldbank.org/public-private-partnership/sites/ppp.worldbank.org/files/documents/PPP%20Reference%20Guide%20Version%203.pdf (accessed on 14 February 2026).

Xue, Y., Chong, H., Zhou, J., & Li, Q. (2019). Concession model for fair distribution of benefits and risks in build-operate-transfer road projects. *Journal of Civil Engineering and Management*, *25*(3), 265–275. [CrossRef]

Yan, M., Pong, C., & Lo, W. (2011). Utility-based multicriteria model for evaluating BOT projects. *Technological and Economic Development of Economy*, *17*(2), 207–218. [CrossRef]

Yuan, J., Xiang, R., & Zhang, A. (2010). Analysis on the management mechanism of public-private partnership (PPP) projects in China. *International Journal of Project Management*, *28*(6), 555–568. [CrossRef]

Zakharina, O. V., Korzhenko, V. V., Kovalenko, N. V., Shashyna, M. V., Tomashevska, A. V., & Mosiichuk, I. V. (2020). Effective public-private partnership models and their application in public policy implementation. *International Journal of Economics and Business Administration*, *8*, 239–247. [CrossRef] [PubMed]

Zhang, Y., Yuan, J., Zhao, J., Cheng, L., & Li, Q. (2022). Hybrid dynamic pricing model for transport PPP projects during the residual concession period. *Journal of Construction Engineering and Management*, *148*(2). [CrossRef]

The Green Economy's Prospects for Employment: Emerging Skills and Economic Change

Burcu Türkcan and Nuri Aytuğ Erdemir

Abstract: The world economy has experienced a remarkable increase in welfare through rapid industrialisation following the First Industrial Revolution. However, it has also experienced a rapid increase in environmental degradation. As the global climate crisis worsened, clearly showing that we were reaching global limits, the UNEP announced the "Green Economy Initiative". It defines the green economy as an economy seeking to achieve improved human well-being and social equality while reducing environmental risks. In this context, it tries to serve sustainable development in several aspects. Employment and economic change are two significant concepts in the green transition. The transition has important implications for employment, requiring the development of new skills and leading to significant economic changes. This chapter examines the green economy's prospects for employment from the aspects of emerging skills and economic change. The findings highlight the increasing demand for environmentally responsible roles and the urgent need to upskill workers to meet the needs of a low-carbon economy. In the light of technological transformations, economic change is substantial in all economies, and this change brings about green jobs. In this manner, this study contributes to the literature by offering policy insights for fostering inclusive, green, and sustainable employment.

1. Introduction

Rapid industrialisation has increased the ecological footprint enormously since the 19th century (Radmehr et al., 2024). Humankind has rapidly reached the limits of the globe by adopting mass production and consumption habits. Recent scientific assessments have shown that the boundaries safeguarding the stability of Earth's key environmental systems provide not only a symbolic perspective but also a concrete framework for assessing ecological pressure. This framework, known as the planetary boundaries, consists of nine critical thresholds, and current analyses indicate that some of them have already been breached. In particular, the safe limits related to climate, biodiversity, land use, and chemical pollution have been exceeded, while other processes such as freshwater cycles and the nitrogen–phosphorus balance are experiencing increasing stress (Stockholm Resilience Centre, 2025). These disruptions are difficult to reverse by using existing policy instruments, and recovery in systems with high inertia, such as climate and biodiversity, is expected to take place only over long timeframes (van Vuuren et al., 2025). This reality caused new quests for sustainability. In this manner, several countries have adopted carbon neutrality targets after the Paris Climate Conference. In this regard, green technology and clean energy have become more important in the agendas of countries (Shan et al., 2021,

p. 1). Green transition has become a must for sustainability, while it has brought about several hardships. These hardships draw attention to new areas of tension within economic structures and labour dynamics, emphasising the social dimensions of the transition.

As countries navigate the challenges of transitioning to a green economy, employment and economic change emerge as critical dimensions. The shift to a green economy involves profound structural adjustments in labour markets and skills development. Green transition has the potential to create new job opportunities—namely "green jobs"—which contribute directly to preserving or restoring environmental quality. However, it also poses challenges for workers in carbon-intensive industries facing job displacement, necessitating proactive strategies for reskilling and upskilling.

This chapter explores the prospects of the green economy for employment, focusing on the dynamics of emerging skills and economic transformation. It examines how green transitions reshape labour markets, emphasising both the opportunities for green and green jobs and the risks associated with workforce disruptions. The analysis draws attention to the dual nature of the transformation: while it promises inclusive and sustainable employment opportunities, it also demands careful management of technological and structural shifts in economies. The findings highlight the increasing demand for environmentally responsible roles and the urgent need for upskilled workers to meet the needs of a low-carbon economy. In the light of technological transformations, economic change is substantial for all economies, and this change brings about green jobs. In this manner, this study contributes to the related literature by offering policy insights for fostering inclusive, green, and sustainable employment.

2. Green Economy and Its Prospects for Employment: Green Jobs and Greening Jobs

Sustainable development is increasingly recognised as a dual imperative: not only minimising environmental risks but also ensuring social justice and universal access to basic needs. Kate Raworth's Doughnut Economics Model encapsulates this vision through two concentric boundaries: the ecological ceiling, representing the environmental thresholds that human activity must not exceed, and the social foundation, defining the minimum standards for human well-being below which no one should fall. In the 21st century, the central challenge of sustainability lies in maintaining societies within this safe space: safeguarding ecosystems while simultaneously upholding social equity. Raworth's model emphasises that green jobs must not only support environmentally responsible production but also align with principles of decent work, equity, and inclusive economic participation. As such, the green transition should be viewed not merely as a technological transformation, but as a broader ethical, social, and institutional shift toward sustainable and just economies (Raworth, 2017).

In this context, some global actions have been taken. As a significant example, the European Union (EU) aims to become climate-neutral by 2050, and hence, it announced the European Green Deal in 2019. Following this, the European Commission, through its Green Deal Industrial Plan and Net-Zero Industry Act proposal, has stated that by 2030, at least 40% of annual deployment needs for net-zero technologies will be met through EU-based manufacturing capacity while also supporting the expansion of green employment opportunities throughout this transformation process (European Commission, 2023). The Green Deal seeks to achieve sustainable energy production while promoting circular products that produce no waste and cause zero pollution (Bauer et al., 2021, p. 80). The Green Deal aims to achieve green transition including cleaner and more energy-efficient production processes with efficient policy mix (Kemp & Never, 2017, p. 66). Empirical findings underline that investing in green technology reduces carbon emissions and contributes to environmental quality (Gao et al., 2018; Zhao et al., 2015). Green technology innovations significantly promote long-term sustainable development (Jiang et al., 2021, p. 1510). Renewable energy and green technologies together play a critical role in environmental sustainability and climate change. Investing in renewable energy and green technologies is fundamental to building a resilient, low-carbon global future.

The green transition is also a process that creates job opportunities. In 2008, the United Nations Environment Programme (UNEP), the International Organisation of Employers (IOE), the International Trade Union Confederation (ITUC), and the International Labour Organisation (ILO) announced the "Green Jobs Initiative" as a joint initiative. Green jobs are defined as jobs that maintain and restore environmental quality by using less energy and raw materials and causing less pollution and waste (Stanef-Puica et al., 2022). Renewable energy technicians, environmental engineers, energy efficiency experts, and recycling workers can be listed as some examples of green jobs (Urban et al., 2023). Across those green jobs, environmental engineers and renewable energy engineers are projected to be among the fastest-growing jobs between 2025 and 2030 (WEF, 2025).

The World Economic Forum (WEF) has published "The Future of Jobs Report 2025", intending to determine future professions and skills by considering the disruptions experienced due to the pandemic in 2020, the economic situation that the world has been in for a while, and recent technological developments. While preparing the report, the opinions of business leaders, senior managers, strategic planning experts, and human resources experts were gathered, and an attempt was made to draw a diagram of how professions will transform by 2030 and what the skills of the future will be. The main findings of the report can be listed as follows:

- It is expected that the increase in digital access will be the biggest transformative trend; artificial intelligence and information processing, robotics and automation, and energy production and distribution will also be transformative.
- The second most important factor is that increasing living costs and changes in global inflation will drive both employers and employees to transform their businesses.
- It is believed that structures aimed at slowing down climate change (focused on green transformation) will be the third most important factor in the transformation of businesses.
- The increase in the ageing population and the decrease in the working-age population, especially in high-income countries, are expected to directly affect global economies and labour markets.
- Geoeconomic divergence and geopolitical tensions (especially trade wars between the US and China) are expected to transform business models (WEF, 2025).

WEF (2025) predicts that expanded digital access will create 9.9 million new jobs, expanding the working-age population (mainly in underdeveloped and developing countries) will create 9.1 million jobs, and climate change adaptation will create 5.5 million jobs. On the other hand, it also proposes that slowing economic growth will cause 1.6 million job losses, while robots and autonomous systems will cause 4.8 million job losses. When all these changes are considered together, the net job creation effect is expected to be positive.

3. Economic Change and Emerging Skills

The transition towards a more sustainable and environmentally conscious global economy has emerged as a defining feature of contemporary economic transformation, especially in terms of labour market transformation. This transformation leads to the contraction of traditional sectors and a decline in certain job types while simultaneously paving the way for the emergence of new occupations and skill profiles in areas such as renewable energy, circular production, green construction, and sustainable agriculture (OECD, 2023; Fuchs, 2024).

The high-carbon economic model that evolved after the Industrial Revolution is now facing both an environmental sustainability crisis and a structural shift in employment. Employment in sectors such as coal mining and fossil fuel-based industries is in decline, while new professions are emerging in fields like solar and wind energy technology, energy efficiency, carbon accounting, and sustainable design (Stroud et al., 2014; Lagorio et al., 2024; Greenspon & Raimi, 2024).

The ILO (2025) describes green jobs as the jobs "promising a triple dividend: sustainable enterprises, poverty reduction, and a job–centred economic recovery". In this manner, the Green Jobs Programme of the ILO concentrates on six priorities: analysis of employment and labour market conditions, practical approaches to greening enterprises, green jobs in waste management and recycling, renewable energy and energy efficiency, transition towards a green economy and a sustainable society, and adaptation to climate change (ILO, 2025). Understanding the employment dimension of the green transition requires more than identifying new types of jobs; it also involves analysing the transformation in skill requirements. The literature classifies the emerging skillsets associated with the green transition into three main categories: (1) technical and sector-specific skills, (2) behavioural and transformative soft skills, and (3) hybrid digital–green skills (OECD, 2023; IMF, 2024; Economist Impact, 2024). This classification reflects global approaches prominent in policy documents and skills taxonomies. Figure 1 shows the emerging skill sets associated with the green transition.

Technical and sector-specific skills pertain directly to the installation and operation of new technologies. Competencies such as solar and wind energy system installation, carbon emission measurement and reporting, circular economy design, waste management processes, green building practices, and electric vehicle systems fall into this category (Lagorio et al., 2024; Bone et al., 2024). These technical skills are increasingly in demand not only in highly specialised fields like engineering but also in technician and mid-level occupational roles.

To better comprehend the country-specific outcomes of this technical transformation, certain environmental indicators offer valuable insights. For example, in terms of carbon intensity per unit of GDP (measured in kg CO_2 per PPP$), Switzerland reported the lowest figure among OECD countries in 2023, at 0.047. In contrast, Türkiye's value for the same year was 0.149 (World Bank, 2023a). This suggests that Switzerland has broadly implemented production processes that minimise carbon emissions, whereas in Türkiye, higher carbon intensity indicates that low-carbon production techniques and the workforce capable of implementing them are still developing. It should be noted that this interpretation is based on benchmarking against the best-performing country in this area.

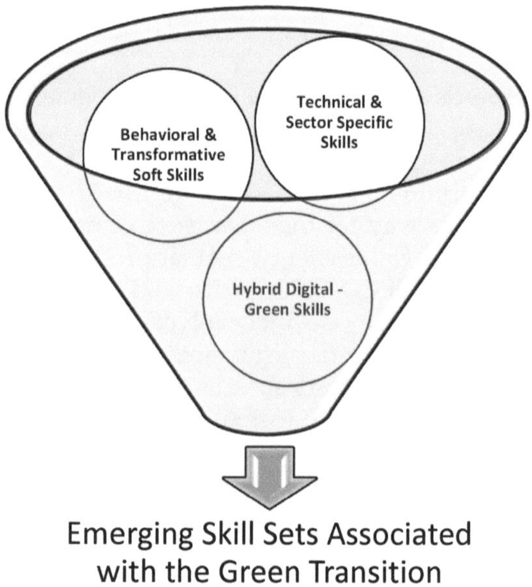

Figure 1. Emerging skill sets associated with green transition. Source: Figure by authors.

The second group of skills—behavioural and transformative soft skills—enables individuals to internalise and act on sustainability values. These include systems thinking (analysing issues as interconnected wholes rather than in isolation), environmental literacy, interdisciplinary problem-solving, empathy, collaborative leadership, conflict resolution, and adaptability (Fuchs, 2024; OECD, 2023; IMF, 2024). Such skills not only shape individual awareness but also influence the institutional capacity to drive societal transformation (ILO, 2025).

The third category—hybrid digital–green skills—emerges at the intersection of technological innovation and environmental sustainability. Key competencies include big data analytics, Internet of Things (IoT), artificial intelligence (AI)-powered environmental monitoring, digital energy efficiency systems, and blockchain-enabled sustainable supply chain traceability (Lagorio et al., 2024; Economist Impact, 2024; Bone et al., 2024). Energy efficiency is a tangible outcome of these skills. As an example, according to World Bank Data, in 2023, Ireland produced approximately USD 50.79 of economic output per kilogram of oil-equivalent energy, whereas Türkiye produced only USD 22.84 (World Bank, 2023b). This 2.2-fold difference can be attributed not only to infrastructural disparities but also to the limited human capital available to manage digital energy efficiency systems. This comparison with Ireland is relevant as it leads the rankings in this indicator.

The literature includes evidence suggesting that individuals equipped with green skills enjoy wage premiums and employment advantages in the labour market. For instance, Bone et al. (2024), using UK job posting data, demonstrated that green skills yield higher wage differentials even in low-skilled occupations, particularly in areas such as carbon auditing, digital energy efficiency, and sustainable supply chains.

Despite these advancements, a significant mismatch persists between the supply of skills and the demand for green jobs. According to LinkedIn data, while the number of workers with green skills increased by only 12.3%, the number of job postings demanding such skills rose by 22.4% (Drašković, 2024). However, the IMF (2024) notes that 20% of men in developed countries are employed in green jobs, compared to only 6% of women, attributing this gap largely to gender disparities in access to STEM (Science, Technology, Engineering, and Mathematics) fields. What is more is that findings by Greenspon and Raimi (2024) from the U.S. context reveal that only 1% of workers from fossil fuel sectors have transitioned into green sectors, underscoring serious deficiencies in social and interpersonal skills. Similarly, Garrote Sanchez and Yanez-Pagans (2024) argue that one in six jobs in the Western Balkans will be affected by the green transition, yet current education systems lack the structural capacity to support this transition effectively.

All these transformations have also changed recruitment practices. Bone et al. (2024) reveal a growing move toward skill-based hiring, whereby short-cycle certifications and workplace assessments are increasingly valued over traditional academic degrees. This shift requires a coordinated redesign of workforce development strategies by both public and private sectors. The OECD (2023) advocates for the restructuring of skills anticipation systems to incorporate the priorities of the green transition, emphasising the need to align national qualifications frameworks with evolving labour market signals. Economist Impact (2025) similarly warns that without such coordination, the green skills gap will likely widen further.

In conclusion, the success of economic transformation depends not only on investments in environmental technologies but also on cultivating a skilled workforce capable of implementing, managing, and integrating these technologies into society. The new generation of green skills—comprising technical, behavioural, and digital competencies—forms the cornerstone not only of sustainable production processes but also of social justice and inclusive development. Accordingly, robust partnerships among educational institutions, industry stakeholders, and policymakers will be key to enabling both economic and societal transformation.

4. Economic Policy Design for the Green Economy's Employment Prospects

For the green transition to result in lasting change across workforce structures and skill systems, it must be underpinned by a broader transformation of the economic architecture that supports it. In this context, it is critical to examine the related theoretical background and apply it to observations. In this context, Tim Jackson's ecological macroeconomic framework should be considered. It offers one of the most comprehensive and realistic alternatives to traditional growth-oriented economic models. Jackson argues that a sustainable future requires a new macroeconomic paradigm—one that safeguards employment, prioritises social investment, reduces inequality, and operates within the limits of the planet's ecological boundaries (Jackson, 2009). Within this framework, green jobs are not only supported through technical upskilling but also through restructuring public investment, redefining financial systems, and reconsidering the purpose and value of work itself. Investing in green jobs may provide both economic growth (namely green growth) and sustainable development (Stilwell & Primrose, 2010, p. 5). Accordingly, economic policy must extend beyond the questions of what to produce and address how to produce, for whom, and within what ecological limits. In this view, the sustainability of green employment depends not only on individual capacity building but on a comprehensive macro-level transformation that reimagines every foundation of economic activity.

The transition to a green economy generates new forms of employment, namely green jobs. Such jobs require new skill sets focusing on the environment and sustainability. An effective policy formation should support these emerging needs of the labour market in a green economy by supporting both green investments and vocational education. At this point, vocational and bachelor's programs for green jobs may play a substantial role. Also, employment structures should be backed up by the legal framework. Governmental support for green jobs (and greening the existing jobs) plays a pivotal role in the green transition in jobs. Some concrete examples can be found in Nordic countries such as Iceland, Finland, and Norway, where sustainable development has been integrated across all subjects in national curricula, making it a foundational element of basic education (Jónsson et al., 2021). In Germany, meanwhile, the expansion of publicly funded vocational training modules in areas such as energy efficiency, sustainable construction, and renewable energy resulted in a 14% increase in the number of new trainees equipped with green skills between 2013 and 2021 (IAB-Forum, 2024).

Another important theoretical implication for the green transition comes from political ecology. The political ecology approach proposes the circular economy view as an alternative to the linear economy understanding. Circular economy tries to characterise a sustainable and circular economic view by combining social and environmental concerns. In this manner, a circular economy is defined as an economy composed of reduction, recycling, reuse, and recovery of materials in production, distribution, and consumption (Kirchherr et al., 2017). Hence, a circular economy is a sustainable, low-carbon, resource-efficient, and competitive economy (European Parliament, 2023). An efficient circularity in the economy is provided by a good combination of lower consumer demand by eliminating unnecessary consumption, waste recycling, smart reuse of materials, renewable energy production and consumption, and reducing ecological footprint (Huyugüzel Kışla et al., 2022; Kirchherr & van Santen, 2019).

At this point, the concept of inclusive green growth has special importance (Shobande et al., 2024). It is not a new concept, but it has gained increasing importance in recent years. It suggests that rapid economic growth can be attained at the same time as the green production and consumption options. Further, poverty elimination can be achieved, and overall welfare can be increased without sacrificing the environment (World Bank, 2012, p. 2). Resource conservation and environmental protection are the key points. And decreasing social inequalities has critical importance to sustain economic growth (Sun et al., 2020). All these points underline the importance of transformational skill updates and labour market reforms. What is more is that empirical findings suggest that public expenditures on education significantly transform the labour market and hence support inclusive green growth (Okombi & Lebomoyi, 2024, p. 22).

When we consider all this theoretical background, it can be said that an effective economic policy for the labour market transformations required by the green economy should have the following components:

- Prioritisation of social investments.
- Reduction in inequalities.
- Adoption of the circular economy approach.
- Support for inclusive green growth.
- Reconfiguration of public investments.
- Harmonisation of financial systems.
- Providing private sector orientation.
- Support for emerging skill sets.
- Improvement in government support for vocational education.

5. Conclusions

The green transition is not only an environmental phenomenon but also a fact that is reshaping labour markets. While the green transition offers significant prospects for job creation through the development of green jobs and greening the jobs, it also demands a fundamental transformation of skills and economic structures. Addressing the mismatch between existing workforce competencies and the requirements of a low-carbon economy is critical for ensuring that no one in society is left behind during this transition. Emerging technical and digital skills are central to equipping individuals for future labour market demands. Moreover, the success of this transformation depends on coordinated policy efforts that integrate vocational education, public investment, and private sector engagement. It seems that governments, industry leaders, and educational institutions must collaborate to create a skilled workforce capable of navigating the complexities of the green transition, ensuring that environmental sustainability and economic prosperity reinforce one another.

There is no doubt that the success of a green transition directly depends on a balanced approach that connects technological innovation, skill development, and inclusive policies. However, some studies show that there are some challenges to the effective green transition. As the IMF (2024) mentioned, there is still a significant gender gap in green jobs. Women's participation lags behind that of men, primarily as a result of their insufficient representation in STEM education. Also, providing a strong legal framework for green transition by supporting structural transformations is a hard job for governments. In such a case, all stakeholders in the economy should be on the side of the green transition. Since it requires some parties to give up their high profit (especially the private sector), governments face opposition and oppression. At this point, governments should inform all stakeholders in the economy about the legal transformations, uncertainties, risks, costs, and benefits (Eurofi, 2025). The European Green Deal is a successful example of transforming European economies into a green economy. The European Commission helps member states to design and implement reforms supporting the green transition (European Commission, 2025). However, the European Green Deal even includes some disparities. Although member states act despite the Deal, there are still regional disparities in green job opportunities. Green industries are located mainly in Northern Europe's city centres. Hence, green job opportunities are evaluated by the workers who can work at those destinations (Eurobrussels, 2025). Since green jobs provide higher wages and better future opportunities, this situation creates regional disparities even in Europe. Such situations are more severe for underdeveloped and developing countries. The Green Jobs Initiative is a joint effort to include such countries in the global green economy transformation, and some other sub-initiatives have also been implemented. The Green Jobs in Asia Project, which was implemented between 2010 and 2012, is a good example (ILO, 2015, p. 3). However, there is still a long way to go for such countries' labour markets to be transformed in terms of green transition.

All these challenges and hardships point out that effective economic policy formation is a must for the green transition, and labour market transformations are critical to attain a successful transition. Jobs have been transformed in response to current and emerging global needs. The global climate crisis warns humanity that the globe has reached its limits. Humankind should adopt more sustainable production and consumption patterns. This creates an urgent need to transform societies and economies. This transformation calls for new job opportunities and new skill sets. An effective economic policy should meet the needs of changing labour markets. In this context, an effective economic policy for the labour market transformations required by the green economy should prioritise social investments and reduce all types of inequalities, adopt a circular economy view and support inclusive green growth, reconfigure public investments and orient the private sector, harmonise financial systems, support emerging skill sets, and invest in vocational education.

Author Contributions: Conceptualisation, B.T. and N.A.E.; methodology, B.T. and N.A.E.; investigation, B.T. and N.A.E.; writing—original draft preparation, B.T. and N.A.E.; writing—review and editing, B.T. and N.A.E.; visualisation, B.T.; supervision. All authors have read and agreed to the published version of the manuscript.

Funding: This research received no external funding.

Conflicts of Interest: The authors declare no conflicts of interest.

Author Names and Affiliations: Burcu Türkcan, Economics Department, Ege University, Izmir, Turkey; Nuri Aytuğ Erdemir, Department of Economics, Izmir Bakırçay University, Izmir, Turkey.

Keywords: green economy; employment; skills; economic change.

References

Bauer, P., Stevens, B., & Hazeleger, W. (2021). A digital twin of earth for the green transition. *Nature Climate Change*, *11*, 80–83. [CrossRef]

Bone, M., Ehlinger, E. G., & Stephany, F. (2024). Skills or degree? The rise of skill-based hiring for AI and green jobs. *Technological Forecasting and Social Change*, *214*, 124042. [CrossRef]

Drašković, D. (2024). *Nurturing green skills*. United Nations Development Programme. Available online: https://www.undp.org/serbia/blog/nurturing-green-skills (accessed on 27 June 2025).

Economist Impact. (2024). *Green skills: Driving the transition to a more sustainable future*. Available online: https://impact.economist.com/sustainability/green-skills-outlook/ (accessed on 8 July 2025).

Economist Impact. (2025). *The green skills atlas: Mapping readiness and demand worldwide.* Available online: https://impact.economist.com/sustainability/green-skills-atlas/ (accessed on 8 July 2025).
Eurobrussels. (2025). *Recruitment challenges in Europe's green job market: A statistical overview.* Available online: https://www.eurobrussels.com/article/818/recruitment-challenges-in-europes-green-job-market-a-statistical-overview (accessed on 30 June 2025).
Eurofi. (2025). *Green transition prospects and challenges.* Available online: https://www.eurofi.net/current-topics/green-transition-prospects-and-challenges/ (accessed on 12 July 2025).
European Commission. (2023). *Proposal for a regulation on establishing a framework of measures for strengthening Europe's net-zero technology products manufacturing ecosystem (Net-Zero Industry Act).* COM(2023) 161 final. Available online: https://eur-lex.europa.eu/legal-content/EN/TXT/?uri=CELEX%3A52023PC0161 (accessed on 14 July 2025).
European Commission. (2025). *Green transition.* Available online: https://reform-support.ec.europa.eu/what-we-do/green-transition_en (accessed on 14 July 2025).
European Parliament. (2023). *Circular economy: Definition, importance and benefits.* Available online: https://www.europarl.europa.eu (accessed on 15 July 2025).
Fuchs, M. (2024). Green skills for sustainability transitions. *Geography Compass, 18*(10), e70003. [CrossRef]
Gao, Y., Tsai, S.-B., Xue, X., Ren, T., Du, X., Chen, Q., & Wang, J. (2018). An empirical study on green innovation efficiency in the green institutional environment. *Sustainability, 10*(3), 724. [CrossRef]
Garrote Sanchez, D., & Yanez-Pagans, M. (2024, October). *Navigating the green transition: Building green skills for a sustainable workforce.* Skills4Dev knowledge digest, issue 13. World Bank.
Greenspon, J., & Raimi, D. (2024). Matching geographies and job skills in the energy transition. *The Extractive Industries and Society, 17,* 101397. [CrossRef]
Huyugüzel Kışla, G. Ş., Türkcan, B., & Ince Yenilmez, M. (2022). Sustainable COVID-19 recovery and circular economy. *Sustainability and Climate Change, 15*(4), 289–295. [CrossRef]
IAB-Forum. (2024). *Vocational training: Occupations with green skills are in high demand.* Available online: https://www.iab-forum.de/en/vocational-training-occupations-with-green-skills-are-in-high-demand/ (accessed on 28 June 2025).
ILO. (2015). *Factsheet—Green jobs in Nepal.* Available online: https://www.ilo.org/resource/project-document/fact-sheet-green-jobs-nepal (accessed on 14 July 2025).
ILO. (2025). *The green jobs programme of the ILO.* Available online: https://www.ilo.org/sites/default/files/wcmsp5/groups/public/%40ed_emp/%40emp_ent/documents/publication/wcms_371396.pdf (accessed on 5 July 2025).
International Monetary Fund. (2024). *Green jobs and the future of work for women and men.* Staff discussion note. Available online: https://www.imf.org (accessed on 6 July 2025).
Jackson, T. (2009). *Prosperity without growth—Economics for a finite planet.* Routledge.
Jiang, T., Ji, P., Shi, Y., Ye, Z., & Jin, Q. (2021). Efficiency assessment of green technology innovation of renewable energy enterprises in China: A dynamic data envelopment analysis considering undesirable output. *Clean Technologies and Environmental Policy, 23,* 1509–1519. [CrossRef]

Jónsson, Ó. P., Guðmundsson, B., Øyehaug, A. B., & Didham, R. J. (2021). *Mapping education for sustainability in the Nordic countries*. Nordic Council of Ministers. [CrossRef]
Kemp, R., & Never, B. (2017). Green transition, industrial policy, and economic development. *Oxford Review of Economic Policy, 33*(1), 66–84. [CrossRef]
Kirchherr, J., Reike, D., & Hekkert, M. (2017). Conceptualizing the circular economy: An analysis of definitions. *Resources, Conservation and Recycling, 127*, 221–232. [CrossRef]
Kirchherr, J., & van Santen, R. (2019). Research on the circular economy: A critique of the field. *Resources, Conservation and Recycling, 151*, 104480. [CrossRef]
Lagorio, A., Colombo, B., Cimini, C., & Gaiardelli, P. (2024). The future of green skills for the manufacturing sector. *IFAC PapersOnLine, 58*(19), 533–538. [CrossRef]
Okombi, I. F., & Lebomoyi, N. E. (2024). Economic complexity and inclusive green growth: The moderating role of public expenditure on education. *Journal of Environmental Studies and Sciences, 15*(3), 666–696. [CrossRef]
Organisation for Economic Co-Operation and Development (OECD). (2023). *Assessing and anticipating skills for the green transition: Unlocking talent for a sustainable future*. OECD Publishing. Available online: https://www.oecd.org/en/publications/assessing-and-anticipating-skills-for-the-green-transition_28fa0bb5-en.html (accessed on 1 June 2025).
Radmehr, R., Shayanmehr, S., Baba, E. A., Samour, A., & Adebayo, T. S. (2024). Spatial spillover effects of green technology innovation and renewable energy on ecological sustainability: New evidence and analysis. *Sustainable Development, 32*(3), 1743–1761. [CrossRef]
Raworth, K. (2017). *Doughnut economics—7 ways to think like a 21st century economist*. Chelsea Green Publishing.
Shan, S., Yılmaz Genç, S., Kamran, H. W., & Dinca, G. (2021). Role of green technology innovation and renewable energy in carbon neutrality: A sustainable investigation from Turkey. *Journal of Environmental Management, 294*, 113004. [CrossRef]
Shobande, O. A., Tiwari, A. K., Ogbeifun, L., & Trabelsi, N. (2024). Demystifying circular economy and inclusive green growth for promoting energy transition and carbon neutrality in Europe. *Structural Change and Economic Dynamics, 70*, 666–681. [CrossRef]
Stanef-Puica, M.-R., Badea, L., Şerban-Oprescu, G.-L., Şerban-Oprescu, A.-T., Francu, L.-G., & Cretu, A. (2022). Green jobs—A literature review. *International Journal of Environmental Research and Public Health, 19*(13), 7998. [CrossRef] [PubMed]
Stilwell, F., & Primrose, D. (2010). Economic stimulus and restructuring: Infrastructure, green jobs and spatial impacts. *Urban Policy and Research, 28*(1), 5–25. [CrossRef]
Stockholm Resilience Centre. (2025). *Planetary boundaries: The state of Earth's resilience*. Available online: https://www.stockholmresilience.org/research/planetary-boundaries.html (accessed on 20 June 2025).
Stroud, D., Fairbrother, P., Evans, C., & Blake, J. (2014). Skill development in the transition to a 'green economy': A 'varieties of capitalism' analysis. *The Economic and Labour Relations Review, 25*(1), 10–27. [CrossRef]
Sun, Y., Ding, W., Yang, Z., Yang, G., & Du, J. (2020). Measuring China's regional inclusive green growth. *Science of the Total Environment, 713*, 136367. [CrossRef]

Urban, P., Rizos, V., Ounnas, A., Kassab, A., & Kalantaryan, H. (2023). *Jobs for the green transition: Definitions, classifications and emerging trends*. TransEuroWorkS working paper 1/2023. Available online: https://transeuroworks.eu/wp-content/uploads/2023/09/Green-Jobs-Report-final_TransEuroWorkS-1.pdf (accessed on 15 June 2025).
van Vuuren, D. P., Doelman, J. C., Schmidt Tagomori, I., Beusen, A. H., Cornell, S. E., Röckstrom, J., Schipper, A. M., Stehfest, E., Ambrosio, G., van den Berg, M., Bouwman, L., Daioglou, V., Harmsen, M., Lucas, P., & van der Wijst, K.-I. (2025). Exploring pathways for world development within planetary boundaries. *Nature, 641*, 910–960. [CrossRef] [PubMed]
WEF. (2025). *Future of jobs 2025 report*. Available online: https://www.weforum.org/publications/the-future-of-jobs-report-2025/ (accessed on 7 June 2025).
World Bank. (2012). *Inclusive green growth—The pathway to sustainable development*. Available online: https://books.google.com.tr/ (accessed on 18 June 2025).
World Bank. (2023a). *World development indicators: Carbon intensity of GDP (kg per 2017 PPP $ of GDP)*. Available online: https://databank.worldbank.org/source/world-development-indicators (accessed on 18 June 2025).
World Bank. (2023b). *World development indicators: Energy use (GDP per kg of oil equivalent)*. Available online: https://databank.worldbank.org/source/world-development-indicators (accessed on 18 June 2025).
Zhao, X., Yin, H., & Zhao, Y. (2015). Impact of environmental regulations on the efficiency and CO_2 emissions of power plants in China. *Applied Energy, 149*, 238–247. [CrossRef]

How Public–Private Partnerships Drive Environmental Performance

Metin Nazlıoğlu and Hasan Yazar

Abstract: This chapter explores the growing role of public–private partnerships (PPPs) in addressing climate change and enhancing environmental performance. As countries face increasing pressure to decarbonise their economies and expand green infrastructure, PPPs have emerged as a crucial governance and financial mechanism for mobilising private sector resources and innovation. The study examines the definitional features of PPPs, their sectoral application, especially in the transition to renewable energy systems and climate-resilient infrastructure, and their contribution to sustainable development goals. Additionally, the study seeks to reveal the link between environmental performance, measured by the Environmental Performance Index, and PPP investment in the environment sector. The findings suggest a positive association between strong environmental outcomes and the utilisation of PPPs in the environment sector. The chapter concludes by highlighting the importance of regulatory clarity, institutional capacity, and inter-sectoral coordination for enhancing the effectiveness of PPPs. It also emphasises the need for future research to explore the causal dynamics between PPPs and environmental performance across various national contexts.

1. Introduction

Climate change has been one of the most pressing and urgent problems in recent years. Around the world, an increasing number of countries are making efforts to reduce their emissions. They commit to net-zero emissions by 2050. To keep warming under 1.5 degrees, emissions need to be cut in half by 2030 (IEA, 2021). Rising greenhouse gas emissions, global warming, dwindling water resources, and issues related to biodiversity not only impact the environment but also pose profound economic and social threats. According to A Global Call for Leadership on Climate Change by the Global Commission on Adaptation, "without adaptation, climate change may depress growth in global agriculture yields up to 30 percent by 2050". Additionally, climate change will threaten approximately 100 million people from around the world, especially those in developing countries below the poverty line, by 2030. This multidimensional and complex issue requires collective responsibility, encompassing not only states but also the private sector, civil society, and international organisations, as climate change is a problem that transcends borders. Also, it is unlikely to be solved through the intervention or effort of a single country (Piazza, 2021; Tosun & Schoenefeld, 2017).

The limitations in resources and capacity that conventional public policies face, as well as problems related to sustainability in long-term investments for the private sector, reveal the necessity for new cooperation models (Casady et al., 2024; Murphy & Bendell, 1997). Here, public–private partnerships (PPPs) can be an efficient model that facilitates the delivery of public goods and services, as well as financing significant infrastructure investments. As investments in addressing climate change require extraordinarily initial expenditures and technical expertise, PPP models have the potential to provide efficient solutions in this regard.

One of the prerequisites for combating climate change is to switch energy systems from fossil fuels to renewable sources such as solar or wind. A significant portion of global greenhouse gas emissions stems from the intensive use of fossil fuels, including coal, oil, and natural gas (Bertrand, 2021). This situation not only has devastating effects on the environment but also poses serious risks to human health, food security, and long-term economic stability (Romanello et al., 2024). Thus, transitioning from energy systems based on fossil fuels to systems relying on more renewable sources is of crucial importance. In addition, implementing these investments quickly and on a large scale means a race against time to prevent the devastating effects of climate change.

However, this transition is not merely a technical process but also one that entails significant costs. Establishing renewable energy plants, transforming energy transmission infrastructure, developing energy storage technologies, and rehabilitating outdated systems require large-scale investments (IEA, 2024). The transition to clean energy alone requires an investment of USD 4.5 trillion per year by the early 2030s (IEA, 2023). On the other hand, the OECD states that between 2016 and 2030, to support growth and sustainable development, USD 95 trillion in public and private investment will be needed in energy, transport, water, and telecommunications infrastructure at a global scale (OECD, 2018).

In this regard, climate-resilient infrastructure plays a crucial role in mitigating and adapting to the effects of climate change. These critical investments have the potential to contribute to reducing emissions and enhancing the resilience of economies against climate-related shocks, such as droughts, floods, heatwaves, and rising sea levels. However, developing and maintaining such infrastructure projects requires substantial and sustainable financial resources, particularly in sectors such as energy, water, transportation, and urban planning (ICSI, 2024; Cadario, 2024). According to the Global Commission on Adaptation 2019 Report, every USD 1 invested in resilient infrastructure yields USD 4 in avoided losses. This situation further highlights the importance of leveraging both public and private finance.

Therefore, it seems unlikely for most countries to move forward with public resources alone; the capital power, technical capacity, and innovative approach of the private sector play a critical role in this process. Accordingly, cooperation is essential to initiate, manage, and complete the sustainable energy transition so that a partnership between the public and private sectors can provide a suitable framework for achieving this objective. While this partnership involves the mobilisation of financial resources, it should also consider long-term responsibility sharing, technical expertise transfer, and risk management. The PPP model holds significant potential to enhance private sector investment incentives and promote alignment between policy measures and environmental goals.

Nowadays, investments in PPP projects, especially in environmental areas such as renewable energy production and climate-resilient infrastructure, have risen (OECD, 2025). This increase shows that PPPs are becoming a strategic tool in addressing climate change. This chapter aims to examine both conceptual and empirical aspects of PPP models in terms of addressing climate change. Additionally, it aims to investigate the impact of PPPs on the government's environmental performance.

2. Public–Private Partnerships in Combating Climate Change

The public sector has been the leading actor in combating climate change. However, governments have faced various challenges in this process, including budget limitations, redistributive issues, high opportunity costs, and political problems resulting from the tax burden. Recently, the private sector has also begun to play a more active role, attracting investments in climate-resilient infrastructure. Nevertheless, it seems unlikely for any actor to succeed in isolation. The scale and complexity of climate change underscore the need for a collaborative approach that leverages the strengths of both sectors. Cooperation between public and private sectors, through structured mechanisms and PPPs, can combine public sector oversight and long-term planning with private sector efficiency, innovation, and financing capacity (Casady et al., 2024; Guijie, 2025).

The Organisation for Economic Co-operation and Development (OECD) identifies PPPs as "long-term contractual arrangements between the government and a private partner whereby the latter delivers and funds public services using a capital asset, sharing the associated risks" (OECD, 2025). "PPPs are a key entry point to mobilise private sector finance to bridge a financing gap in adaptation actions. They must be resilient to climate change and work to build the resilience of the communities they serve. The involvement of the private sector can lead, beyond investment capacity and finance, to innovative thinking and new expertise"(Climate-ADAPT, 2025).

PPPs refer to diverse forms of collaboration between public and private entities, including legally binding contracts, cooperative agreements, and a wide range of institutional arrangements. The core characteristics of these arrangements, categorized by their form, purpose, and shared responsibilities, are summarized in Table 1. These partnerships provide a basis to develop, finance, or maintain public infrastructure and services. A defining element of PPPs is their long-term orientation, facilitating sustained cooperation over the lifecycle of a project. Both sectors share not only responsibilities and resources but also risks, costs, and potential rewards. The involvement of the private sector is crucial for the success of PPPs, especially when aligned with clearly defined public objectives. Goal alignment, private sector engagement, and a shared focus on outcomes are essential factors contributing to the effective implementation of these partnerships (Pinilla-De La Cruz et al., 2022).

Table 1. Key features of PPPs as derived from their definitions.

Form	- Contract - Cooperation - Collaboration - Agreement - Legally binding contract - Broad assortment of relationships
Purpose	- Public assets/infrastructure and/or services - Funding, construction, renovation, management, and maintenance of infrastructure or service
Timeframe	Long-term
Stakeholders	Public and private entities
Risk, reward, resource, and responsibility sharing	Sharing responsibilities, risks, revenue, and costs
Critical success factors	- Engagement of the private sector - Focus on a specific goal - Goal alignment

PPPs—public–private partnerships. Source: Authors' compilation based on data from Pinilla-De La Cruz et al. (2022).

2.1. Climate-Resilient Infrastructure and PPPs

Infrastructure is essential for functioning societies and economies, as it enables the movement of people, goods, services, and information. However, climate-related disasters, such as floods, heatwaves, and storms, increasingly threaten to cause widespread infrastructure failures and economic losses, especially in developing countries that are vulnerable due to limited financial and technical capacity. To tackle these challenges, governments at all levels must systematically incorporate climate resilience into infrastructure planning and decision-making, emphasising sustainable and adaptive projects to lower long-term societal and economic risks (OECD, 2024). This urgent and expanding need underscores the importance of innovative financing and implementation models. In this context, PPPs serve as an essential way to mobilise the resources and expertise needed to develop and sustain climate-resilient infrastructure, ensuring both sustainability and efficiency amid increasing climate-related risks.

In recent years, international organisations have increasingly acknowledged the strategic value of leveraging PPPs to promote climate-resilient infrastructure. For example, the Global Centre on Adaptation has developed a specialised training program and certification for infrastructure practitioners, aimed at enhancing institutional ability to design and manage resilient infrastructure projects (Global Center on Adaptation, 2025). Likewise, the World Bank's PPP Legal Resource Centre provides a comprehensive inventory of legal and technical resources to assist with planning, implementation, and governance of climate-resilient PPPs (World Bank, 2025). These initiatives reflect a growing consensus among global stakeholders that PPP mechanisms can play a pivotal role in achieving sustainable infrastructure goals.

As climate risks become more frequent and severe, international efforts to equip both the public and private sectors with the necessary tools and frameworks for building resilient infrastructure are becoming increasingly essential.

Due to limited public budgets and substantial infrastructure gaps, PPPs are becoming increasingly important for many governments to deliver infrastructure projects (Mills et al., 2020). This reliance on PPPs not only addresses funding challenges but also provides a strategic opportunity to embed long-term sustainability and resilience into infrastructure planning. One of the most crucial areas where PPPs can play a significant role in combating climate change is in developing climate-resilient infrastructure. Due to the immense scale and high cost of infrastructure projects, especially in sectors such as energy, water, transportation, and urban development, governments often encounter significant budgetary issues and technical limitations. In this context, PPPs serve as an effective means of attracting private capital and expertise for long-term infrastructure investments aimed at mitigating and adapting to climate-related risks (Kennedy & Corfee-Morlot, 2012).

PPPs are mechanisms that compel the government and private sector actors to recognise the long-term costs by preventing them from concentrating solely on the construction phase of infrastructure projects. PPP contracts, typically spanning 25 to 30 years, encourage private parties to evaluate the entire lifecycle of a project and the risks that may arise throughout its duration, especially those related to climate change. This lifecycle-focused approach helps create infrastructure that is more resilient to climate-related events. Additionally, PPP projects require coordination among multiple stakeholders, including developers, public authorities, investors, and operators, all of whom work together toward common goals. This type of collaborative process facilitates the creation of more innovative and sustainable solutions in response to climate risks. Moreover, financial institutions participating in PPPs conduct due diligence to determine if the project can generate sufficient revenue to service its debt. This also necessitates a thorough analysis of climate risks. In this regard, the robust risk assessment at the heart of every successful PPP project provides a framework for effectively managing climate and disaster risks (Mills et al., 2020).

2.2. Transition to Renewable Energy Systems and PPPs

The transition to renewable energy is one of the most critical pillars of global efforts to mitigate and adapt to climate change, as well as reduce dependence on fossil fuels. Fossil fuels continue to dominate global energy production, accounting for over 80 percent of the total, while cleaner energy alternatives are steadily advancing. At present, approximately 29 percent of electricity is generated from renewable sources (United Nations, 2023). Fossil fuel-based energy production is a significant contributor to greenhouse gas emissions, which in turn contribute to global warming, air pollution, and environmental degradation. Renewable energy sources, such as solar, wind, hydro, and geothermal, provide clean and sustainable alternatives that can significantly reduce carbon footprints while enhancing energy security and price stability (Edenhofer et al., 2011). Furthermore, integrating renewables into energy systems enhances long-term economic resilience, fosters the creation of green jobs, and aligns with the global goal of achieving net-zero emissions as outlined in the Paris Agreement. In many countries, particularly those experiencing rapid growth in energy consumption, the transition to renewable energy sources is crucial for ensuring universal access to affordable and reliable electricity (IEA, 2021; PNNL, 2021).

By 2022, the fossil fuel industry had received approximately USD 7 trillion in subsidies, while the annual investment required for renewable energy was only USD 4.5 trillion. However, it is estimated that a clean energy transition could save up to USD 4.2 trillion annually by 2030, simply by reducing environmental and health impacts. The costs of solar and wind energy technologies have fallen by 85% and 56%, respectively, from 2010 to 2020, making renewable energy the most affordable option for electricity generation in many countries. According to the International Renewable Energy Agency (IRENA), 90% of the world's electricity could be generated from renewable sources by 2050. Furthermore, every USD 1 invested in clean energy creates three times as many jobs as in the fossil fuel sector. As we work towards reaching net-zero targets, 14 million new jobs are expected to be created in the clean energy sector alone by 2030. All this data demonstrates that renewable energy serves as a strategic lever not only in combating climate change but also in promoting economic growth, job creation, and energy security (United Nations, 2023).

The transition to renewable energy systems forms is the cornerstone of the global transformation towards a low-carbon, sustainable development model. However, this transformation requires significant restructuring of energy systems and, consequently, substantial financial investments (Cheng et al., 2021). One of the primary challenges, particularly in realising the potential of green energy investments, is securing adequate financing. Given that the public sector often lacks financial capacity to meet the growing demand for energy investment, alternative financing tools have gained increasing importance (Lu et al., 2022). In this regard, PPPs have emerged as an alternative tool to mobilise resources for renewable energy projects, especially under conditions of limited budgets. Beyond providing capital, PPPs enable the integration of private expertise and efficiency into public service delivery, thereby supporting the achievement of broader sustainability goals. As a result, many countries are increasingly recognising the crucial role of PPP investments in advancing energy efficiency and realising their long-term climate and development objectives (Cheng et al., 2021).

PPPs are crucial in the transition to renewable energy systems. This model integrates public policies with financial resources and the technical expertise of the private sector, enabling the achievement of long-term goals such as enhancing energy security and reducing carbon emissions. Unlike traditional infrastructure projects, PPPs focus not only on building and operating projects but also on their long-term performance driven by output. These structures typically include mechanisms such as purchase guarantees, power purchase agreements, and contracts for differences to encourage private sector investment. This provides investment opportunities for biofuels and other renewable technologies that are not yet cost-effective. Despite their initial costs, PPPs significantly contribute to the sustainable energy transition by facilitating the adoption of environmentally friendly alternatives (Akhavan, 2025).

2.3. Scale and Value of PPPs

PPPs offer a wide range of advantages, which have made them attractive to the public sector, especially in Europe. Timely delivery and cost efficiency of large-scale infrastructure projects are among the most distinguishing benefits of PPPs. PPPs encourage a service-oriented approach and promote innovation and competition. In doing so, they help minimise lifecycle costs and facilitate the transfer of lifecycle risks to the private sector. Furthermore, PPPs promote the robustness of projects by involving independent funding bodies that enhance project evaluation and ensure suitable due diligence. Finally, PPPs provide a basis for higher quality standards, cross-border competitiveness, outcome-based planning, long-term value for money, and elimination of the taxpayer burden (European PPP Expertise Centre, 2009; Guijie, 2025).

PPPs for infrastructure projects can include private sector involvement throughout all phases of the project, such as development, financing, construction, operation, maintenance, and eventual transfer, deconstruction, or redesignation of public infrastructure (Kennedy & Corfee-Morlot, 2012).

The reports by European PPP Expertise Centre (EPEC) reveal that 1749 PPP projects reached financial close between 1990 and 2016 in the European market, worth EUR 336 billion. In this period, the United Kingdom, France, Spain, Portugal, and Germany were the leading countries. The United Kingdom had an outstanding record with over 1000 PPP projects worth approximately EUR 160 billion. France followed it with 175 PPP projects worth almost EUR 40 billion (European Court of Auditors, 2018).

A review of the European PPP market in 2010 by EPEC reveals that the value of PPP transactions reaching financial close in the European market was EUR 18.3 billion. Following the 2008 global financial crisis, 2010 saw an increase. The value of PPP transactions in 2009 was approximately EUR 15 billion. It is worth noting that in the record years 2005, 2006, and 2007, the value ranged between EUR 26 billion and EUR 30 billion.

In 2024, a total of PPP projects reached financial close, with a combined value of EUR 11.47 billion, a 17% decrease from 2023. As illustrated in Figure 1, the number of projects nearing financial close increased by almost 3%, reaching 39 projects compared to 38 in 2023. The transportation sector had the highest transaction value in 2024, reaching approximately EUR 6.8 billion (EIB, 2025).

While PPPs have traditionally concentrated on transport, telecommunications, and education, there has been increasing interest in applying this model to promote collaboration between public authorities and private stakeholders in tackling environmental challenges, especially in developing climate-resilient infrastructure. To achieve sustainable objectives for climate change mitigation and adaptation, PPPs have become a vital tool.

PPP investments in the environment sector experienced a decrease from EUR 2.1 billion in 2023 to EUR 805 million in 2024 (EIB, 2025). Environment-related PPP projects in 2024 are the redevelopment of an energy-from-waste plant in France, energy efficiency improvements for the French Ministry of Defense, and an offshore wind farm energy transmission project in the United Kingdom.

Figure 2 illustrates the evolution of PPP projects in the environment sector between 2010 and 2024, both in terms of project number and total project value. Starting from relatively low levels in 2010, there was a peak in 2013. This period likely reflects a growing interest in environmental investments and the implementation of large-scale projects. However, between 2014 and 2017, a notable decline was observed in both indicators. From 2018 onwards, the trend shows signs of recovery, with 2021 and particularly 2022 marking a resurgence in project activity. In 2022, both project numbers and value reached high levels, indicating renewed momentum driven by global efforts to combat climate change and develop green transition policies. In 2023, while the number of projects declined, the overall value remained high, suggesting a shift to fewer but larger-scale investments. In 2024, both project numbers and value dropped significantly. The observed decline in certain years may be attributed to the natural completion of previously initiated projects.

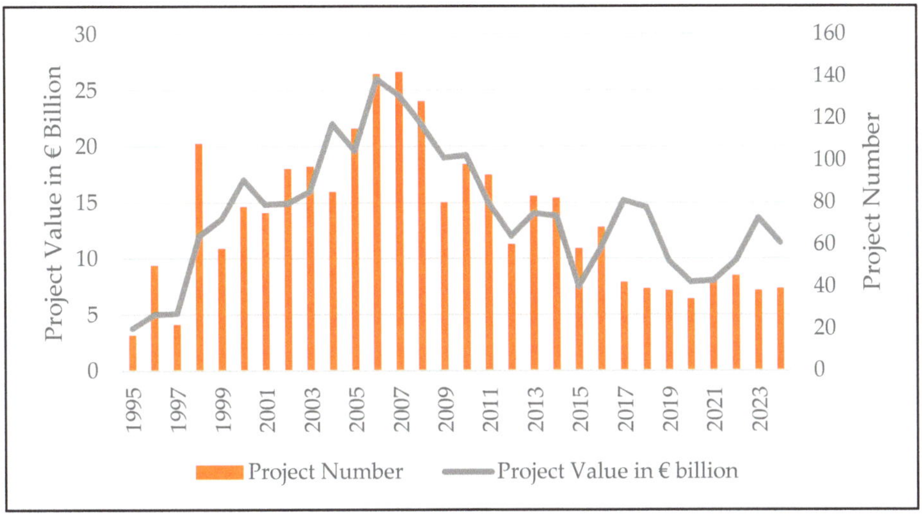

Figure 1. Thirty years of view of the European public–private partnership market by number of projects and value (1995–2024). Source: Authors' compilation based on data from EIB (2025).

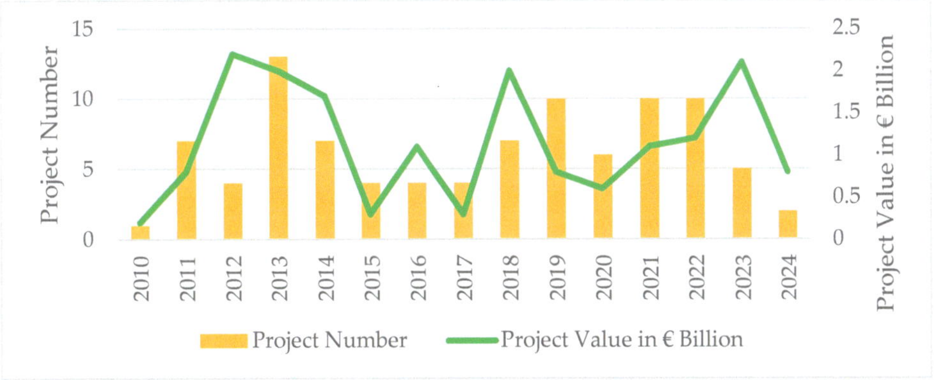

Figure 2. Evolution of the main public–private partnership in the environment sector by project number and project value (2010–2024). Source: Authors' compilation based on data from the EIB (2025).

3. Case Studies

3.1. National Level

The Greater Manchester Waste Project in the UK was one of the first examples of a partnership between public and private partners, the Private Finance Initiative (PFI), in the waste sector. The project aims to support the regional waste disposal authority in gradually achieving its targets for recycling/composting, and diversion from landfills through its contractual agreement with Viridor Laing Ltd., a partnership between Viridor and John Laing. The project helps to ensure that the UK complies with its requirements under EU Directives. The project is developed under a PFI/P3 agreement, valued at GBP 631 million (EIB, 2006). Staffordshire Waste PFI and Western Riverside EFW were another notable PPP examples in the UK that addressed climate change.

Germany has been a pioneer in investments related to combating climate change, not only through national policies but also by implementing innovative and cooperative PPP models. One distinguishing example is the Emschergenossenschaft river basin restoration. It was a long-term collaboration between public authorities and private actors. The EUR 5.5 billion project transformed the Emscher River from a concrete wastewater canal into a natural river ecosystem by modernising its sewage infrastructure and integrating flood management measures. This project plays a crucial role in implementing the European Green Deal, improving water quality, hydro-morphology, and biodiversity, and has contributed mainly to combating flooding and droughts (Climate-ADAPT, 2024). Another great example is that Hannover Region Administrative Building (Regionhaus) is developed under a Design–Build–Finance–Operate (DBFO) PPP model. The building was constructed according to Energy-Optimised Construction (EnOB) standards with strict energy efficiency targets. These targets are embedded in all phases, from planning and construction to long-term operation, leading to a significant carbon emission reduction (Federal Ministry for Economic Affairs and Energy, 2021). Both projects highlight how PPP frameworks in Germany have been strategically utilised to achieve climate adaptation and mitigation goals.

The Seine Aval Wastewater Treatment Plant in Archeres stands out as one of Europe's most important environmental infrastructure projects and exemplifies a Design–Build–Operate–Maintain (DBOM) PPP model. The EUR 392 million DBOM contract was awarded to OTV, a subsidiary of Veolia, under a long-term PPP agreement with the public authority SIAAP (Syndicat Interdépartemental pour l'Assainissement de l'Agglomération Parisienne). Through this project, the facility was upgraded with energy-efficient technologies and an integrated sludge treatment system that helps mitigate climate change and improve water quality (WaterWorld, 2007). In 2013, supported by EUR 600 million in funding from the European Investment Bank, the plant continued to modernise its facilities, highlighting the strategic role of PPPs in developing large-scale, climate-resilient environmental infrastructure in France (European Investment Bank, 2013).

India, as a signatory to the Paris Agreement, expanded its electricity generation capacity before the 2030 target year. To reach 500 GW, it deployed a large-scale renewable energy project. The project, the Pavagada Solar Park, spans 53 square kilometres in Tumkur district and operates under a PPP model designed to attract private investments in climate infrastructure. The project made a significant contribution to the country's net-zero emission targets. It was completed in 2019 with a total cost of USD 2.1 billion. The project was developed and implemented by Karnataka State Power Development Corporation Ltd. (KSPDCL). KSPDCL is a parastatal joint venture between the Solar Energy Corporation of India, the Government of India, and Karnataka Renewable Energy Development Limited, representing the Government of Karnataka. Additionally, various private companies, including Azure Power, Tata Power Renewable Energy, SB Energy, ReNew Power, Fortum, and Avaada Power, played critical roles (Haldar et al., 2024).

Benban Solar Park in Egypt is the largest solar project in Africa. The project is a solar energy initiative that uses photovoltaic panels to produce 200 megawatts of renewable electricity. Thanks to this project, Egypt will be able to reduce its CO_2 equivalent emissions by 285,050 metric tons each year. It is a joint government venture supported by international financing institutions and involving around 100 Egyptian companies. The project cost was USD 4 billion (EcoConServ Environmental Solutions, 2016). Overall, this project serves as an excellent example of collaboration between the government and the private sector in advancing the energy transition and combating climate change.

The Menengai Geothermal project is a 35 MW greenfield geothermal project. The project is developed to provide clean, affordable, and sustainable energy to half a million Kenyan households (African Development Bank Group, 2024). Steam for the project will be provided by the Geothermal Development Company, which is a state-owned company in Kenya, through a 25-year agreement covering project implementation and steam supply. After becoming operational, the electricity will be sold to Kenya Power, the national distribution company, under a power purchase agreement spanning the same 25-year period (Globeleq, 2023). The project also received assistance and financial support from the African Development Bank, the European Investment Bank, the United States Agency for International Development, the Japan International Cooperation Agency, and the French Development Agency (Geothermal Development Company, 2025).

Case studies from Mongolia, Australia, Maryland (USA), and Puerto Rico showcase diverse uses of PPPs in climate-resilient and technologically adaptive infrastructure projects, each with distinct features and scales. In Mongolia, PPPs were employed to advance renewable solar energy, encompassing 29 solar PV projects with a combined capacity of over 150 MW. Australia's Victoria Desalination Plant, built under a 30-year PPP with the AquaSure consortium, ranks as one of the largest reverse osmosis desalination facilities worldwide, incorporating advanced membrane technology and adaptability for future upgrades. The I-495 and I-270 PPP in Maryland is the largest highway PPP of its kind, spanning 70 miles and planned to include autonomous vehicle infrastructure through an innovative two-phase procurement process. Lastly, Puerto Rico's PR-22 and PR-5 toll roads, structured as a 50-year lease PPP, involved USD 1.08 billion in upfront payments and USD 350 million in capital improvements, including dynamic toll lanes and advanced gantry systems. These cases collectively highlight the adaptability of PPPs in addressing emerging climate and technological challenges, while striking a balance between fiscal responsibility and service innovation (World Bank, 2022).

3.2. Subnational and Local Level

Porto Alegre, Brazil, is progressing its urban resilience efforts by integrating conventional infrastructure funding with private sector investment via PPPs. The city, in partnership with the World Bank, is exploring ways to access international resilience funding, potentially through local banks serving as intermediaries (World Bank, 2020, City Resilience Program). The local government, supported by the Chief Resilience Officer's team, is taking a central role in mobilising stakeholders from various sectors. Recent legislative changes have increased the PPP investment cap from 1–2% of public GDP to 7%, aligning with the federal level and boosting the city's ability to finance resilient urban projects (International Finance Corporation, 2018).

In Japan, local governments are increasingly utilising PPPs as a strategic tool to address both ageing infrastructure and the growing impacts of climate change. Many municipalities in Japan face fiscal constraints, declining populations, and disaster risks. PPPs provide a way to leverage private sector expertise and finance for climate-resilient infrastructure, especially in water and sanitation. Several cities exemplify Japan's approach to local PPPs (Febiola et al., 2024):

- The Yokohama municipality has developed comprehensive PPP frameworks focused on transparency, data sharing, and robust regulatory oversight. These efforts have fostered innovative solutions and long-term resilience in urban water and sanitation services.
- Hamamatsu implemented a PPP model to rehabilitate and operate its water treatment facility. The project enabled the city to integrate advanced technologies and improve operational efficiency, while ensuring sustainable water management.
- Amagasaki partnered with private firms to manage wastewater treatment services. Through this collaboration, energy-saving technologies were adopted, resulting in reduced operating costs and a lower environmental impact, and contributing to the city's climate goals.

Bhubaneswar city in India adopted a PPP model for street lighting as part of its USD 700 million urban renewal plan, with USD 400 million anticipated from private investment. Supported by the International Finance Corporation (IFC) and DevCo, the project links the private sector operator's revenue to energy savings, incentivising efficiency. Approximately 20,000 streetlights have been upgraded to energy-efficient systems. Similar PPPs in cities such as Cuttack and Jaipur are projected to cut greenhouse gas emissions by 50,000 metric tons each year and draw more than USD 20 million in private investment (International Finance Corporation, 2018).

Semarang, a coastal city in Indonesia, deals with growing challenges associated with flooding, land subsidence, and rapid urbanisation. In response, the city has made substantial efforts to embed resilience into its planning processes, including the creation of a City Resilience Strategy and the incorporation of climate initiatives into its Medium-Term Urban Development Plan. Although most climate-resilient initiatives in Semarang, such as early flood warning systems, mangrove restoration, and renewable energy, have primarily been funded by public sources and donors, the city is now increasingly seeking involvement from the private sector. Semarang is notably proposing a PPP for a street lighting project, involving energy service companies and backed by the Ministry of Energy and Mineral Resources. This initiative presents a strategic opportunity to enhance private investment in climate-smart infrastructure, thereby supporting broader urban sustainability and emissions reduction goals (International Finance Corporation, 2018; Energy Transition Partnership, 2022). Like the Semarang case, cities in Vietnam, such as Hanoi and Ho Chi Minh City, face risks from floods, storms, and intense rainfall. To address this, PPPs have been developed to finance and build drainage networks, resilient water and energy systems that enhance urban resilience against climate-related shocks (DAI, 2024).

PPPs serve as an essential platform to foster cooperation and collaboration between governments and private sector entities, especially when addressing increasing climate challenges. This variety of examples, including the Greater Manchester Waste Project, the Emschergenossenschaft River Restoration, India's

Pavagada Solar Park, and Egypt's Benban Solar Park, shows how PPPs mobilise private sector financial resources, technical expertise, and operational capabilities while supporting public climate objectives. These cases underscore PPPs' ability to bridge institutional and financial gaps by distributing risks and responsibilities, ensuring long-term sustainability. Whether it is the deployment of advanced wastewater treatment in France, energy-efficient infrastructure in Germany, or large-scale renewable energy projects in Africa and Asia, PPPs encourage innovation and long-term commitment. Therefore, PPPs not only facilitate the implementation of climate-resilient infrastructure but also institutionalise cooperative governance frameworks that enhance mutual trust, accountability, and policy alignment between the public and private sectors.

3.3. Environmental Performance and PPPs

In this study, we state that there can be an association between environmental PPPs and environmental performance. To explore this, we begin with an indicator that will demonstrate the environmental performance. The Environmental Performance Index (EPI), created by combining the environmental indicators of various countries, is a comprehensive measurement we refer to. We include environmental PPPs immediately following the section on the Environmental Performance Index, comparing the data of both.

The Environmental Performance Index (EPI), developed through a collaboration between Yale University and Columbia University, is built upon three main themes: climate change, environmental health, and ecosystem vitality. It comprises a total of 58 indicators under these themes and ranks 180 countries based on their environmental performance using this data. The performance indicator in question is aligned with the UN Sustainable Development Goals and the targets of the Paris Climate Agreement. Thus, the index provides insights into how close countries are to achieving environmental goals. Its detailed and comparative perspective enables researchers to conduct analyses in various environmental domains (Block et al., 2024).

According to Figure 3, 2024 EPI scores, Estonia ranks first, followed by Luxembourg, Germany, Finland, and the United Kingdom. Thus, Europe stands out as a group of countries with strong performance in this measurement. The country with the worst performance is Vietnam, followed by Pakistan, Laos, Myanmar, and India, respectively.

There are numerous lessons to be drawn from EPI scores. One of these pertains to the size of economies. In the United States, one of the world's largest economies, emissions are declining at a slow pace. In contrast, countries such as China, India, and Russia continue to experience rising emissions. As illustrated in the global distribution of scores in Figure 4, an examination of EPI scores suggests a strong correlation between the size of a country's economy and its environmental performance. The results also indicate that some countries stand out from their peers in terms of economic development (Block et al., 2024).

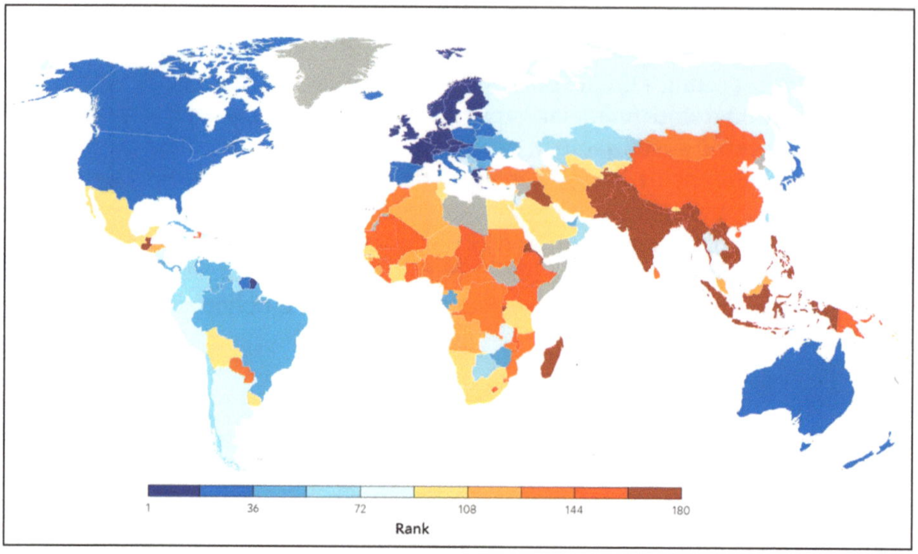

Figure 3. Rankings in the 2024 Environmental Performance Index. Source: Reprinted from Block et al. (2024), used with permission.

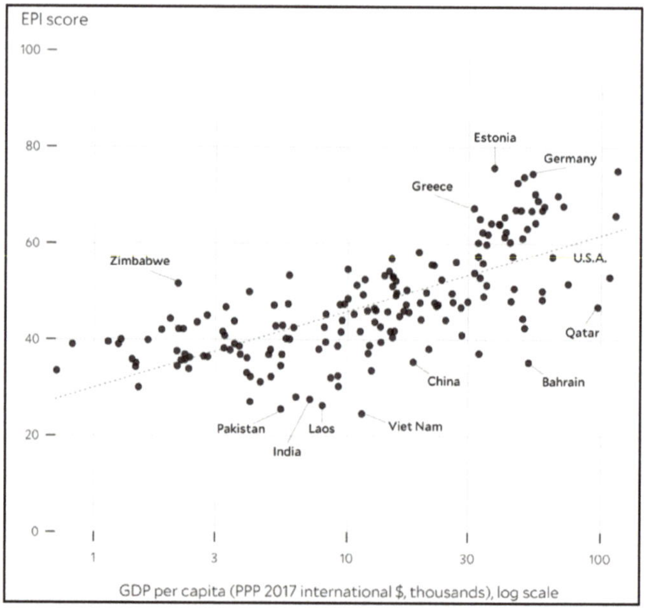

Figure 4. The Environmental Performance Index (EPI) and countries' GDP. Source: Reprinted from Block et al. (2024), used with permission.

Globally, public infrastructure projects are often not adequately implemented due to financial constraints. Consequently, PPPs serve as an effective alternative for addressing financial challenges and find application in various sectors. One such application is supporting environmental projects. In recent years, PPPs for environmental projects such as water and solid waste management have been rapidly gaining momentum (Kanakoudis & Tsitsifli, 2012). The public sector uses various tools, like subsidies, to improve environmental quality. However, in the context of environmental quality, the implementation of PPPs is generally more effective than subsidies (Buso & Stenger, 2018). Government–industry R&D partnerships pave the way for innovation and technological advancement in the relevant field. This leads to high sectoral efficiency while also contributing to the development of low-pollution technologies in terms of environmental impact (Sperling, 2001). When used effectively, PPPs contribute to social and environmental development alongside economic growth. Therefore, PPPs play a critical role in addressing infrastructure gaps and ensuring sustainability (Guijie, 2025).

Environmental PPPs significantly contribute to improving environmental performance. However, they face several challenges in implementation. Inadequate and unclear regulatory frameworks are major obstacles to PPP implementation. Unequal risk distribution between the public and private sectors, negative private perception of the public sector, and high costs are additional issues. Nevertheless, opportunities such as new technological advancements, improved governance, capacity building, and increased investment make environmental PPPs highly significant (Lee, 2025).

The literature on PPPs and environmental performance confirms that PPPs yield highly positive results. Tang et al. (2021) conducted a study examining the service quality of PPPs in the context of China's urban wastewater treatment sector. Based on detailed data from firms in Jiangsu Province, it is claimed that the implementation of PPPs contributes to pollutant treatment performance, thereby enhancing environmental performance.

Guijie (2025) examines the role of PPPs in sustainable infrastructure projects. The analysis compares the traditional model with the PPP model, focusing on project completion rates, cost efficiency, service quality, sustainability, and public satisfaction. The results confirm that PPP models are more advantageous than traditional models across all these aspects.

Thellbro et al. (2018) conducted interviews with project leaders from 38 randomly selected PPP projects out of 245 in Sweden's mountainous region. These interviews explored the status of sustainability goals in PPPs. The results confirm that PPPs are highly effective in achieving these goals. Li et al. (2020) examined urban water environment treatment public–private partnership (UWETP-PPP) projects in Xuchang City, China. Using the fuzzy logic method, their study found that UWETP-PPPs in Xuchang City encompass indicators such as energy efficiency, utilisation of construction waste, renovation of project facilities, and waste recycling. These results highlight the contribution of Xuchang City's UWETP-PPPs to sustainability and environmental quality. The superior performance of these models across various indicators compared to traditional methods is further supported by the comparative data presented in Figure 5. Anwar et al. (2021) conducted a study in China from 1990 to 2018, examining the impact of PPP investments in the transportation sector, renewable energy consumption, and urbanisation on carbon emissions. They employed the Quantile Autoregressive Distributed Lagged (QARDL) method for this purpose. The results confirm a negative relationship between carbon emissions in the transportation sector and PPPs used in transportation. This finding aligns with the positive contribution of PPPs to environmental performance. Hou et al. (2023) examined data from 284 cities in China between 2003 and 2020. They used a staggered difference-in-difference (DID) model to test the relationship between carbon intensity and PPPs. The findings indicate that PPPs are highly effective in reducing carbon intensity. Therefore, their study presents PPPs as a toolkit for achieving environmental improvement. Additionally, it argues that local governments are more successful in implementing these projects and should be encouraged to do so. Ha (2025) used data from 38 countries between 2010 and 2022 to test the dynamic relationship between green logistics and PPPs in the energy sector. The findings confirm that green logistics has significant short-term impacts on energy-related PPPs.

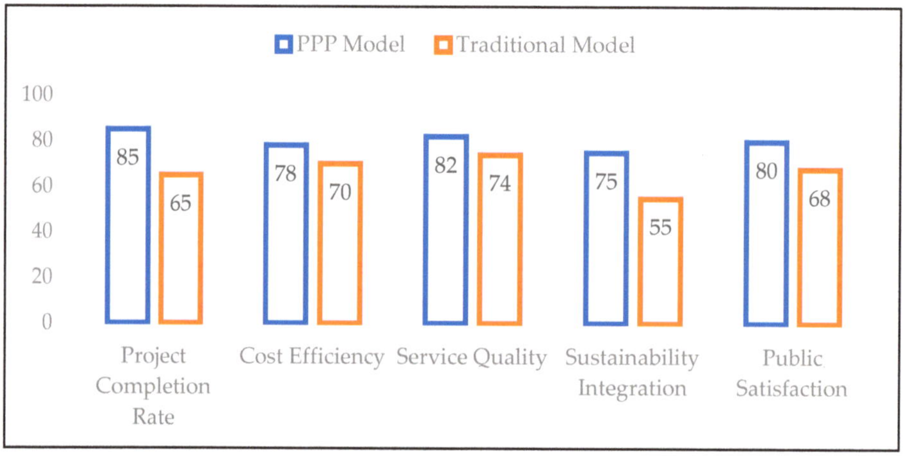

Figure 5. PPPs model vs. traditional model in sustainable infrastructure development. Source: Authors' compilation based on data from Guijie (2025).

In this study, consistent with the literature, we propose a positive relationship between environmental performance and PPPs. To this end, we first focused on the Environmental Performance Index. We observed that European countries generally rank high in the Environmental Performance Index. This observation led us to investigate whether environmental PPPs exist in European countries. In the European Investment Bank database, we found evidence of the monetary value of environmental PPPs in some European countries between 1990 and 2025. This finding provides an answer to the research question of this study.

Upon careful examination of the data, countries with high performance in the Environmental Performance Index (EPI) also have significant project values for environmental PPPs. As depicted in Figure 6, the most notable country is the United Kingdom, which ranks third in the EPI, holding a strong position. At the same time, the value of its environmental PPPs is approximately EUR 13.3 billion. In Spain, ranked 20th, this value is EUR 3.1 billion. France, ranked 11th, has a value of EUR 2.1 billion. In the Netherlands, ranked 13th, the monetary value of environmental PPP projects is EUR 1.725 billion. Italy, ranked 29th, has a project value of EUR 1.466 billion. The graph shows that environmental PPP projects are also being implemented in other European countries. These data indicate that countries with relatively good environmental performance place value on environmental PPP projects. Their investment in environmental PPP projects also reflects the government's commitment to improving environmental performance.

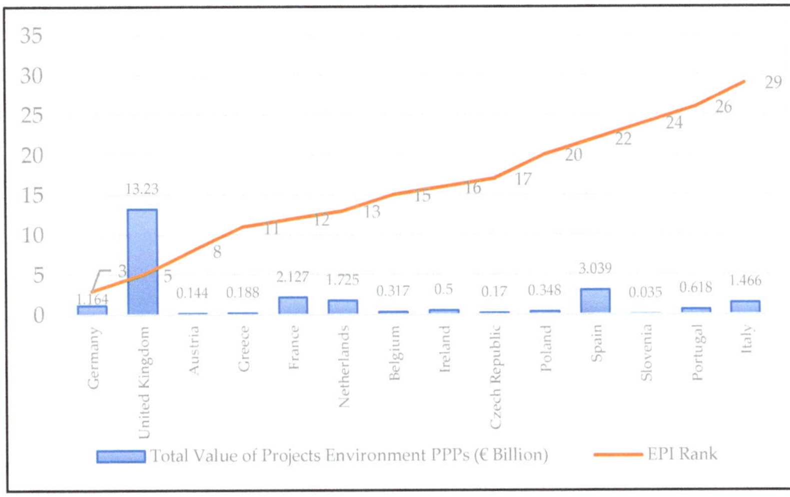

Figure 6. Total value of environmental PPPs and EPI ranking in some European countries. Source: Figure by authors.

The significant role of Europe's climate targets lies behind the development of environmental PPPs in Europe. Tvarnø (2020) argues that climate PPPs, one type of environmental PPP, play a critical role in achieving Europe's climate goals. However, in his article, he asserts that multiple conditions are necessary to achieve an effective climate PPP. These include a balance in bargaining power within the PPP contracts, the dominant influence of government participation in the decision-making process, and the structuring of tenders and climate PPP contracts to ensure mutual benefit and efficiency.

Environmental PPPs have emerged as a strategic tool to support countries in achieving better environmental performance. As demonstrated by EPI, which measures countries' achievements across climate change, environmental health, and ecosystem vitality, countries with strong environmental outcomes, especially in Europe, tend to exhibit a high level of investments in environmental PPPs. For instance, the UK, France, and the Netherlands not only rank highly in the EPI but also have implemented environmental PPPs worth billions of euros. This correlation suggests that governments committed to environmental goals actively leverage PPP to enhance infrastructure for mitigating and adapting to climate change. Empirical studies confirm that PPP contributes positively to environmental performance by improving service quality, reducing emissions, and fostering innovation in green technologies. Despite the challenges such as regulatory uncertainty and risk imbalances, environmental PPPs offer a promising avenue for aligning financial investment with sustainability objectives, particularly when supported by clear governance frameworks, private sector engagement, and transparent procurement processes.

4. Conclusions

As the urgency of climate change grows, PPPs have become a key strategy for mobilising capital, improving technical skills, and fostering innovation in environmental infrastructure services. This chapter showed that PPPs, especially in climate-resilient infrastructure and the transition to renewable energy systems, not only help close infrastructure and financing gaps but also act as collaborative governance mechanisms aligned with long-term sustainability goals.

A key contribution of this study is highlighting the potential connection between a country's environmental performance and its involvement in environmental PPPs. The data suggest that countries with higher EPI scores, including the UK, Germany, and the Netherlands, tend to exhibit greater investments in environmental PPPs. This observed correlation indicates that governments prioritising environmental goals are more likely to use PPPs as a tool for achieving them. In this regard, PPPs may not only be a consequence of strong environmental governance but also a driver of improved environmental outcomes.

Given the relevance of this correlation, future research should focus on empirically testing the strength, direction, and causality of the relationship between EPI scores and the scope or quality of environmental PPPs. Are countries that invest more in PPPs truly achieving better environmental outcomes, or are PPPs simply more common in already high-performing countries? Longitudinal and cross-country comparative analyses, along with econometric models, could offer solutions to these questions. Furthermore, future research could examine sector-specific differences, such as whether PPPs in energy, water, or waste management have varying effects on environmental indicators.

Additionally, this research yields important implications for policymakers seeking to improve both environmental outcomes and investment efficiency. First, PPP regulatory frameworks must be strengthened to reduce uncertainty and enhance private sector confidence. This includes clear rules on risk sharing, transparent procurement processes, and mechanisms for long-term accountability (OECD, 2025). Second, institutional capacity-building is paramount, particularly in developing countries, so that public agencies can effectively design, negotiate, and monitor complex PPP arrangements. Finally, governments should consider linking PPP project performance to environmental targets, for instance, by embedding climate indicators into contract clauses and performance-based payments.

As the global community advances toward more ambitious climate goals, enhancing the strategic use of PPPs and understanding their role in overall environmental performance will be vital. Therefore, progressing the research and policy agenda at the intersection of PPP implementation and environmental performance is both timely and essential for developing evidence-based, climate-smart governance in the coming years.

Author Contributions: Conceptualisation, M.N. and H.Y.; validation, M.N. and H.Y.; investigation, M.N. and H.Y.; data curation, H.Y.; writing—original draft preparation, M.N.; visualisation, H.Y. and M.N. All authors have read and agreed to the published version of the manuscript.

Funding: This research received no external funding.

Conflicts of Interest: The authors declare no conflicts of interest.

Author Names and Affiliations: Metin Nazlıoğlu, Department of Public Finance, Manisa Celal Bayar University, Manisa, Turkey; Hasan Yazar, Department of Public Finance, Manisa Celal Bayar University, Manisa, Turkey.

Keywords: public-private partnerships; institutional capacity; inter-sectoral coordination; green infrastructure; renewable energy.

References

African Development Bank Group. (2024). *Kenya's Menengai geothermal project to power half a million homes with clean energy*. African Development Bank Group. Available online: https://www.afdb.org/en/success-stories/kenyas-menengai-geothermal-project-power-half-million-homes-clean-energy-74832 (accessed on 29 July 2025).

Akhavan, K. (2025). *How public-private partnerships can accelerate the energy transition*. Wood Mackenzie. Available online: https://www.woodmac.com/news/opinion/how-public-private-partnerships-can-accelerate-the-energy-transition/ (accessed on 29 July 2025).

Anwar, A., Sharif, A., Fatima, S., Ahmad, P., Sinha, A., Rehman Khan, S. A., & Jermsittiparsert, K. (2021). The asymmetric effect of public private partnership investment on transport CO_2 emission in China: Evidence from quantile ARDL approach. *Journal of Cleaner Production, 288*, 125282. [CrossRef]

Bertrand, S. (2021). *Climate, environmental, and health impacts of fossil fuels. Environmental and energy study institute*. Available online: https://www.eesi.org/papers/view/fact-sheet-climate-environmental-and-health-impacts-of-fossil-fuels-2021 (accessed on 29 July 2025).

Block, S., Emerson, J. W., Esty, D. C., Sherbinin, A., & Wendling, Z. A. (2024). *Environmental performance index*. Yale Center for Environmental Law & Policy. Available online: https://epi.yale.edu/ (accessed on 19 June 2025).

Buso, M., & Stenger, A. (2018). Public-private partnerships as a policy response to climate change. *Energy Policy, 119*, 487–494. [CrossRef]

Cadario, A. (2024). *Infrastructure and NbS*. Global Center on Adaptation. Available online: https://gca.org/programs/infrastructure-and-nbs/ (accessed on 30 July 2025).

Casady, C. B., Cepparulo, A., & Giuriato, L. (2024). Public-private partnerships for low-carbon, climate-resilient infrastructure: Insights from literature. *Journal of Cleaner Production, 470*, 143338. [CrossRef]

Cheng, G., Zhao, C., Iqbal, N., Gülmez, Ö., Işik, H., & Kirikkaleli, D. (2021). Does energy productivity and public-private investment in energy achieve carbon neutrality target of China? *Journal of Environmental Management, 298*, 113464. [CrossRef]

Climate-ADAPT. (2024). *The Emscher restoration: A contribution to climate adaptation*. Available online: https://climate-adapt.eea.europa.eu/en/mission/solutions/mission-stories/the-emscher-restoration-story19 (accessed on 30 July 2025).

Climate-ADAPT. (2025). *Private-public partnerships (PPPs) for adapting and maintaining infrastructure and services*. Available online: https://climate-adapt.eea.europa.eu/en/metadata/adaptation-options/private-public-partnerships-ppps-for-adapting-and-maintaining-infrastructure-and-services (accessed on 30 July 2025).

DAI. (2024, December 18). *The climate-resilient city*. DAI Publications. Available online: https://dai-global-developments.com/articles/climate-resilient-city/ (accessed on 30 July 2025).

EcoConServ Environmental Solutions. (2016). *SESA Benban 1.8 GW PV solar park final report*. EcoConServ Environmental Solutions.

Edenhofer, O., Pichs-Madruga, R., Sokona, Y., Seyboth, K., Matschoss, P., Kadner, S., Zwickel, T., Eickemeier, P., Hansen, G., Schloemer, S., & von Stechow, C. (2011). *Renewable energy sources and climate change mitigation*. IPCC. Available online: https://www.ipcc.ch/report/renewable-energy-sources-and-climate-change-mitigation/ (accessed on 30 July 2025).

EIB. (2006). *MANCHESTER WASTE PPP*. European Investment Bank. Available online: https://www.eib.org/en/projects/all/20060299 (accessed on 30 July 2025).

EIB. (2025). *Market update review of the European public-private partnership market in 2024*. Available online: https://www.eib.org/en/publications/20250010-market-update-review-of-the-european-public-private-partnership-market-in-2024 (accessed on 20 February 2026).

Energy Transition Partnership. (2022). *Diagnostic review and analysis of energy efficiency development in Indonesia*. Energy Transition Partnership.

European Court of Auditors. (2018). *Special report 09/2018: Public private partnerships in the EU: Widespread shortcomings and limited benefits*. Available online: http://www.eca.europa.eu/en/publications/sr18_09 (accessed on 30 July 2025).

European Investment Bank. (2013). *France: EUR 600 million for the upgrading of the Seine Aval sewage treatment plant*. European Investment Bank. Available online: https://www.eib.org/en/press/all/2013-082-france-600-meur-pour-la-modernisation-de-la-station-depuration-de-seine-aval (accessed on 30 July 2025).

European PPP Expertise Centre. (2009). *European PPP report 2009*. DLA Piper.

Febiola, M., Parekhelashvili, N., Namba, Y., Basar, B., & Ram, K. S. (2024). *Local private sector involvement in public–private partnerships for sustainable water and sanitation in Asia*. Asian Development Bank Institute. [CrossRef]

Federal Ministry for Economic Affairs and Energy. (2021). *Public-private partnership finances new energy-efficient administrative building*. Available online: https://www.energieforschung.de/en/project/public-private-partnership-finances-new-energy-efficient-administrative-building (accessed on 30 July 2025).

Geothermal Development Company. (2025). *Menengai geothermal project*. Geothermal Development Company. Available online: https://www.gdc.co.ke/menengai/ (accessed on 30 July 2025).

Global Center on Adaptation. (2025). *Knowledge module on PPPs for climate-resilient infrastructure*. Global Center on Adaptation. Available online: https://gca.org/knowledge-module/ (accessed on 25 June 2025).

Globeleq. (2023). *Menengai geothermal plant*. Globeleq. Available online: https://globeleq.com (accessed on 16 February 2026).

Guijie. (2025). Public-private partnerships for sustainable infrastructure development. *Journal of Lifestyle and SDGs Review*, *5*(5), e06622. [CrossRef]

Ha, L. T. (2025). An application of panel VAR technique to explore a link between commitments to energy projects in public–private partnerships and green logistic management. *Asia Pacific Journal of Marketing and Logistics*, *37*(11), 3535–3563. [CrossRef]

Haldar, S., Hoffman, J., Verma, M., Peddibhotla, A., & Bazaz, A. (2024). Reimagining energy infrastructure for justice: Power, politics, and institutional work in India's 2.05 GW Pavagada solar park. *Energy Research & Social Science*, *116*, 103645. [CrossRef]

Hou, X., Li, W., Li, D., & Peng, J. (2023). Public–private partnerships and carbon reduction targets: Evidence from PPP investments in energy and environmental protection in China. *Environment, Development and Sustainability, 27*(3), 6567–6597. [CrossRef]

ICSI. (2024). *The climate resilient infrastructure report*. ICSI.

IEA. (2021). *Net zero by 2050*. IEA. Available online: https://www.iea.org/reports/net-zero-by-2050 (accessed on 13 July 2025).

IEA. (2023). *World energy outlook 2023—Analysis*. IEA. Available online: https://www.iea.org/reports/world-energy-outlook-2023 (accessed on 12 July 2025).

IEA. (2024). *World energy outlook 2024—Analysis*. IEA. Available online: https://www.iea.org/reports/world-energy-outlook-2024 (accessed on 13 July 2025).

International Finance Corporation. (2018). *Climate investments oppurtunities in cities: An IFC analysis*. International Finance Corporation.

Kanakoudis, V., & Tsitsifli, S. (2012). Urban water services public infrastructure projects: Turning the high level of the NRW into an attractive financing opportunity using the PBSC tool. *Desalination and Water Treatment, 39*(1–3), 323–335. [CrossRef]

Kennedy, C., & Corfee-Morlot, J. (2012). *Mobilising investment in low carbon, climate resilient infrastructure*. OECD environment working papers 46. OECD. [CrossRef]

Lee, S. (2025). *The environment and PPPs*. Available online: https://www.numberanalytics.com/blog/environmental-public-private-partnerships (accessed on 9 July 2025).

Li, H., Xia, Q., Wang, L., & Ma, Y. (2020). Sustainability assessment of urban water environment treatment public-private partnership projects using fuzzy logic. *Journal of Engineering, Design and Technology, 18*(5), 1251–1267. [CrossRef]

Lu, Q., Farooq, M. U., Ma, X., & Iram, R. (2022). Assessing the combining role of public-private investment as a green finance and renewable energy in carbon neutrality target. *Renewable Energy, 196*, 1357–1365. [CrossRef]

Mills, A., Frisari, G. L., Silva Zuniga, M. C., Shepherd, C., Ham, M., Donadi, E., & Pohl, I. (2020). *Climate resilient public private partnerships: A toolkit for decision makers*. Inter-American Development Bank. [CrossRef]

Murphy, D. F., & Bendell, J. (1997). *In the company of partners: Business, environmental groups and sustainable development post-Rio*. Policy Press.

OECD. (2018). *Subnational public-private partnerships*. OECD. Available online: https://www.oecd.org/en/publications/responding-to-the-infrastructure-challenge_9789264304864-en.html (accessed on 15 July 2025).

OECD. (2024). *Infrastructure for a climate-resilient future*. OECD. Available online: https://www.oecd.org/en/publications/infrastructure-for-a-climate-resilient-future_a74a45b0-en.html (accessed on 14 July 2025).

OECD. (2025). *Recommendation of the council on principles for public governance of public-private partnerships*. Available online: https://legalinstruments.oecd.org/en/instruments?mode=advanced&committeeIds=863 (accessed on 15 July 2025).

Piazza, A. (2021). Collective responsibility in the cooperative governance of climate change. *Sustainability, 13*(8), 4363. [CrossRef]

Pinilla-De La Cruz, G. A., Rabetino, R., & Kantola, J. (2022). Unveiling the shades of partnerships for the energy transition and sustainable development: Connecting public–private partnerships and emerging hybrid schemes. *Sustainable Development, 30*(5), 1370–1386. [CrossRef]

PNNL. (2021). *Renewable integration.* Pacific Northwest National Laboratory. Available online: https://www.pnnl.gov/explainer-articles/renewable-integration (accessed on 13 July 2025).

Romanello, M., Walawender, M., Hsu, S.-C., Moskeland, A., Palmeiro-Silva, Y., Scamman, D., Ali, Z., Ameli, N., Angelova, D., Ayeb-Karlsson, S., Basart, S., Beagley, J., Beggs, P. J., Blanco-Villafuerte, L., Cai, W., Callaghan, M., Campbell-Lendrum, D., Chambers, J. D., Chicmana-Zapata, V., & Costello, A. (2024). The 2024 report of the Lancet Countdown on health and climate change: Facing record-breaking threats from delayed action. *The Lancet, 404*(10465), 1847–1896. [CrossRef] [PubMed]

Sperling, D. (2001). Public-private technology R&D partnerships: Lessons from US partnership for a new generation of vehicles. *Transport Policy, 8*(4), 247–256. [CrossRef]

Tang, Y., Liu, M., & Zhang, B. (2021). Can public-private partnerships (PPPs) improve the environmental performance of urban sewage treatment? *Journal of Environmental Management, 291*, 112660. [CrossRef] [PubMed]

Thellbro, C., Bjärstig, T., & Eckerberg, K. (2018). Drivers for public–private partnerships in sustainable natural resource management—Lessons from the Swedish mountain region. *Sustainability, 10*(11), 3914. [CrossRef]

Tosun, J., & Schoenefeld, J. J. (2017). Collective climate action and networked climate governance. *WIREs Climate Change, 8*(1), e440. [CrossRef]

Tvarnø, C. D. (2020). Climate public private partnerships in the EU: A climate law and economic perspective. *European Procurement & Public Private Partnership Law Review, 15*(3), 200–208. Available online: https://www.jstor.org/stable/27067349 (accessed on 10 July 2025).

United Nations. (2023). *Renewable energy—Powering a safer future. United Nations.* United Nations. Available online: https://www.un.org/en/climatechange/raising-ambition/renewable-energy (accessed on 12 June 2025).

WaterWorld. (2007, August). *Seine aval, Europe's largest wastewater plant, opens nitrification unit.* WaterWorld. Available online: https://www.waterworld.com/wastewater-treatment/article/16201029/seine-aval-europes-largest-wastewater-plant-opens-nitrification-unit (accessed on 16 June 2025).

World Bank. (2020). *City resilience program.* Available online: https://www.worldbank.org/en/topic/disasterriskmanagement/brief/city-resilience-program (accessed on 17 June 2025).

World Bank. (2022). *Public-private partnership (PPP) contracts in an age of disruption.* World Bank.

World Bank. (2025). *Legal and regulatory issues concerning PPPs.* Available online: https://ppp.worldbank.org/legal-framework (accessed on 21 June 2025).

Climate Justice: Local Voice and Global Challenges in Bangladesh

Parimal Kumar Roy, Md. Moshiur Rahman and Md. Shakhawat Hossain Sojib

Abstract: This chapter examines the historical background of SDGs localisation and its related challenges, with a particular emphasis on SDG 13 localisation in promoting social justice globally. It seeks ways to enhance the future progress of public welfare through a social justice perspective introduced by the ILO. Methodologically, the study follows the indigenous community perspective model, aligning with established frameworks. An analysis of Bangladesh's Voluntary National Report (VNR) assesses progress using relevant indicators. The result shows dissatisfaction with positional progress. Further, this chapter investigates and highlights the gaps between SDG targets and actual achievements in Bangladesh through a global lens. Finally, we conclude with recommendations for futuraction, addressing strategic and financial constraints. These recommendations are based on a review of the existing literature and VNR data, considering global challenges.

1. Introduction

We indeed live in a regime of Sustainable Development Goals, and their thriving leads us to a rethink of the role of community development. The social phenomena analysed in academic texts emphasise ensuring social justice through accountability. In this context, this chapter discusses the climate justice process aimed at building strong social institutions. The document we present fits into the general proposition of the anthropology of public policies which is oriented towards the ethnographic discovery of the "constellations of actors, activities, and influences..." (Wedel et al., 2005, p. 30). Our focus is on the climate policies outlined by Bangladesh as a nation state, intending to protect vulnerable groups and promote social welfare.

The SDGs are the legacy of the environmental issues highlighted after the establishment of the Club of Rome in 1968. The academic discussion at the time concluded that promoting growth should be limited since it is doing an injustice to the environment (Meadows et al., 2018). The SDGs are an international document from 2015 and were adopted by the Government of Bangladesh (GoB) and align with this framework. The GoB formulated and implemented a policy in line with its local context.

2. Analytical Frameworks

To address environmental issues, policymakers should acknowledge the cultural and economic vulnerability before taking action to protect and preserve the people for future generations. This study, hence, proposes a potential solution—the indigenous community perspective model (Roy, 2025)—to ensure the voices of vulnerable ethnic communities, for example, the Santals. Their voices are vital in climate policy and action decisions. Vulnerable groups in Bangladesh are experiencing complicated and wide-ranging effects of climate change, and efforts must be made to address these issues thoroughly and culturally. Indeed, there is a need for a multifaceted approach that considers these communities' diverse needs and circumstances and recognises the substantial role these communities play in developing solutions to the climate crisis.

Indigenous Community Perspective Model Linked with Climate Justice

This model proposes 4Rs (Respect, Relational, Relevancy, and Reliability) to minimise the complexities of climate change in society. Without aligning the 4Rs, vulnerable [ethnic] groups would not be capable of facing adverse climatic hazards at the community level.

The indigenous community perspective model emphasises the integration of traditional ecological knowledge, cultural values, and community-led decision-making into social justice frameworks. This model challenges Western-centric approaches by centring lifeworld views in climate adaptation and mitigation strategies, instead of the predominant worldview (Roy, 2025; Datta & Kairy, 2024; Cajete, 2020; Datta et al., 2024).

A key feature of this model is the community-based approach, which directly involves Indigenous peoples in identifying climate vulnerabilities and developing locally relevant solutions. For example, research with the Santal community in Bangladesh highlights how customary laws, knowledge, and cultural practices—such as community-based disaster risk reduction and social cohesion—enhance climate resilience. This approach not only produces context-specific, sustainable solutions but also empowers Indigenous communities as key stakeholders in climate policy and action (Roy, 2025; Roy et al., 2023a, 2023b).

Furthermore, this model calls for the integration of Indigenous and scientific knowledge systems in climate research and policy. Such integration must be ethical, participatory, and attentive to issues of 4Rs, cultural autonomy, and social justice. By centring Indigenous perspectives, climate justice efforts can address historical inequalities, promote sustainability, and ensure that adaptation and mitigation strategies are both practical and equitable based on 4Rs (Roy, 2025; Orlove et al., 2023).

Against this backdrop, Indigenous community perspectives offer transformative pathways for climate justice by valuing traditional knowledge, fostering community leadership, and advocating for inclusive, decolonised climate action (Ashraf et al., 2019).

3. Social Justice Model and Its Link to Climate Justice

The International Labour Organization (ILO) has long supported a social justice model rooted in the promotion of decent work, fundamental rights, and inclusive social dialogue. This model, formalised through key declarations such as the 1998 Declaration on Fundamental Principles and Rights at Work and the 2008 Declaration on Social Justice for a Fair Globalization, positions social justice as central to both national and international policy frameworks (Reynaud, 2018; Dreval, 2025; Kohiyama, 2018). The ILO's approach emphasises the importance of strong institutions, legal frameworks, and participatory mechanisms that involve the participation of people [employers, workers, and governments] in shaping labour standards and addressing emerging global challenges, including climate change (Dreval, 2025).

A core mechanism of the ILO's social justice model is social dialogue—negotiation, consultation, and information exchange among all stakeholders in the world of work (www.ilo.org, last accessed on 20 September 2025). This process is not only fundamental for improving labour relations but is also seen as essential for consolidating democratic and strong institutions and ensuring sustainable governance. The ILO's model advocates for comprehensive mechanisms that integrate legal, communicative, institutional, and educational tools to implement social justice principles effectively.

Climate justice is increasingly recognised as a critical dimension of social justice. The ILO's recent work highlights the need for social protection systems that shield vulnerable populations from the impacts of climate change, such as extreme weather and rising temperatures, while also supporting a just transition to a green economy (Razavi et al., 2025). Climate justice demands that those most responsible for emissions—typically wealthier nations—support low-income countries and marginalised groups who bear the brunt of climate impacts (Patterson et al., 2018). This includes closing social protection gaps, redistributing resources, and ensuring that climate policies are fair, inclusive, and attentive to historical inequalities (Amorim-Maia et al., 2022).

4. Literature Review: Climate Justice and Global Policy Frameworks

Climate justice has become a central concern in global climate policy, particularly within the frameworks established by the United Nations Framework Convention on Climate Change (UNFCCC) and the Paris Agreement. The literature highlights that justice debates—especially those around distributive and procedural fairness—have significantly shaped international climate negotiations, with persistent divisions between developed and developing countries over historical responsibility, equity, and the allocation of mitigation and adaptation burdens (Okereke & Coventry, 2016; Huggel et al., 2016; Resnik, 2022; Sengupta, 2023).

The Paris Agreement marked a milestone by explicitly referencing climate justice, yet the operationalisation of justice within global policy remains fraught. Key challenges include the tension between state sovereignty and collective action, the procedural imbalance in knowledge and representation between the Global North and South, and the limited effectiveness of current mechanisms to address loss and damage or ensure fair climate finance (Huggel et al., 2016; Onifade, 2021).

Scholars emphasise that climate justice is not only about the distribution of burdens and benefits but also about inclusive decision-making and the recognition of vulnerable groups, such as low-income populations and indigenous communities (Resnik, 2022; Cairney et al., 2023). The literature also notes in Table 1 (see details in Table 1) that while global frameworks increasingly acknowledge justice, implementation often falls short, and active engagement from civil society and marginalised voices is crucial to ensure that climate policies do not perpetuate existing inequalities (Resnik, 2022; Cairney et al., 2023).

Overall, advancing climate justice within global policy frameworks requires bridging normative ideals with practical mechanisms, strengthening accountability, and fostering more inclusive, equitable governance. Based on the mentioned discussion, we can summarise the key themes, such as distributive justice and climate finance (details in Table 1), in climate justice scenarios with policy frameworks in the table below.

Table 1. Key justice themes in global climate policy frameworks.

Theme	Key Insights	Example
Distributive Justice	Persistent North–South divides over responsibility and burden-sharing	(Okereke & Coventry, 2016; Huggel et al., 2016; Resnik, 2022; Sengupta, 2023)
Procedural Justice	Need for inclusive, transparent, and participatory decision-making	(Huggel et al., 2016; Resnik, 2022; Cairney et al., 2023)
Climate Finance	Justice in funding flows and addressing historical inequities	(Huggel et al., 2016)
State Sovereignty vs. Collective Action	National interests often hinder robust, justice-oriented global agreements	(Onifade, 2021; Okereke & Coventry, 2016; Sengupta, 2023)
Role of Civil Society	Essential for holding policymakers accountable and amplifying marginalised voices	(Resnik, 2022; Cairney et al., 2023)

Source: Table by authors.

5. Climate Justice: Integrating Local Voices and Challenges in Regional Contexts

Climate justice research highlights global inequities, emphasising the disproportionate burdens on vulnerable regions and Indigenous communities (see details in Table 2). Local voices, especially from marginalised groups, are often sidelined in policy, yet their participation is crucial for equitable, context-sensitive solutions that address both global and regional climate challenges (Gifford & Knudson, 2020).

Table 2. Regional, local, and Indigenous perspectives in climate justice.

Focus Area	Highlighted Area	Example
Global–Local Inequities	Disproportionate impacts on developing regions and marginalised groups	Sultana (2021) Codato et al. (2024) Wilkens and Datchoua-Tirvaudey (2022)
Indigenous Perspectives	Indigenous knowledge and leadership are vital but often marginalised in policy processes	Parsons and Crease (2024) Martinez et al. (2024)
Policy and Governance	Regional contexts require inclusive, decolonial, and context-sensitive climate governance	Codato et al. (2024) Wilkens and Datchoua-Tirvaudey (2022) Parsons and Crease (2024)

Source: Table by authors.

6. MDGs to SDGs: A Journey of Localisation in Bangladesh

Bangladesh's transition from the Millennium Development Goals (MDGs) to the Sustainable Development Goals (SDGs) reflects a shift toward inclusive, locally driven development. While Bangladesh made significant progress on MDGs—reducing poverty, improving maternal and child health, and increasing educational access—the

SDGs demand broader, more integrated action, including climate, inequality, and sustainable growth. Localisation is central: local governments, especially union parishads, are now recognised as key actors for SDG implementation, given their proximity to marginalised communities and understanding of local needs. However, challenges persist—limited resources, capacity gaps, and insufficient decentralisation hinder effective localisation. Bangladesh's policy frameworks, such as integrating SDGs into Five-Year Plans and forming local SDG committees, aim to empower local actors and foster participatory, context-sensitive development, as mentioned in Table 3, the evolution of the global frameworks. Continued progress depends on strengthening local institutions, resource allocation, and stakeholder engagement.

Table 3. Bangladesh's MDG achievements and SDG localisation.

Aspect	Description
MDG Achievements	Poverty reduction, health, education gains
SDG Localisation	Local governments central to implementation
Policy Innovations	Integration into Five-Year Plans, local SDG committees

MDG—Millennium Development Goals; SDG—Sustainable Development Goals. Source: Table by authors.

Bangladesh has made significant strides in aligning national policies with the Sustainable Development Goals (SDGs), but critical gaps persist between global ambitions and local realities. These gaps stem from institutional, financial, governance, and capacity challenges that hinder effective SDGs localisation and implementation.

7. GAPs: Local vs. Global SDGs Implementation Challenges

7.1. Institutional and Governance Gaps

Ambiguous mandates and overlapping jurisdictions among ministries and divisions create confusion, conflicts of interest, and lack of cohesion, impeding coordinated SDG action.

Weak local government capacity: Local governments (LGs) are closest to communities but lack adequate resources, authority, and technical skills to implement SDGs effectively.

Top-down policy approach: National-level planning often fails to reflect local needs, resulting in poor alignment between global SDG targets and local priorities.

7.2. Resource and Capacity Constraints

Insufficient funding and resource mobilisation: The scale of investment required for SDG achievement far exceeds available government resources, especially at the local level.

Limited technical and administrative capacity: Local institutions often lack the expertise for data collection, monitoring, and innovative policy implementation.

7.3. Stakeholder Engagement and Inclusivity

Inadequate stakeholder analysis and participation: Key local actors, including marginalised groups, are often excluded from planning and decision-making, undermining the "leave no one behind" principle.

Weak multi-stakeholder partnerships: Collaboration between government, civil society, academia, and the private sector is limited, especially at the grassroots.

7.4. Policy and Data Gaps

Policy incoherence and misalignment: National policies may not address local realities, leading to suboptimal outcomes and missed synergies among the SDGs (as noted in Table 4).

Table 4. Key gaps in SDGs implementation in Bangladesh.

Gap Type	Local Level Example	Global/National Level Example
Institutional	Weak LG capacity, lack of authority	Overlapping ministry mandates
Resource/Capacity	Insufficient funding, skills	National resource mobilisation
Stakeholder Engagement	Exclusion of local actors	Limited cross-sector partnerships
Policy/Data	Poor local data, policy misfit	National policy misalignment
Contextual/Environmental	Rural–urban divide, climate risks	National focus on economic growth

LG—local government. Sources: Authors' compilation based on data from Rahman (2021); Roy et al. (2023a, 2023b).

Data unavailability and poor monitoring: Lack of reliable, disaggregated data at the local level hampers progress tracking and evidence-based decision-making are clearly seen in the following table (Table 4).

7.5. Contextual and Environmental Challenges

Urban–rural disparities: Rural areas face greater challenges in SDG localisation due to poverty, low digital literacy, and climate vulnerability.

Trade-offs between SDGs: Competing priorities (e.g., economic growth vs. environmental protection) are not always managed effectively, especially in sensitive regions like coastal Bangladesh.

8. Conclusions

Bangladesh's SDGs progress is hampered by a persistent disconnect between global/national strategies and local realities. Addressing these gaps requires empowering local governments, improving resource allocation, fostering inclusive partnerships, and ensuring policies are context-sensitive and data-driven. Bridging these divides is essential for achieving the SDGs by 2030.

Author Contributions: Conceptualisation, first draft, revision and project administration, P.K.R.; data visualisation and editing, M.M.R. and M.S.H.S. All authors have read and agreed to the published version of the manuscript.

Funding: No external funding for this research.

Conflicts of Interest: The authors declare no conflict of interest.

Author Names and Affiliations: Parimal Kumar Roy, Bangladesh Public Administration Training Centre, Savar, Bangladesh; Md. Moshiur Rahman, Bangladesh Public Administration Training Centre, Savar, Bangladesh; Md. Shakhawat Hossain Sojib, Capacity Building Training-Research, Dhaka, Bangladesh.

Keywords: social justice; climate change; SDGs; community development; climate challenges.

References

Amorim-Maia, A., Anguelovski, I., Chu, E., & Connolly, J. (2022). Intersectional climate justice: A conceptual pathway for bridging adaptation planning, transformative action, and social equity. *Urban Climate*, *41*, 101053. [CrossRef]

Ashraf, M., Ullah, L., Shuvro, M., & Salma, U. (2019). Transition from millennium development goals (MDGs) to sustainable development goals (SDGs): Blueprint of Bangladesh for implementing the sustainable development goals (SDGs) 2030. *Medicine Today*, *31*(1), 46–59. [CrossRef]

Cairney, P., Timonina, I., & Stephan, H. (2023). How can policy and policymaking foster climate justice? A qualitative systematic review. *Open Research Europe*, *3*, 51. [CrossRef]

Cajete, G. (2020). Indigenous science, climate change, and indigenous community building: A framework of foundational perspectives for indigenous community resilience and revitalization. *Sustainability*, *12*(22), 9569. [CrossRef]

Codato, D., Peroni, F., & De Marchi, M. (2024). The multiple injustice of fossil fuel territories in the Ecuadorian Amazon: Oil development, urban growth, and climate justice perspectives. *Landscape and Urban Planning*, *241*, 104899. [CrossRef]

Datta, R., Chapola, J., Owen, K., Hurlbert, M., & Foggin, A. (2024). Indigenous land-based practices for climate crisis adaptions. *Explore*, *20*, 103042. [CrossRef]

Datta, R., & Kairy, B. (2024). Decolonizing climate change adaptations from indigenous perspectives: Learning reflections from munda indigenous communities, coastal areas in Bangladesh. *Sustainability*, *16*(2), 769. [CrossRef]

Dreval, Y. (2025). Mechanisms for implementing the principles of social dialogue in the activities of the International Labour Organization. *Bulletin of Kharkiv National University of Internal Affairs*, *108*(1), 136–145. [CrossRef]

Gifford, L., & Knudson, C. (2020). Climate finance justice: International perspectives on climate policy, social justice, and capital. *Climatic Change*, *161*(2), 243–383. [CrossRef]

Huggel, C., Wallimann-Helmer, I., Stone, D., & Cramer, W. (2016). Reconciling justice and attribution research to advance climate policy. *Nature Climate Change*, *6*, 901–908. [CrossRef]

Kohiyama, T. (2018). Role of international organizations in driving rule-making: The example of the international labour organization. In *Proceedings of the ASIL annual meeting* (Vol. 112). Cambridge University Press. [CrossRef]

Martinez, D., Meadow, A., Manning, B., & Maldonado, J. (2024). Climate justice and climate adaptation in California: Indigenous community climate adaptation leadership and opportunities for scientific collaboration. *Weather, Climate, and Society*, *16*(3), 399–409. [CrossRef]

Meadows, D. H., Meadows, D. L., Randers, J., & Behrens, W. W. (2018). The limits to growth. In *Green planet blues* (pp. 25–29). Routledge.

Okereke, C., & Coventry, P. (2016). Climate justice and the international regime: Before, during, and after Paris. *Wiley Interdisciplinary Reviews: Climate Change*, *7*(6), 834–851. [CrossRef]

Onifade, T. (2021). Climate justice under the Paris agreement: Framework and substance. *Carbon & Climate Law Review*, *15*(3), 233. [CrossRef]

Orlove, B., Sherpa, P., Dawson, N., Adelekan, I., Alangui, W., Carmona, R., Coen, D., Nelson, M., Reyes-García, V., Rubis, J., Sanago, G., & Wilson, A. (2023). Placing diverse knowledge systems at the core of transformative climate research. *Ambio*, *52*(9), 1431–1447. [CrossRef]

Parsons, M., & Crease, R. (2024). Indigenous climate justice in Aotearoa New Zealand: The dangers of (mis)recognition within climate policymaking. *Inland Waters*, *14*(3), 204–219. [CrossRef]

Patterson, J., Thaler, T., Hoffmann, M., Hughes, S., Oels, A., Chu, E., Mert, A., Huitema, D., Burch, S., & Jordan, A. (2018). Political feasibility of 1.5 °C societal transformations: The role of social justice. *Current Opinion in Environmental Sustainability*, *31*, 1–9. [CrossRef]

Rahman, M. (2021). Achieving sustainable development goals of Agenda 2030 in Bangladesh: The crossroad of the governance and performance. *Public Administration and Policy*, *24*(2), 195–211. [CrossRef]

Razavi, S., Behrendt, C., Bischler, J., & Orton, I. (2025). At home in the world: Putting European eco-social policies in their global context. *Global Social Policy*, *25*(1), 170–175. [CrossRef]

Resnik, D. (2022). Environmental justice and climate change policies. *Bioethics*, *36*(7), 735–741. [CrossRef] [PubMed]

Reynaud, E. (2018). *The international labour organization and globalization: Fundamental rights, decent work and social justice*. International Labour Office.

Roy, P. K. (2025). Climate policy reform through the indigenous lens of the institutional analysis and development framework: A case of the Bangladeshi santals. In R. A. Doon (Ed.), *Transitioning to climate action* (pp. 215–239). MDPI. [CrossRef]

Roy, P. K., Abd Wahab, H., & Hamidi, M. (2023a). A philosophical discussion of sustainable development: A case from the Bangladeshi Santal community. In *Handbook of research on implications of sustainable development in higher education* (pp. 97–114). IGI Global Scientific Publishing.

Roy, P. K., Abd Wahab, H., & Hamidi, M. (2023b). Achieving the sustainable development goals: A Case study of the ministry of Chittagong hill tracts affairs, Bangladesh. In *Positive and constructive contributions for sustainable development goals* (pp. 161–180). IGI Global Scientific Publishing.

Sengupta, S. (2023). Climate change, international justice and global order. *International Affairs*, *99*(1), 121–140. [CrossRef]

Sultana, F. (2021). Critical climate justice. *The Geographical Journal*, *188*(1), 118–124. [CrossRef]

Wedel, J. R., Shore, C., Feldman, G., & Lathrop, S. (2005). Toward an anthropology of public policy. *The American Academy of Political and Social Science*, *600*(1), 30–51. [CrossRef]

Wilkens, J., & Datchoua-Tirvaudey, A. (2022). Researching climate justice: A decolonial approach to global climate governance. *International Affairs*, *98*(1), 125–143. [CrossRef]

Cooperative Strategies for Climate Change Mitigation and Adaptation

Aykut Balcı

Abstract: In this section, the issue of climate change is addressed in a multi-dimensional way, and the tools for combating this problem at the national and international levels are analysed. In the first part of the chapter, the concept of climate change, its causes, and its effects are defined to create a theoretical framework. Subsequently, the struggles waged at the international level are examined within a historical process. The establishment of the United Nations Environment Program (UNEP), the adoption of the United Nations Framework Convention on Climate Change (UNFCCC), the activation of scientific structures such as the Intergovernmental Panel on Climate Change (IPCC), the Kyoto Protocol, and the Paris Climate Agreement have been concrete outcomes of this international struggle. In light of current debates in the academic literature, the financial dimension of combating climate change, namely climate finance, is considered a cornerstone for the transition to a low-carbon economy and enhancing resilience. The literature extensively examines the obstacles in transferring financial resources from developed to developing countries and the role of innovative financing instruments like green bonds. However, macroeconomic modelling studies used to predict the economic impacts of climate policies provide policymakers with strategic roadmaps by analysing the trade-off between emission reduction targets and GDP growth. Sectoral adaptation studies focus on technological and structural transformations that will increase resilience, particularly in areas most vulnerable to climate shocks, such as agriculture, energy, and water management. The literature emphasises the importance of developing customised adaptation strategies for each sector based on its unique risk profile. In addition to these technical and economic processes, the concept of climate justice has become central to scientific discussions. Climate justice advocates for the rights of communities that have contributed the least to the climate crisis but are most affected by its impacts (particularly women and low-income populations in the Global South), reminding us that responsibilities and burdens must be shared equitably at the global level. Additionally, the roles of states, local governments, non-governmental organisations, and the private sector in combating climate change are discussed. Public–private partnerships (PPPs), which are an important tool, especially in combating climate change, have been examined through field examples, and the importance of PPPs in effectively combating climate change has been emphasised. Recent findings in the literature indicate that public–private partnerships not only provide financing but also accelerate sectoral alignment through technology transfer and risk sharing and produce more inclusive outcomes when blended with climate justice principles.

1. Introduction

Climate change, one of the most significant social problems on a global scale, is a critical issue that needs to be addressed for the world we live in. With the increase in the use of fossil energy sources due to the industrial revolution, the accumulation of greenhouse gases in the atmosphere has risen, leading to increased temperatures, melting glaciers, and a proliferation of natural disasters such as floods and droughts. These developments indicate that the climate is changing due to human influence, deviating from its natural course. Just as human actions are the main cause of this climate change, the solution is also being sought in human actions.

Climate change, which has extremely negative and destructive effects on the future of the world, was addressed locally and nationally for a long time under the warnings and guidance of scientists. However, with the recognition that the problem is a global reality and that countries' production–consumption patterns and lifestyles have universal consequences, the fight against climate change has been elevated to the international level. The establishment of the United Nations Environment Programme (UNEP), the adoption of the United Nations Framework Convention on Climate Change (UNFCCC), the creation of scientific bodies like the Intergovernmental Panel on Climate Change (IPCC), the Kyoto Protocol, and the Paris Climate Agreement have been concrete outcomes of this international struggle.

Today, a new governance paradigm has been adopted in the fight against climate change, and the solution is no longer sought solely by governments and central administrations, but within a multi-stakeholder structure encompassing actors such as local governments, non-governmental organisations, private sector organisations, and universities. This arrangement, where each stakeholder assumes a significant role and responsibility, is considered essential in the global fight against climate change.

In this new governance paradigm, public–private partnerships have become an increasingly prominent tool for tackling challenges. The financial resources, technological infrastructure, and innovative initiatives of the private sector have come together with the regulatory role of the public sector to combat climate change, reduce vulnerabilities, increase resilience, and implement ecologically compatible and sustainable projects in collaboration. Thus, concrete and observable progress has been made in combating climate change.

Based on all these points, this section will first establish a theoretical foundation by discussing the concept, causes, and consequences of climate change. In the second section, what has been done in the international fight against climate change will be discussed historically. Subsequently, the roles of governments (central administration), local administrations, the private sector, civil society, and universities will be detailed, and multi-actor governance in combating climate change will be discussed. The final section will focus on the role and practices of public–private partnerships in combating climate change. In the Conclusion Section, a general assessment will be presented, and future recommendations for combating climate change will be made.

2. Global Climate Change

Climate change is one of the most important environmental problems threatening the world today. Although climate change in the world has existed for thousands of years, long-term averages or normals did not change, and this situation indicated that the climate was naturally changeable and there was no problem. However, with the role of human activities in climate change, these changes have become an important problem, and it has been accepted that, in addition to natural changes, humans have a determining effect on climate at the regional and global scale (Kadıoğlu, 2001). After this acceptance, global climate change was defined in the United Nations Framework Convention on Climate Change as "a change in climate because of human activities that directly or indirectly disrupt the composition of the global atmosphere, in addition to the natural climate change observed in comparable time periods. The term 'global' is used because the area of the climate alteration caused by human activities encompasses the entire atmosphere" (UNFCCC, 1992). This is because, even if environmental problems occur within the borders of a country, the resulting destruction affects water resources, the atmosphere, or the ozone layer, which cross borders. Therefore, environmental problems are global in nature (Erçandırlı, 2019).

Today, it is seen that human activities that increase climate change are increasing. Humans have a negative impact on the environment in two dimensions. The first dimension is the problems caused by the consumption of natural resources and the lack of resources. The second dimension is pollution of the environment. While resource consumption is carried out more slowly, pollution of the environment is gaining speed, and its effects are much more negative (Çelebi, 2014). Factors such as the increase in industrialisation and urbanisation, and the accompanying environmental pollution, increase in fossil fuels and population growth increase the deterioration in the climate. These factors increase the accumulation of greenhouse gases in the atmosphere and thin the ozone layer. As a result, the energy balance on earth changes and causes a global temperature increase (Doğan & Tüzer, 2011).

According to the AR6 Synthesis Report, a climate change report prepared by the United Nations Intergovernmental Panel on Climate Change (IPCC) in 2023, greenhouse gas emissions increased due to human activities between 2011 and 2020, and the global temperature increased by 1.1 °C compared to the 1900s. When the last 2000 years are considered, it can be stated that, since 1970, temperatures have increased faster than in any other 50-year period, and there will be an average increase of 1–3.5 °C by 2100. The same report cites increased energy use, land-use changes, and inappropriate land use as primary causes, in addition to the rise in greenhouse gases. However, inequalities in lifestyle, production, and consumption activities between regions and countries are also cited as contributing factors (IPCC, 2023).

Climate change caused by global warming and environmental destruction has caused widespread negative impacts on nature and human life. Melting of glaciers and sea level rise, change in precipitation regimes, heat waves, drought and desertification are the most obvious problems. Due to these changes in the ecosystem, hundreds of local species have been lost on land and in the oceans, and living diversity has irreversibly decreased. Agriculture has become inefficient, food and water insecurity has started to occur in countries, and human health has been adversely affected. In addition, human deaths and forced migrations have increased due to floods caused by the changing precipitation regime, droughts due to temperature increase, and climate-related epidemics (IPCC, 2023; Kumari Rigaud et al., 2018).

As can be seen, each of the negative situations caused by global climate change is essentially a secondary disaster. Because the environmental problems we experience penetrate much faster than societies can adapt and because their negative effects are gradually increasing, combating environmental problems from the local to global dimension has come to the forefront, and important steps have been taken by governments and international organisations in this regard. For this reason, in the next section, efforts to combat climate change will be presented.

3. International Struggle Against Global Climate Change

Climate change and its accompanying problems have an international character, and their effects are being felt increasingly more day by day. It disrupts the balance of the ecosystem. To build a more liveable world, countries have tried to put forward multi-dimensional mechanisms in cooperation, and initiatives to combat climate change have gained momentum. In this context, the United Nations Environment Programme, United Nations Framework Convention on Climate Change, Intergovernmental Panel on Climate Change, Kyoto Protocol, and Paris Climate Agreements will be discussed.

3.1. United Nations Environment Programme (UNEP)

With the occurrence of acid rain in the 1960s and the increase in pollution in the Baltic Sea, environmental problems started to be discussed at the international level for the first time, and the importance of inter-state cooperation was pointed out. As a result of this idea, the "Conference on the Human Environment" was convened in Stockholm in 1972 with the active participation of states, and the Stockholm Declaration, the first international declaration on the environment, was published (Sands, 2003). The most concrete and successful outcome of the declaration was the establishment of the United Nations Environment Programme (UNEP). Established in 1972 by the United Nations (UN) General Assembly Resolution No. 2997, the UNEP was the first international body created solely with a focus on the environment, and its stated purpose was "to increase international co-operation on the environmental issues, to to advise on environmental policies, and to guide countries by fostering cooperation on environmental issues within the UN" (Murphy, 2006). The UNEP, which had 58 members when it was first established, has been expanded to include all UN member states as of 2013 and has reached 193 member states.

Since the UNEP has the aim of responding to the environmental needs and problems of developing countries, its headquarters was determined to be in Nairobi, in Kenya, a developing country (Wakefield, 1982). Today, it has offices in Africa, Asia and the Pacific, Europe, Latin America and the Caribbean, North America, Western Asia, and New York. The UNEP carries out its main activities in the fields of climate action, nature action, chemicals and pollution action; air quality, energy, disasters, digital transformation, resource efficiency, green economy, oceans and coasts, environmental law, and environmental management (UNEP, 2025).

3.2. United Nations Inter-Governmental Panel on Climate Change (IPCC)

The United Nations Inter-Governmental Panel on Climate Change (IPCC) was established by UNEP in 1988. The panel, which is an intergovernmental organisation, has 195 member countries.

The main mission of the panel is to prepare scientifically valid reports in the field of climate and environment through scientists. In this context, Global Environment

Assessment reports have been published for 37 years with the work of scientists from member states. The first report of the Panel was published in 1990 and the last report, the Sixth Assessment Report, was published in 2023.

The Panel, which has a great contribution in the field of environment, has developed a large part of the terminology in climate studies. The reports and statistics prepared by this Panel were also influential in the preparation of the Kyoto Protocol and the Paris Climate Agreement. Moreover, the Panel received the Nobel Peace Prize in 2007 for addressing the human impact on climate, combating climate change, and putting forward measures. Therefore, it is seen as one of the most important international organisations on the environment and climate (Sharma & Ravindranath, 2019).

3.3. United Nations Framework Convention on Climate Change (UNFCCC)

After the establishment of the UNEP, the increasing interest in environmental problems pushed countries to hold various climate meetings and solution partnerships, and many conferences were held in this process. However, the first important step was taken in 1979 to reduce the negative effects of increasing carbon dioxide accumulation in the atmosphere. In 1979, the First World Climate Conference was held under the organisation of the World Meteorological Organization (WMO). Subsequently, two more congresses were held in 1985 and 1987 in order to evaluate the effects of greenhouse gases on climate change and to determine the mitigation options, and thus preparations for the Second World Climate Conference were made. The Second World Climate Conference was held in Geneva in 1990 and at the end of the conference, a Ministerial Declaration on greenhouse gas emissions and climate change was signed by 137 countries (Türkeş, 2001).

Following all these developments, the World Conference on Environment and Development was held in Rio and the "United Nations Framework Convention on Climate Change (UNFCCC)" was prepared and opened for signature. In 1994, 194 countries, including Turkey, became parties to the convention, and their signatures were completed and the convention entered into force (UNFCCC, 2025).

The main purpose of the convention is to stop the concentration of greenhouse gases in the atmosphere at a level that can prevent human-induced hazards on the climate system. When the effects are stabilised at such a level, natural adaptation to climate change will be achieved, and this level should be reached in a timeframe that allows development to continue sustainably (Eckersley, 2016). In the Convention, both the common responsibilities of the countries and their objectives and responsibilities according to their national and regional development priorities are addressed. However, all countries party to the convention are jointly responsible for reducing greenhouse gas emissions and preventing climate change. There are two additional lists in the Convention. The countries in Annex I (OECD, Russia and Eastern European countries) are responsible for limiting greenhouse gas emissions, strengthening greenhouse gas sinks and taking measures to prevent climate change and report the policies and activities they implement. Annex II consists only of OECD countries, and Annex II countries are responsible for transferring environmentally compatible technologies to developing countries and providing the necessary financing in addition to their duties in the first list (Görmez, 2020).

Within the scope of the UN Framework Convention on Climate Change, a meeting was held every year under the name of conference of parties (COP) and the Kyoto Protocol was adopted at the Third Conference of the Parties (COP3) held in 1997.

3.4. Kyoto Protocol

The "Kyoto Protocol to the United Nations Framework Convention on Climate Change" was put forward at the Third Conference of the Parties (COP3) held in Kyoto, Japan, on 11 December 1997. The protocol, which specifies binding objectives for reducing greenhouse gas emissions, was opened for signature in New York in 1998 and signed by 169 countries. Since the Russian Federation ratified the protocol in 2004, the protocol entered into force in 2005, 7 years after its signature. Today, there are 191 countries that are parties to the protocol, and these countries fight against greenhouse gas emissions by taking a common stance.

The Kyoto Protocol is an environmental treaty containing concrete and binding provisions supported by sanctions for the first time. The protocol envisages the restriction of all gases that have a greenhouse effect, and with the protocol, emissions limitations and reduction obligations have been set for countries with developed industries. The countries that are parties to the protocol aim to reduce greenhouse gas emissions and the Earth's temperature level by 5 per cent below the 1990 level and will switch to alternative energy sources and systems that enable energy saving instead of fossil fuels (Demir, 2006).

There are two commitment periods in the Kyoto Protocol: the 2008–2012 period and the 2013–2020 period. The first commitment period has two agendas, namely the realisation of the targets by implementing the protocol as specified and the permanence of the regime, i.e., the continuation of the regime after 2012. The results of the first commitment period are important as they shape the future of climate practices in the world (Mazlum, 2008). In the first commitment period, country emissions in 1990 were accepted as the starting point, and greenhouse gas emissions at the end of the period were realised within the limits set. However, Russia, Australia, Japan, and Canada, which fulfilled their obligations in the first period, have stated that they would not commit to these limits in the second period (Eckersley, 2016).

The existence of flexibility mechanisms plays a role in the Kyoto Protocol, becoming a fundamental strategy for climate change. By creating a mechanism for emission trading, the countries party to the Protocol considered carbon as a commodity, and a cap-and-trade approach to gas emissions was formed. In this emission trade, companies that emitted below a certain limit started to sell the difference in emissions to other companies that failed to meet the target. Thus, economically binding targets have become more acceptable for countries and companies (Heywood, 2014).

The Kyoto Protocol lost its validity in 2012, and there are some reasons for this. The main reason is that countries such as China and Brazil, which have a considerable share in greenhouse gas emissions, were excluded from the obligations required by the protocol since they are classified as developing countries. As China has grown economically and technologically, its greenhouse gas emissions have also increased, but the Chinese government has not signed the protocol, stating that countries such as the USA, which have had a greater impact on climate change in the historical process, should take responsibility. The fact that this conflict between the USA and China was not resolved and the developed countries that were parties to the protocol stepped back at the end of the commitment period gradually rendered the protocol ineffective, and its validity was lost. However, at the Doha Conference held on 7 December 2012, a call was made to the party countries that efforts should be made regarding global climate change, and after the conference, it was decided to continue the Kyoto Protocol and the second commitment period, which expires at the end of 2020, started (Kaya, 2020; Eckersley, 2016).

3.5. Paris Climate Agreement

At the 21st Conference of the Parties (COP-21) held in Paris, the need for an agreement to cover the new process after the end of the Kyoto Protocol was emphasised. As a result of this conference, the Paris Climate Agreement was adopted by the unanimous vote of the states party to the UN Framework Convention on Climate Change, and a new era in the international climate issue started. The unanimous adoption of the Paris Climate Agreement shows that it is a more accepted agreement compared to the Kyoto Protocol. The Paris Climate Agreement is a historic agreement; it is a critical agreement with features that will fundamentally change economies, societies, and the environment at local, national, regional, and global scales.

The main goal of the 2015 Paris Climate Agreement was to reduce global warming and, at the same time, limit the increase in the Earth's temperature to a maximum of 1.5–2 °C. In order to achieve this goal, no country should enter into a trade on climate, and carbon trade markets should be prevented. In other words, nature should be at the forefront in the balance of economic gain and nature (Böhm & Sıddhartha, 2011). If the global warming value exceeds 2 °C, dangerous consequences will emerge, the temperature will rise to record levels, and droughts will increase. Therefore, it is essential for the signatory countries to change their production and consumption habits (Başkaya, 2020). For this reason, all countries that have signed the convention have taken obligations to reduce greenhouse gas emissions. Developed countries will reduce their emissions more and developing countries will reduce their emissions according to their current situation. However, when the year 2050 and beyond is considered, it is expected that all countries, especially developed countries, will reach a point where they will achieve zero emissions. Again, according to the agreement, developed countries will provide financing and technological support to developing countries to reduce the negative impacts of development on climate, and low-carbon, climate-resilient development will be ensured (UNFCCC, 2015).

One of the important elements in achieving the targets in the Paris Climate Agreement is the "Intended Nationally Determined Contribution" (INDC) committed to by countries. Of the parties, 187 have submitted mitigation plans (INDCs). By complying with the INDC plan, using material resources in a way to reduce natural pollution, and supporting climate-sensitive development, healthier and stronger steps can be taken against climate change (Bozoğlu, 2019).

However, despite all these positive developments and targets, greenhouse gas emissions reached the highest level in 2018, the third year after the agreement entered into force. The reason given was the acceleration of economic growth as of 2016 (World Meteorological Organisation, 2018). At this point, new co-operations are needed to achieve the objectives set by the agreement and to ensure the balance between economy, development and nature. These collaborations need to be realised not only between governments, but also by involving all actors at local, regional, national and global scales. Therefore, in the next section, all actors and their roles and responsibilities in combating climate change will be discussed.

4. New Governance Paradigm in the Climate Crisis

Combating climate change is not an issue that governments can address alone, neither nationally nor internationally. Climate change is a multidimensional, complex, and holistic issue.

Global problems such as the increase in greenhouse gases, air pollution, decrease in water resources, drought, and climate change cannot be solved at national scales, and the management approach, in which states act alone, is insufficient in combating climate change. A holistic and multidimensional approach to climate change requires integration and coordination between different sectors and institutions. Based on this view, a paradigm shift has taken place in climate management, and a new governance understanding has developed, and the concept of environmental governance has come to the fore as a collaborative, participatory, multi-stakeholder solution search. Nowadays, combating climate change is considered as practice that should be continued around this governance model.

As a result of the United Nations Conference on Environment and Development organised by the United Nations in Rio De Janeiro in 1992, Agenda 21 was established, and an action plan was published. Many institutions and organisations have been assigned responsibility in the Agenda 21 action plans. The roles and responsibilities of United Nations organisations, economic development institutions, non-governmental organisations, and local governments have been defined. The importance of global partnership in solving the problems has been emphasised. Thus, the classical and one-dimensional management approach has been replaced by a new collaborative and participatory governance approach (Aydınlı, 2004).

According to the new governance paradigm, the fight against climate change is based on a multi-centred structure in which all official and non-official actors are included in the process, based on multiple networks and policy channels, covering all dimensions from the national to the global level (Gregorioa et al., 2019). In addition to the effectiveness of the state and central governments, a way of struggle in which the roles of local governments in the process are increased, non-state actors, namely non-governmental organisations and private organisations, are included in climate governance, carbon control, efficient use of resources, adaptation and resilience and security issues have gained importance (Bulkeley & Betsill, 2013). According to the new governance approach, in addition to increasing the efficiency of the public sector, states should open space for the private sector and non-governmental organisations through legal regulations and contribute to their struggle against climate change by supporting these institutions. The new governance approach, which is multi-stakeholder (central government, local government, private sector, non-governmental organisations, universities, public) and multi-dimensional (from local to global), facilitates the solution of possible problems that may arise in decision-making processes carried out between global, regional and local levels (Kern & Alber, 2008). For example, the greenhouse gas reduction target set by the central government is implemented by local governments and the level of success is determined by the practices of local governments. Therefore, strong cooperation and coordination between the central government and local governments minimise the problems experienced in this field.

In this multi-actor and multi-dimensional governance model, communication and co-operation between governance actors is ensured both vertically and horizontally in order to eliminate implementation differences between different units. While vertical cooperation refers to the cooperation between all administrative units in a structure extending from the centre to the local level, horizontal cooperation refers to the mutual work between units at the same level but with different roles and functions (Corfee-Morlot et al., 2009). However, in order to minimise the vulnerability of individuals and societies, all actors of governance address climate change and its consequences with a holistic perspective covering environmental, economic, social and psychological dimensions. Based on all these, we can say that the new governance model in climate change has a strong quality.

The main stakeholders included in the climate change governance model are states (central government), local governments, private sector, civil society organisations, universities and the public. The importance, roles and responsibilities of climate governance actors are given below.

States (Central Government)

States are the most important actors in the fight against climate change. Decisions and practices taken on climate change cannot be fully realised by the market mechanism, i.e., the private sector. State intervention is essential to mitigate, adapt to, and gain resilience to climate change because what needs to be done to become resilient to climate change is part of public services. However, the things to be done in combating climate change such as reducing the use of fossil fuels, reducing carbon emissions, building environmentally friendly cities, etc., require the use of additional resources rather than being profit-making. Therefore, the intervention of the public sector, i.e., the state, in this process, which should be carried out with the understanding of social benefit, is absolutely essential (Satterthwaite et al., 2007).

Agreements that have an important place in the fight against climate change are constructed by states. At this point, conducting international negotiation processes, preparing global scale action plans, and harmonising these action plans with the national dimension are under the responsibility of states. Again, states are responsible for developing national strategies and action plans on combating climate change, sharing strategies with stakeholders, determining roles and responsibilities and monitoring the process. States are also primarily responsible for developing innovative and environmentally friendly methods in the use of energy and resources, which have an important place in combating climate change (Delibaş, 2021; Aslan & Bulut, 2022).

However, states are the main actors in the continuation of "sustainability". Due to the increase in ecological and environmental problems, sustainability has become an internationally accepted concept and sustainability goals have been set by the United Nations. When we look at the United Nations Sustainable Development Goals, ending poverty, protecting the environment, taking measures against the climate crisis, fair sharing of welfare and peace are the main themes. States are committed to taking the necessary measures to protect the environment and minimise the effects of the climate crisis. Sustainability has imposed duties on the public sector, i.e., states, such as producing policies, ensuring coordination between institutions in the field of environment and climate, carrying out social responsibility projects, publishing climate-related reports within the principle of transparency and accountability, designing ecological products compatible with the environment, and making production processes ecological. In other words, states are obliged to provide the infrastructure of sustainability (Qureshi et al., 2015).

Local Governments

One of the most important actors in the fight against climate change is local governments. In case of climate change and any natural disasters that will occur for this reason, the impact will be felt most in cities and local governments are the closest management units to the living population. For this reason, they are at a critical point in both preventing climate change and mitigating its impacts (Puppim, 2009). Since climate change also involves many different areas such as marine and coastal environment, agriculture, energy, industry, transport, waste, water, it is imperative that local governments take an active role in this issue. However, since local governments are the units closest to the public, it is easier for them to produce and implement services in harmony with ecology, to raise awareness of individuals about the environment and to create climate-friendly cities.

Local governments adopt two basic strategies in combating climate change: adaptation and mitigation. Mitigation strategies aim to minimise the use of fossil fuels, reduce greenhouse gas emissions, and reduce environmental and air pollution while increasing energy efficiency, waste management, using renewable energy sources, creating ecological cities, and developing sustainable transport systems (Davarcıoğlu & Lelik, 2017). Adaptation strategies, on the other hand, include making cities more resilient in the face of the possible and unavoidable effects of climate change, making them ready in terms of infrastructure and technical equipment, strengthening cities to reduce the effects of floods and natural disasters, increasing green areas, and managing water and energy resources (Measham et al., 2011). The implementation of these two strategies in an integrated manner with each other enables individuals, societies and cities to increase their resilience against climate change.

The success of adaptation and mitigation strategies by local governments depends on the existence of certain conditions. First of all, the legal framework should be strengthened, and the construction of climate-friendly cities should be made compulsory. At this point, the decision-making capacities of local governments should be strengthened, and the support and cooperation of central governments is very important for the implementation of strategies and action plans prepared for combating climate change. Central and local governments should proceed in a coordinated manner and the financial support needed by local governments should be provided. At this point, finance models used through public–private partnerships have an important place.

Another important role of local governments in combating climate change is awareness and awareness raising activities. Since human actions have an impact on climate change and the increase in earth temperatures, one of the important methods in combating climate change is to educate, raise awareness, and train individuals on climate, environment and nature. For this reason, local governments can organise seminars in schools, neighbourhood headmen's offices, city squares, and raise awareness on this issue with posters and brochures.

In summary, local governments play a key role in the implementation of climate change strategy and action plans determined by central governments, prevention of environmental and air pollution, climate-friendly urban planning, waste management and recycling, water management, energy saving and use of renewable energy sources, making transportation services environmentally friendly, and raising climate awareness among citizens.

Civil Society Organisations

Civil society organisations are an important stakeholder in the fight against climate change. The impact of non-governmental organisations, which work in cooperation with public institutions and private sector organisations, raise awareness against the climate crisis, carry out protective–preventive activities, and assume the role of advocacy in the development of climate policies, is increasing day by day.

Non-governmental organisations providing services in the field of environment take action to produce solutions to social, economic, and political problems in the face of environmental problems such as natural disasters, nuclear and chemical threats, drought, desertification, melting of glaciers, increase in greenhouse gas emissions, water crisis, and damage to natural resources, especially the climate crisis (Mavi, 2021).

According to environmentalist non-governmental organisations shaped by environmentalist movements, climate change is a universal problem and global action should be taken to solve it. At this point, global environmentalist movements and non-governmental organisations have started to contribute to the solution of problems in a short time by providing international organisation; they have expanded their sphere of influence by receiving the support of societies and have become an important actor in the fight against climate change (Kalouche & Mielants, 2008).

When the roles adopted by civil society organisations in combating climate change are evaluated, we can state that they basically undertake the roles of raising awareness and raising awareness, advocacy activities and involvement in policy-making processes, social solidarity, conducting research on the causes, consequences and solutions to climate change, presenting scientific data, and providing social, economic, psychological, and financial support in times of crisis.

Universities contribute to the struggle against climate change by informing all stakeholders, presenting the most up-to-date and scientific data, putting the solution process on a scientific basis, combining theoretical knowledge with practical knowledge, and educating the public in all dimensions from the individual to the society. The public, which is most affected by climate change and the accompanying negativities, has an important place in supporting the struggle of all stakeholders in the process and making an individual contribution by ensuring adaptation.

Private Sector Organisations

Private sector organisations, companies and businesses appear as actors that support the public sector and share secondary responsibility for solving environmental problems. In cases where ecological and humanitarian responsibility is the primary priority for private sector organisations instead of competition and economic interests, the fight against climate change can be carried out in a much healthier way.

Today, climate change is being actively combated, but attempts to manage the climate crisis are being made on the axis of neoliberal policies. As crisis management tools, policies and practices that incentivise companies with economic instruments to reduce environmental damage are used (Dent, 2022). Since neoliberal policies are capital-oriented, they may be insufficient to ensure ecological justice. For this reason, market mechanisms alone are not effective in ensuring environmental transformation and state intervention plays a critical role. At this point, what is meant by state intervention is the implementation of tax policies against private sector organisations that harm the environment while carrying out their activities, the implementation of environmental regulations, and the promotion of green investments (Klein, 2015). With such an approach, that is to say, by ensuring the balance between profit orientation and environmental responsibility through the activation of the regulatory role of the state alongside neoliberal policies, the effectiveness of the private sector in combating the climate crisis is increased. With this understanding, it is ensured that private sector organisations become an active actor in the fight against climate.

Today, private sector organisations tend towards environmentally friendly investments through mechanisms such as green financing practices, carbon trading, and renewable energy investments. However, while these mechanisms give private sector organisations the opportunity to engage in environmentally responsible activities, they also allow them to continue their environmentally insensitive activities. Therefore, the balance here needs to change with a focus on environmental awareness.

Providing environmentally friendly products and services to combat climate change, preferring renewable energy systems to reduce greenhouse gas emissions, and increasing nature- and ecology-oriented studies through public–private partnerships are the main responsibilities of private sector organisations. At this point, the understanding of public–private partnerships comes to the fore.

Climate Action Through Public–Private Partnerships

Public–private partnerships, which are essentially the participation of the private sector in services provided by the state, refer to "the realisation of investments and services based on a contract by sharing the costs, risks and returns of the project in a balanced manner between the public and private sectors". Although public–private partnerships were once considered a method developed to provide the financial resources required to meet the infrastructure investments of countries in the first periods of their implementation, their sphere of influence has expanded over time and today they are accepted as a model in which the private sector's operating capabilities are utilised and the public sector assumes responsibility in areas such as coordination, planning, and supervision of investments (Republic of Turkey Ministry of Development, 2016).

Public–private partnerships are based on the principle that the public sector aims to transfer its resources, income, and market share to the private sector for reasons such as not having the resources to finance the infrastructure projects it wants to realise, wanting to keep expenditure at a minimum level, wanting to make the private sector a partner by involving the private sector in the process, or wanting to postpone the expenditure. Public–private partnerships have become a preferred model both nationally and internationally for reasons such as reducing the expenditures of the public sector on investments and sharing the risk and responsibility between the public and private sectors in a balanced manner (Kalaycı, 2018).

Public–private partnership models provide services such as energy generation and distribution, communication and transport systems, irrigation systems, schools, stadiums, hospitals, information technologies, agriculture, tourism, mining, construction works, and infrastructure investments of public administrations. In addition to the UK and the USA, they have become a frequently preferred method in European countries such as Germany, Sweden, Canada, Ireland, South Africa, Italy, the Netherlands, and Spain (Yılmaz & Karakaş, 2011).

The advantages of the public–private partnership model can be expressed as follows (Acartürk & Keskin, 2012):

- Balanced allocation of risk and responsibility among stakeholders (public and private sector);
- Utilising the expertise and business skills of the private sector;
- Providing quality public services in a shorter time;
- Facilitating access to investment and funding sources;
- Providing the opportunity to transfer public resources to different areas;
- Increasing competition and adopting accountable and transparent management processes;
- Directing national and international capital to infrastructure projects.

Public–private partnerships are also a critical tool in combating climate change with the advantages they provide because combating climate change is not an issue that can be addressed only in the context of environmental policies and action strategies. It is intertwined with areas such as social welfare, social justice, economic growth and profitability, and national–international competition. Therefore, since it is not a process that can be carried out with the limited funds of states, new partnerships, financial and managerial models are needed. Public–private partnerships have come to the forefront in the fight against climate change as a result of this need.

It is estimated that several trillion dollars of investment will be needed each year to achieve the United Nations Sustainable Development Goals and to finance climate action (Barua, 2020). According to another estimate on climate action, between 300 and 500 billion dollars of financing will be required annually between 2030 and 2050 for the establishment of climate-resilient infrastructure (Adhikari & Chalkasra, 2021). It is unlikely that these figures needed to combat climate change can be met with the existing financial resources of the countries or by the private sector taking financial responsibility alone. For this reason, governments, the financial sector, and investors must come together to share ecological investment budgets.

The concept of green finance, which opens space for public–private partners, has an important place in the action to combat climate change and to realise the Sustainable Development Goals in this context. Green finance is an innovative understanding that aims to produce without any harm to the environment and to provide financial return by working with the responsibility of providing social benefit. Private sector institutions that adopt the green finance approach increase their capital transfers to partnerships and projects with social and ecological benefits while gradually moving away from unsustainable and environmentally damaging projects and investments (Thomson, 2021). With the understanding of green finance, it becomes easier to establish public–private partnerships in projects and investments necessary to minimise the effects of climate change and to take measures against its consequences.

Renewable energy resources are in a very important position in combating global climate change, and most public–private partnerships are established through renewable energy projects. When we look at the world in general, it is noticeable that there is a trend towards transforming energy resources. In order to reduce greenhouse gas emissions and ensure environmental and economic sustainability, the use of innovative and environmentally compatible renewable energy sources is encouraged (Şerbetçi & Fettahlıoğlu, 2024).

When the examples of public–private partnerships realised within the scope of combating climate change and sustainable development targets across the world are examined, it can be said that energy investments come to the forefront. The South East Asia region is a region where the green finance approach is dominant, and ecological investments based on public–private partnerships are actively used. In 2019, the 100 MW(e) Cambodia Solar Park Project, with a total investment value of USD 26.7 million, the Energy from Waste Project, with an investment value of USD 151.13 million, and other projects developed for green sustainability in Georgia, Thailand, Indonesia, and the Philippines were financed by the Asian Development Bank and contributed to the fight against climate change (Mehta & Andrich, 2021).

Acciona, a Spanish wind energy company, signed a 20-year agreement with Cemex, a Mexican company, to realise a wind farm project in Mexico. The energy produced will be purchased by Cemex and transferred to the national grid. Part of the project financing will be covered by the public bank. This will encourage the use of renewable energy and reduce the impact of energy sources that are not sustainable and increase greenhouse gas emissions (Mathews et al., 2010).

Public–private partnerships are also widely realised in Central Asian countries such as Kazakhstan, Turkmenistan, Uzbekistan, Kyrgyz Republic and Uzbekistan, and projects such as energy transformation, improvement in food and agriculture, and water management are financed and implemented by public funds and investors such as the Green Climate Fund, the Global Environment Facility, and the Clean Development Fund (CAREC, 2020).

In Latin America and the Sub-Saharan Countries region, projects in the region are supported by many public institutions, especially the World Bank, and public–private partnerships are established with investors to protect biodiversity, support sustainable development by using renewable resources, and create climate-resilient cities by changing climate vulnerability in the region (Bhattacharyya, 2021).

In countries such as Italy, Germany, Canada, South Korea, Turkey, and the USA, green infrastructure investments are encouraged, public–private partnerships are increased to achieve the United Nations 2030 Sustainable Development Goals, and regulations are made to reduce climate vulnerability and encourage green infrastructure investments, especially renewable energy investments, low-carbon transport, and waste and water management.

5. Conclusions

Combating climate change has become vital to minimising the effects of climate change, a global problem, and reducing its negative, destructive consequences. Today, climate change has become a multifaceted issue, transcending its status as a purely environmental problem to encompass social, economic, political, and even psychological dimensions. As shown in this context, significant mechanisms have been developed at the international level to combat climate change, and a wide range of policy instruments have been implemented, from UNEP's coordination of environmental actions to the UNFCCC's creation of a global agreement framework, the IPCC's provision of a solid scientific basis, and the roadmaps of the Kyoto and Paris agreements, which contain concrete commitments.

However, despite these international efforts, the desired progress in combating climate change has not been achieved. The speed of implementation of current policies has lagged behind the growing momentum of the climate change crisis; the gap between emission reduction targets and actual emissions has widened. This situation has brought about a search for a new paradigm, and multi-stakeholder and innovative solutions have begun to be sought in the fight against climate change. The solution has evolved into a multi-stakeholder process, carried out collectively around a structure that now includes not only governments and central administrations but also actors such as local administrations, non-governmental organisations, private sector organisations, and universities. This new understanding of governance makes it possible to produce more effective, sustainable, and socially acceptable solutions by creating synergy from different knowledge, resources, and capabilities.

Specifically, public–private partnerships (PPPs) have formed one of the key building blocks of this new era and have been viewed not only as financing instruments but also as actors with shared responsibility. The transformation required to combat climate change (especially the transformation of infrastructure, transportation, water and waste management, and energy sources) is quite extensive. The financing required for sustainable transportation infrastructure, renewable energy facilities, smart water systems, and waste management is quite costly, and this transformation cannot be achieved solely with public budgets. The financial resources, experience, technological infrastructure, and social responsibility goals of private sector organisations have been brought together through public–private partnerships and have begun to be actively and efficiently implemented in concrete projects across many areas, from combating climate change and sustainable transportation infrastructure to renewable energy facilities and smart water systems. These collaborations provide a framework that allows for the sharing of risk, the dissemination of innovative technologies, the effective management of projects throughout their lifecycle, and the safeguarding of public interest.

As a result, climate change has also brought about a search for common solutions and collaborations. Everyone, from governments to local administrations, from the private sector to civil society, and from academia to individuals, has a responsibility and role in this process. In the coming period, a new and green world order can be built by increasing public–private sector collaborations focused on combating climate change and implementing projects that are compatible with the ecosystem and aim for social benefit. At the heart of this system there should lie a circular economy approach, low-carbon production systems, climate-resilient cities, and effective climate governance at all levels. Only in this way can a liveable, just, and sustainable planet be ensured for current and future generations.

Funding: This research received no external funding.

Conflicts of Interest: The author declares no conflicts of interest.

Author Name and Affiliation: Aykut Balcı, Vocational School of Social Sciences, Tekirdag Namik Kemal University, Tekirdağ, Turkey.

Keywords: climate change; mitigation; corporate strategies.

References

Acartürk, D., & Keskin, S. (2012). Public-private partnership model in the health sector in Türkiye. *Süleyman Demirel University Journal of Faculty of Economics and Administrative Sciences*, *17*(3), 25–51.

Adhikari, B., & Chalkasra, L. S. S. (2021). Mobilizing private sector investment for climate action: Increasing ambition and scaling up implementation. *Journal of Sustainable Finance & Investment, 13*(2), 1110–1127.

Aslan, M. M., & Bulut, Y. (2022). Innovative approaches to building climate resilient cities: Climate change governance and energy efficient buildings. *Journal of Urban Academy, 15*(3), 1023–1035.

Aydınlı, H. İ. (2004). *Municipalities in the period of socio-economic transformation* (1st ed.). Nobel Publication.

Barua, S. (2020). Financing sustainable development goals: A review on challenges and mitigation strategies. *Business Strategy & Development, 3*(3), 277–293.

Başkaya, F. (2020). *Climate crisis and ecological devastation with young people.* Yordam Kitap.

Bhattacharyya, R. (2021). Green finance for energy transition, climate action and sustainable development: An overview of concepts, practices, implementation and challenges. *Green Finance, 4*(1), 1–35. [CrossRef]

Bozoğlu, B. (2019). *21st century climate crisis, Paris agreement and climate change adaptation.* Dorlion Publishing House.

Böhm, S., & Sıddhartha, D. (2011). Commentary: Fault lines in climate policy: What role for carbon markets? *Climate Policy, 11*(6), 1389–1392. [CrossRef]

Bulkeley, H., & Betsill, M. M. (2013). Revisiting the urban politics of climate change. *Environmental Politics, 22*(1), 136–154. [CrossRef]

Central Asia Regional Environmental Center (CAREC). (2020). *Financing climate action in central Asia: A study on international and local investments.* Available online: https://zoinet.org/wp-content/uploads/2020/10/CA-climate-finance-en.pdf (accessed on 13 July 2025).

Corfee-Morlot, J., Kamal-Chaoui, L., Donovan, M. G., Cochran, I., Robert, A., & Teasdale, P.-J. (2009). *Cities, climate change and multilevel governance.* OECD environmental working paper No. 14. OECD Publishing, OECD.

Çelebi, H. (2014). Environmental problems. In H. Çakmak (Ed.), *International relations: Introduction, concepts and theories.* Doğu Kitabevi.

Davarcıoğlu, B., & Lelik, A. (2017). Global climate change and adaptation studies: Evaluation in terms of Turkey. *Journal of Professional Sciences, 6*(2), 94–105.

Delibaş, A. (2021). *The impact of geopolitics of energy on international climate change governance* [Master's thesis, Ankara University, Institute of Social Sciences].

Demir, İ. (2006). Changes that may occur in world energy use in the way of reaching the objectives of Kyoto protocol. *Gazi University Journal of Faculty of Economics and Administrative Sciences, 8*(2), 241–251.

Dent, C. M. (2022). Neoliberal environmentalism, climate interventionism and the trade-climate nexus. *Sustainability, 14*(23), 15804. [CrossRef]

Doğan, S., & Tüzer, M. (2011). Combating global climate change: General approaches and international efforts. *Istanbul Journal of Sociological Studies, 44*, 157–194.

Eckersley, R. (2016). Green theory. In T. D.-M. Kurki, & S. Smith (Eds.), *International relations theories discipline and diversity.* Sakarya University Kültür Yayınlar.

Erçandırlı, Y. (2019). Global environmental problems and politics. In M. S. Erol, & M. Ekşi (Eds.), *Current issues in international relations.* Akçağ Publications.

Görmez, K. (2020). *Environmental problems.* Nobel Yayınları.

Gregorioa, M. D., Fatorelli, L., Paavola, J., Locatelli, B., Pramova, E., Nurrochmat, D. R., May, P. H., Brockhaus, M., Sari, I. M., & Kusumadew, S. D. (2019). Multi-level governance and power in climate change policy networks. *Global Environmental Change, 54*, 64–77. [CrossRef]

Heywood, A. (2014). *Global politics* (N. Uslu, & H. Özdemir, Eds.). Adres Publications.

IPCC. (2023). Summary for policymakers. In Core Writing Team, H. Lee, & J. Romero (Eds.), *Climate change 2023: Synthesis report. Contribution of working groups I, II and III to the sixth assessment report of the intergovernmental panel on climate change* (pp. 1–34). IPCC. [CrossRef]

Kadıoğlu, M. (2001). *Bildiğiniz havalarin sonu global climate change and turkey*. Güncel Publishing.

Kalaycı, İ. (2018). Public-private partnership (PPP) model in energy investments: Theoretical framework. *Eurasian Journal of Social and Economic Research, 5*(4), 48–61.

Kalouche, F., & Mielants, E. (2008). The transformation of anti-system movements 1968–2005. In W. G. Martin (Ed.), *Toplumsal hareketler 1750–2005* (K. Deniz, Trans.; pp. 219–283). Versus Yayınları.

Kaya, H. E. (2020). Global climate policies from Kyoto to Paris. *Meriç International Journal of Social and Strategic Research, 4*(10), 165–191.

Kern, K., & Alber, G. (2008, October 9–10). *Governing climate change in cities: Modes of urban climate governance in multi-level systems*. Competitive Cities and Climate Change OECD Conference Proceedings, Milan, Italy. Available online: http://www.oecd.org/governance/regional-policy/44232251.pdf (accessed on 13 July 2025).

Klein, N. (2015). *This changes everything: Capitalism* vs. *the climate* (576p). Simon & Schuster.

Kumari Rigaud, K., Sherbinin, A., Jones, B., Bergmann, J., Clement, V., Ober, K., Schewe, J., Adamo, S., McCusker, B., & Midgley, S. H. (2018). *Groundswell: Preparing for internal climate migration*. The World Bank.

Mathews, J. A., Kidney, S., Mallon, K., & Hughes, M. (2010). Mobilizing private finance to drive an energy industrial revolution. *Energy Policy, 38*, 3263–3265. [CrossRef]

Mavi, İ. (2021). Global environmentalist movements as an example of new social movements in the context of global climate change. *Nişantaşı University Journal of Social Sciences, 9*(2), 116–126. [CrossRef]

Mazlum, S. C. (2008). International climate policy: An assessment on the axis of equity and sustainability. In E. Karakaya (Ed.), *Global warming and Kyoto protocol: Scientific, economic and political analysis of climate change*. Bağlam Publishing.

Measham, T. G., Preston, B. L., Smith, T., Brooke, C., Gorddard, R., Withycombe, G., & Morrison, C. (2011). Adapting to climate change through local municipal planning: Barriers and challenges, Mitigation and Adaptation Strategies. *Global Change, 16*(8), 889–909.

Mehta, A., & Andrich, M. L. (2021). *The asian development bank's green finance initiatives and their impacts*. Available online: https://www.adb.org/sites/default/files/institutional-document/691951/ado2021bn-adb-green-finance-initiative.pdf (accessed on 22 June 2025).

Murphy, S. (2006). *Principles of international law*. Thomson-West, United States.

Puppim, D. O., & Jose, A. (2009). The implementation of climate change related policies at the subnational level: An analysis of three countries. *Habitat International, 33*, 253–259. [CrossRef]

Qureshi, M. I., Rasli, A. M., Jusoh, A., & Kowang, T. O. (2015). Sustainability: A new manufacturing paradigm. *Jurnal Teknologi (Sciences & Engineering)*, *77*(22), 47–53. [CrossRef]
Sands, P. (2003). *Principles of international environmental law*. Cambridge University Press.
Satterthwaite, D. H., Saleemul, R., Hannah, P., Mark, R., & Patricia, L. (2007). *Adapting to climate change in urban areas: The possibilities and constraints in low- and middle-income nations. Human settlements discussion paper series: climate change and cities 1*. International Institute for Environment and Development (IIED).
Sharma, J., & Ravindranath, N. H. (2019). Applying IPCC 2014 framework for hazard-specific vulnerability assessment under climate change. *Environmental Research Communications*, *1*, 1–7. [CrossRef]
Şerbetçi, A., & Fettahlıoğlu, T. (2024). Financing green energy investments in emerging market economies. *Premium e-Journal of Social Sciences (PEJOSS)*, *8*(49), 1723–1730.
Republic of Turkey Ministry of Development. (2016). *Developments regarding public private partnership practices in the world and Turkey 2015*. General Directorate of Investment Programming Monitoring and Evaluation.
Thomson, S. (2021). *Green and sustainable finance principles and practice*. Kogan Page.
Türkeş, M. (2001). Global climate protection, framework convention on climate change and Turkey. *Tesisat Engineering, TMMOB Chamber of Mechanical Engineers, Periodical Technical Publication*, *61*, 14–29.
UNEP. (2025). *Where we work*. Available online: https://www.unep.org/ (accessed on 25 June 2025).
UNFCCC. (1992). *Completion of a framework convention on climate change, united nations climate change*. Available online: https://unfccc.int/sites/default/files/resource/docs/1992/a/eng/l14a01.pdf (accessed on 22 June 2025).
UNFCCC. (2015). *The Paris agreement*. Available online: https://unfccc.int/process-and-meetings/the-paris-agreement (accessed on 22 June 2025).
UNFCCC. (2025). *Status of ratification*. Available online: https://unfccc.int/process/the-paris-agreement/status-of-ratification (accessed on 22 June 2025).
Wakefield, P. (1982). Is UNEP still a good investment? *Environment: Science and Policy for Sustainable Development*, *24*(4), 7–38. [CrossRef]
World Meteorological Organisation (WMO). (2018). *Global carbon Baget shows rise in emissions*. Available online: https://wmo.int/media/news/global-carbon-budget-shows-rise-emissions#: :text=Global%20CO2%20emissions%20are%20expected,from%20the%20Global%20Carbon%20Budget (accessed on 22 June 2025).
Yılmaz, F. Y., & Karakaş, D. G. (2011, May 6–7). *Structural/cyclical and turkey-specific causes of public-private partnership in health*. Symposium on Public-Private Partnership in Health, Bursa, Turkey.

MDPI AG
Grosspeteranlage 5
4052 Basel
Switzerland
Tel.: +41 61 683 77 34

MDPI Books Editorial Office
E-mail: books@mdpi.com
www.mdpi.com/books

www.ingramcontent.com/pod-product-compliance
Lightning Source LLC
Chambersburg PA
CBHW040852230926
51850CB00012BA/2931
9783725844029